50% OF
Online PHR Prep Course!

By Mometrix

Dear Customer,

We consider it an honor and a privilege that you chose our PHR Study Guide. As a way of showing our appreciation and to help us better serve you, we are offering **50% off our online PHR Prep Course.** Many PHR courses cost hundreds of dollars and don't deliver enough value. With our course, you get access to the best PHR prep material, and **you only pay half price.**

We have structured our online course to perfectly complement your printed study guide. The PHR Prep Course contains **in-depth lessons** that cover all the most important topics, over **1,000 practice questions** to ensure you feel prepared, and over **350 digital flashcards**, so you can study while you're on the go.

Online PHR Prep Course

Topics Include:
- Business Management
    - Vision, Mission, Values, and Structure of the Organization
    - Employee Communications
- Talent Planning and Acquisition
    - Federal Laws and Regulations
    - Planning Concepts and Terms
- Learning and Development
    - Theories and Applications
    - Adult Learning Process
- Total Rewards
    - Job Pricing, Pay Structures, and Non-Cash Compensation
    - Benefits Programs
- Employee and Labor Relations
    - General Employee Relations Activities and Analysis
    - Human Relations, Culture, and Values

Course Features:
- PHR Study Guide
    - Get content that complements our best-selling study guide.
- 8 Full-Length Practice Tests
    - With over 1,000 practice questions, you can test yourself again and again.
- Mobile Friendly
    - If you need to study on the go, the course is easily accessible from your mobile device.
- PHR Flashcards
    - Our course includes a flashcard mode consisting of over 350 content cards to help you study.

To receive this discount, visit our website at mometrix.com/university/phr or simply scan this QR code with your smartphone. At the checkout page, enter the discount code: **phr50off**

If you have any questions or concerns, please contact us at support@mometrix.com.

SCAN HERE

FREE Study Skills Videos/DVD Offer

Dear Customer,

Thank you for your purchase from Mometrix! We consider it an honor and a privilege that you have purchased our product and we want to ensure your satisfaction.

As part of our ongoing effort to meet the needs of test takers, we have developed a set of Study Skills Videos that we would like to give you for <u>FREE</u>. These videos cover our *best practices* for getting ready for your exam, from how to use our study materials to how to best prepare for the day of the test.

All that we ask is that you email us with feedback that would describe your experience so far with our product. Good, bad, or indifferent, we want to know what you think!

To get your FREE Study Skills Videos, you can use the **QR code** below, or send us an **email** at <u>studyvideos@mometrix.com</u> with *FREE VIDEOS* in the subject line and the following information in the body of the email:

- The name of the product you purchased.
- Your product rating on a scale of 1-5, with 5 being the highest rating.
- Your feedback. It can be long, short, or anything in between. We just want to know your impressions and experience so far with our product. (Good feedback might include how our study material met your needs and ways we might be able to make it even better. You could highlight features that you found helpful or features that you think we should add.)

If you have any questions or concerns, please don't hesitate to contact me directly.

Thanks again!

Sincerely,

Jay Willis
Vice President
<u>jay.willis@mometrix.com</u>
1-800-673-8175

PHR

Study Guide
2025-2026

3 Full-Length Practice Tests

Secrets Prep Book for the
HRCI PHR
Certification Exam

7th Edition

Copyright © 2025 by Mometrix Media LLC

All rights reserved. This product, or parts thereof, may not be reproduced, stored in a retrieval system, or transmitted in any form or by any means—electronic, mechanical, photocopy, recording, scanning, or other—except for brief quotations in critical reviews or articles, without the prior written permission of the publisher.

Written and edited by the Matthew Bowling

Printed in the United States of America

This paper meets the requirements of ANSI/NISO Z39.48-1992 (Permanence of Paper).

Mometrix offers volume discount pricing to institutions. For more information or a price quote, please contact our sales department at sales@mometrix.com or 888-248-1219.

Mometrix Media LLC is not affiliated with or endorsed by any official testing organization. All organizational and test names are trademarks of their respective owners.

Paperback
ISBN 13: 978-1-5167-2794-0
ISBN 10: 1-5167-2794-0

Dear Future Exam Success Story

First of all, **THANK YOU** for purchasing Mometrix study materials!

Second, congratulations! You are one of the few determined test-takers who are committed to doing whatever it takes to excel on your exam. **You have come to the right place.** We developed these study materials with one goal in mind: to deliver you the information you need in a format that's concise and easy to use.

In addition to optimizing your guide for the content of the test, we've outlined our recommended steps for breaking down the preparation process into small, attainable goals so you can make sure you stay on track.

We've also analyzed the entire test-taking process, identifying the most common pitfalls and showing how you can overcome them and be ready for any curveball the test throws you.

Standardized testing is one of the biggest obstacles on your road to success, which only increases the importance of doing well in the high-pressure, high-stakes environment of test day. Your results on this test could have a significant impact on your future, and this guide provides the information and practical advice to help you achieve your full potential on test day.

Your success is our success

We would love to hear from you! If you would like to share the story of your exam success or if you have any questions or comments in regard to our products, please contact us at **800-673-8175** or **support@mometrix.com**.

Thanks again for your business and we wish you continued success!

Sincerely,
The Mometrix Test Preparation Team

Need more help? Check out our flashcards at:
http://mometrixflashcards.com/HRCI

Table of Contents

Introduction _____ 1
Secret Key #1 – Plan Big, Study Small _____ 2
Secret Key #2 – Make Your Studying Count _____ 3
Secret Key #3 – Practice the Right Way _____ 4
Secret Key #4 – Pace Yourself _____ 6
Secret Key #5 – Have a Plan for Guessing _____ 7
Test-Taking Strategies _____ 10
Business Management _____ 15
   General Business Environment _____ 15
   Relationships with Cross-Functional Stakeholders _____ 20
   Risks and Best Practices _____ 24
   Metrics and Data _____ 32
   Organizational Culture, Core Values, and Ethics _____ 35
Workforce Planning and Talent Acquisition _____ 41
   US Federal Laws and Organizational Policies Related to Hiring _ 42
   Sourcing Methods _____ 47
   Talent Acquisition Lifecycle _____ 51
Learning and Development _____ 61
   Career Development and Professional Growth _____ 61
   Succession Planning _____ 63
   Learning and Development Programs _____ 65
Total Rewards _____ 73
   Total Rewards Programs _____ 73
   Non-Monetary Rewards _____ 80
   Benefits _____ 81
   US Federally Compliant Compensation and Benefit Programs _____ 90
Employee Engagement _____ 98
   Enhancing Employee Participation and Engagement _____ 98
   Performance Management _____ 102
   Performance and Employment Activities _____ 108
Employee and Labor Relations _____ 115
   Outreach and Diversity, Equity, and Inclusion (DEI) _____ 115
   US Federal Health, Safety, Security, and Privacy Laws _____ 123
   Organizational Policies and Procedures _____ 131
   Employee Complaints, Concerns, and Conflicts _____ 133
   Employee and Labor Relations _____ 140
HR Information Management _____ 146
   HR Database Content and Technologies _____ 146

    Using Information Obtained from HR Databases _____ 150
    Security Best Practices _____ 154

PHR Practice Test #1 _____ 157
Answer Key and Explanations for Test #1 _____ 183
PHR Practice Test #2 _____ 195
Answer Key and Explanations for Test #2 _____ 221
PHR Practice Test #3 _____ 235
Answer Key and Explanations for Test #3 _____ 263
How to Overcome Test Anxiety _____ 275
Additional Bonus Material _____ 281

Introduction

Thank you for purchasing this resource! You have made the choice to prepare yourself for a test that could have a huge impact on your future, and this guide is designed to help you be fully ready for test day. Obviously, it's important to have a solid understanding of the test material, but you also need to be prepared for the unique environment and stressors of the test, so that you can perform to the best of your abilities.

For this purpose, the first section that appears in this guide is the **Secret Keys**. We've devoted countless hours to meticulously researching what works and what doesn't, and we've boiled down our findings to the five most impactful steps you can take to improve your performance on the test. We start at the beginning with study planning and move through the preparation process, all the way to the testing strategies that will help you get the most out of what you know when you're finally sitting in front of the test.

We recommend that you start preparing for your test as far in advance as possible. However, if you've bought this guide as a last-minute study resource and only have a few days before your test, we recommend that you skip over the first two Secret Keys since they address a long-term study plan.

If you struggle with **test anxiety**, we strongly encourage you to check out our recommendations for how you can overcome it. Test anxiety is a formidable foe, but it can be beaten, and we want to make sure you have the tools you need to defeat it.

Secret Key #1 – Plan Big, Study Small

There's a lot riding on your performance. If you want to ace this test, you're going to need to keep your skills sharp and the material fresh in your mind. You need a plan that lets you review everything you need to know while still fitting in your schedule. We'll break this strategy down into three categories.

Information Organization

Start with the information you already have: the official test outline. From this, you can make a complete list of all the concepts you need to cover before the test. Organize these concepts into groups that can be studied together, and create a list of any related vocabulary you need to learn so you can brush up on any difficult terms. You'll want to keep this vocabulary list handy once you actually start studying since you may need to add to it along the way.

Time Management

Once you have your set of study concepts, decide how to spread them out over the time you have left before the test. Break your study plan into small, clear goals so you have a manageable task for each day and know exactly what you're doing. Then just focus on one small step at a time. When you manage your time this way, you don't need to spend hours at a time studying. Studying a small block of content for a short period each day helps you retain information better and avoid stressing over how much you have left to do. You can relax knowing that you have a plan to cover everything in time. In order for this strategy to be effective though, you have to start studying early and stick to your schedule. Avoid the exhaustion and futility that comes from last-minute cramming!

Study Environment

The environment you study in has a big impact on your learning. Studying in a coffee shop, while probably more enjoyable, is not likely to be as fruitful as studying in a quiet room. It's important to keep distractions to a minimum. You're only planning to study for a short block of time, so make the most of it. Don't pause to check your phone or get up to find a snack. It's also important to **avoid multitasking**. Research has consistently shown that multitasking will make your studying dramatically less effective. Your study area should also be comfortable and well-lit so you don't have the distraction of straining your eyes or sitting on an uncomfortable chair.

The time of day you study is also important. You want to be rested and alert. Don't wait until just before bedtime. Study when you'll be most likely to comprehend and remember. Even better, if you know what time of day your test will be, set that time aside for study. That way your brain will be used to working on that subject at that specific time and you'll have a better chance of recalling information.

Finally, it can be helpful to team up with others who are studying for the same test. Your actual studying should be done in as isolated an environment as possible, but the work of organizing the information and setting up the study plan can be divided up. In between study sessions, you can discuss with your teammates the concepts that you're all studying and quiz each other on the details. Just be sure that your teammates are as serious about the test as you are. If you find that your study time is being replaced with social time, you might need to find a new team.

Secret Key #2 – Make Your Studying Count

You're devoting a lot of time and effort to preparing for this test, so you want to be absolutely certain it will pay off. This means doing more than just reading the content and hoping you can remember it on test day. It's important to make every minute of study count. There are two main areas you can focus on to make your studying count.

Retention

It doesn't matter how much time you study if you can't remember the material. You need to make sure you are retaining the concepts. To check your retention of the information you're learning, try recalling it at later times with minimal prompting. Try carrying around flashcards and glance at one or two from time to time or ask a friend who's also studying for the test to quiz you.

To enhance your retention, look for ways to put the information into practice so that you can apply it rather than simply recalling it. If you're using the information in practical ways, it will be much easier to remember. Similarly, it helps to solidify a concept in your mind if you're not only reading it to yourself but also explaining it to someone else. Ask a friend to let you teach them about a concept you're a little shaky on (or speak aloud to an imaginary audience if necessary). As you try to summarize, define, give examples, and answer your friend's questions, you'll understand the concepts better and they will stay with you longer. Finally, step back for a big picture view and ask yourself how each piece of information fits with the whole subject. When you link the different concepts together and see them working together as a whole, it's easier to remember the individual components.

Finally, practice showing your work on any multi-step problems, even if you're just studying. Writing out each step you take to solve a problem will help solidify the process in your mind, and you'll be more likely to remember it during the test.

Modality

Modality simply refers to the means or method by which you study. Choosing a study modality that fits your own individual learning style is crucial. No two people learn best in exactly the same way, so it's important to know your strengths and use them to your advantage.

For example, if you learn best by visualization, focus on visualizing a concept in your mind and draw an image or a diagram. Try color-coding your notes, illustrating them, or creating symbols that will trigger your mind to recall a learned concept. If you learn best by hearing or discussing information, find a study partner who learns the same way or read aloud to yourself. Think about how to put the information in your own words. Imagine that you are giving a lecture on the topic and record yourself so you can listen to it later.

For any learning style, flashcards can be helpful. Organize the information so you can take advantage of spare moments to review. Underline key words or phrases. Use different colors for different categories. Mnemonic devices (such as creating a short list in which every item starts with the same letter) can also help with retention. Find what works best for you and use it to store the information in your mind most effectively and easily.

Secret Key #3 – Practice the Right Way

Your success on test day depends not only on how many hours you put into preparing, but also on whether you prepared the right way. It's good to check along the way to see if your studying is paying off. One of the most effective ways to do this is by taking practice tests to evaluate your progress. Practice tests are useful because they show exactly where you need to improve. Every time you take a practice test, pay special attention to these three groups of questions:

- The questions you got wrong
- The questions you had to guess on, even if you guessed right
- The questions you found difficult or slow to work through

This will show you exactly what your weak areas are, and where you need to devote more study time. Ask yourself why each of these questions gave you trouble. Was it because you didn't understand the material? Was it because you didn't remember the vocabulary? Do you need more repetitions on this type of question to build speed and confidence? Dig into those questions and figure out how you can strengthen your weak areas as you go back to review the material.

Additionally, many practice tests have a section explaining the answer choices. It can be tempting to read the explanation and think that you now have a good understanding of the concept. However, an explanation likely only covers part of the question's broader context. Even if the explanation makes perfect sense, **go back and investigate** every concept related to the question until you're positive you have a thorough understanding.

As you go along, keep in mind that the practice test is just that: practice. Memorizing these questions and answers will not be very helpful on the actual test because it is unlikely to have any of the same exact questions. If you only know the right answers to the sample questions, you won't be prepared for the real thing. **Study the concepts** until you understand them fully, and then you'll be able to answer any question that shows up on the test.

It's important to wait on the practice tests until you're ready. If you take a test on your first day of study, you may be overwhelmed by the amount of material covered and how much you need to learn. Work up to it gradually.

On test day, you'll need to be prepared for answering questions, managing your time, and using the test-taking strategies you've learned. It's a lot to balance, like a mental marathon that will have a big impact on your future. Like training for a marathon, you'll need to start slowly and work your way up. When test day arrives, you'll be ready.

Start with the strategies you've read in the first two Secret Keys—plan your course and study in the way that works best for you. If you have time, consider using multiple study resources to get different approaches to the same concepts. It can be helpful to see difficult concepts from more than one angle. Then find a good source for practice tests. Many times, the test website will suggest potential study resources or provide sample tests.

Practice Test Strategy

If you're able to find at least three practice tests, we recommend this strategy:

UNTIMED AND OPEN-BOOK PRACTICE

Take the first test with no time constraints and with your notes and study guide handy. Take your time and focus on applying the strategies you've learned.

TIMED AND OPEN-BOOK PRACTICE

Take the second practice test open-book as well, but set a timer and practice pacing yourself to finish in time.

TIMED AND CLOSED-BOOK PRACTICE

Take any other practice tests as if it were test day. Set a timer and put away your study materials. Sit at a table or desk in a quiet room, imagine yourself at the testing center, and answer questions as quickly and accurately as possible.

Keep repeating timed and closed-book tests on a regular basis until you run out of practice tests or it's time for the actual test. Your mind will be ready for the schedule and stress of test day, and you'll be able to focus on recalling the material you've learned.

Secret Key #4 – Pace Yourself

Once you're fully prepared for the material on the test, your biggest challenge on test day will be managing your time. Just knowing that the clock is ticking can make you panic even if you have plenty of time left. Work on pacing yourself so you can build confidence against the time constraints of the exam. Pacing is a difficult skill to master, especially in a high-pressure environment, so **practice is vital**.

Set time expectations for your pace based on how much time is available. For example, if a section has 60 questions and the time limit is 30 minutes, you know you have to average 30 seconds or less per question in order to answer them all. Although 30 seconds is the hard limit, set 25 seconds per question as your goal, so you reserve extra time to spend on harder questions. When you budget extra time for the harder questions, you no longer have any reason to stress when those questions take longer to answer.

Don't let this time expectation distract you from working through the test at a calm, steady pace, but keep it in mind so you don't spend too much time on any one question. Recognize that taking extra time on one question you don't understand may keep you from answering two that you do understand later in the test. If your time limit for a question is up and you're still not sure of the answer, mark it and move on, and come back to it later if the time and the test format allow. If the testing format doesn't allow you to return to earlier questions, just make an educated guess; then put it out of your mind and move on.

On the easier questions, be careful not to rush. It may seem wise to hurry through them so you have more time for the challenging ones, but it's not worth missing one if you know the concept and just didn't take the time to read the question fully. Work efficiently but make sure you understand the question and have looked at all of the answer choices, since more than one may seem right at first.

Even if you're paying attention to the time, you may find yourself a little behind at some point. You should speed up to get back on track, but do so wisely. Don't panic; just take a few seconds less on each question until you're caught up. Don't guess without thinking, but do look through the answer choices and eliminate any you know are wrong. If you can get down to two choices, it is often worthwhile to guess from those. Once you've chosen an answer, move on and don't dwell on any that you skipped or had to hurry through. If a question was taking too long, chances are it was one of the harder ones, so you weren't as likely to get it right anyway.

On the other hand, if you find yourself getting ahead of schedule, it may be beneficial to slow down a little. The more quickly you work, the more likely you are to make a careless mistake that will affect your score. You've budgeted time for each question, so don't be afraid to spend that time. Practice an efficient but careful pace to get the most out of the time you have.

Secret Key #5 – Have a Plan for Guessing

When you're taking the test, you may find yourself stuck on a question. Some of the answer choices seem better than others, but you don't see the one answer choice that is obviously correct. What do you do?

The scenario described above is very common, yet most test takers have not effectively prepared for it. Developing and practicing a plan for guessing may be one of the single most effective uses of your time as you get ready for the exam.

In developing your plan for guessing, there are three questions to address:

- When should you start the guessing process?
- How should you narrow down the choices?
- Which answer should you choose?

When to Start the Guessing Process

Unless your plan for guessing is to select C every time (which, despite its merits, is not what we recommend), you need to leave yourself enough time to apply your answer elimination strategies. Since you have a limited amount of time for each question, that means that if you're going to give yourself the best shot at guessing correctly, you have to decide quickly whether or not you will guess.

Of course, the best-case scenario is that you don't have to guess at all, so first, see if you can answer the question based on your knowledge of the subject and basic reasoning skills. Focus on the key words in the question and try to jog your memory of related topics. Give yourself a chance to bring the knowledge to mind, but once you realize that you don't have (or you can't access) the knowledge you need to answer the question, it's time to start the guessing process.

It's almost always better to start the guessing process too early than too late. It only takes a few seconds to remember something and answer the question from knowledge. Carefully eliminating wrong answer choices takes longer. Plus, going through the process of eliminating answer choices can actually help jog your memory.

Summary: Start the guessing process as soon as you decide that you can't answer the question based on your knowledge.

How to Narrow Down the Choices

The next chapter in this book (**Test-Taking Strategies**) includes a wide range of strategies for how to approach questions and how to look for answer choices to eliminate. You will definitely want to read those carefully, practice them, and figure out which ones work best for you. Here though, we're going to address a mindset rather than a particular strategy.

Your odds of guessing an answer correctly depend on how many options you are choosing from.

Number of options left	5	4	3	2	1
Odds of guessing correctly	20%	25%	33%	50%	100%

You can see from this chart just how valuable it is to be able to eliminate incorrect answers and make an educated guess, but there are two things that many test takers do that cause them to miss out on the benefits of guessing:

- Accidentally eliminating the correct answer
- Selecting an answer based on an impression

We'll look at the first one here, and the second one in the next section.

To avoid accidentally eliminating the correct answer, we recommend a thought exercise called **the $5 challenge**. In this challenge, you only eliminate an answer choice from contention if you are willing to bet $5 on it being wrong. Why $5? Five dollars is a small but not insignificant amount of money. It's an amount you could afford to lose but wouldn't want to throw away. And while losing $5 once might not hurt too much, doing it twenty times will set you back $100. In the same way, each small decision you make—eliminating a choice here, guessing on a question there—won't by itself impact your score very much, but when you put them all together, they can make a big difference. By holding each answer choice elimination decision to a higher standard, you can reduce the risk of accidentally eliminating the correct answer.

The $5 challenge can also be applied in a positive sense: If you are willing to bet $5 that an answer choice *is* correct, go ahead and mark it as correct.

Summary: Only eliminate an answer choice if you are willing to bet $5 that it is wrong.

Which Answer to Choose

You're taking the test. You've run into a hard question and decided you'll have to guess. You've eliminated all the answer choices you're willing to bet $5 on. Now you have to pick an answer. Why do we even need to talk about this? Why can't you just pick whichever one you feel like when the time comes?

The answer to these questions is that if you don't come into the test with a plan, you'll rely on your impression to select an answer choice, and if you do that, you risk falling into a trap. The test writers know that everyone who takes their test will be guessing on some of the questions, so they intentionally write wrong answer choices to seem plausible. You still have to pick an answer though, and if the wrong answer choices are designed to look right, how can you ever be sure that you're not falling for their trap? The best solution we've found to this dilemma is to take the decision out of your hands entirely. Here is the process we recommend:

Once you've eliminated any choices that you are confident (willing to bet $5) are wrong, select the first remaining choice as your answer.

Whether you choose to select the first remaining choice, the second, or the last, the important thing is that you use some preselected standard. Using this approach guarantees that you will not be enticed into selecting an answer choice that looks right, because you are not basing your decision on how the answer choices look.

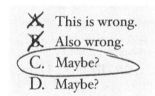

This is not meant to make you question your knowledge. Instead, it is to help you recognize the difference between your knowledge and your impressions. There's a huge difference between thinking an answer is right because of what you know, and thinking an answer is right because it looks or sounds like it should be right.

Summary: To ensure that your selection is appropriately random, make a predetermined selection from among all answer choices you have not eliminated.

Test-Taking Strategies

This section contains a list of test-taking strategies that you may find helpful as you work through the test. By taking what you know and applying logical thought, you can maximize your chances of answering any question correctly!

It is very important to realize that every question is different and every person is different: no single strategy will work on every question, and no single strategy will work for every person. That's why we've included all of them here, so you can try them out and determine which ones work best for different types of questions and which ones work best for you.

Question Strategies

⊘ Read Carefully

Read the question and the answer choices carefully. Don't miss the question because you misread the terms. You have plenty of time to read each question thoroughly and make sure you understand what is being asked. Yet a happy medium must be attained, so don't waste too much time. You must read carefully and efficiently.

⊘ Contextual Clues

Look for contextual clues. If the question includes a word you are not familiar with, look at the immediate context for some indication of what the word might mean. Contextual clues can often give you all the information you need to decipher the meaning of an unfamiliar word. Even if you can't determine the meaning, you may be able to narrow down the possibilities enough to make a solid guess at the answer to the question.

⊘ Prefixes

If you're having trouble with a word in the question or answer choices, try dissecting it. Take advantage of every clue that the word might include. Prefixes can be a huge help. Usually, they allow you to determine a basic meaning. *Pre-* means before, *post-* means after, *pro-* is positive, *de-* is negative. From prefixes, you can get an idea of the general meaning of the word and try to put it into context.

⊘ Hedge Words

Watch out for critical hedge words, such as *likely, may, can, sometimes, often, almost, mostly, usually, generally, rarely,* and *sometimes*. Question writers insert these hedge phrases to cover every possibility. Often an answer choice will be wrong simply because it leaves no room for exception. Be on guard for answer choices that have definitive words such as *exactly* and *always*.

⊘ Switchback Words

Stay alert for *switchbacks*. These are the words and phrases frequently used to alert you to shifts in thought. The most common switchback words are *but, although,* and *however*. Others include *nevertheless, on the other hand, even though, while, in spite of, despite,* and *regardless of*. Switchback words are important to catch because they can change the direction of the question or an answer choice.

⊘ FACE VALUE

When in doubt, use common sense. Accept the situation in the problem at face value. Don't read too much into it. These problems will not require you to make wild assumptions. If you have to go beyond creativity and warp time or space in order to have an answer choice fit the question, then you should move on and consider the other answer choices. These are normal problems rooted in reality. The applicable relationship or explanation may not be readily apparent, but it is there for you to figure out. Use your common sense to interpret anything that isn't clear.

Answer Choice Strategies

⊘ ANSWER SELECTION

The most thorough way to pick an answer choice is to identify and eliminate wrong answers until only one is left, then confirm it is the correct answer. Sometimes an answer choice may immediately seem right, but be careful. The test writers will usually put more than one reasonable answer choice on each question, so take a second to read all of them and make sure that the other choices are not equally obvious. As long as you have time left, it is better to read every answer choice than to pick the first one that looks right without checking the others.

⊘ ANSWER CHOICE FAMILIES

An answer choice family consists of two (in rare cases, three) answer choices that are very similar in construction and cannot all be true at the same time. If you see two answer choices that are direct opposites or parallels, one of them is usually the correct answer. For instance, if one answer choice says that quantity *x* increases and another either says that quantity *x* decreases (opposite) or says that quantity *y* increases (parallel), then those answer choices would fall into the same family. An answer choice that doesn't match the construction of the answer choice family is more likely to be incorrect. Most questions will not have answer choice families, but when they do appear, you should be prepared to recognize them.

⊘ ELIMINATE ANSWERS

Eliminate answer choices as soon as you realize they are wrong, but make sure you consider all possibilities. If you are eliminating answer choices and realize that the last one you are left with is also wrong, don't panic. Start over and consider each choice again. There may be something you missed the first time that you will realize on the second pass.

⊘ AVOID FACT TRAPS

Don't be distracted by an answer choice that is factually true but doesn't answer the question. You are looking for the choice that answers the question. Stay focused on what the question is asking for so you don't accidentally pick an answer that is true but incorrect. Always go back to the question and make sure the answer choice you've selected actually answers the question and is not merely a true statement.

⊘ EXTREME STATEMENTS

In general, you should avoid answers that put forth extreme actions as standard practice or proclaim controversial ideas as established fact. An answer choice that states the "process should be used in certain situations, if…" is much more likely to be correct than one that states the "process should be discontinued completely." The first is a calm rational statement and doesn't even make a definitive, uncompromising stance, using a hedge word *if* to provide wiggle room, whereas the second choice is far more extreme.

✓ Benchmark

As you read through the answer choices and you come across one that seems to answer the question well, mentally select that answer choice. This is not your final answer, but it's the one that will help you evaluate the other answer choices. The one that you selected is your benchmark or standard for judging each of the other answer choices. Every other answer choice must be compared to your benchmark. That choice is correct until proven otherwise by another answer choice beating it. If you find a better answer, then that one becomes your new benchmark. Once you've decided that no other choice answers the question as well as your benchmark, you have your final answer.

✓ Predict the Answer

Before you even start looking at the answer choices, it is often best to try to predict the answer. When you come up with the answer on your own, it is easier to avoid distractions and traps because you will know exactly what to look for. The right answer choice is unlikely to be word-for-word what you came up with, but it should be a close match. Even if you are confident that you have the right answer, you should still take the time to read each option before moving on.

General Strategies

✓ Tough Questions

If you are stumped on a problem or it appears too hard or too difficult, don't waste time. Move on! Remember though, if you can quickly check for obviously incorrect answer choices, your chances of guessing correctly are greatly improved. Before you completely give up, at least try to knock out a couple of possible answers. Eliminate what you can and then guess at the remaining answer choices before moving on.

✓ Check Your Work

Since you will probably not know every term listed and the answer to every question, it is important that you get credit for the ones that you do know. Don't miss any questions through careless mistakes. If at all possible, try to take a second to look back over your answer selection and make sure you've selected the correct answer choice and haven't made a costly careless mistake (such as marking an answer choice that you didn't mean to mark). This quick double check should more than pay for itself in caught mistakes for the time it costs.

✓ Pace Yourself

It's easy to be overwhelmed when you're looking at a page full of questions; your mind is confused and full of random thoughts, and the clock is ticking down faster than you would like. Calm down and maintain the pace that you have set for yourself. Especially as you get down to the last few minutes of the test, don't let the small numbers on the clock make you panic. As long as you are on track by monitoring your pace, you are guaranteed to have time for each question.

✓ Don't Rush

It is very easy to make errors when you are in a hurry. Maintaining a fast pace in answering questions is pointless if it makes you miss questions that you would have gotten right otherwise. Test writers like to include distracting information and wrong answers that seem right. Taking a little extra time to avoid careless mistakes can make all the difference in your test score. Find a pace that allows you to be confident in the answers that you select.

⊘ Keep Moving

Panicking will not help you pass the test, so do your best to stay calm and keep moving. Taking deep breaths and going through the answer elimination steps you practiced can help to break through a stress barrier and keep your pace.

Final Notes

The combination of a solid foundation of content knowledge and the confidence that comes from practicing your plan for applying that knowledge is the key to maximizing your performance on test day. As your foundation of content knowledge is built up and strengthened, you'll find that the strategies included in this chapter become more and more effective in helping you quickly sift through the distractions and traps of the test to isolate the correct answer.

Now that you're preparing to move forward into the test content chapters of this book, be sure to keep your goal in mind. As you read, think about how you will be able to apply this information on the test. If you've already seen sample questions for the test and you have an idea of the question format and style, try to come up with questions of your own that you can answer based on what you're reading. This will give you valuable practice applying your knowledge in the same ways you can expect to on test day.

Good luck and good studying!

Business Management

General Business Environment

MISSION AND VISION STATEMENTS

Mission statements and vision statements are similar in that they are both intended to clarify the objectives of the organization. However, a mission statement is only intended to define the broad mission an organization is attempting to carry out on a daily basis. A vision statement is intended to define the specific goals an organization hopes to achieve in the future.

A mission statement is a declaration of the reason an organization exists. This is important in determining standards, values, strategies, and other organizational aspects and serves as a guideline for establishing the processes to achieve goals. For example, the mission statement of a retail chain might be "to provide the best shopping experience possible for our customers." As a result, a decision might be made to implement standards and practices that promote high levels of customer service.

A vision statement is a declaration of the goals the organization wishes to achieve at some future point, which is important in designing and implementing the strategies necessary to meet those goals. For example, the vision statement of a retail chain might be to become the largest retail chain in the United States. As a result, the decision might be made to implement strategies that allow for rapid expansion, like finding and purchasing new locations and training new personnel quickly.

BUSINESS TERMS AND CONCEPTS

COMPETITIVE ADVANTAGE

An organization may seek to produce goods or provide services better than those of a similar organization, or to produce specialized goods or services to focus on a specific target market. **Competitive advantage** is what sets one organization above another in the eye of the consumer. Competitive advantage leads to higher profit margins and increased value for the organization and its shareholders. This advantage can originate in numerous ways, such as having access to developing technology or other resources not readily available to others, employing a highly skilled workforce, and leading in price points. There are four key areas for building competitive advantage:

- **Cost leadership** is the ability of an organization to offer the same quality product or service as the competition but at a lower price. Companies will often look for the best way to produce goods and services with minimal inefficiencies and well-developed production methods.
- **Differentiation leadership** is another key area to establishing competitive advantage. It entails marketing products and services that are significantly different than offerings from competing organizations. This method requires continuous improvement and investment in research and development.
- **Cost focus** is a strategy similar to cost leadership, but with emphasis on a specific market. It involves offering a quality product/service at a low price with a targeted market segment in mind. Using the cost focus strategy helps an organization establish brand awareness more readily in that market.
- **Differentiation focus** is a strategy like differentiation leadership, in that they both offer specific or custom products, but the differentiation focus strategy offers those specialized products/services to a narrow and targeted market.

Revenue

For an organization, **revenue** is the total amount of money brought in, measured over a specific time period. The revenue of an organization is its gross income before subtracting any expenses. Revenue is calculated as the total of the company's earnings plus gained interest and increased equity over a specified period, such as a quarter or year. Calculation and analysis of revenue is critical to understanding the financial success of the organization.

Profit and Loss

The difference between revenue and expenses that determine if the company made or lost money is referred to as the **profit and loss**. Profit and loss can be simply explained as the money brought into an organization and the money going out of an organization, respectively. Net profit and loss can be calculated by finding the difference between gross profit/loss and the sum of indirect income/expenses of the organization. If the difference is positive, the company is making a profit. If the difference is negative, the company is experiencing a loss for the calculated period. There are many expenses that come out of the revenue of an organization, such as compensation, advertising/marketing, utilities, licensing, building fees (rent/mortgage), the cost of making a product or providing a service, and insurance. These expenditures are often tracked through a **profit and loss statement**, which helps the organization determine if the business is generating revenue or losing revenue.

Financial Projections

Financial projections are a collection of financial statements used to forecast future expenses and revenue. These projections have numerous uses both internally and externally. Additional funding can be secured using financial projections. An organization can also analyze overall business performance and determine areas for improvement. Financial projections are used to demonstrate what an organization plans to do with its money, and what its growth expectations look like. Financial projections are made up of external and internal data. Internal data included in the projection should include an income statement, a cash flow statement, and a balance sheet. The **income statement** displays expenses, revenue, and profit for a set time period. The **cash flow statement** details incoming and outgoing cash. The **balance sheet** shows business assets, liabilities, and equity. External data included in the projection can include market growth rates, historical growth trends in the market, and consumer demand.

Quality

The **quality** of an organization plays a large role in the image, branding, and reputation of the organization to the public and consumers. It can have various definitions, depending on how the word is applied. For example, it can be defined as how well an organization meets the expectations and needs of its customers. This metric can be measured using customer satisfaction surveys, customer complaints, and other methods of feedback. Some business areas have specific ways to measure quality. In manufacturing, for example, there are set standards related to the reliability and safety of a product and customer satisfaction with the product. In a service business area, quality may be measured based on response time, how complaints are addressed and resolved, and levels of customer service.

Service-Level Agreements

A **service-level agreement (SLA)** is a contract between at least two parties, where one party (or group) provides a service to another party (or group). SLAs can be informal contracts, such as between departments, or they can be formal and legally binding contracts between one organization and another. There are three main types of **SLAs:** customer-based, service-based, and multilevel.

- A **customer-based** SLA exists between a vendor and a customer. It details the level of service that will be delivered to the customer. An agreement between a customer and a payroll service is an example of a customer-based SLA.
- An **internal** SLA can exist between departments to outline the roles and responsibilities of the teams so that there is a clear understanding of expectations. An SLA between the marketing and sales departments might detail lead requirements from marketing to sales in order to reach goals.
- A **multilevel** SLA is divided into different tiers or sections based on the level of access or service provided. For example, a software-as-a-service (SaaS) provider might offer basic email services to all individuals within an organization, and access to additional features or software such as word processing or storage options to those in specific departments.

FIXED AND VARIABLE COSTS

Organizations are responsible for both fixed and variable costs related to the operations of the business. **Fixed costs** do not change in relation to the activity of a business; they remain the same regardless of how much or how little a company produces. Property taxes, rent, licensing, and insurance are examples of common fixed costs. **Variable costs** do change based on business activity. These costs increase as production increases, and lower as production shrinks. Utilities, raw materials, and payroll are examples of common variable costs.

SUPPLY AND DEMAND

The term **supply and demand** refers to the economic relationship involving the cost of a product, product availability, and buyer demand for the product. **Supply** is the amount of the product that is being sold on the market by companies producing that item or service. When the price point is high, it is profitable for an organization to increase supply. Supply can be impacted by numerous factors, including cost of production and availability of raw material. **Demand** is how many goods buyers are willing to purchase at different prices. If the price point is higher, fewer items will be demanded. As the price point lowers, demand increases. Factors that can impact demand can include pricing, the buyer's expectation, and the buyer's budget.

NET INCOME

The amount of money that a business makes after deducting the costs of raw goods/materials, taxes, wages, and operating expenses is its **net income**. This measurement is concrete and, for a publicly traded organization, is used to help calculate the earnings per share. This calculation is also the "bottom line" on an income statement and is used to understand how profitable a business is.

ANALYZING AND INTERPRETING BUSINESS DOCUMENTS
STRATEGIC PLANS

A **strategic plan** defines and communicates the direction that an organization will take over the course of three to five years. The plan contains the company's mission and vision, organizational goals and objectives, and the actions that it plans to take to achieve those goals. A strategic plan differs from a business plan in that strategic plans are recommended for companies that are already established. There are three main elements in the strategic planning process:

- **Forming the strategy.** Assess the current situation using internal and external audits. These assessments gather data in areas such as relevant industry data, employee feedback, and **SWOT** (strengths, weaknesses, opportunities, and threats) analysis. This information helps stakeholders determine where to allocate company resources for maximum return, which markets should be pursued or abandoned, and how growth and expansion should occur.
- **Implementing the strategy.** Once the strategy is formed, the organization needs to establish objectives and targets related to achieving the desired strategy outcome. Key performance indicators (KPIs) should be used to map out the processes and help monitor progress. Communication about the plan and changes throughout its implementation is key to success. Communicating the desired results and updates will help garner "buy-in" from individuals, helping to ensure the success of the initiatives.
- **Evaluate and revise the strategy.** Internal and external factors affecting strategy implementation need to reviewed, as does the success of the objectives and targets. When necessary, corrective steps should be taken and revisions should be made to make the strategy most effective.

Each of these three elements need to occur throughout all levels of the business, so that each area is aligned with the others. Communication and feedback throughout the organization are critical to help the organization function more effectively as a team. Establishing strong strategic plans allows an organization to move from a reactive approach to a proactive approach, which means that the company may have the opportunity to influence a situation versus just responding to it.

Contracts

Documents that define binding agreements between two or more individuals or groups, **contracts** are vital to the success of an organization. They help outline and define interactions between parties, which helps to eliminate ambiguity and friction. Contracts should include guidelines for how to handle issues and problems that may arise over time and outline expectations for vendors, employees, and partners. Contracts are also utilized to prevent proprietary information from being leaked or keep trade secrets internal. For a contract to be legally binding, it must contain several elements:

- **Offer.** The terms of the contract such as parties involved, length of service, value or price, and the scope of services.
- **Acceptance.** The involved parties agree on the offer.
- **Consideration.** The parties in the contract exchange something of value. If the buyer contracts for a recognition program, the buyer receives the program. The seller receives money based on the terms outlined in the offer.

When properly implemented and utilized, business contracts help manage business expectations and aid in avoiding unnecessary liability.

Grants

A business **grant** is money distributed to a company to be used for growth, hiring, development, or expansion. Grants are frequently bestowed on businesses that require research funding, are looking to expand, or that are starting up. There are two types of grants: grants from the government and private grants from other organizations or corporations. Grant programs have specific criteria and application requirements. In order to obtain a grant, a business needs to state the need for the grant money, that the grant money will be used for business purposes, and that there is a set purpose and goal outlined. Additionally, the business needs to follow the application process and provide any documentation or information requested. Grants are typically reserved for small businesses.

BUSINESS PLANS

A **business plan** is a detailed outline and definition of an organization's objectives and how the organization plans to achieve its goals. Business plans are used to identify metrics and priorities within a company. This document can be used for both internal and external audiences. Internally, it can be used to drive the company toward achieving its objectives and goals. Externally, it can be used to obtain investments or lending opportunities. No two business plans are exactly alike, but many share common key parts:

- **Executive summary.** This section introduces the company, including the mission statement and detailed information about employees, location, leadership, and operations.
- **Products and services.** This section introduces the products/services the company offers, including information like pricing, benefit to the customer, and how long the product will last. Companies can also use this section to highlight research and development or trademarks/patents specific to the organization. Information about the manufacturing or production process can also be included.
- **Market analysis.** The company should detail its strengths and weaknesses here. Expected demand should be listed, as should opportunity to gain market share. The company may also detail its competition and how it fits into that particular market.
- **Market strategy.** Advertising and marketing campaigns should be outlined, including the channels that will be used to target audiences. The company should also detail how it intends to attract and keep its customer base.
- **Financial planning.** Balance sheets, revenue projections/estimates, and financial statements should be provided, along with a detailed analysis of each, to describe the current and projected financial state of the organization.
- **Budget.** This area of the business plan includes costing information related to development, marketing, production, staffing, and any other related business expenses.

The information in the business plan can serve as a guide for how the organization should run.

BUSINESS CONTINUITY PLANS

A **business continuity plan (BCP)** is a set of standards and guidelines that an organization uses to ensure proper risk management and to prevent and recover from potential company threats such as natural disasters or cyber threats. The BCP should protect both personnel and assets. It should also guide the company on how to react quickly and continue to function when faced with a threat. The planning process for the BCP should contain the following steps:

- **Business impact analysis.** Functions and resources that are critical or time-sensitive should be identified.
- **Recovery.** Critical or time-sensitive business functions must have guidelines and implementation steps for recovery.
- **Plan development.** Framework plans should be developed and documented, and teams should be assigned to carry out required roles.
- **Training.** Teams assigned to required roles should complete exercises that review the plan and ensure that they are prepared to react.

Having a proper BCP in place will allow an organization to reduce company downtime and loss in the face of a threat or disaster.

Relationships with Cross-Functional Stakeholders

ORGANIZATIONAL STRUCTURES

Organizational design and organizational charts are related, but not the same. An organizational chart could be a part of the overall organizational design process. Organizational design is a process that aligns processes, functions, and people in a way that reduces dysfunction and inefficiencies. It requires an understanding of the work that is currently happening, roles and responsibilities, and future-oriented strategic goals. An understanding of these factors can help define what roles are needed for the future. From there, an organizational structure can develop, from which an organizational chart can be made. An organizational chart shows the organizational structure as a hierarchy. It shows each individual's position and displays reporting structure (who reports to who).

FUNCTIONAL ORGANIZATIONAL STRUCTURE

Functional organizational structure is often considered the most traditional structure. It is easily recognizable as being hierarchal—showing executives at the top, managers in the middle, and lower-level employees at the bottom. The organizational structure is divided into "functions," meaning employees are grouped by their skills, their knowledge, and the type of work that they do. In this type of structure, it would be common to see a hierarchy for general departments—sales, IT, administration, finance, etc. An advantage of the functional structure is the clarity that comes with knowing the exact chain of command. One disadvantage of this structure is the tendency for workers and leaders to operate without much interaction or partnering with the other functions. In such cases, functions become separate "silos," causing power struggles when business units must work together.

MATRIX ORGANIZATIONAL STRUCTURE

The matrix organizational structure is a combination of more traditional structures. Matrix structures are often identified by additional lines in an organizational chart, where a person has a direct (main) reporting responsibility to a department but also has a temporary or secondary reporting responsibility shown as a horizontal line. Matrix structures are common in the project management arena. As a project is starting, stakeholders are identified from cross-functional teams. Then a matrix structure is built to identify the reporting structure within the project team. This exists while project team members continue to have direct reporting responsibilities in their own departments. Matrix structures can also occur in roles that are not project based. For example, an HR professional may have a matrix reporting line to the geographical division they support while having a direct reporting line to the HR department. This helps to maintain consistency within HR processes while addressing the individualized needs of the supported division.

Matrix Organization Chart

DIVISIONAL ORGANIZATIONAL STRUCTURE

A divisional organizational structure aligns the company in a way that separates the company by product line or geographical region. The goal of this structure is to provide each division autonomy (within reason) to run its business. Ultimately, the structure is meant to allow "local" decision-making to be more responsive to customer needs. Often, each division is assigned its own administrative support, such as a dedicated HR partner. Besides local decision-making, one advantage of this structure is that it clearly identifies who is accountable for what. It also fosters internal competition—particularly if the divisions are divided geographically. One disadvantage of this structure is that it creates some redundancies across the organization, so it is typically more expensive. Ideally, organizations recoup this expense through increased customer commitment and sales.

Divisional Organization Chart

FLAT ORGANIZATIONAL STRUCTURE

A flat organizational structure can be understood easily by looking at an applicable organizational chart. Managers lead more employees in a flat organization, and more autonomy is given to lower-level workers. Advantages of this structure are that there are fewer layers of management and lower decision-making points. A flatter organization is often seen as being "lean," as there are fewer management-level salaries to pay. In addition, such organizations are seen as more adaptable because they have fewer layers of hierarchy. Flat organizational structures are easier for smaller organizations to implement. The larger an organization becomes, the more it needs structure and specialized workers. In addition, collaboration and communication are key to a flat organization's success, and both of these become more challenging as an organization grows.

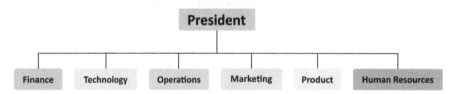

NETWORK ORGANIZATIONAL STRUCTURE

A network organizational structure is designed to keep all focus on the core business of the company. All supportive work is outsourced. Therefore, functions that might typically be kept in-house in a more traditional structure, such as IT, accounting, HR/recruitment, and facilities management, are all completed by third parties. This structure is advantageous because there are few internal distractions from the strategic business. On the other hand, this structure requires staff to have keen contract management skills to manage such a diverse group of contractors. This type of structure can also become unrealistic as an organization grows. For example, the organization may need an accountant who thoroughly understands the business, and over time, it may be more cost-effective to bring that skill in-house.

CHAIN OF COMMAND AND SPAN OF CONTROL

Organizational charts display both chain of command and span of control. The easiest way to understand the difference is that chain of command is shown "up and down" while span of control is shown "across." The term *chain of command* is commonly associated with the military, but it is also widely used in organizations. **Chain of command** specifies who reports to who and should explain who is "in charge." An example of chain of command would be a line worker who reports to the supervisor, who reports to the manager, who reports to a vice president, who reports to the CEO. Meanwhile, **span of control** shows how broad a manager's area of responsibility is. A manager with only two direct reports has a narrow span of control. On the other hand, a chief administrative officer who has responsibility for several different types of departments (such as facilities, HR, IT, and security) has a wide span of control.

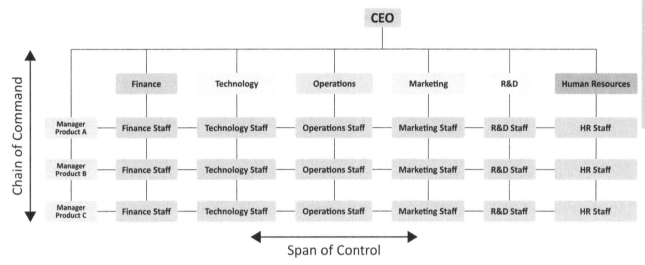

CENTRALIZATION

Centralization and decentralization have to do with how an organization wants decisions to be made. Centralization takes a more "command and control" approach. In other words, decisions are made higher up in the organization, or if it is a multisite organization, decisions are made in the corporate office. On the other hand, decentralization pushes decision-making further down in the organization. Decentralization is seen more often in divisional or flat organizations—where decision authority is pushed to lower levels. Neither type is necessarily good or bad. The choice is simply based on leadership preference or company need at the time. Organizations that are going through considerable change or conflict may need a more centralized approach to decision-making for consistency and structure. Meanwhile, organizations that operate in unique geographical regions may benefit from decentralization of decision-making.

CENTER OF EXCELLENCE (CoE)

A **center of excellence (CoE) HR model** features internal groups of consultants that have expertise in different HR functional areas, such as payroll and benefits. Their main role is to provide each company location with guidance driven by best practices and assistance with problem-solving. Generally, business units must utilize this in-house resource before seeking external help.

SHARED SERVICES

Some larger organizations have begun to centralize certain business functions into **shared service centers**, such as finance, information technology, or HR. Shared services are essentially the merging and streamlining of business operations that are used by multiple units of the same organization. This helps business units retain more control and identifies ways to work more efficiently, improving service quality and the credibility of each function. For example, an HR shared services center may process all employment-related changes for an entire enterprise within the company's human resource information system (HRIS) at the request of HR staff at each location.

Risks and Best Practices

Risk management refers to the process of identifying, analyzing, and prioritizing **risks or potential uncertainties** while developing strategies to protect the financial interests of a company. Risks or potential uncertainties may include workplace safety, workers' compensation, unemployment insurance, security, loss prevention, health and wellness, data management, privacy protection, project failures, and contingency planning. Depending upon the size of the company or severity of the threat, some or all of these areas might be assigned to HR. The underlying goal of risk management is to mitigate the costs of these uncertainties as much as possible.

RISK TYPES

- **Hazard risk** involves potential liability or loss of property and is generally mitigated by insurance. Workplace accidents, fires, and natural disasters are examples of risk that fall into this category.
- **Financial risk** involves potential negative impacts to a firm's cash flow. A major customer not paying invoices on time is an example of this type of risk.
- **Operational risk** involves the impact to a firm's ability to function effectively and may include technology failures, process breakdowns, and human error.
- **Strategic risk** involves a firm's plans becoming outdated due to shifts in the economy, politics, customer demographics, or the overall competitive landscape.

RISK ASSESSMENTS

Risk assessments are a critical element of risk management. A **quantitative risk assessment** will allow the business to assign actual dollar amounts to each risk based on value, exposure, single loss expectancy, annualized rate of occurrence, and annualized loss expectancy. **Single loss expectancy** is measured when a value is placed on each asset, and the percentage of loss is determined for each acknowledged threat. The **annualized loss expectancy** can be calculated by multiplying the single loss occurrence and the annualized rate of occurrence. In these calculations, potential loss amounts are used to consider whether implementing a security measure is necessary. **Qualitative risk assessment**, on the other hand, does not assign a defined monetary value to the risk. It uses descriptive statements to describe the potential impact of a risk, which can include a general reference to financial loss. For example, a major system breach would result in customer data being compromised, severe damage to the firm's reputation, and a significant financial blow to the organization due to handling the crisis, shoring up the system to prevent further issues, and responding to possible lawsuits by those affected.

RISK MANAGEMENT

Enterprise risk management (ERM) refers to a variety of techniques used to identify and minimize the effects of risks that may prevent the achievement of objectives. The process usually takes place after the organization has identified threats or opportunities related to a particular objective from a SWOT or PEST analysis. Once the threat or opportunity is identified, an assessment can be made to determine the risk. The organization can then determine the appropriate response based on the level of risk associated with the threat or opportunity.

There are five response strategies an organization can use to respond to a risk: reducing the amount or the potential effects of the risk, transferring the risk, sharing the risk, avoiding the risk, or accepting the risk. **Reducing the risk** includes any action taken to make the risk less likely to occur or less likely to cause significant harm to the organization. **Transferring the risk** includes any action that transfers some of the risk to another business entity (such as by transferring the risk to an insurance company by purchasing an insurance policy). **Sharing the risk** involves distributing the risk across multiple entities in order to lessen the risk to any particular one. **Avoiding the risk** refers to discontinuing any activities associated with the risk in order to eliminate the risk entirely. **Accepting the risk** refers to monitoring the risk because the potential benefits of the opportunity outweigh the potential cost.

It is important for an HR professional to be able to manage risk effectively because a great deal of the organization's financial risk will be related to human resources. Some of the more costly risks are related to liability and legal concerns. These concerns include being held liable for the unethical, illegal, or inappropriate actions of employees, fines for not submitting required government forms, or filling them out incorrectly. Since many of these risks can be controlled through careful monitoring and intelligent risk management, it is essential for an HR professional to be able to identify risks as they appear and to find ways to reduce the chance that those risks will affect the organization.

There are a variety of methods an HR professional can use to identify potential risks to the organization, but the most common method is an HR audit. An **HR audit** consists of a checklist, survey, or similar communication designed to assess whether a particular employee or department understands and is adhering to the policies, procedures, and regulations set by the organization. An HR audit is designed to ensure each employee is adhering to all laws and regulations set by the local, state, and federal government. The format used for an HR audit will vary to adapt to a wide range of risks or to make sure that a specific risk, such as fines associated with a newly passed law, can be avoided.

EPLI

Employment practices liability insurance (EPLI) is a risk management tool used to share financial risk associated with employee lawsuits. EPLI is insurance purchased to protect against some of the legal costs faced if an employee brings a civil suit against the organization. There are many situations in which an employee may bring a lawsuit because of perceived rights violations. If they do, the organization will pay huge costs in legal fees, even if it wins the suit. EPLI can be extremely useful in covering these unexpected costs.

COMPLIANCE AUDITS

A **compliance audit** ensures that an organization is meeting guidelines established by the company, the government, or a regulatory agency. The audit checks the organization's current state against all applicable bylaws, controls, or policies. Audit reports cover such functions as:

- Security
- Production
- Finances
- Human resources
- Risk management
- Compliance
- Processes and controls
- Health and safety

A finalized audit report assesses performance against a base standard, identifies gaps, and provides recommendations for resolving outstanding issues.

An audit or **investigative plan** includes a list of what risks will be assessed, results from previous audits to check compliance or resolutions, and any significant changes in the organization over the audit period. The plan includes a list of the team members who will perform the audit, assignments of duties, and outlines for interviews with key stakeholders, as well as a timeline for completion.

Corrective Actions

An audit will identify failures to comply, gaps in compliance, weaknesses in processes, and any other non-conformity in the elements assessed. When an issue is recognized, the audit should also recommend a **corrective action** to bring the area into compliance. Corrective actions should clearly identify the **five Ws**:

- **Who:** the party responsible for taking the corrective action
- **What:** the exact failure or non-conformity that has been identified
- **Where:** the location of the failure, whether geographic or digital, to be corrected
- **When:** the timeframe within which the corrective action must be taken
- **Why:** the reason for the corrective action and the reason that compliance is required

Clearly identifying the specifics required to correct the failure will ensure that the right issue is being addressed and that the team is fully informed on the issue.

Internal/External Threats
SWOT Analysis

A SWOT (strengths, weaknesses, opportunities, threats) analysis is a tool that is often used in the strategic planning process. Though participants in the planning process may complete the analysis independently, it is often used to facilitate group discussion. A SWOT analysis looks at all areas of a company, from its people to its financials, and at external factors that could impact the business.

- Strengths are areas that are seen as company highlights or as being better than the competition.
- Weaknesses include company areas that need improvement.
- Opportunities include areas that the company could explore and ultimately turn into strengths. Examples are new revenue streams, people, actions, or restructuring.
- Threats are external factors that, without monitoring or management, could cause challenges for the company. These could be regulations, economic conditions, competition, or other external factors.

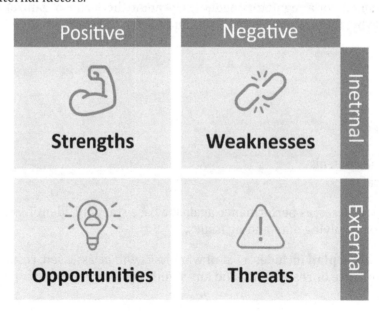

PEST ANALYSIS

A PEST (political, economic, social, technological) analysis is a tool that can be used in the strategic planning process. Though participants in the planning process may complete the analysis independently, it is often used to facilitate group discussion. A PEST analysis looks at external factors that could impact the business. Items identified in a PEST analysis are often viewed as opportunities or threats to an organization. Therefore, PEST is sometimes used as a tool to do an in-depth review of the opportunities and threats portions of the SWOT analysis.

- **Political** considerations include upcoming elections and current/potential legislation.
- **Economic** analysis could look at a wide range of factors, including but not limited to supply chain, interest rates, or unemployment rates.
- **Social** aspects are any aspects concerning external people that impact the business. This could include cultural changes, customer activity, or demographic changes.
- **Technological** factors include any technology changes that impact customers, competitors, or the industry as a whole.

PORTER'S FIVE FORCES

Porter's five forces is a model by which organizations can analyze external forces that may impact a business and can determine its potential in a certain industry. The components analyzed are as follows:

- **Competitive rivalry** involves comparing the organization to all viable competitors in terms of services offered and quality.
- **Supplier power** involves reviewing current supplier information, such as cost and supplier availability.
- **Buyer power** involves analysis of the number of interested and available customers. The more customers, the more power for the organization. Fewer customers means more power for the buyer.
- **Threat of substitution** involves knowing how viable it would be for customers to replace the product provided by the organization, by means such as automation or outsourcing.
- **Threat of new entry** involves knowing how easily a competitor could enter the organization's market. Does it require significant capital? Is the industry highly regulated? The easier it is to enter the industry, the more likely it is that there will be an increase in competition.

SAFETY

WORKPLACE VIOLENCE

Due to the growing number of workplace assaults and homicides, it is suggested that human resource managers be prepared and implement policies such as the following:

- **Zero tolerance:** prohibit any act of violence in the workplace, including verbal threats
- **Prevention:** present strategies and training to help managers recognize danger signs
- **Crisis management:** create plans for responding to threats or acts of violence
- **Recovery:** provide support and counseling for victims and survivors that may suffer lasting trauma

To reduce the likelihood that a troubled employee might become violent, managers should be encouraged to practice the following:

- Discipline employees one-on-one as a private matter as opposed to in public.
- Provide employees with an opportunity to explain or tell their side of the story.
- Ensure that managers refrain from disciplining employees when the manager is angry. Even if the employee's behavior may warrant immediate action, the employee should be removed from the scene, and disciplinary action should be discussed and decided at a later meeting.
- Try to calm angry workers or have a friend accompany them when leaving.

FRAUD AND THEFT

A serious concern for all companies is illegal or dishonest behavior, such as theft, embezzlement, falsifying records, or misuse of company property. Committing **fraud** often involves at least one of three main forces: situational pressure, opportunity to commit fraud, or personal integrity. When employees are suspected of stealing, the company must decide whether to conduct an investigation or prosecute. Investigations and prosecutions can be costly; however, most cases should be investigated. Some investigations will result in termination, whereas others may result in prosecution.

Organizations may also adopt **anti-fraud programs** to increase early detection and decrease opportunities. These programs often contain the elements of reporting, oversight, prudence, communication, compliance, enforcement, prevention, and advocating personal integrity. Companies prone to theft and dishonest behavior, such as retail corporations, often have **loss prevention departments** dedicated to protecting assets and cash while minimizing and detecting inventory shrinkage.

CORPORATE ESPIONAGE

When employees give corporate trade secrets to another organization, they are committing **corporate espionage**. They give the receiving firm a competitive advantage and may cause the first company to lose customers, sales, human capital, market share, or all of the above. Firms can protect themselves from corporate espionage by requiring employees to sign nondisclosure or noncompete agreements. These agreements outline what information is protected and what happens when an employee (or former employee) violates the agreement. Companies should also restrict their most important classified information to a small group of personnel that need it to do their jobs.

SABOTAGE

Workplace **sabotage** is the act of destroying or disrupting business operations. It can be overt, through behaviors such as erasing important files, intentionally failing to complete certain key tasks, or spreading rumors. It can also be much more subtle, and occur through behaviors such as taking a meeting off topic, practicing perfectionism, or being totally unwilling to bend the rules for overall gain or greater good. To combat deliberate sabotage efforts, firms should have a code of conduct in place that forbids such behavior and spells out what happens when an employee violates the code. To address the less-direct forms of sabotage, leaders should be trained to detect the behaviors at an early stage and firmly take charge to nip them in the bud.

KIDNAPPING AND RANSOM

When employees are kidnapped and ransomed, it is a terrifying ordeal for them, their families, and the organization. However, the firm can take several steps to both prevent a **kidnapping** from occurring and handle it effectively should it happen. First and foremost, the company should address the threat of kidnapping in a given area. It should also create a clear plan for how it would negotiate in a hostage situation. If an area is high-risk, the firm should consider whether it is worth having personnel there at all. If employees are sent to or are located in that area, the firm should teach them how to detect threats and be mindful of their surroundings. They should also be trained how to act if they are kidnapped. Best practices include speaking about their personal lives and families so that kidnappers see them as humans and not as a commodity for sale. Those who are kidnapped should avoid speaking about hot-button issues like politics or religion. Companies should also teach employees what to do when they are rescued. For example, employees should not run toward the rescue team because they might be mistaken as being a part of the enemy group. During a kidnapping situation, the company should provide support to the hostage employee's family and keep a low media profile. The media can make things worse, depending on what information gets released and is seen by the kidnappers. Finally, companies should consider purchasing kidnap and ransom insurance, which will help cover the cost of the **ransom** should a kidnapping occur.

ACTIVE SHOOTERS

Preparations for **active shooters** are unfortunately becoming more common and more of a necessity. Similar to any other emergency preparedness plan, the key is having a plan and ensuring that employees know the safety protocol. When developing an active shooter plan, it is prudent for organizations to involve local law enforcement to discuss the plan and coordinate responses. Companies should develop processes and procedures to be able to lock down facilities and prohibit access at the entrances during a lockdown. The active shooter plan should identify areas of the building for visitors or guests to gather during an event, and a critical response team to activate during an incident. As with all emergency plans, this plan should be documented, communicated, and practiced on a regular basis. After each drill, there should be a de-brief and assessments of the strengths and weaknesses of the plan to allow for improvements. If an active shooter event should occur, management should immediately make counseling resources available to the employees.

INSIDER THREATS

The risk of a threat coming from inside the organization is real and serious. An **insider** is anyone who has access to a company's resources, such as data, personnel, information, buildings, equipment, and networks. While many insiders are employees, other insiders include anyone who gained access to a badge, passwords, or access controls such as a vendor, contractor, or repair person. An **insider threat** is a person or persons who use that access to harm the organization. Harm can be intentional or unintentional, but always results in negative consequences to the organization. Insider threats can take the form of:

- Unauthorized disclosure of information
- Sabotage
- Workplace violence
- Corruption
- Espionage

Organizations can make efforts to deter insider threats by developing best practices to define, detect, identify, assess, and manage the risk. The identification and detection of potential risks is the most critical prevention method. Employees must be trained to watch for and report potential incidents or concerns.

DATA BREACHES

A **data breach** is an incident in which unauthorized individuals gain access to sensitive company data such as personnel data, customer data, or financial data. A breach is when that information is viewed or shared without the permission of the organization. There are steps that a company should take to prevent such incidents, including educating employees on proper procedures for protecting data, ensuring that all security standards and systems are up-to-date and documented, continually monitoring the systems and networks for intrusions or issues, ensuring that all data is backed up to allow for restoration, and having information technology experts on staff to set up and monitor security protocols.

In the event that a data breach does occur, the speed at which an organization responds is critical. The breach must be identified, a response plan should be activated, all evidence must be collected and analyzed, attempts at containment or recovery should be executed when appropriate, and affected people and organizations should be notified. When it is over, a post-event analysis should be executed to identify the lessons learned.

CHANGE MANAGEMENT

LEADERSHIP BUY-IN

Buy-in is support or endorsement for something. In the case of change, leadership buy-in is critical. Often, their support is necessary to get the change movement started because they may need to approve the use of resources or major modifications to business operations. If the change requires their endorsement, and they will not give it, then the change is defeated before it can get started. Additionally, leadership buy-in is necessary to champion the change across the organization. If the leaders believe in the effort, they can communicate their enthusiasm for it and model the new desired behavior, making it easier for the change to take root.

BUILDING A CASE FOR CHANGE

One useful way to approach organizational change activities is the **action research model**. Once a problem has been identified, there are six basic steps that follow: data gathering, feedback of data to the target group, data discussions and diagnosis, action planning, action, and recycling. **Data gathering** involves collecting information about the problem from sources such as observations, interviews, surveys, and archived data. **Feedback of data to a target group** involves making the gathered data openly available and sharing it with a group through presentations. **Data discussions and diagnosis** involve a roundtable conversation and analysis by the target group to diagnose a root cause and to explore alternatives or viable solutions. **Action planning** involves creating a plan to implement solutions, which may require outside parties. **Action** involves the execution of new changes. Finally, **recycling** involves reviewing and repeating the processes to ensure problems do not reoccur.

ENGAGING EMPLOYEES

For changes to be implemented successfully, the employees need to embrace them (or at least understand them). This can be accomplished by engaging them in the change process and ensuring that they remain engaged overall as employees. Engaging them in the change process includes asking for and using their feedback (when possible) before, during, and after the change. Doing this shows that the organization values their opinion and places an importance on collaboration and transparency. When employees can help shape the change, they are far more likely to go along with it. Additionally, when employees are truly engaged at work, they will have an easier time adapting to change (even if unpleasant) because of their strong emotional commitment to the company.

COMMUNICATING CHANGE

Provide clear communication to employees and all stakeholders as early as possible. Keep communications simple, and explain both the necessity and the timeline for the change. Let employees know what will be staying the same, and proactively counter any negative reactions that can be anticipated. Develop opportunities for **two-way communications**. This provides employees with the chance to ask questions. Then, repeat communications, and explain how employees will be kept informed throughout the process to manage expectations. Finally, have leadership get involved to advocate for the change and lead by example to keep morale high.

REMOVING BARRIERS

HR practitioners must be cognizant of any barriers to organizational change. Change actions can be thwarted by barriers such as staff attitudes or behaviors that discourage implementing new ideas, insufficient skills or technologies, and distances or obstacles between formal structures. These barriers can be eliminated by regularly communicating the rationale and timeline of the change, implementing new training programs or technologies, involving employee advocates in decision-making processes, and welcoming feedback from all levels.

ENSURING CHANGE MANAGEMENT IS SUCCESSFUL AND AVOIDING FAILURES

These tactics are recommended to accomplish a successful change effort:

- Have a change sponsor lead the initiative.
- Communicate a clear need for the change.
- Create a shared vision of the organization post-change.
- Rally commitment or request participation from all involved.
- Integrate past systems, structures, policies, and procedures into the new normal.
- Monitor progress and benchmark results against other successful companies.
- Make change sustainable by having a clear plan and rewarding desired behavior.

Some important reasons that **change efforts fail** include the following:

- Change was not strategically aligned with organizational goals or mission.
- Change was not communicated meaningfully or was perceived as a superficial, quick fix.
- Change was unrealistic given the current economic and political environment.
- Change leaders were inadequate or lacked the necessary commitment.
- Measurable goals and timelines were not established.
- Resistance to the change thwarted change efforts.

GAP ANALYSIS

A **gap analysis** compares the expected outcomes of a practice or behavior to the actual outcomes of that practice or behavior. The difference between the expectations and the actual outcomes is the gap. This type of analysis can be a useful tool in the monitoring and evaluating stage of the strategic planning process, which occurs after the plan is set. The tool can vary in its style or format but should always show the difference between what is expected and the actual outcomes. While the actuals can be compared to the initial expectations set in the plan, they can also be compared to industry standards. In fact, using industry standards is often recommended since the strategic planning process typically covers three to five years, and the business environment will likely change during that time. Once the gap analysis is completed, it should be evident whether the plan progress is on track or if adjustments need to be made.

Metrics and Data

RETENTION AND TURNOVER METRICS

A company's **retention rate** is the percentage of employees that are employed at the company throughout an entire measurement period, such as a quarter or a year. A critical metric for tracking purposes, **turnover** provides good insight into the work culture, efficacy of hiring and onboarding policies/procedures, and management of employees. There are various ways to calculate turnover. The **turnover rate** is the number of employees who left the company during the measurement period compared to the average number of employees throughout the measurement period.

$$\text{Retention rate} = \frac{\text{Number of employees employed for entire measurement period}}{\text{Number of employees at start of measurement period}} \times 100\%$$

$$\text{Turnover rate} = \frac{\text{Number of employees who left during measurement period}}{\text{Average number of employees during measurement period}} \times 100\%$$

DIVERSITY METRICS

As a tangible means to demonstrate not just shifting practices but also improved business outcomes, **diversity metrics** can be an integral piece of DEI efforts and projects in the workplace. Metrics associated with DEI interventions can help to evaluate the impact of the interventions and demonstrate any tangible financial returns. Metrics can also be used to test an intervention's impact on a social or operational level. One way to test for **adverse impact** in a given process is to utilize the **four-fifths rule**. According to this rule, if the selection rate of a protected group is less than four-fifths of the selection rate of a nonprotected group for the same process (e.g., promotion), the disparity could have an adverse impact on the protected group. Examples of diversity metrics, some of which can be tested using the four-fifths rule, include:

- Demographic ratios at varying hierarchical levels
- Retention or turnover rates categorized by various diversity dimensions
- Recruiting ratios of different diversity dimensions compared to the corresponding community or candidate pool
- Compensation audit data across diversity dimensions
- Net promoter scores among employees across diversity dimensions

APPLICANT-TO-INTERVIEW-TO-OFFER METRICS

One of the most critical metrics used in the talent acquisition field is the calculation of both the time and cost of bringing a new employee on board. There are multiple components to that long, tedious path, which will be broken down below:

Time from vacancy identification to job posting. Identification of an opening or vacancy in the organization is the first step in hiring. Partnering between managers and HR is critical in anticipating when and where vacancies occur and determining the requirements to fill the position; this requires forecasting, planning, and aligning with the organizational strategy.

Time from posting to applicants. Once the vacancy is identified and the job description is properly updated, the job advertisement must be posted; then the organization waits for applicants from internal or external sources. The hurdles to this process can be driven by process, policy, and regulation. Submitted applications must be initially reviewed either by HR or the hiring manager. All applications should be acknowledged, typically with a return email. Non-qualified candidates should be eliminated and acknowledged. Qualified candidates may be ranked, rated, or otherwise assessed based on the match of their qualifications to the job description. HR or the manager can identify the candidates who will be offered interviews.

Time from application to interview. After identifying the candidates to be reviewed, interview offers should be extended and scheduled. Managers may use HR to screen candidates, interview candidates themselves, schedule panel interviews, or any combination of the above. Many times, especially in technical or management positions, multiple interviews are required.

Time from interview to offer. The interview process should narrow down the candidates to the top one or two. The top candidate may be offered a position verbally at first, but all final offers should be issued in writing. A negotiation period may require some time to go back and forth on the compensation package.

Time from offer to onboarding. Upon acceptance of a final offer package, the candidate will typically have to give notice at their current employer, and can establish a start date after that. For companies who have set new-hire orientations, the candidate's timeline must be coordinated with that schedule.

Time to fill. All of the steps above, from vacancy to onboarding, are then combined to calculate an offer metric of "time to fill." Some organizations may also have to include a security review process between offer and onboarding, which can add weeks, months, or even years to the process. Talent acquisition analysts will dissect all of the steps above to determine where bottlenecks exist and where process improvement or process automation can assist in getting past them.

Cost per hire. All of the steps above cost the organization time and money. Talent acquisition analysts will identify the most time-consuming parts of the process and the costliest elements of the process. They will partner with HR and management to work to achieve more efficient and effective processes.

The steps from position vacancy to a filled position has both time and money implications. However, the talent acquisition analyst will also look at how the process works in terms of the number of candidates in the pipeline. Each of the above steps is also reviewed to assess how effectively the organization is making decisions on the candidates in each step of the process. For example, if the organization starts with 200 applicants, it takes both HR and management time to review, qualify, and downselect the number of candidates who will ultimately be interviewed, which is the costliest part of the process, both in time and money.

With the end goal of getting the most qualified three to five candidates to the manager to interview, HR must have processes in place to move through the downselect process efficiently but effectively. The qualifications for the position must be clearly identified. A metric or rating system may be employed to move through the process in an objective manner; these systems can be automated.

RETURN ON INVESTMENT (ROI)

The **return on Investment (ROI)** is usually shown as a percentage that measures how beneficial a new tool or practice has been compared to its initial investment. The **ROI** can be calculated as:

$$\text{ROI} = \frac{\text{Net return on investment}}{\text{Cost of investment}} \times 100\%$$

HR professionals may be asked about ROI to determine the effectiveness of training programs, recently implemented software, or supplementations to the workforce. However, it is important to consider all associated costs. For example, the ROI of a harassment training seminar should include the travel costs to get employees to the seminar. Total costs associated with the seminar can then be compared to alternatives such as videos or webinars. Another strategy is to compare the firm's ROI with the ROI of other companies. If there is a competitive return, strategic plans should not be drastically changed. However, if the ROI is much lower than that of competitors, a new strategy is in order. It should also be noted that when making decisions among investments, an estimated ROI is used.

SUCCESS OF TRAINING

Three of the most common types of metrics that an organization might use to measure the effectiveness of a training program are cost-benefit measures, financial measures, and production measures.

Cost-benefit measures are any metrics that an organization can use to compare the advantages associated with a training program with the disadvantages or costs associated with the program. Cost-benefit measures are usually identified through a cost-benefit analysis, and the specific measures that an organization can use will vary from program to program.

Financial measures measure the effect that the training program has had on the organization's financial resources. Financial measures include metrics such as return on investment, profit margins, and cash flow.

Production measures measure the effect of the training program on the organization's amount or quality of production. Production measures include metrics such as the number of items produced per day, the number of items produced that do not meet specifications, and the number of orders filled per day.

COST/BENEFIT ANALYSIS

Although training and development programs should be viewed as an extremely valuable capital investment, they should also provide measurable returns. Simple calculations can be used to measure the costs and benefits of training.

Costs should include both direct costs (e.g., materials, facilities) and indirect costs (e.g., lost production time). The overall costs of training and development programs might include staff hours, program materials, hardware or software, videos, and production losses (e.g., training time and associated salaries).

Benefits of training should be evaluated according to how well the training will increase productivity, advance product quality, reduce errors, improve safety, or reduce operating costs. One calculation for measuring training is the cost per trainee, in which the total cost of training is divided by the total number of trainees.

Regardless, the long-term benefits of training should outweigh the costs, and this can be determined through a **cost/benefit analysis**. There are creative adjustments that can be used to reduce training costs. The size of training classes can be increased, and materials can be reused when this does not violate copyrights. Expenses can be further reduced by making training available online or using videoconferencing.

CONTINUOUS IMPROVEMENT

BALANCED SCORECARD

The **balanced scorecard (BSC)** is a strategic metric that is used to recognize and manage internal processes and their external outcomes to provide continuous improvement. This tool is used for planning and aligning day-to-day duties with company strategy. The BSC has four key areas used to develop goals, objectives, and to measure key performance indicators (KPIs):

- **Finance** details areas such as sales, costs, and income to get a clear picture of how the organization is performing financially.
- **Customer/stakeholder** covers the organizational performance from the customer or stakeholder point of view. This area relies on feedback from customers or stakeholders to determine satisfaction related to quality, availability, and service.
- **Internal process** relates to how smoothly the organization is running. This section targets reducing waste, improving delivery of products/services, and minimizing waste.
- **Learning and growth** considers the corporate culture, technology, training, and how efficiently those areas are leveraged to perform competitively.

KEY PERFORMANCE INDICATORS (KPIS)

Quantifiable metrics used to measure the long-term performance of particular areas, **key performance indicators (KPIs)** are used to gauge the efficiency of operational and strategic plans within an organization or department. These metrics help stakeholders and management to make data-based decisions that will improve performance and profitability. KPIs allow organizations to identify areas for improvement, assess actual performance against goals, and determine how to best allocate available resources. KPIs can be used in almost all business areas, including sales, customer service, production, human resources, and information technology. It is helpful to be familiar with and understand the following types of KPIs:

- **Leading KPIs** can be used to help project future outcomes based on the available data. The percentage of growth in a sales pipeline is a leading indicator for increased sales revenue.
- **Lagging KPIs** measure performance after the event has taken place and are used to support long-term trends. For example, an employee's sales average (percent of consultations that resulted in a closed deal) is a lagging indicator.
- **Functional unit KPIs** are used to measure specific functions or areas within an organization, providing information on whether that area is achieving its objectives and performing well. Customer service response time is a functional unit KPI.
- **Operational KPIs** measure performance over a short term (such as month over month) to give insight into efficiency and how operational objectives are being met. How quickly inventory is turned over is an example of an operational KPI.
- **Strategic KPIs** typically track big-picture and high-level goal progression. They really indicate how the organization is doing. Return on investment is a major strategic KPI.

Organizational Culture, Core Values, and Ethics

EMPLOYER BRANDING

The act of marketing an image that makes people want to work for the organization is called **employment branding**. This image stems from the organization's **employer value proposition (EVP),** which is what they have to offer as compared to other firms. The EVP may include the work environment, internal opportunities, benefits, and compensation. Employers should consider **active branding** because it can increase the talent pool, firm productivity, and team morale while reducing the turnover rate.

An organization can showcase a positive EVP and brand in the following ways:

- Describing their benefits, perks, and culture on their website, in their job ads, and in other promotional materials
- Sharing current employee testimonials about how great it is to work there
- Doing charity work in the community and demonstrating a commitment to corporate social responsibility

CULTURE

As a part of employment branding within the EVP, it is imperative to help potential candidates get a feel for the **culture** of the organization. Organizational culture is the set of shared beliefs and values that embody the organization, drive employee behavior, and direct how employees do their jobs in the workplace. Values and beliefs are created, communicated, and reinforced by the leaders of the company in the formal and informal systems and norms that establish the working environment.

Culture underlies the standards set by the company leaders, is evident in the attitudes of the managers, and can impact the firm's reputation in the market. Potential employees should seek to identify an organization with a culture that fits well with their own beliefs and values systems. The reputation and culture of an organization are critical elements of the EVP and employment branding.

SOCIAL MEDIA

Social media **branding** is a great marketing tool that can be used to engage, entice, and expand an organization's target market and demographic. With this practice, social media promotion and marketing are used together to establish a consistent message and experience across various platforms. Successful branding sets an organization apart from its competitors on any given platform. Regular posting and interaction will increase hits and results. The brand is the lifeblood of the organization, so clear instructions and policies should be established regarding what content is posted, how audience engagement occurs, and what partnerships can be established. Choosing to partner with an individual or organization with a questionable reputation can damage the organization, so due diligence should be completed before such a thing occurs.

ETHICAL AND PROFESSIONAL STANDARDS

TRANSPARENCY

Transparency is the free sharing of nonconfidential information. It results in better-informed and more engaged employees. Most employees appreciate it when management is transparent with information, such as healthcare costs, pay increase schedules, or future changes on the horizon. **Transparency** can be a tool for removing obstacles to diversity, as employees will be better able to understand one another. Being transparent and openly communicating with staff during decision-making processes can also build employee trust and be leveraged as a recruiting or retention tool. The internet now provides job seekers with transparent information about a company's culture, benefits, average pay, and interview process. It's always better for employees to hear this information directly from the employer so that the firm can ensure accuracy and address any questions or concerns head-on.

CONFIDENTIALITY

Confidentiality is vital in human resources practices. Maintaining the confidentiality of all **employee records** is imperative. This may include social security numbers, birth dates, addresses, phone numbers, email, benefits enrollment, medical or leave details, earnings history, garnishments, bank account information, disciplinary action, grievances, and employment eligibility data. When employee record information is requested for legitimate purposes, a written release signed by the employee should be obtained and kept on file. Examples of these requests might include bank loans, mortgage applications, or employment verification. Companies should also consider implementing **confidentiality or nondisclosure agreements** so employees are aware that databases, client lists, and other proprietary information must be protected and sharing these records will have serious consequences.

Anonymity

Anonymity is similar to confidentiality. It provides employees the ability to partake in activities without their names being disclosed. Employers may have employees take a survey or evaluate their managers under anonymity to eliminate any fear of retaliation. Individuals may also anonymously report any complaint or ethics violation.

Personal Integrity

Personal integrity comes from developing and sticking to an internal code of ethics that determines what is right and what is wrong. It is strengthened by choosing thoughts and actions that are based upon an individual's moral principles and personal values. Some character traits of those with high **personal integrity** might include honesty, trustworthiness, kindness, courage, respect, and loyalty. An example of personal integrity in action would be helping an elderly neighbor with yard work or home repairs, even when it might not be convenient. It is these types of behaviors that develop an individual's personal integrity and reputation. Those with high personal integrity are not generally motivated by popularity, nor are they compelled to seek ill-gotten gains. The stronger one's sense of personal integrity, the less likely one is to succumb to corruption.

Professional Integrity

Professional integrity involves choosing actions that adhere to moral principles and codes of ethics (both internal and organizationally imposed) while at work. It originates from an individual's personal integrity. Professional integrity avoids corruption or any potential conflicts of interest and develops professional credibility. An example of professional integrity in action would be telling the CEO that you've made a major mistake, even though you will likely face consequences. Professional integrity often leads to high professional standards, resulting in an increased quality of work. Moreover, leaders who demonstrate unyielding professional integrity frequently have a greater following of employees and customers.

Ethical Agent

Ethics and compliance officers ensure that business is conducted in accordance with rules, legal regulations, and industry standards of practice. Additionally, an ethical agent makes moral judgments based on fundamental ethical principles that are rooted in their personal character, not based on a situation's potential gains. Ethical dilemmas occur when a corporation or individual is faced with a conflict of interest, or actions that are blatantly wrong, deceptive, or may have uncertain consequences. Many ethical conflicts value profit over moral principles. Over the past few decades, ethics and business conduct have received increasing attention that has led to more stringent compliance regulations, like the Sarbanes-Oxley Act.

CONFLICTS OF INTEREST

A **conflict of interest** occurs when someone with a responsibility to act in the best interest of the company may also be in the position to derive personal benefit at the expense of the company. Some examples include:

- Utilizing company resources for personal financial gain
- Forming relationships or obligations that compromise objectivity when conducting duties
- Disclosing company information to interfere with bidding, negotiating, or contracting
- Exerting influence in business transactions that benefit the individual or a relative
- Traveling at vendors' or customers' expense
- Accepting gifts, services, or favors from company stakeholders

Conflicts of interest should be avoided. Clear policies should be in place, and all employees should be held to them.

PRIVACY PRINCIPLES

With technology now a part of every business transaction, it is essential that companies and employees adhere to strict confidentiality practices and **privacy principles**. From employee monitoring to asking interview questions, employers need to carefully avoid invading personal privacy. Legal regulations that inform best practices and internal privacy policies should be consulted regularly for guidance. On the other hand, companies should consider implementing confidentiality or nondisclosure agreements so employees are aware that databases, client lists, and other proprietary information must be protected and that the sharing of these records externally is strictly prohibited.

CODE OF CONDUCT

A **code of conduct** is a set of behavioral rules rooted in moral standards, laws, and best practices that a company develops, adopts, and communicates to employees. It outlines expected behavior and defines what behavior will not be tolerated. The document should also state what disciplinary actions employees could face if they violate the code.

Employee involvement in the development of a code of conduct will lead to greater employee buy-in and adherence. The code should be written in clear language that can be applied to specific situations as they arise. Upon finalization, the code should be shared with all employees. Employees should then be required to sign a document acknowledging receipt and understanding of the new code.

> **Review Video: Ethical and Professional Standards**
> Visit mometrix.com/academy and enter code: 391843

DEVELOPING AND MAINTAINING A POSITIVE ORGANIZATIONAL CULTURE

Organizational culture should be a focal point beginning with new hire orientation. Introductory training materials should discuss the culture and provide examples of it in action within the firm. From there, managers should regularly coach and train staff so that the culture stays top of mind. Finally, leaders should live the company culture in all that they do. Employees may be influenced by their behavior.

Organizational culture should be communicated frequently, clearly, and consistently. If employees see inconsistencies in this communication, they may distrust leadership or be less engaged at work.

An organization's **values** are the foundation of its culture. Therefore, leadership must establish them early on. Human resources should hire candidates that embody the firm's values. Any new policies and procedures should reflect the same principles. Finally, discipline and rewards systems should be built upon these core values.

Maintaining Organizational Culture

Culture encompasses every facet of an organization and comprises four **key elements:** norms, artifacts, values, and core assumptions. Shared **norms** are not always defined or obvious but often inferred from specific situations. For example, norms of punctuality and professionalism are demonstrated by leaders who practice them. Likewise, the collective beliefs, ideals, and feelings of the members of an organization construct its cultural **values**. Cultural **artifacts**, such as behaviors, language, and symbols, are tangible traits that portray core values. An organization's shared **core assumptions** reveal the basis of how its people think. This can be reflected by the extent of controls that management impose upon line staff. Organizational culture can be maintained through employee selection and disciplinary procedures, rewards systems, recognition ceremonies, stories, symbols, and leadership reactions to achievements and problems.

Influence of Culture on Organizational Outcomes
Organizational Performance

Studies have long demonstrated that organizational culture plays a significant role in **organizational performance**. How well a company is doing (based on how many tasks and objectives are successfully completed), heavily depends on the internal environment—the company culture. Organizations that prioritize engagement, training, and development are much more likely to see higher sales and customer satisfaction. The more invested an organization is in its employees, the more invested the employees will be in the organization, driving higher organizational performance.

Organizational Learning

The process of how an organization acquires, retains, and transfers new skills, processes, and knowledge for continued growth and development, or **organizational learning**, is a key area for business success. The organizational culture heavily impacts organizational learning. A culture that promotes continuous learning and development will have a much stronger basis for organizational learning versus an organization where training and learning are not highly emphasized. Similarly, cultures that value the sharing and transferring of organizational knowledge will foster more collaboration and exchanging of ideas than a culture where certain areas and concepts are siloed. A culture of organizational learning helps to empower employees, retain employees, and keep individuals engaged while also simultaneously breeding innovation and strategic growth.

Innovation

A culture of **innovation** and the ability to think outside the box is required for organizations to remain competitive and attract new talent. The ways of working are always changing, so being able to innovate and stay on top of changes and trends deeply impacts the ability of a business to remain solvent. Organizations that develop a culture of challenging assumptions, experimentation, failure, learning, and acceptance of new ideas are likely to be innovative. Cultures where employees are expected to accept the way things are done, simply because that is the way they have always been done, are less likely to breed innovation and will be unable to keep up with the changing business landscape.

Risk-Taking

Development and growth do not exist without risk. **Risk-taking**, or doing something with an uncertain outcome, is necessary for competition and progress. Organizations that foster a culture where failure and success are accepted, challenging the status quo is allowed, and thinking of less-conventional solutions is encouraged, are organizations that are open to at least some level of risk-taking. Having a risk-averse culture can stifle creativity, limit growth, and increase turnover. Employees who do not feel that they have a voice or say in one organization are more prone to leave for one where they feel they do.

Workforce Planning and Talent Acquisition

Because the specific skills and knowledge needed to perform tasks vary from organization to organization, from department to department, and from position to position, workforce planning is essential. The needs of an organization can change as its size or environment changes, making it important to identify available human resources and human resources for future needs.

Some of the most common activities an organization might perform in the workforce planning process include conducting staffing forecasts, establishing staffing goals and objectives, conducting job analyses, and establishing plans to meet staffing goals and objectives. Many organizations begin by conducting a staffing forecast, which refers to any analysis determining how staffing needs might change. Once an organization has conducted a staffing forecast, the organization may set specific staffing goals and objectives describing current and future positions to fill. After staffing goals and objectives are established, each position is analyzed to determine specific qualifications needed. Finally, a plan is established to find and hire individuals to fill these positions.

FORECASTING METHODS

The two main types of forecasting methods an organization might use to evaluate changing labor needs are qualitative forecasting methods and quantitative forecasting methods. Qualitative forecasting methods include any forecasting method based on the opinions or analyses of managers or experts in the industry. Quantitative forecasting methods are based on actual data, such as past trends or employee to output ratios. The difference between the two types is that qualitative forecasting is based on knowledge and opinion and quantitative forecasting is based on statistics or mathematical data.

The most common qualitative forecasting methods include management forecasts and a variety of techniques associated with expert forecasting. Management forecasts determine future staffing needs by asking managers of each department to discuss staffing needs at a meeting or to submit reports. Expert forecasting methods (such as the Delphi method) seek the opinion of experts outside the organization. This allows information to be obtained about the effects of changes in the industry or changes from a variety of sources. That information is then formed into a report about possible changes in staffing needs.

Some of the most common quantitative forecasting methods include historical ratio analyses, trend analyses, turnover analyses, and probability models. A **ratio analysis** is a type of analysis comparing current employment ratios (such as the number of employees required to produce a certain number of products) with past ratios to determine if staffing needs might change in the future. **Trend analyses** compare a single current employment variable (such as the number of employees) with a past employment variable, rather than comparing two ratios. **Turnover analyses** examine the rate employees leave the organization during a given period compared to previous turnover rates. **Probability models** allow the organization to chart and predict data related to changes in the organization.

The two most important factors to consider when deciding which forecasting method to use are how far in the future the organization is attempting to plan and if the organization needs to change at a steady rate. Qualitative methods are usually effective for short-term forecasts or for constantly changing staffing needs, while quantitative methods are more effective for long-term forecasts in organizations that have staffing needs that change at a steady rate. Most organizations need both short-term and long-term forecasts.

US Federal Laws and Organizational Policies Related to Hiring

TITLE VII

Title VII of the Civil Rights Act, which was originally passed in 1964 and amended in 1972, 1978, and 1991, is designed to prevent unlawful discrimination in the workplace. This section of the Civil Rights Act makes it unlawful to discriminate against or segregate any aspect of an individual's employment based on any of the following:

- Race
- Color
- National origin
- Religion
- Gender

In other words, Title VII legislation prevents an employer from discriminating with regard to any condition of employment based on these criteria, including recruiting, hiring, and firing. Furthermore, Title VII prohibits an employer from limiting the opportunities for an employee with regard to compensation, career promotions, training, and other employment avenues for advancement or progress. Title VII also makes it unlawful for an employer to discriminate against individuals who are pregnant, are about to give birth, or have any similar medical condition.

Title VII of the Civil Rights Act applies to any employer who has more than 15 employees. Exceptions include religious organizations, which can choose to hire only individuals within that religion, or to consider individuals of that religion for employment before individuals of other religions; and Indian reservations, which can choose to hire or consider Native Americans living on or near a reservation for employment before other individuals.

EEOC

The **Equal Employment Opportunity Commission (EEOC)** was formed by Title VII of the Civil Rights Act to protect certain groups of individuals from unlawful discrimination. The EEOC is a federal agency designed to encourage equal employment opportunities; to train employers to avoid practices and policies that could cause unlawful discrimination; and to enforce the laws included in the Civil Rights Act, the Age Discrimination in Employment Act, and laws included in other similar anti-discrimination legislation.

Discriminatory practices by an employer are either intentional (like an employer advertisement saying they will not hire a certain race) or unintentional (such as banning hats for reasons unrelated to safety, being discriminatory against those who wear a head covering for religious purposes). Equal opportunity laws prohibit both intentional and unintentional discrimination. The EEOC attempts to obtain settlements from employers for actions that the commission deems to be discriminatory. If the employer will not settle with the EEOC, the EEOC will continue their attempt to enforce the law by filing a lawsuit against the employer on behalf of the victim of the discrimination.

DISCRIMINATION AND UNLAWFUL EMPLOYMENT PRACTICES

Discrimination refers to the process of making a decision about a particular individual or thing based on the specific traits that make the person or thing different from other individuals or things. Because the practice of discrimination is a type of decision-making, it is only illegal under certain conditions. Unlawful employment practices are specific business actions involving hiring, training, employee compensation, and other factors related to an individual's employment that are prohibited by law. These practices are specifically prohibited when they prevent individuals with certain characteristics from obtaining a position, performing the duties related to a position, or receiving all of the benefits and respect from the employer normally associated with the position.

The word *discrimination* by itself only refers to the practice of making a decision regarding a person or thing based on the characteristics of that particular person or thing, which is a practice most organizations perform legally on a daily basis. Discrimination is only unlawful if the employer's decision regarding a particular individual is based on a characteristic considered protected. For example, if an employer decides to only hire people under the age of 40, the employer is unlawfully discriminating against employees based on their age. On the other hand, if the employer decides to only hire people with a certain type of college degree and the college degree is required by law or the knowledge associated with that degree is necessary to perform the tasks related to that position, the employer is legally discriminating based on the individual's characteristics.

Disparate impact is a type of discrimination in which an employer institutes a policy that appears to be reasonable, but prevents individuals of a certain color, national origin, race, religion, or gender, or individuals with certain disabilities or military status, from receiving employment or any of the benefits associated with employment, such as promotions or pay. It refers to a policy that may seem to make sense, but is unfair because it makes things more difficult for individuals of a certain group to receive the job or benefit. For example, a policy stating that individuals applying for an office job must be at least 5'10" and weigh at least 185 pounds may create a disparate impact if it makes it more difficult for women to get the job. However, a physical attribute directly linked to the work that must be performed is not discriminatory so long as it correlates with the essential job requirements. For example, a firefighter has to fulfill certain physical requirements to perform the essential functions of the job. Disparate impact discrimination was first identified by the Supreme Court in *Griggs v. Duke Power Co.*

Disparate treatment is a type of discrimination in which an employer deliberately treats an individual differently because of that individual's age, color, disability, military status, national origin, race, religion, and/or sex. It refers to any instance where an employer uses a different set of procedures, expectations, or policies than he would normally use simply because the individual belongs to a particular group. For example, a business that required female employees to follow a strict dress code while the male employees of the business could wear whatever they liked would be guilty of disparate treatment because of treating employees differently based on gender. This type of discrimination was first identified by Title VII of the Civil Rights Act.

ADEA

The Age Discrimination in Employment Act (ADEA), which was originally passed in 1967 and then later amended in 1991, is designed to prevent discrimination against individuals over the age of 39. This act makes it unlawful to base decisions related to an individual's employment (such as pay or benefits) on the age of the individual if that individual is at least 40 years old. This act applies to any business, employment agency, labor organization, or state or local government agency with more than 20 employees. Exceptions include individuals age 40 or over who do not meet the occupational qualifications required to perform the tasks reasonably necessary to the business's operations, termination due to reasonable cause, employment of firefighters or police officers, retirement of employees with executive positions, or tenured educators under certain conditions. Pre-employment inquiries about an individual's age are not recommended because it could deter an older worker from applying for a position, and could indicate discriminatory intent by the employer on the basis of age. Someone's age can be determined after the employee is hired.

Under the Age Discrimination in Employment Act, any individual may waive the right to protection from age discrimination by signing a waiver of rights. To be legal, the waiver must be written in a clear and concise manner and state that the individual should consult with an attorney prior to signing the waiver. Secondly, the employee must be allowed at least 21 days to consider the terms of the waiver and at least 7 days to change his or her mind and terminate the waiver after signing. Finally, the waiver must offer consideration such as pay or benefits in addition to anything the individual would normally receive.

Under the Age Discrimination in Employment Act, early retirement or incentive programs encouraging individuals to leave the organization must meet certain requirements. First, the waiver must be written in a clear and concise manner, must state that the individual should consult with an attorney prior to signing the waiver, must allow the individual at least 45 days to consider the terms of the waiver, and must allow the individual to have at least 7 days to change his or her mind after signing. The employee must be informed of eligibility factors, time limits associated with the program, and the job titles and ages of each person who is eligible or has been chosen, and the ages of each person ineligible or has not been chosen to take part in the program.

ADA

The **Americans with Disabilities Act** (ADA), which was passed in 1990, is designed to prevent discrimination against individuals with disabilities. A disability, as defined by the ADA, is a mental or physical impairment that impedes one or more life activities. Examples might include, but are not limited to, mobility and personal hygiene. A qualified person with a disability should be able to perform the essential functions of a job with or without reasonable accommodations. This act makes it unlawful to base decisions related to aspects of an individual's employment (such as pay or benefits) on whether the individual is disabled. This act also requires the business, employment agency, or labor organization to ensure the disabled individual has access to his or her place of employment unless making these changes will cause the business significant harm.

VEVRAA

The Vietnam Era Veterans' Readjustment Assistance Act (VEVRAA) is designed to prevent discrimination against veterans. This act makes it unlawful for federal contractors or subcontractors with $25,000 or more in federal contracts or subcontracts to base employment decisions on the fact that the individual is a veteran. It also requires federal contractors or subcontractors meeting these requirements to list open positions with state employment agencies and requires these employers to institute affirmative action plans for veterans. However, in order for this act to apply, the veteran must have served for more than 180 days, with at least part of that time occurring between August 5, 1964, and May 7, 1975; have a disability or group of disabilities that are rated at 10-30 percent or more, depending on the severity or circumstances of their disability; and be eligible for compensation from the Department of Veterans Affairs; or have served on active duty for a conflict with an authorized campaign badge.

IRCA

The **Immigration Reform and Control Act** (IRCA) is designed to prevent discrimination based on nationality. This act makes it unlawful for an employer to base employment decisions (such as pay or benefits) on an individual's country of origin or citizenship status, as long as the individual can legally work within the United States. This act also makes it unlawful for an organization to intentionally hire individuals that cannot legally work in the United States and requires completion of the I-9 form for all new employees. This act specifically requires the employer to obtain proof of the employee's eligibility to work in the United States for the I-9 form, but the employee must be allowed to provide any document or combination of documents considered acceptable by the IRCA.

MERITOR SAVINGS BANK V. VINSON

The Supreme Court case known as Meritor Savings Bank v. Vinson recognized sexual harassment as a form of unlawful discrimination. The case was brought against Meritor Savings Bank by Mechelle Vinson because the bank's vice president had created a hostile work environment through a series of repeated unwelcome sexual advances and acts. Prior to this case, the protections offered by Title VII of the Civil Rights Act of 1964 for discrimination based on sex had been related solely to economic or other tangible discrimination. However, after the Meritor decision, any disparate treatment that causes a hostile work environment for a member of a protected class constitutes a form of unlawful discrimination.

PREGNANCY DISCRIMINATION IN EMPLOYMENT ACT OF 1978

There are two main clauses of the **Pregnancy Discrimination Act** (PDA) of 1978. The first clause applies to Title VII's prohibition against sex discrimination, which also directly applies to prejudice on the basis of childbirth, pregnancy, or related medical conditions. The second clause requires that employers treat pregnant women the same as others for all employment-related reasons. In short, the PDA makes it illegal to fire or refuse to hire or promote a woman because she is pregnant; to force a pregnancy leave on women who are willing and able to perform the job; and to stop accruing seniority for a woman because she is out of work to give birth. If a pregnant woman is not able to perform her job because of a medical condition related to the pregnancy, the employer must treat the pregnant woman the same way it treats all other temporary disabilities, which includes providing reasonable accommodations. In addition to the PDA of 1978, employers should be aware of any other state regulations that may afford pregnant women more protections.

VOCATIONAL REHABILITATION ACT

The Vocational Rehabilitation Act was intended to increase occupational opportunities for disabled individuals and to prohibit discrimination against "handicapped" persons. The **Rehabilitation Act** applies to federal government contractors and subcontractors holding contracts or subcontracts of $10,000 or more. Contractors and subcontractors with greater than $50,000 in contracts and more than 50 employees must develop written affirmative action plans that address hiring and promoting persons with disabilities. Although there are regulations that protect those engaged in addiction treatment, this act does not protect against individuals who currently suffer with substance abuse that prevents them from performing the duties of the job or whose employment would constitute a direct threat to the safety and property of others.

UGESP

The Uniform Guidelines on Employee Selection Procedures (UGESP), which were passed in 1978, are actually a collection of principles, techniques, and procedures designed to help employers comply with federal anti-discrimination laws. The primary purpose of these guidelines is to define the specific types of procedures that may cause disparate impact and are considered illegal. The UGESP relates to unfair procedures that make it much less likely that an individual belonging to a protected class would be able to receive a particular position.

GRIGGS V. DUKE POWER CO. (1971)

Prior to the 1964 Civil Rights Act, Duke Power Co. segregated employees by race. Once the act passed, the company started requiring a high school diploma and a certain score on an IQ test to qualify for any positions above manual labor. As a result, many African Americans could not obtain the higher-paying jobs. This 1971 case determined that employers must be able to demonstrate that position requirements are actually linked to being able to perform the work. It also determined that employers may be charged with discrimination, even if they did not intend to discriminate. This is known as disparate impact.

PHILLIPS V. MARTIN MARIETTA CORP. (1971)

Linked to the 1964 Civil Rights Act, this case ruled that a company cannot refuse to employ women with young children if they employ men with young children unless there is a legitimate business necessity.

EMPLOYEE POLYGRAPH PROTECTION ACT OF 1988

The **Employee Polygraph Protection Act of 1988** was designed to protect individuals seeking employment from being required to submit to polygraph tests. This act specifically forbids private employers from basing hiring decisions on polygraph tests unless the individual is seeking a position involving pharmaceuticals, working in an armored car, or serving as a security officer. This act does not apply to any government agency or federal contractor or subcontractor with Federal Bureau of Investigation, national defense, or national security contracts. If an employer requires a polygraph test and the position is not related to one of these areas, the company can be fined up to $10,000.

USERRA

The **Uniformed Services Employment and Reemployment Rights Act** (USERRA) of 1994 is applicable to all employers, both public and private. USERRA forbids employers from denying employment, reemployment, retention, promotion, or employment benefits due to service in the Armed Forces, Reserves, National Guard, and other uniformed services, including the National Disaster Medical System and the Commissioned Corps of the Public Health Service. In other words, this statute is designed to prevent those in the uniformed services from being discriminated against or otherwise disadvantaged in the civilian workplace because of their military service or affiliation.

Employees absent in uniformed services for less than 31 days must report to the employer within 8 hours after arriving safely home. Those who are absent between 31 and 180 days must submit an application for reemployment within 14 days. Those who are absent 181 days or more have 90 days to submit an application for reemployment.

Employees are entitled to the positions that they would have held if they had remained continuously employed. If they are no longer qualified for or able to perform the job requirements because of a service-related disability, they are to be provided with a position of equal seniority, status, and pay. Moreover, the escalator principle further entitles returning employees to all of the seniority-based benefits they had when their service began, plus any additional benefits they would have accrued with reasonable certainty if they had remained continuously employed. Likewise, employees cannot be required to use accrued vacation or PTO during absences. USERRA requires all healthcare plans to provide COBRA coverage for up to 18 months of absence and entitles employees to restoration of coverage upon return. Pension plans must remain undisturbed by absences as well. However, those separated from the service for less-than-honorable circumstances are not protected by USERRA.

INDEPENDENT CONTRACTORS

Organizations must be diligent when classifying workers as **employees** versus **independent contractors**. Courts are more likely to favor employee classifications than independent contractor relationships to be sure that employers are not inappropriately avoiding income taxes, Social Security contribution matches, unemployment or workers' compensation protection, and healthcare costs. The difference between an employee and independent contractor is determined

by the entire working relationship. The Internal Revenue Service (IRS) looks at several factors when evaluating a worker's classification: behavioral control, financial control, and type of relationship.

If the company directs the workers on how to act or perform their work, the court is likely to label them as employees. If, on the other hand, the company allows the worker to reach a mutually agreed-upon objective in the manner that they see fit, they're more likely to be classified as an independent contractor. In terms of financial control, if the firm provides the worker with the necessary equipment to perform the work, that worker is more likely to be an employee. Conversely, if the workers purchase their own tools and supplies, they are probably independent contractors. In terms of the relationship, if the company offers the worker benefits, that worker is an employee. However, if the firm does not provide any benefits, the worker may be an independent contractor. The IRS views the relationship between the parties holistically and weighs every detail before making a determination.

CHILD LABOR

The Fair Labor Standards Act established child labor regulations designed to prevent children from entering the workforce before they are mature enough to do so, from working in hazardous environments, from working for long periods, and from working instead of attending school. These regulations prohibit employers from hiring anyone under the age of 14 unless the individual is working for a parent or for a farm and from hiring individuals under the age of 18 for any kind of work deemed hazardous by law. These regulations also prevent individuals under the age of 16 from working in any manufacturing or mining-related job, working during school hours, working more than 3 hours a day or 18 hours a week during a school week or 8 hours a day and 40 hours a week during a non-school week, and working before 7:00 a.m. or past 7:00 p.m. during the school year or working before 7:00 a.m. or past 9:00 p.m. during the summer.

Sourcing Methods

The three main ways an organization recruits potential employees are external recruiting, internal recruiting, and alternative recruiting. **External recruiting** attempts to encourage individuals from outside to seek employment with the organization. This type of recruiting usually consists of strategies that stress the advantages of working for the organization. **Internal recruiting** attempts to encourage individuals from within to seek transfers or promotions into vacant positions the organization needs to fill. **Alternative recruiting** refers to the process of finding interns, telecommuters, or temps to perform specific tasks.

Most external recruiting strategies rely on advertising that appeals to potential candidates by promoting the organization's benefits (pay, insurance, product discounts) and improving the organization's image (with the public and employees). These factors will make it easier to find skilled employees.

There are several recruiting strategies an organization might use to find qualified individuals from within the organization to fill vacant positions, but some of the most common strategies include internal job announcements, job bidding, and promotion/succession plans. **Internal job announcements** are job postings only available to individuals within the organization. This includes job postings that are available to employees before they are made available to the general public. Internal job announcements are usually posted as new positions become available. **Job bidding** is a process in which employees inform the organization of their interest in transferring to another position. **A promotion/succession plan** is a chart or list detailing each employee, their skills and training, and the specific positions they are qualified to fill. These positions are filled by offering promotions or additional training to these qualified individuals.

EMPLOYEE REFERRAL PROGRAMS

One of the quickest ways to fill a position is through employee referrals. Because referrals can save not only time but also budgeted recruitment dollars, employers are often interested in incentivizing employees to refer their contacts to open jobs. The employer should define the goals of a referral program early in the program development. First, the employer should be clear as to whether all open jobs or just hard-to-fill positions are available for incentives. Next, the employer should define the worth of a successful referral. Typically, this scenario involves a monetary award. Once the incentive is defined, the program should be advertised internally. Finally, the program should be measured to see if the intended results were achieved. The employer could measure time-to-fill improvement, number of qualified referral candidates, number of referrals, and any other factors defined as goals.

COLLEGE RECRUITMENT

College and university recruitment is a relationship business, combining technology and personal contact strategies. To determine the dollars that will be budgeted for the process, an employer should have a plan as to how many college graduate hires are needed. If there is a significant need, employers should implement the multichannel recruitment tools that college graduates use. Utilizing a company website, social media, blogs, and email campaigns can create interest using mediums that college students gravitate to. However, personal relationships are still critical to the recruitment process. Phone calls, on-campus interviewing days, and job fairs are all ways for an employer to use personal contact to show college candidates who they could work with.

PASSIVE CANDIDATES

Passive candidates are individuals who are not actively seeking a new job. It is difficult for traditional advertisements to be effective if qualified candidates aren't looking at them. Using a professional-oriented social media platform, such as LinkedIn, is one way to find a passive candidate. After searching such a site for individuals who hold certain skills, employers can reach out to those candidates through that medium. Also, using personal connections such as employee referrals and hiring manager referrals can connect a person who is not actively looking for a job. Finally, constantly marketing the company so there is brand awareness, even when the need for employees is down, can create recognition for a passive job seeker once a job does open up.

SOCIAL MEDIA

Social media is a cost-effective way to attract employment candidates. Traditional advertisements, such as job postings and print advertisements, are much more expensive. Often recruiters use a combination of the two by posting the job on a traditional job board and enhancing the posting's reach by sharing it on social media. Recruiters can also ask other employees to share the posting on their social media accounts to reach even more candidates. Sharing the posting on LinkedIn, Twitter, Facebook, and other platforms increases the chance a passive candidate learns about the opening. Moreover, an employer's consistent use of social media—not just during hiring times—strengthens the brand and creates awareness of the company.

INTERNAL RECRUITMENT

Internal recruiting is using current staff as part of the candidate pool when an opening occurs. This is often through an internal posting process or career development activities—or, ideally, a combination of both. An internal posting process starts with defining the way employees learn about open positions. This is often accomplished through job postings shared on the employee self-service page of the company's human capital management system, and/or on the company's intranet. Many companies stress the desire to "grow people" within the company. The most successful internal recruiting tactics are intentional and in place before a position opens. Career ladder programs prepare employees to become proficient in certain areas and ultimately prepare the employee for the next-level position.

EXECUTIVE RECRUITERS

There are many reasons why companies use executive recruiters when filling senior-level or specialized-skill positions. First, executive recruiters are experts in that level of work. They have the contacts needed to seek out executives, who are typically so busy that they do not have time to work through the traditional application process. Another reason to use a recruiter is for roles that require specialty skills. Recruiters often specialize in a certain niche or industry. Executive recruiters are also useful in times when confidentiality is needed. For example, if a current role is already filled but the company expects a vacancy in the near future, an executive recruiter can conduct a confidential search so that concerns are not raised inside the company. Finally, because of the connections available to executive recruiters, filling critical roles often takes less time. While executive recruiters are expensive, companies may see finding senior-level or specialized talent as worth the expense.

OUTSOURCING

Outsourcing refers to the practice of hiring third-party companies or contractors to perform tasks traditionally performed by the organization itself. There are a variety of situations in which it might be better to outsource. Crucial factors to consider when deciding whether or not to outsource include the cost of performing the task in-house, the cost of a third party performing the task, the level of difficulty associated with the task, the level of quality control necessary for the task, the level of quality control available from outside sources, the impact on the organization if the task is not completed when expected or as expected, and how much control the organization needs to maintain.

There are a variety of factors that an organization should consider before choosing a third-party vendor regardless of the specific task. However, four of the most important factors to consider are the costs associated with doing business with the vendor, the quality of the vendor's product or service, the ability of the vendor to meet the organization's needs for the specific task, and the vendor's experience as it relates to the specific task. The **costs** associated with doing business with a particular vendor are all of the costs potentially incurred with a particular vendor. The **quality** of the vendor's product or service refers to the vendor's ability to perform the service or manufacture the product to the standards set by the organization. Finally, the ability of the vendor to meet the **organization's needs** and the **vendor's experience** as it relates to the task are both ways of determining if the vendor will be able to consistently perform the task as expected.

OFFSHORING

Offshoring is a process similar to outsourcing because it refers to hiring an individual or company located in another country to perform a task the organization would normally perform domestically. Usually, organizations hire offshore, overseas, or in a different country because it can be more cost effective. Offshoring differs from outsourcing because it is possible to have an offshore division that is actually a part of the organization.

STAFFING AGENCIES

Temporary agencies are used in a few different ways. First, organizations use temporary agencies when there is a temporary need for staff. For example, if a critical employee is going to be absent for several weeks, hiring a temporary employee may be the best way to ensure the work continues. Second, organizations may use staffing services temporarily to supplement traditional recruitment methods if a large number of employees are needed at one time. This could occur if an organization is opening a new department with more positions than the internal HR department has the capacity to fill. Finally, some organizations use a staffing service for ongoing recruitment needs for positions that are consistently open. This can happen in lower-level positions, such as machine operators or customer service positions. Organizations can request a staffing agency to send a constant stream of candidates to fill the open positions. This creates a "try before you buy" scenario, where the employer can see if an individual is a good fit before hiring the person as a regular employee.

MEASURING EFFECTIVENESS

There are a variety of different business metrics that an organization might use in order to measure the effectiveness or efficiency of a recruiting strategy. Three of the most common effectiveness/efficiency metrics for recruiting are the quantity of applications, the cost per hire, and the time to fill. The **quantity of applications** simply refers to the number of employment applications that the organization has received for a particular position or group of positions. The **cost per hire** refers to the estimated amount that the organization spends on recruiting for each employee that is hired by the organization. The **time to fill** refers to the number of days that a specific position remains open before the organization is able to hire an individual to fill the open position.

REMOTE/HYBRID WORK SOLUTIONS
FLEXIBLE WORKPLACE POLICIES

With a diverse workforce can come diverse personal and professional needs; organizations that are able to offer **flexible benefits and workplace policies** are better equipped to care for all of their employees. Remote or hybrid work options can help employees reduce commuting costs (in both time and money), reduce their environmental footprints, and improve their abilities to balance home and work responsibilities. Remote work can be especially useful for jobs that are measured in outcomes rather than in time spent. Unconventional scheduling may be a valuable option for employees seeking to work compressed hours or alternative hours such as nights or weekends to help balance their work and home lives. **Job sharing** may be a viable option if there are employees seeking part-time work for positions that are traditionally full time. Some companies also benefit from unlimited vacation time policies, which encourage employees to take the time they want or need but put a premium on effective communication and work outcomes. Flexibility in workplace policies can add to an employer brand when attracting new talent. Flexibility in workplace policies can also reduce stress outside of work, so employees are better able to perform at work. When mindfully designed and executed, flexible workplace policies can shift the focus from transactional and administratively driven work interactions to transformational and business-impact-driven work interactions.

REMOTE WORK

Companies need to consider many implications before making a decision to move employees from office-based to **remote work**:

- **The impact to recruiting and retention.** While many employees want to work remotely, there are those who do not embrace that arrangement. Employers should carefully assess the type of work required, the corporate culture, the support of management, and the geographical location of the job to understand how current and future employees will react to moving jobs remotely.
- **Corporate culture.** It can be very difficult to establish a strong corporate culture when employees are located remotely. There must be practices and procedures intentionally instilled that will support remote workers. Management must be fully on board.
- **Results over time worked.** In a remote environment, employees perform successfully when they are given a task and a deadline, and then are allowed to get the job done without constant oversight. If it is not absolutely essential to dictate the hours worked, employees should be given flexibility to achieve their tasks.

Employees who work remotely can be highly effective, but management needs to be trained on supervision approaches, employee support, and performance management.

Talent Acquisition Lifecycle

JOB ANALYSIS AND IDENTIFICATION OF JOB REQUIREMENTS

A **job analysis** is an essential part of any workforce planning process because it identifies specific skills, knowledge, and traits required to meet staffing goals and organizational objectives. It outlines what a worker needs to be successful in a given role and also establishes the relative importance of each role to the company.

The three main parts of a job analysis are job competencies, job specifications, and job descriptions. **Job competencies** are detailed lists of all broad skills and traits (such as leadership ability) needed for a particular position. **Job specifications** are detailed descriptions of all specific qualifications (such as experience or education) an individual must have to perform the role. A **job description** is a detailed written breakdown of all tasks that a worker in that role must complete, along with the job competencies and job specifications required for a worker to be qualified for that role. Equal Employment Opportunity Commission (EEOC) guidelines encourage employers to prepare written job descriptions listing the essential functions of each job.

Some of the major uses of job analysis include the following:

- **Human resource planning,** to develop job categories
- **Recruiting,** to describe and advertise job openings
- **Selection,** to identify skills and criteria for selecting candidates
- **Orientation,** to describe activities and expectations to employees
- **Evaluation,** to identify standards and performance objectives
- **Compensation,** to evaluate job worth and develop pay structures
- **Training,** to conduct needs assessments
- **Discipline,** to correct subpar performance
- **Safety,** to identify working procedures and ensure workers can safely perform activities

- **Job redesign,** to analyze job characteristics that periodically need updating
- **Legal protection,** to identify essential functions that must be performed to protect the organization against claims

ESSENTIAL FUNCTIONS IN A JOB DESCRIPTION

Essential functions are documented within a **job description**, detailing what a job applicant unquestionably must be able to do because it is essential to the job. Capturing all essential functions in a job description is important because they are used to determine the legal rights of an employee with a disability under the American with Disabilities Act (ADA). If an employee cannot perform the essential function, even with reasonable accommodations, then that employee is not qualified for the job and cannot be safeguarded from discrimination as outlined in the ADA. In other words, a person cannot bring a disability lawsuit against an employer if the person, due to a disability, could not perform the essential functions as documented in the job description. A job analysis is significant in determining essential functions because if an essential function is not truly an essential function, then the employer cannot exclude a person with a disability from the given position because they cannot perform the function. The following are some guidelines to consider when documenting essential functions for every task:

- Ensure the task is truly a requirement to perform the job.
- Evaluate and determine the frequency and time spent performing a task.
- Evaluate whether not performing the task would be detrimental to the employer.
- Determine whether the task could be redesigned, conducted in a different manner, or altered in a way that doesn't severely compromise the end product or service.
- Decide whether the task could be accomplished by a similar employee.

After drafting a job's essential functions, the employer should carefully consider whether the functions are truly essential or marginal. The words "essential function" are part of a typical job description and should clearly state that those functions are essential to perform the job.

COMPONENTS OF JOB DESCRIPTIONS

There is not a specific template for any job description because it is dependent on the particulars of the job and the organization. However, a job description is usually standardized in appearance in most organizations. The following are some of the most important elements that should be included in a job description:

- Job title.
- Classification (exempt, nonexempt, contractor).
- Date when the job description was written.
- Summary of the job and key objectives.
- Listing of all essential functions, knowledge, skills, and abilities (KSAs). KSAs may or may not be included in essential functions. If not, there should be a separate section for competencies.
- Level of supervision—Whether the role has direct reports (and, if so, how many) or is an individual contributor with no supervisory responsibilities.
- Work environment conditions such as temperature and noise, and physical demands such as bending, sitting, and lifting.
- Hours—The hours to be spent working on-site and remotely; and/or the percentage of travel required, if applicable.
- Education and/or experience required, including college, certifications, and/or number of years of experience in a specific industry or environment.

- Salary range for the position.
- Affirmative action plan and/or equal employment opportunity statement. These are especially necessary if the position is a federal contractor, but are usually common practice.

SELECTION PROCESS

Selection methods and tools are an essential part of an organization's hiring process because the goal is to find groups of acceptable employees and then choose the best candidates from those groups. However, even if an organization has located a suitable group of potential employees, it can be extremely difficult for an interviewer to separate the most qualified individual from the rest of the group based on applications and resumes alone. As a result, it is necessary to have a set of well-defined selection tools and methods that are both valid and reliable.

The **selection process** is sequential and includes a series of steps; each systematically screens out unsuccessful individuals who will not continue to the next round. The order of steps is often organized based on a cost/benefit analysis, with the most expensive steps at the end of the process. Steps of the selection process may include introductory screening, questionnaires, initial interviews, employment testing, final interviews, selection decisions, reference checks, drug testing, post-offer medical exams, and placement. The **two basic principles of selection** that influence the process of making an informed hiring decision are 1) past behaviors and 2) reliable and valid data. Past behavior is the best predictor for future behavior. **Reliable data** is consistently repeated, whereas **valid data** measures performance.

TYPES OF VALIDITY

The three main types of validity that an HR professional may have to evaluate in order to determine if a screening or selection tool is valid are construct validity, content validity, and criterion validity. A screening or selection tool is considered to have **construct validity** if the tool actually assesses whether or not the individual possesses the specific traits that have been shown to indicate success within a particular position. In other words, the screening or selection tool must test for specific characteristics that can be shown as indicators of job performance in order to be considered valid in this sense. A screening or selection tool is considered to have **content validity** if the tool actually assesses whether or not the individual possesses the skills and knowledge necessary to perform the tasks associated with a particular position. Finally, a screening or selection tool is considered to have **criterion validity** if the tool can be used to reasonably predict how an individual will behave in the workplace based on the individual's score on a written or verbal test.

The two types of criterion validity that an HR professional may have to evaluate in order to determine if a screening or selection tool is valid are concurrent validity and predictive validity. A screening or selection tool is considered to have **concurrent validity** if it can be proven that the individual's score on a written or verbal test indicates that the individual currently possesses the desired trait or will behave in the desired fashion during a different test. For example, if a person's score on a written test indicates they will remain calm in stressful situations, and that same person remains calm in a stressful situation during a different test, these two tests have concurrent validity. That is, both tests are in agreement in their assessment of the individual. A screening or selection tool will be considered to have **predictive validity** if it can be proven that the individual's score on a written or verbal test indicates that the individual will possess the desired trait or will behave in the desired fashion at some point in the future.

Preemployment Tests

Two of the most common types of preemployment tests are aptitude tests and in-box tests. An **aptitude test** is an examination designed to determine if an individual has the basic knowledge to perform the tasks associated with a particular position. For example, an aptitude test for a bank teller might consist of a series of basic math problems related to specific banking activities (e.g., determining an account balance after several deposits and withdrawals).

During an **in-box test**, also called an in-basket test, the individual must determine the appropriate way to handle particular problems. For example, a person applying for a position as head bank teller might be asked to describe the appropriate way to handle a check deposited into the wrong account.

The two main advantages associated with preemployment tests are that they allow the organization to have more control over the information gathered, and they make it easier to gather information in a consistent way. Preemployment tests comprise premade questions that assess an individual's ability to use specific skills and areas of knowledge. The results will either support or refute the information gathered during the interview. Preemployment tests provide consistent results as long as each applicant takes the exam under the same conditions.

There are some disadvantages associated with using a preemployment test. First, it is easy to unintentionally cause a disparate impact to a protected class if questions are not relevant to the position for which the individual is applying. A series of poorly worded or irrelevant questions may make it more difficult for members of a particular group of people to get the job, which may make the organization legally liable. Second, preemployment tests do not allow for flexibility because the same questions are asked of every applicant. An interviewer is able to ask questions specifically related to each individual applicant, whereas a preemployment test cannot.

Assessment Centers

An **assessment center** is a standardized system of tests designed to gauge candidates' knowledge, skills, abilities, and behaviors in relation to the position for which they are being considered. The assessment center may include interviews, psychological tests, simulations of scenarios typical to the role, and other forms of measurement. A firm employing this screening approach may use live raters. However, technological advances, such as objective computerized tests, have made it possible to rate candidates without human intervention, resulting in a more cost- and time-effective process.

Reference Checks

Reference checks are an important part of any organization's hiring process for two reasons. First, reference checks verify that individuals have the skills and knowledge necessary to perform the position for which they are being hired. Second, they allow an organization to protect itself from lawsuits and damage to its operations or reputation from employees who are inept or dishonest. References may identify past problems that may not show up on a resume or application.

The two main types of references an organization would normally need to check are educational and employment. **Educational references** are certifications, degrees, diplomas, professional licenses, scholarly awards, or other documents used to prove the individual's knowledge. Universities or certification organizations may provide specific information about performance such as grades, but most educational reference checks are only used to verify education and the dates each degree, certification, or license was earned. **Employment references** refer to previous employers, co-workers, or customers who can verify experience. An organization will usually seek on-the-job performance information from previous employers and co-workers in addition to position, pay, and length of employment.

CRIMINAL RECORD CHECKS

It is important to check criminal records because individuals who have caused problems in the past will often cause problems in the future, which could lead to damage or liability to an organization. Criminal records will indicate if the individual has been convicted of a crime so that a determination can be made if those crimes relate to the position. In many cases, the crime the individual committed may not be relevant to how the individual will perform in a particular position. However, employers may want to think twice before hiring an individual with a history of violent crimes, theft, or substance abuse.

EMPLOYER CONSIDERATIONS REGARDING PRE-EMPLOYMENT BACKGROUND CHECKS

Many employers will conduct pre-employment background checks on candidates to ensure that employees have sound judgment and are unlikely to engage in improper conduct and/or do not have a criminal record. HR departments often order credit checks or criminal record searches through online service providers and then review results. The Fair Credit Reporting Act, like many legal regulations, requires not only that employers notify applicants that they administer background checks, but also that applicants must sign a written release consenting that the employer may receive their personal information. Furthermore, when implementing a pre-employment background check, employers must consider if doing so may be discriminatory, and therefore must validate the business necessity.

Many states have joined the Ban the Box movement, which prohibits employers from asking about an applicant's criminal history at the time of application. If an offense is found, employers are urged to consider the severity of the offense, the amount of time elapsed since the offense, and whether the offense is related to the nature of the job. Applicants must also have the opportunity to contest or explain adverse results before officially being turned down for employment. The prospective employer must furnish a copy of the report to the applicant. The Federal Trade Commission advises employers to give the applicant five days to respond before sending them an official letter of rejection.

INTERVIEWS

After making it through the resume and job application review round, and possibly a phone screening, the applicant advances to the interview phase of the selection process. Some reasons for conducting interviews are to obtain information about the applicant, to sell and provide information about the company, and to build relationships.

There are many different types of interviews. A **structured, or patterned, interview** allows the interviewer to ask a series of prepared questions and may even contain a list of multiple-choice answers. In a **semi-structured interview**, the interviewer follows a guide of prepared questions, but can ask follow-up questions to evaluate qualifications and characteristics. Situational interviews that gauge responses to hypothetical problems, and behavioral interviews that question previous or anticipated behavior, are frequently semi-structured. An **unstructured, or nondirective, interview** is more conversational and allows more freedom so the applicant may determine the course of the discussion. To be successful, the interviewer should listen carefully without interruption.

Due to technological advancements and the rise of telecommuting, the number of **virtual interviews** has increased. These may involve the candidate sitting in front of a webcam and answering recorded questions, or both the candidate and the interviewer speaking in real time from their respective locations. These interviews are often less expensive and more convenient and can provide both personality and standardized evaluations.

Sometimes interviews involve many parties. **Group interviews** involve multiple candidates, whereas **panel interviews** and **board interviews** involve multiple interviewers. Finally, candidates may be required to go through additional screening, such as preemployment testing, a physical examination, drug testing, a background investigation, academic achievement verification, and/or reference checking.

There are two main disadvantages associated with a selection interview. First, it can be heavily affected by the interviewer's own biases. Regardless of how much experience or training an interviewer has, preconceived ideas of a particular candidate or a particular type of candidate can influence the evaluation. Second, even the best-planned interview can be rendered useless when intelligent applicants, wanting to cast themselves in the best possible light, control the interview. Further, when the interviewer does not ask the right questions, the applicant may appear to be a viable candidate even though he or she lacks the necessary skills or traits to do the job.

JOB OFFERS AND CONTRACTS
NEGOTIATIONS

Negotiation is a vital technique for every business professional. New or expired contracts and changing behaviors require skillful **negotiations**. Human resource practitioners must know how to handle negotiations to successfully avoid conflicts, improve relations, secure pay rates, and evaluate contracts. It is paramount to note that negotiations are only possible when all parties are open to compromise and finding solutions that are mutually satisfying.

Some tips for successful negotiation might include: be prepared, listen carefully, be flexible, be patient, be alert, be persuasive, be considerate, be professional, be respectful, remain confident, keep communications honest, encourage taking steps forward, manage expectations, always have an alternative plan, think outside the box to find creative solutions, remain task oriented, strive to build relationships, avoid delays, and review details.

Once a candidate has been selected, the salary must be **negotiated** before a formal offer can be made. An employee agreement often includes the first day of work, starting salary, company benefits, and other terms or conditions. The following techniques may be used to improve negotiations:

1. Consider the interests and expectations of both parties.
2. Plan a negotiation strategy that addresses minimum requirements and discussion points.
3. Be creative. Include low-cost incentives such as people, culture, and time off, as well as opportunities for growth and development.
4. Address compromises or trades and avoid making biased concessions to encourage fairness. Think, "If we give you this, we will expect that in return."
5. Know your limitations and when to walk away. Allow time for contemplation.

WRITTEN EMPLOYMENT CONTRACTS

Many employment details may be explained in **written contracts or job offer letters**. The contract should summarize what position is being offered, rate of pay, benefits, perks, expectations regarding performance, probationary periods, and proprietary information. Written employment contracts will frequently include some combination of these elements:

- **The length of the contract**—if agreement is for a specified period of time
- **Duties and responsibilities**—if not included in a job description
- **Career opportunities**—succession planning or likelihood of advancement
- **Compensation**—hourly or salary rate and sign-on bonus inclusions
- **Benefits and bonus incentives**—relocation assistance, commissions, bonus potential, stock options, and paid time off
- **Restrictive covenants**—limitations such as confidentiality and noncompete disclosures
- **Severance payments**—if employees can expect any promised pay at the end of an assignment
- **Dispute resolution**—arbitration requirements and payment of legal fees
- **Change of control**—in the event of a merger or acquisition

> **Review Video: Written Employment Contracts**
> Visit mometrix.com/academy and enter code: 407808

APPROACHES TO EMPLOYEE ONBOARDING

There are many approaches to **onboarding** newly hired employees, from the interview, to orientation, through the 90-day review. However, all companies do things a bit differently, and the size of or engagement from the welcoming committee will vary. A majority of the responsibility will fall upon HR in most cases, but the hiring manager and information technology personnel often share some responsibilities as well. Here are a few steps that might appear on an onboarding checklist for new hires:

- **Phone interview:** brief 10- to 30-minute screening of applicants (HR)
- **Live interview**: more in-depth discussion, often lasting one to three hours (HR/hiring manager)
- **Offer letter:** formal written offer to finalist (HR)
- **Computer access:** workstation set up with email, phone, and systems access (information technology)
- **Keys, equipment, and business cards:** order/log equipment usage (operations)
- **Welcome email:** introductory email welcoming new hires with tips for success (HR)
- **Federal paperwork:** employment eligibility and tax forms (HR)
- **Company paperwork:** handbook, policies, nondisclosure agreements, and benefits acknowledgments (HR)
- **Orientation:** thorough company and policy overview and required training (HR/hiring manager)
- **Position overview and mentoring/training:** buddy assignment, job expectations, and process manual (hiring manager)
- **Introductions:** site tour, staff introductions, and icebreaker questionnaires or games (HR/hiring manager)
- **30-/60-/90-day reviews**: summary of how the new hire is assimilating into the new role (HR/hiring manager)

ORIENTATION

While all of the initial paperwork and equipment set-up is vital to ensuring success for the new employee, the new hire **orientation** is an opportunity for the organization to communicate its mission, vision, values, and objectives. The orientation is typically designed as a one-time event to bring newly hired employees together and share information that allows employees to quickly receive the information they need to start functioning within the organization.

Some of the core information shared at a new hire orientation should be organization charts, phone lists, performance review schedules, policies and procedures, and a calendar of critical company events.

Orientations create a connection to the organization and its goals. Employees should be able to see how they fit in and how their work adds value to the overall objectives. The meeting sets up communication channels for new employees to seek guidance and assistance.

Employees should be provided with a copy of their job description to ensure that they fully understand the requirements of the position. Available training opportunities can be shared to assist employees in any areas of weakness or development.

The orientation should establish a communication channel for the new employees to help them fit in and provide them with resources to go to for questions, concerns, ideas, and suggestions.

BUDDY SYSTEM

Starting a new job can be a very exciting period for the employee, but it can also be very stressful. A positive program that employers can implement is a **buddy system**. HR, or the manager for each new employee, identifies an experienced employee to partner with the new employee for some period of time. It is beneficial if the buddy is from the same work area as the new hire. Buddies can offer the new employee some of the following benefits:

- Help in navigating the organization, including how different business elements integrate.
- Guidance on identifying relevant stakeholders of the organization or project to which the new employee is assigned.
- Advice on assimilating into the corporate culture.
- Determining how his or her role fits within the team.
- Counsel for thinking strategically when approaching work issues.
- Offering an ear for questions, issues, or concerns, and advice from a trusted source.

A buddy system can significantly increase employee satisfaction for both the new employee and the buddy, which drives improved productivity and retention.

PERSONALIZATION

Onboarding that is done well can be an effective tool for setting up new employees for success, therefore adding great value to the organization. However, as diversity, equity, and inclusion programs expand and become more integrated in organizations, organizations will start to embrace changes in new hire orientation programs. Treating every new hire the same way, presenting information in the same manner, and assuming that everyone will benefit equally from it is missing the opportunity to **personalize** the new hire orientation in ways that reach individual employees more efficiently and effectively. Some of the approaches to personalizing new hire programs are:

- Use data tagging software to customize each employee's journey through the online onboarding process. Landing pages, training pages, and letters can be customized with the employee's name, job title, email address, and start date.

- Administer a personality assessment test as part of onboarding. This can help HR and managers understand some traits that may impact the willingness of a candidate to ask questions or push back if they don't understand the material.
- Group new hires by career paths or goals. Similar employees onboarding together, whether in face or remotely, can create a sense of comradery and bonding that will help the employees feel more welcome and give them a familiar face with which to interact.
- Personalize the onboarding process. Employees straight out of college may need more information, more background, and more support starting their first job. Late-career employees need less information about the job but may benefit from learning more details about the company culture and customers.

Taking the time to get to know the incoming employees and tailoring the onboarding process to be inclusive and personalized will help the employees integrate and settle into their positions more quickly and easily. This will benefit productivity and long-term retention.

Managing Cultural Integration
Reverse Mentorships

In a **reverse mentorship**, a junior employee is paired with a more senior employee so that the junior employee can share advice, experience, and skills with the senior mentee. This practice can be especially helpful with new and emerging technologies and work practices. Senior employees may have more tenure within the organization or the workforce, but partnering with junior employees provides them with opportunities to pick up on new skills and perspectives. Senior employees may benefit by gaining more tangible skills, and junior employees gain leadership skills, confidence, and opportunities for continued growth and development. Reverse mentoring improves workplace relationships, increases employee engagement, and helps broaden skills and improve learning.

Sensitivity Training

The goal of **sensitivity training** is to create a more open and collaborative working environment by helping individuals within an organization become aware of attitudes, behaviors, and biases that may impact others. This training can involve employees gathering to participate in group activities and discussions in order to develop greater acceptance within the group. Many trainings are directed toward diversity, while others focus on various forms of harassment. Sensitivity training can help workers to develop emotional intelligence, provide guidance on how to deal with difficult or opposing personalities, and review appropriate workplace conversations and interactions. Companies that implement strong sensitivity training programs can benefit because these programs can lead to a more respectful and accountable workforce.

Focus Groups

A great method to collect qualitative data on different workplace topics, in a **focus group** employee feedback is gathered to provide the employer with insight into the employees' ideas and opinions. A focus group is made up of several individuals who participate in a moderated discussion aimed at gathering information and data regarding a particular topic, issue, or initiative. The moderator asks open-ended questions to encourage conversation. Focus groups are beneficial because they provide the employer with important data while also empowering employees by allowing them a voice in decision-making processes. Focus groups can help identify both weaknesses and strengths within the organization. Holding focus groups and taking action on information discovered in this fashion also shows employees that their feedback is valued and the organization is committed to improvement.

Barrier Removal

Global and **cultural barriers** are increasing as businesses spread across oceans and countries. When two different cultures clash, gestures can be misinterpreted and communications can be misunderstood. For example, although Americans shake hands when meeting new people, other countries might bow, hug, or kiss. Similarly, making eye contact or expressing emotional sensitivity might be considered offensive in some cultures. As operations grow and the company turns to outsourcing or sending manufacturing overseas, language and other barriers can make finding the best resources difficult and delay communications. **Inclusive cultures** are key to removing these barriers because they welcome individuals regardless of culture, age, race, ethnicity, sexual orientation, religious belief, disability, or any other factor. Inclusive cultures foster understanding and ensure that appropriate accommodations are made in the workplace. Companies dedicated to fostering an inclusive culture also provide team members with regular training to underscore the value of cultural diversity and instill a sense of acceptance.

Assimilation

During a job transition process, employees are separated from their previous roles and gradually initiated into their new roles. **Assimilation** is the final stage of the transition process, when the individual has overcome any initial shock and successfully integrates into the new role and company culture. During this stage, individuals become part of the group and begin to fit in while new expectations are formed. To ensure that the process is a success, new employees should be partnered with long-tenured staff who can show them the ins and outs of the organization. The new employee should be given ample time to ask questions, make and correct mistakes, and adapt to the new environment. They should also be immediately included in office events and meetings.

Learning and Development

Career Development and Professional Growth

CAREER LADDERS AND CAREER PATHS

Career ladders and career paths are similar tools in employee development and often overlap. **Career ladders** outline the traditional "steps" of moving up in an organization. In a manufacturing plant, a basic ladder may outline how an employee could move up from machine operator to supervisor to plant manager.

A **career path** is less straightforward. It encompasses all of the turns a career could take in an organization. For example, it could outline the traditional career ladder steps, but it also includes more nontraditional development opportunities—including lateral moves into other departments. A manufacturing example of a career path could illustrate how an employee could move from machine operator to the shipping/receiving department, or could increase their technical knowledge to become a draftsperson. An employee who understands all the development options available and pursues a nontraditional path could become a more well-rounded employee.

CAREER DEVELOPMENT
STAGES OF WORKING AND PROFESSIONAL CAREER DEVELOPMENT

Professional careers and trade careers both involve four stages of career development. For **professional careers**, the stages are internship, independent contributor, mentor, and sponsor.

- **Interns** are individuals who are learning under the supervision of experienced professionals.
- **Independent contributors** are autonomous workers whose success is based upon how well they take initiative, meet objectives, and exceed expectations.
- **Mentors** have displayed their ability to perform, supervise, and coach others.
- **Sponsors** make strategic decisions while providing organizational guidance, influence, and accountability.

For **trade or working careers**, the stages are exploration, establishment, maintenance, and decline.

- The **exploration stage** describes individuals who are just beginning their careers, often between the ages of 15 and 24, who are still working on trade programs or courses and who may be prone to frequently changing positions while trying to explore interests and abilities against job demands.
- The **establishment stage** describes individuals, often between the ages of 25 and 44, who are striving to create a more stable position within their chosen occupation to establish work and build a reputation.
- The **maintenance stage** describes individuals, often between the ages of 45 and 64, who are concerned with job security and survival.
- The **decline stage** describes individuals, often older than 65, who are approaching the end of their career and entering retirement.

Individual Career Development

Commonly used methods of individual career development include coaching programs, employee counseling and support programs, and training workshops. Coaching programs are designed to provide each employee with a specialist to help learn new skills or understand how to handle work-related problems or situations. Employee counseling and support programs are designed to provide help if the employee is experiencing problems that may be affecting performance or the ability to seek other opportunities. Training workshops that offer employees the opportunity to learn the knowledge and skills associated with other positions within the organization can also be helpful.

There are a variety of methods a manager or supervisor can use to further an individual's career development. Some methods commonly used are coaching, counseling, mentoring, and evaluating. Employees can be coached to perform new tasks, handle certain problems outside of the scope of their current positions, and develop communication and leadership. Employees can also be offered counseling, advice, or emotional support. Managers or supervisors can act as mentors by helping employees apply for promotions, suggesting them for promotions, and offering guidance about other positions. Finally, managers or supervisors can help further an employee's career by candidly evaluating and discussing strengths and weaknesses.

There are a variety of methods individuals can use for their own career development. Some of the most important methods include attending training workshops, networking, and seeking additional education. Many organizations offer training workshops to help individuals seek management positions or positions in other departments, but most of these workshops are optional, so they will only help if an individual takes the time to attend the program and learn the material. Networking is a necessary skill because it is nearly impossible to progress in an organization if there is unwillingness or an inability to establish relationships with managers, supervisors, coworkers, or customers. Finally, when the knowledge or educational background required for a particular position is lacking, the best way to develop a career is to seek additional education from colleges, universities, or seminars.

Techniques for Career Development

Career pathing or mapping is a plan for employees to progress within the organization. It involves a management-guided employee self-assessment of interests, motivations, knowledge, and skills. Potential matching roles within the organization will be identified, such as a promotion or lateral move. Plans will be created to fill gaps in skills and knowledge needed for the potential roles. When the identified opportunities arise, employees will further explore and pursue them if ready.

Coaching and Mentoring Techniques

Coaching

Coaching in business is a method of training in which an experienced individual provides an employee with advice to encourage his or her best possible performance and career. Having a strong **coaching culture** among strategic goals often leads to increased organizational performance and engagement. Coaching is a personal, one-on-one relationship that takes place over a specific period. This method is often used in performance management, but it can be applied to many business objectives. For example, coaching may be used to prepare individuals for new assignments, improve behavior, conquer obstacles, and adapt to change. Coaching might also be used to support diversity initiatives, such as generational differences, behavioral styles, or awareness and inclusion.

EXECUTIVE COACHING

An **executive coaching** relationship is between an individual and a professional coach or consultant. The goal of this relationship is to help the individual develop key skills, improve motivation, gain self-awareness, and achieve development objectives. Executive coaches help the individual work with both strengths and weaknesses. The coaching or consulting is totally individualized, designed to meet the needs and skillset of the individual and his or her unique circumstances. Executive coaches challenge assumptions, provide resources, help identify and guide toward meeting and completing goals, and act as a sounding board for the individual. Individuals who receive executive coaching are often able to better support other leaders and employees while also honing their ability to successfully support business strategies and objectives.

MENTORING

Mentoring is a career development method in which a new or less experienced employee is paired with an experienced leader for guidance. **Formal mentoring programs** need to be measurable and integrated into the culture, without being seen as rigid, forced systems. These programs typically establish goals at the onset and track progress throughout. Similar to coaching, mentoring is a partnership that takes place over a specific period, and both coaching and mentoring need a customized approach that fits the receiver. However, mentoring carries a history of recognition for having considerable impact with the power to positively transform career trajectory. Successful mentors are able to support, encourage, promote, and challenge while developing deep connections.

Mentoring can also happen more informally, where the mentee looks up to and takes the advice of the mentor without there being defined goals or objectives. This happens naturally, and often the people involved don't know the mentor–mentee relationship existed until later reflection.

Succession Planning

Succession planning is a method of planning how management and executive vacancies will be filled so a company has highly trained replacements available to fill available vacancies. First, determine what the requirements are for key positions and create profiles that outline responsibilities. The experience, education, career progress, and future career interests of managerial candidates should also be reviewed. Then, the performance of prospective managers should be assessed to determine whether they are promotable or not and to identify developmental objectives to prepare for advancement opportunities. Performance should be evaluated based on traditional goals and standards. Developmental objectives might include seminars, training programs, special projects, or temporary assignments.

IDENTIFYING HIGH-POTENTIAL EMPLOYEES

As part of any workforce analysis, HR and management must pay special attention to key positions and high-performance and high-potential employees. A **high-potential employee** is an employee who demonstrates the traits and qualities that the organization values. These can be an understanding of the business environment, special customer insight, excellent business values, leadership skills, strong ethics, or outstanding communication skills.

These high-potential employees may not be the top producers, as they may still be learning and working their way up in the organization, but they are clearly aligned with the future direction of the organization and align with the company culture.

HR should have a process whereby they work with management to identify these high-potential employees and involve them in mentoring, succession planning, and retention plans.

IDENTIFYING HIGH-PERFORMANCE EMPLOYEES

As with high-potential employees, **high-performance employees** have all the attributes and skills that the organization values, but high-performance employees have also demonstrated job performance. Four characteristics of high-performance employees are that they:

- Consistently accomplish established goals and frequently seek out additional assignments.
- Constantly work to improve their knowledge and skills.
- Actively seek feedback to improve job performance.
- Adhere to a very high standard of quality work at all times.

High-performance employees are an asset to the organization and should be identified and included in succession planning, promotion opportunities, and retention plans.

HIGH-POTENTIAL DEVELOPMENT PROGRAMS

Firms may offer targeted training and other enrichment opportunities to their best and brightest employees. These **high-potential development programs** should serve as career road maps, cultivating leadership skills and allowing employees to take on meaningful work so that they can see their impact. Some components of this program may include challenging assignments to promote professional growth, opportunities to mentor others, access to on-demand learning modules, and invitations to networking events both within and outside of the firm. To ensure the program's success, participating employees must receive regular and detailed feedback about their performance. Done well, a high-potential development program enables firms to get the best ROI from their staff while keeping them engaged and attracting new waves of high-potential employees for the future.

STRETCH ASSIGNMENTS

A **stretch assignment** is a learning opportunity for an employee to work on a task or a project that exceeds that individual's current level of skill, knowledge, or experience. The stretch assignment helps demonstrate the employee's adaptability, flexibility, and problem-solving skills to management. Throughout the assignment, employees may be given a heightened level of responsibility, and be challenged to work in an unfamiliar area or with unfamiliar content. Stretch assignments can also provide the employee with a break from his or her norm, opening new opportunities and areas of interest. These assignments can be used by management to test an employee who may be ready for promotion or advancement. An example of a stretch assignment could be representing the company during an audit or organizing a meeting or company event.

9-BOX GRID

The 9-box grid is a tool for identifying leadership potential. The tool is facilitated by senior leaders and/or HR and assesses potential leaders of the organization. It is a visual tool presented as a square divided into nine boxes. An employee is assessed on their potential and their past performance. This assessment is best completed when feedback is obtained from multiple leaders. Once the feedback is completed individually, the group of raters meets to discuss the results. Once adjustments have been made, the employee's name is placed in one of the nine boxes. The vertical axis of the square represents the employee's assessed potential, while the horizontal axis represents the employee's assessed performance. Each box has a label, ranging from high performer/high potential to low performer/low potential. Once the employee's box is identified, development plans can be created accordingly.

	Low Performer High Potential	Moderate Performer High Potential	High Performer High Potential
Potential	Low Performer Moderate Potential	Moderate Performer Moderate Potential	High Performer Moderate Potential
	Low Performer Low Potential	Moderate Performer Low Potential	High Performer Low Potential

Performance

When facilitated appropriately, the 9-box grid can provide a company with valuable information and a guide for development actions. The results from the 9-box grid should identify future leaders, helping to determine where development dollars would be best spent. The 9-box grid can also indicate if someone is in the appropriate position. For example, if someone has high potential but low to medium performance, the employee may be best suited to change roles. The 9-box process can also encourage senior leaders to have difficult conversations. For example, if company leaders have never had candid conversations about potential leaders of the organization, the process may push senior leaders to collaborate. It also helps senior leaders identify talent gaps in the organization, which can lead to recruitment plan development. Or the senior leaders could identify a high-potential employee to develop so the talent gaps can be filled.

Learning and Development Programs

NEEDS ANALYSIS

There are several reasons that it is important for an organization to perform a **needs analysis** before designing a training program. First, it is imperative for an organization to accurately identify problems. Second, even if a particular problem is known prior to the analysis, it can be difficult to identify the cause of that problem. Third, and most importantly, it is impossible to design an effective training program without first identifying the specific knowledge, skills, and abilities required to correct a problem or achieve other goals. A needs analysis can be an essential part of the training development process because it helps to identify and detail problems so that possible solutions can be found.

There are a variety of steps that might be taken during a needs analysis, but most begin by collecting data related to the performance of each part of the organization. This information is usually gathered from surveys, interviews, observations, skill assessments, performance appraisals, and so on. Once this information is collected, problems are identified within specific areas of the organization and solutions are proposed. Advantages and disadvantages of each solution are then identified and the plan that seems to provide the greatest benefit for the lowest cost is chosen.

PERSON

A **person needs analysis** is a type of needs analysis that determines several key items, such as how well an employee performs a task compared to expectations. Not all individuals within the organization will require training, so performing a person analysis establishes which specific employees need training or development. Once individuals are identified for training, the type of training can be selected.

ORGANIZATION

An **organization needs analysis** is conducted to ensure that training is aligned with the overall business strategy as well as making sure that there are adequate resources and support available for training.

TRAINING

A **training needs analysis** is completed to identify any gaps that may exist in the actual knowledge, skills, and abilities in a role versus the desired levels. The difference between the actual competency and the standard determines the training that may be required.

COST/BENEFIT ANALYSIS

Although training and development programs should be viewed as extremely valuable capital investments in themselves, they also provide measurable returns. Simple calculations can be used to measure the costs and benefits of training. **Costs** should include both direct costs (e.g., materials, facilities, etc.) and indirect costs (e.g., lost production time). The overall costs of training and development programs might contain staff hours, program materials, hardware or software, videos, and production losses such as training time and respective salaries. **Benefits** of training should be evaluated according to how well the training will increase productivity, advance product quality, reduce errors, improve safety, or reduce operating costs. One calculation for measuring training is the **cost per trainee**, in which the total cost of training is divided by the number of trainees. Regardless of this cost, the long-term benefits of training should outweigh the total costs, and this can be determined through a **cost/benefit analysis**. There are creative adjustments that can be used to reduce training costs. The size of training classes can be increased, and materials can be reused, as long as copyrights are not violated. Expenses can be further eliminated by making training available online or using videoconferencing.

SURVEYS

Learning and development surveys can help organizations determine which growth opportunities are desired by employees and which training method is preferred. They can also help organizations analyze how successful training and development programs are, and how satisfied employees are with current training and development options. These surveys can also help identify if employees feel that there is access to learning opportunities, if management supports learning and development, if there is adequate time for training, and if the organization offers learning and development that will help the employee grow in his or her role as well as in his or her field.

Surveys can also gauge retention and recall of training and presentations, allowing the organization to determine the efficacy of a particular training. Surveys can be offered at various time intervals. For example, learning and development satisfaction questions can be included with an annual employee survey. Shorter **pulse surveys** targeted at determining training effectiveness can be offered soon after the training ends. Other surveys can be sent out when the organization is reviewing the learning and development budget or the budget of the organization overall.

OBSERVATIONS

Managers and leaders can track employee development over time using **observations**. This allows the manager or leader to identify areas where improvement may be needed. Observations may also be used to determine the efficacy of a particular training by watching whether employees display specific behaviors. The individual performing the observation identifies different scenarios that best demonstrate the skill or knowledge that either requires development or has recently been the subject of training. For example, if there was a training just conducted on handling customer complaints cordially and effectively, the observer could listen in to an employee addressing a customer complaint and determine where changes in the training program may be needed. Similarly, if data shows a concerning trend with how customer complaints are handled, individuals taking customer complaints can be observed, and methods or responses can be viewed and noted to highlight areas for improvement. One of the most important aspects of observation is the feedback that follows the observation period. When the observation is complete, the leader should provide feedback that will both empower the employee and address areas where he or she may be struggling or lagging.

INTERVIEWS

One use for a **learning and development interview** is to collect more-detailed information and feedback on the current learning and development opportunities within the organization. Leaders can meet with employees one-on-one to ask specific questions to solicit feedback on the learning and development that is currently offered, has been completed, or the employee would like to see. This allows the organization to determine if the current learning and development program and initiatives truly meet the needs of the organization and the employees.

An interview is more detailed and personal than a survey, and the in-depth feedback can assist in making any changes or adjustments to the programs. Learning and development interviews can also be used to create more-personalized development plans for each employee. This interview should be conducted by the employee's direct supervisor. The supervisor will discuss career goals, professional goals, motivation, strengths, areas of improvement, and positions of interest. This will allow for a more-tailored development plan, establishing a more-meaningful relationship between the employee and supervisor and a stronger level of commitment from the employee to the organization.

LEARNING AND DEVELOPMENT APPROACHES AND TECHNIQUES

There are three main types of learning, each with different suitable training methods. If teaching **motor responses**, such as physical acts that involve muscle groups, a training method that involves exploration, demonstration, activity practice, and corrective guidance works best. If teaching **rote learning**, such as memorization, a training method that involves familiarity, patterns or associations, repetition, and timely feedback works best. If teaching **idea learning**, such as operant conditioning or learning complex ideas, a training method that involves sequential concepts, with practice or exhibition, progressive mastery, and reinforcement at each step works best.

ADDIE Model of Training

The **ADDIE** model of training reflects the three primary phases of learning— assessment, training and development, and evaluation—in detail:

A	**Analysis.** Gather data and identify problems, needs, or discrepancies between current capacities and desired performance.
D	**Design.** Determine learning objectives and goals, decide course content or exercises, and plan delivery methods.
D	**Development.** Create training materials or purchase and modify existing training materials to meet objectives.
I	**Implementation.** Deliver the training program tools to the target audience and observe changes.
E	**Evaluation.** Compare training program results of knowledge and behavior to the course objectives.

Employee Development Methods

Methods of employee development include the following:

- **Literacy training**: Basic education programs offered by companies, such as English-as-a-second-language training, how to interpret engineering designs, or how to make basic computations.
- **Competency training**: Teaching skills, abilities, and behaviors essential for executing responsibilities effectively and for successful performance.
- **Mentoring**: When a more experienced individual teaches valuable job skills and provides encouragement or emotional support.
- **Attitude change**: Group communications through lectures, video presentations, or similar methods to accomplish increased customer service, diversity training, ethical behavior, or harassment training.

Training Formats

Choosing the appropriate training methods for an organization should start with a needs assessment. A needs assessment is a systematic assessment of the roles, individuals, and business to determine the characteristics and needs of the intended audience.

Technology has transformed training and development and provides new ways for organizations to help employees learn. Traditionally, in-house training programs were in high demand: content was created by internal teams with or without the help of external partners. Today, there are a number of development strategies that can be used to train, re-skill, and upskill existing teams. A few of these methods include the following.

Traditional Classroom Training

A traditional classroom training is conducted in a teaching space and allows for face-to-face instruction. This mode of training can take place internally at an employer's work site, externally at a training facility, or possibly at an industry conference. Classroom training offers many options to deploy multiple learning modalities. To begin, a classroom can be conducive to teaching new information to a small or large number of students. A classroom presentation can be made lecture-style, with or without visual aids; or it can include demonstrations of material, allowing for multiple formats to teach information. If the group is small enough, classroom training can be an environment for interactive discussion, whereby the instructor gauges students understanding and immediately changes course if needed. Depending on the training, classroom training can permit employees to interact with one another, thereby enhancing the learning experience. Lastly, a classroom environment provides a human element that is challenging to capture in other training delivery formats.

ON-THE-JOB TRAINING (OJT)

On-the-job training (OJT) is usually provided by managers or supervisors utilizing real-time demonstration of the material or equipment the employee will be using to complete job tasks. This hands-on approach is sometimes more effective than lecturing or a theoretical approach. Seeing and being allowed to perform the desired function is a simple and cost-effective method for learning. This method also allows for immediate feedback and helps to ensure the employee is immediately productive.

However, there can be disadvantages to OJT. First, the person teaching may not be a certified trainer, but rather someone who knows how the work needs to be accomplished. Teaching requires clear communication and patience, and not everyone possesses necessary teaching skills. Second, another reason for OJT is to get the new employee up to speed quickly, but in doing so, there could be safety issues and the potential for accidents. This is especially true of high-risk jobs. Lastly, OJT could be distracting to coworkers, creating work disturbances and causing lack of concentration, especially in a space-constrained environment.

E-LEARNING OR VIRTUAL LEARNING

E-learning, also known as virtual learning, is a training delivery format that permits students to learn via a form that utilizes technology. E-learning can take a number of different formats, including web-based, mobile computer applications, and virtual classrooms. E-learning can be synchronous, in which the instructor and students are interacting in real time. Alternatively, e-learning can be asynchronous, enabling students to access the same training and related materials on demand at different days and times.

There are many benefits to using e-learning, such as delivering a large volume of information quickly, assisting globalization efforts through virtual learning, scheduling flexibility, and cost effectiveness. However, there are considerations that should be examined, including technology constraints and user access, concerns about intellectual property, lack of face-to-face interaction possibly causing uneasiness with students, and the potentially significant costs involved in training development.

BLENDED LEARNING OR HYBRID FORMAT

A blended learning or hybrid format combines multiple methods of delivering training material. Research suggests that a mix of learning strategies and formats might be more effective than one single method. Typically, blended or hybrid learning involves face-to-face, traditional classroom instruction combined with an online, technological component that might also give the student control over their pace of learning. The following are two examples of blended or hybrid learning:

- A course with synchronous learning in a virtual setting using video, as well as independent, web-based, self-paced learning modules that complement classroom instruction.
- A training program that involves a web-based book with case studies, as well as traditional face-to-face classroom instruction coupled with a mobile application for simulation exercises.

Blended learning or hybrid instruction has many advantages: it works well with different student learning styles, enables both independent and collective learning, supports learning in a global workforce, and provides scheduling flexibility. On the other hand, there are some concerns that must be addressed; for example, more advanced planning is necessary, students need to be organized in how they will attend, students potentially need more motivation with this format, there may be feelings of not being connected and needing more encouragement, and development costs can be higher. This integrated, blended learning environment is constantly evolving as technology affords the organization more options.

DELIVERY TECHNIQUES

How work gets done continues to change thanks to macro trends toward globalization, digitization, and changes brought on by the COVID-19 pandemic. With continued focus on collaboration and working across team and cultural boundaries, HR professionals should be well versed in multiple approaches to increase training effectiveness. Some popular styles include:

- **Role play**: This allows the learner to act and speak like the character they are trying to portray. Benefits include practice, which builds experience, and more chances for real-time feedback, which can be applied to enhance performance.
- **Facilitation**: This allows learners to be introduced to the content by a facilitator who guides learners through the content, asks questions, and steers the overall discussion. This style promotes real-time feedback.
- **Case studies**: This involves reviewing a real-life historical situation to learn from others' lived experiences. This can occur in person, online, or in a blended learning situation. This approach gives learners perspective and insights into unique challenges and allows for low-stakes learning opportunities.
- **Games and simulations**: These bring the strategies, rules, and social experiences of game play into a learning setting. This style incorporates digital and gamification tools into learning content and delivers training in a way that increases engagement with learners.

IN-HOUSE VS. EXTERNAL TRAINING SERVICES

A critical question that comes up when assessing the learning needs of an organization is whether the training should be developed and delivered in-house or through a third party. Deciding whether all elements or specific components of the instructional design will be outsourced will help to clarify the value proposition of the training program. Companies can choose to partner with external vendors on specific elements ranging from content creation to design, illustration, voice-over, translation, and accessibility services.

Some important considerations when deciding whether to insource or outsource learning content include:

- Type of training (e.g., legally required, role-specific, business-specific)
- Length and duration of training (how often learners will need to retest)
- Location of training audience (whether multiple languages are needed)
- Data privacy and accessibility (single sign-on or externally hosted site)
- Trademark and copyright considerations
- Feedback mechanisms needed to get input on the end users' experience

Techniques to Assess Training Program Effectiveness
Kirkpatrick's Four-Level Learning Evaluation Model

It's important to analyze the effectiveness of training programs so you don't waste resources. Donald Kirkpatrick introduced a **four-level training evaluation model** for planning, evaluating, and preserving. The four levels of the evaluation model are:

- **Reaction**: Measures how people react to the training, often a survey upon completion that asks for feedback or satisfaction levels on the subject, the material, the instructor, and so on
- **Learning**: Measures what objectives people have learned from the training program (could be in the form of a questionnaire, assessment, etc.)
- **Behavior**: Measures how far the performance or behavior of people that received the training has changed and observes how they apply what has been learned to their environment
- **Results**: Analyzes noticeable effects of training, such as changes in production, efficiency, and quality

Brinkerhoff's Stages of Evaluation

Robert Brinkerhoff's Six Stages of Evaluation model is a six-step process that an organization can use to ensure that a program is effective.

1. **Goal setting**: Identify the specific problem that the program is going to address, and set the specific goals that the organization hopes to achieve as a result of the program.
2. **Program design**: Design the program in order to achieve the goals set in the first stage of the process.
3. **Implementation**: Implement the program in order to determine whether the program actually accomplishes the goals the organization set out to achieve.
4. **Immediate outcomes**: Test each employee in order to determine whether or not the program succeeded in teaching the information that the program was designed to teach.
5. **Intermediate outcomes**: Monitor each employee's behavior in order to make sure that each individual is actually applying the information that the program taught.
6. **Impacts and worth**: Measure the value of the program based on the organization's progress toward the goals that the program set out to achieve versus the cost of implementing the program.

Learning and Development Technologies
Learning Management Systems

A **learning management system (LMS)** is a software system that handles the creation, management, distribution, and analytics of educational content. An LMS can be cloud-based and hosted by a vendor, or it can exist on the company server. With an LMS, administrators can upload content, deliver lessons and training, send out notifications and announcements, and share data with specific parties. There are many analytic features available to administrators, who can track how many individuals have completed training, which training leads to the best results, what offerings are popular, and how active employees are on the system. An LMS is used throughout multiple aspects of the employee life cycle, including onboarding, training, professional development, and compliance training. Specific training can be automated for certain times of the year to help establish a training calendar. An LMS allows for on-demand training options and easy access, and helps the organization create a culture of learning.

Artificial Intelligence

As **artificial intelligence (AI)** becomes more readily available and evolved, it will have a tremendous impact on learning and development. Already, organizations can see how AI has impacted the learning and development landscape by helping to personalize learning pathways. AI can help training programs adapt to each employee. The learning process can be adjusted to meet the needs of the employee. AI can automate learning platforms, so all employee content is stored, delivered, and tracked. AI can also make training more accessible, as it is available around the clock without constraints. AI is also more cost-effective than physical in-person trainers.

Virtual Reality

Another technology experiencing rapid expansion and improvement is **virtual reality (VR)**. VR can offer many benefits to learning and development offerings. It allows the learner to become totally immersed in the training, removed from external distractions and stimuli and focused purely on the content, which improves retention. VR also heavily relies on simulation, or experiential learning through doing, which is one of the most effective ways to present material for retention and comprehension. VR learning can also utilize gamification, which makes it more fun and interesting, motivating the learner to complete the module. Immediate feedback and analysis are available on VR training, which helps to track its efficacy. VR training is also on-demand and does not come with the expense of hosting on or off-site training.

Chatbots

An effective learning and development tool that can help personalize a user's learning experience, a **chatbot** can help walk the user through the learning process and help make the learning experience feel more one-on-one by creating a back-and-forth dialogue. This tool can be passive, simply waiting in the background until the user needs assistance. Alternatively, the tool can be programmed to prompt targeted topics at designated times, keeping the process moving. Chatbots are available around the clock and do not lose patience with the learner. Additionally, when a chatbot is faced with a question it cannot answer, it can try to redirect or refer the learner to other available resources. Chatbots help encourage engagement throughout the learning process by prompting the user on what to do and offering relevant feedback. Chatbots are a way to quickly access and deliver content and information at a cost that is greatly reduced compared to a live trainer.

Total Rewards

The concept known as **total rewards** refers to all of the compensation and benefits received for performing tasks related to each position. Total rewards packages include things that employees typically think of when considering a job, like compensation, benefits, time off (PTO and holidays), and bonuses. Beyond those basics, the package also includes things not always thought of, including flexibility, free parking, gym memberships, and employee discount programs. In times of low unemployment and smaller talent pools, providing total rewards summaries during the recruitment process is essential.

It is important to have an effective total rewards program for two main reasons. First, it encourages employees to join and then stay with the organization. Second, there are legal concerns associated with the minimum amount of compensation an individual can receive for a certain amount of work, making it essential to consider these concerns to avoid unnecessary fines or litigation. When taking total rewards into account, the whole of an employee's compensation can be seen, not just monetary compensation.

> **Review Video: Total Rewards and Compensation**
> Visit mometrix.com/academy and enter code: 502662

Total Rewards Programs

PAY STRUCTURES AND PROGRAMS
IMPORTANCE OF PAY STRUCTURES

Pay structure is the way an organization groups jobs and defines the compensation associated with a collection of jobs. Pay structure is critical because every organization needs qualified and talented individuals to build and run a business. One of the best ways to obtain and retain good talent is through a fair and attractive pay structure. Additionally, as in most areas of HR, pay structure needs to demonstrate that an organization has fair and consistent policies surrounding all aspects of pay. This structure will help an organization meet necessary compliance requirements, as well as clearly demonstrate fair practices related to pay opportunities for all employees.

One of the most important considerations in pay structure is the balance between internal and external pay equity. Internal pay equity is how an employee's pay compares to the pay of others in similar positions within the organization. External pay equity is the comparison of pay to similar jobs outside the organization. A balance indicates the pay is fair, which will help attract new employees and also help retain existing employees in the organization.

CREATING A PAY STRUCTURE

Methods of creating a pay structure can vary greatly, but most organizations begin the process by conducting a job evaluation for each position. A **job evaluation** is the process whereby the value of a job to the organization is determined—it is how a job's worth is established. Once all positions are evaluated and assigned a value, they are categorized based on their importance to the organization. The organization will usually gather information from salary surveys to determine the market median for each category and the wages an individual would receive at the midpoint of a similar pay category for another organization. Finally, using all of this information as a guide, a **pay range** is developed for each category.

Pay ranges can be a challenge because this is a very fluid process. Occasionally, an employee is paid above the range maximum or below the range minimum. When an employee is paid above a range maximum, it is called a **"red-circle rate"** and could mean that an employer's pay range is below the market value and should be researched to remain competitive. If the pay rate is below the range minimum, it is called a **"green-circle rate"** and should also be re-examined.

Pay Grades and Banding

A **pay grade** refers to a compensation job grouping, by level, with similar responsibilities, authority, and experience. This grouping means that within an organization, similar jobs have approximately the same relative value and are therefore paid at similar rates within a pay range. Some compensation structures break out pay grades or ranges into separate **bands** (or levels) so the company can maintain pay equity and stay within budget. This is done by conducting a job analysis and grouping titles into families. For example, those that fall into the first pay grade may have a pay band of $20,000 to $35,000, the second pay grade may have a band of $30,000 to $50,000, and the third pay grade may have a band of $50,000 to $100,000. Jobs may also be evaluated and ranked based upon overall responsibilities and worth to the organization.

Although pay bands are broken out based upon job duty and skill level, it is important to recognize whether the company tends to lead, lag, or match current market rates. Matching or leading the market is best for recruitment and retention. The sizes of pay bands tend to grow as you move up the managerial ladder, with executives having the largest pay levels.

Traditional Salary Structure

A **traditional salary structure** could have multiple pay ranges that correlate to differences in a position. The way it typically works is that a new employee will be offered a salary on the lower end of the pay range, and then hopefully advance to a higher pay range depending on their performance evaluation or other means of evaluating the employee. The benefit of an organization using a traditional salary structure is that it provides the organization and its employees an easy-to-understand "ladder" or hierarchical system for an employee to advance or be promoted from one pay grade to another. Typically, an organization will first set the minimum and maximum salary range for each grouping. Then, based on the number of groupings, the organization will figure out the logical number of pay grades in their salary structure.

Broadband Salary Structure

A **broadband salary structure** takes multiple pay grades that only have a modest difference between the minimum and maximum pay scale and combines them into a single band with a much broader difference in the spread. In effect, the organization is collapsing multiple ranges in order to obtain a larger spread between the minimum and maximum point for a salary range. An organization might use a broadband salary structure if they wish to remove hierarchical levels and thereby limit the levels of management, a process sometimes referred to as "flattening" an organization. For example, an organization may have had 10 levels of management, with a narrow salary range in each level. They then decide to adopt a broadband salary structure and reduce the levels from 10 to 5, thereby also allowing the organization to increase the difference in the salary range. Existing employees are then moved to the most appropriate level within the five options.

Companies may also choose a broadband salary structure in a large organization if managing too many pay grades becomes complex and difficult to equitably administer.

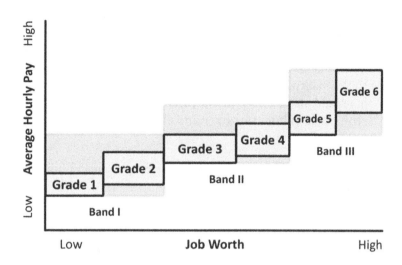

MARKET-BASED PAY STRUCTURES

A **market-based pay structure** can be thought of as a combination of traditional and broadband structures, except market-based pay is a pay scale based on what similar employers in similar geographic locations pay employees. In other words, appropriate pay is determined by an employer evaluating data from various sources in the job market that summarize pay for similar jobs. Sources include the US Bureau of Labor Statistics and some private companies that offer salary surveys for a fee. Like traditional and broadband, the market-based pay structure also has a pay range for specific jobs. However, what usually happens is that the pay range, minimum to maximum, is too slim to be competitive with similar jobs in the external market, while the salary range is usually too high, like the broadband structure. A large majority of businesses utilize a market-based pay structure in their organization.

VARIABLE PAY

Variable pay is employee pay that changes based on predetermined parameters or goals set by an employer. Variable pay is most often used as a monetary incentive to achieve business objectives and reward employees, and is usually a supplement to base salary or wages. An organization that wants to use variable pay to incentivize behavior or performance can accomplish this goal based on criteria such as sales revenue, customer satisfaction scores, percentage increase in clients, and pieces produced. Variable pay is frequently either a dollar amount or percentage based on target objectives and is included in an employee's overall compensation plan. The following are some examples of how variable pay might work:

- An electrician paid hourly could be paid $30 extra for every referral made.
- An account executive could be paid a salary and, for every quarter that his or her team exceeds their sales objective by 10 percent, could receive an additional $5,000.
- An assembly line worker who exceeds his or her pieces built per hour by 10 percent or more (with no defects) could receive an extra $100 per day.

PAY COMPRESSION

Pay compression occurs when a senior employee has a salary that is only slightly more, or in some cases less, than a new hire in the same position. This is a situation in which beginning salaries for new hires are too close to the salaries for existing employees in the same job. In some cases, it is not exactly the same job—this could also occur if a new hire makes more money than their manager. Pay compression can be the cause of high turnover and employee disengagement. Causes of pay compression may include the following:

- An organization increases wages to attract new hires and doesn't adjust wages for existing employees according to market changes.
- Internal compensation is not aligned with real-world market salary data.
- There are issues with existing organizational pay grades, levels, and bands.

The answer to pay compression is easy, but its implementation and fallout are challenging. The answer is to adjust the inequities and pay employees fair market-value wages. This is a costly proposition for most organizations, but if they do not adjust wages accordingly, they risk losing good workers and facing the challenges and costs that come with replacing them.

JOB EVALUATION/CLASSIFICATION

Job evaluation is the process a company uses to identify the relative worth (in terms of monetary value) of each position.

Common methods used to evaluate and classify jobs include:

- **Ranking method**—Ranking begins by listing all an organization's jobs in order, from the highest value or difficulty to the lowest value or difficulty. Those that have the highest value or difficulty receive the highest pay, with compensation adjusted accordingly as the level of value or difficulty decreases.
- **Classification method**—Rather than starting with individual jobs, classification involves establishing multiple pay grades and writing a broad description for each grade. Next, each job description is compared to the description of each grade and assigned to the closest match.
- **Point method**—The point method involves identifying various compensable factors that will be evaluated to determine how much individual jobs should pay. Points are assigned for each compensable factor and compared to benchmark positions within the company.
- **Factor comparison method**—Factor comparison involves evaluating each job against a benchmark position in relation to a set group of five predetermined factors, which are usually defined as skill level, responsibility, mental requirements, physical requirements, and working conditions.

Ranking and classification are non-quantitative classification methods, while the point method and factor comparison method are quantitative.

PAY ADJUSTMENTS

Pay adjustments are not generally required by law, except when necessary to match minimum wage increases. However, pay adjustments are an important part of a company's compensation strategy for positions at all levels.

Employees expect to be rewarded with pay increases as time goes by as a reward for their hard work, loyalty, and contributions. Without pay increases, employees may feel unappreciated—which can negatively impact job performance, engagement, and retention. A company also needs to consider the fact that the cost of living changes over time, a factor that can reduce the overall value of employee compensation.

It is common for companies to consider pay adjustments on an annual basis, though some employers do so more or less frequently.

- For salaried employees, pay adjustments are ordinarily awarded as a percentage of current compensation, though a company can opt to award a specific dollar amount.
- For hourly workers, an employer may opt to adjust pay as a flat per-hour increase or as a percentage of the current hourly rate.

DIFFERENTIAL PAY

Differential pay is when an organization pays an employee an extra wage for working undesirable shifts or hours. This could mean working through the night or maybe on the weekend or a holiday. Organizations are not legally obligated to offer differential pay; rather, they offer it to incentivize people to work those shifts. However, if a worker works over 40 hours in a week, regardless of shift, then they are entitled to overtime pay according to the Fair Labor Standards Act (FLSA). Most employers offer differential pay as a percentage. For example, suppose XYZ Supermarket offers 20% differential for the overnight shift, and the normal day rate of pay is $15 an hour. Multiplying 20% by the normal rate of pay ($15 \times 0.20 = 3$) indicates that the differential would be an additional $3 per hour, meaning the worker doing the overnight shift would earn $18 an hour.

COST-OF-LIVING ADJUSTMENT (COLA)

A **cost-of-living adjustment** (COLA) is designed to counteract and stabilize inflation by declaring a percentage increase in Social Security and supplemental income. Usually, a COLA is equal to the percentage rise in the consumer price index for urban wage earners and clerical workers (CPI-W) for a predefined period of time, a calculation that frequently aligns with the calculation for inflation. For example, if a person received $20,000 in Social Security and the COLA was evaluated at 3.1%, then their benefits would be $20,620 for the year. COLA began in 1975 in response to high inflation and is evaluated every year. The Social Security Administration uses COLAs to protect compensation-based benefits from inflation.

BONUS PAY

Bonus pay is similar to variable pay in that an employee is paid a sum of money based on criteria set by the organization, but not necessarily linked to a clear objective. For example, at the end of the year, an organization might pay employees a bonus, perhaps a percentage of pay or just a lump sum not based on wages. This type of bonus could be offered because the business or the individual achieved certain goals, or the bonus could be made at a manager's discretion to reward the employee(s). Discretion-based bonuses could be given at any interval of time—perhaps by a manager when an employee successfully handled the closing of a deal. Additionally, a bonus could be shared among an entire department, region, team, etc., for a goal achieved or any other valued display of work.

There is only a subtle difference between bonus pay and variable pay. Bonuses may be linked to an achievement of predetermined metrics or factors, such as a holiday bonus or manager discretion bonus. Generally, bonuses reward past activities or achievements, whereas variable pay encourages future performance.

MERIT PAY

Merit pay is money awarded to an employee, via a base pay increase, based on predetermined and performance-related goals. The FLSA does not require or manage merit pay; the management and distribution of merit pay is between the employer and the employee. The overarching goal of merit pay is to motivate employees to meet and hopefully exceed individual predetermined goals. A merit pay program can drive individuals to be more productive and hence an organization more successful. The difference between merit pay and other incentive pay programs (variable, commission, etc.) is that it is incorporated into an employee's base salary rather than being a one-time occurrence. Merit increases can vary based on the organization and circumstances, but typically are under 5 percent of base salary.

There are many advantages to merit pay, such as monetarily rewarding high performers, assisting with the retention of top talent, and differentiating individual contributions versus team contributions to company goals. On the other hand, there are some issues to be aware of when administering a merit pay program, including making sure there are predefined, clear, measurable performance objectives, as well as managing merit awards in a fair, consistent manner.

PAYROLL PROCESSES

Payroll processing is a system that an employer utilizes to manage the payment of wages to its employees. Payroll processing is more than just issuing a paycheck. There are other components that need to be addressed, such as legal compliance with all federal, state, and local laws and regulations, including reporting requirements; the time period for record retention of information; and all aspects of control and security. Generally, the major steps involved in payroll processing include gathering the time worked per employee for a designated time period, calculating and applying cost of benefits and deductions, distributing paychecks (direct deposit or paper check), and following retention procedures. The employer must then file and remit payroll taxes. An organization can face expensive penalties if payroll taxes are not accurate and on time. Most organizations use payroll software or outsource to a third-party payroll processing service.

INFORMATION NEEDED TO PROCESS A PAYROLL

There are many documents and information needed to process a payroll. They include but are not limited to the following:

- Completed **W-4** form (for employees)—This form is completed by an employee before or on their first day of work. It documents employee withholding information needed so that the employer can deduct the correct amount of federal income tax from their wages.
- Completed **I-9** form—This form is for employment eligibility verification, and must be completed by an employee's first day of work. It requires showing the employer a combination of identification documents that prove they can legally work in the US.
- **Job application**—This contains consistent, detailed information about an employee such as name, address, education, and dates of employment, which are used to enter information into a payroll system.
- **Bank account information**—This is usually used by an employer to directly deposit an employee's pay into their bank account(s).

- **Medical insurance** form—This form details the amount to be deducted from an employee's pay and their permission for the deduction (usually requires a signature).
- **Retirement plan** form—This form details the amount being deducted for various retirement plan options. As with medical insurance, an employee signature is required for an employer to deduct from an employee's pay.

Payroll Cycle

A **payroll cycle** or schedule refers to the frequency that an employer issues pay to an employee. The most common cycle is biweekly, or every other week, for a total of 26 paychecks per year. However, an organization could also offer a weekly cycle, meaning 52 paychecks a year; or possibly a monthly cycle, with 12 paychecks a year; etc. An organization can choose their payroll schedule as long as it is in compliance with all federal, state, and local laws and regulations. Many states require employers to pay their employees biweekly, others have more specific requirements, and some have no specified schedules. However, an organization must also consider what the employees would prefer. Most employees prefer to get paid more frequently as compared to less frequently, especially those employees earning low wages. Employers must also weigh the cost of processing payroll more frequently, because it will cost more. An organization must decide and communicate a consistent payroll schedule.

Payroll Policy

A payroll policy is a set of guidelines and protocols established to ensure that payroll is accurate, processed on time, and conducted with strict adherence to all payroll laws and regulations.

- To comply with the Fair Labor Standards Act (FLSA), a **standard work week** needs to be defined and usually constitutes seven consecutive 24-hour periods. A work week doesn't have to start on Monday, but can begin on any day of the week.
- There should be a system in place, electronic or paper, to **accurately record employee hours** worked, with an approval process to verify the information is correct. State laws and regulations may require employers to give breaks from work for rest, meals, etc., after a given number of hours worked. These breaks also need to be reflected in total hours worked.
- **Overtime hours** must also be outlined, including who is eligible and how much they will be paid for hours worked over 40 in one work week. Overtime is usually paid at a rate of one and one-half times the regular pay rate per hour. However, this can vary from state to state—usually in favor of the employee receiving more wages.
- **How often employees are paid** should be detailed—whether biweekly, weekly, monthly, etc.—and what days they will receive their pay.
- A **payroll policy** should also explain deductions: mandatory deductions, such as Social Security and other taxes, and voluntary deductions, like health insurance and retirement plans. In addition, it should give further explanation of pre- and post-tax information. All the different wage structures should be explained, such as hourly pay, salary, bonuses, commission, and stock options.
- Finally, all time periods for **payroll recordkeeping** should be documented, as well as applicable security measures.

Incentive Programs

In addition to base pay, a company may include incentives in its compensation strategy. Incentives should be strategically aligned with the company's goals and objectives, while also providing a way for employees to increase their earnings.

Some incentive programs are specific to certain types of jobs, while others may be open to all types of employees. Examples of commonly used approaches to incentive compensation include:

- **Sales commission**—Sales professionals often earn a percentage of each sale they make as part of their compensation package.
- **Customer referral**—To encourage non-sales employees to refer customers, a company may incentivize other team members by paying a finder's fee for new customers they refer.
- **Employee referral**—To boost its applicant pool, an employer may incentivize current employees by paying a bonus when an applicant they refer joins the company.
- **Signing bonus**—For hard-to-fill jobs, an employer may induce applicants to join their company by offering a signing bonus.
- **Skill-based pay**—A company seeking to have highly trained employees who are prepared for multiple roles in the company may incentivize employees to master new skills.
- **Shift differentials**—Companies with multiple shifts may incentivize employees to accept hard-to-staff shifts with a higher rate of pay for those time slots.
- **Profit sharing**—Some organizations have structured incentive programs that provide profit sharing bonuses on a quarterly or annual basis.
- **Gain sharing**—A company looking for ways to decrease expenses may incentivize employees to increase efficiency by sharing cost savings with them.
- **Year-end bonus**—Some companies offer a year-end bonus to employees as a way of saying thank you for their hard work and service throughout the year.

Non-Monetary Rewards

COMPANY-WIDE INCENTIVE PLANS

Profit-sharing and gainsharing programs reward employees based on the performance of the entire organization. In **profit-sharing plans**, employees receive a share of the company's profits in addition to their regular pay. These may be cash plans, in which payments are made after the close of a specified period, such as a quarter or year, or tax-advantageous deferred plans, in which funds are invested. If deferred, funds are a tax-deductible expense for the company for the year in which they are contributed, and employees are not taxed until their funds are received. In **gainsharing plans**, employees receive bonuses based on improved productivity as opposed to profits. Gainsharing plans often fall into three categories: Scanlon Plans, Rucker Plans, or Improshare Plans. **Scanlon plans** are most popular in union environments, and combine gainsharing with an employee recommendation system. These plans base payouts on a standard ratio of labor costs as a percentage of revenue. **Rucker plans** are similar, but the employee gains are based on production. These plans base payouts on the ratio of labor costs to the result of production minus the cost of materials. **Improshare Plans**, or improved productivity through sharing, provide bonuses to employees based on the amount of time saved compared to a baseline.

ESOPs

An **employee stock ownership plan (ESOP)** is created by establishing a trust into which the business makes tax-deductible contributions of cash or stock. Employees are then granted the ability to purchase this stock or allocate funds into individual employee accounts. The stock is held in an **employee stock ownership trust (ESOT)**, and the business can make regular contributions, typically up to 25 percent of its annual payroll. ESOPs became popular because it is believed that employees who have an ownership interest in the business will work more diligently and have a vested interest in the company's efficiency and profitability. Although this logic is debatable, many studies have shown that ESOPs actually do motivate employees and support business growth.

TUITION ASSISTANCE

Organizations may offer employer-sponsored **tuition assistance**, or **tuition reimbursement**, to employees. Tuition assistance helps employees pursue education, training, and skill development. There are several different forms of tuition assistance. Some companies will cover classes regardless of their content. Other companies will only cover courses that directly relate to the employee's current or next role in the organization. Most commonly, the employee pays for tuition, books, and lab fees (if applicable) up front, and the employer will reimburse the employee after receiving proof of a passing grade, typically a "C" or higher. In many cases, there is a cap on the amount that the employer will reimburse per year. Additionally, many organizations require employees to sign an agreement to return the reimbursement if the individual leaves employment before a certain amount of time passes.

RECOGNITION PROGRAMS

Recognition programs are an important part of the employee experience that enhance employee engagement and help positively shape company culture. Recognition should be tailored to the organization and its employees—there is not a one-size-fits-all plan. However, the goal of most recognition programs is to help make employees feel valued or appreciated, and they frequently serve as an incentive to strive toward. Recognition programs can reward any number of desirable attributes or events, such as going above and beyond, team effort, wellness objectives, innovation, quality improvements, and career celebrations. Recognition rewards can vary, but may include the following:

- A heartfelt, verbal (or written) thank-you
- A meal celebration
- A point-based system for employees to choose a reward
- Treats or candy
- Gift cards
- Unique experiences such as concerts, sporting events, or shows

A recognition program provides an employer with the ability to create a workplace of choice where employees thrive. Recruitment and employee retention is positively influenced by an effective recognition program. Successful recognition has the following characteristics: recognition is genuine, all employees have an opportunity to give and receive recognition, the reward is given in a timely manner, it is specific, it is connected to the company's purpose, and it is presented in a public forum. There are also software programs and vendors that can help an organization design and administer recognition programs.

Benefits

Employee benefits are an important aspect of a company's compensation program. They add financial value to the wages and any incentives a company offers, and they meet important health and wellness needs for employees and their families.

Benefits packages usually include access to group health coverage, as well as other kinds of group benefits like dental insurance, vision plans, term life insurance, and more. Without access to group health coverage or other types of group benefits, employees who want coverage would have to purchase individual plans on the open market. Individual plans tend to be much more expensive than group plans.

In some cases, offering benefits also helps employers comply with regulatory requirements. For example, companies with 50 or more employees are subject to financial penalties if they don't offer health insurance that meets the requirements of the Patient Protection and Affordable Care Act (PPACA).

Benefit Programs
Non-Discretionary vs. Discretionary Benefits

Benefits fit under two basic categories: non-discretionary and discretionary. **Non-discretionary** benefits are benefits that an employer must offer and are mandated under various legal statutes. These benefits can include, but are not limited to, unemployment insurance, workers' compensation, unpaid family medical leave, and COBRA.

Discretionary benefits are those benefits that an employer chooses to offer—and thus are not mandated by legal regulations—in order to attract and retain talent. Generally, discretionary benefits comprise three primary areas:

- **Health benefits**—This includes everything under the healthcare umbrella, including medical, dental, vision, prescription, employee assistance programs, disability insurance, and life insurance.
- **Deferred compensation**—This area includes any type of employer-offered retirement plan whereby the benefit is received at a later date than when work is performed.
- **Other** discretionary benefits—This includes perks that do not fit into health benefits or deferred compensation, such as paid time off for holidays, paid vacation time, flexible work schedule, tuition reimbursement, and childcare.

Flexible Benefit Programs

Flexible benefits are programs offered by an employer that enable an employee to select and create their own customized benefits based on their preferences. In recent years, employees have come to expect benefits that promote work-life balance and support families. To that end, an increasing number of employers offer telecommuting, flex time, and compressed work week options to help workers juggle all of life's different demands. In addition, many workplaces now offer benefits like paid parental leave and designated lactation rooms, making it easier on new parents. Additionally, some employers have started offering paid caregiver leave, which allows workers to care for parents and other relatives without worrying about their paychecks. Small and large businesses alike recognize that flexible benefits are necessary to remain competitive in the marketplace.

Pensions or Retirement Plans

Pensions and company retirement plans fund an individual's retirement by providing deferred payments for prior services. These accounts may be funded by the employer through a variety of means. Retirement benefits are accumulated by the total amount contributed plus interest and market earnings. These defined contribution benefit plans are the traditional company-provided plans, such as 401(k)s, 403(b)s, simplified employee pensions (SEPs), SIMPLEs, and IRAs. A defined contribution benefit plan requires separate accounts for each employee participant, and funds are most often contributed by both the employee and the employer.

Some employers will implement an auto-enroll policy in which new employees are automatically enrolled and minimum contributions to the plan are withheld from payroll. The contribution rates may even automatically increase on an annual basis. However, the Pension Protection Act of 2006 provides employees with a 90-day window to opt out of these plans and recover any funds contributed on their behalf.

Managed Care Healthcare Plans

Employers usually provide managed care healthcare plans, which are defined as care that ensures an individual receives appropriate and necessary treatment in the most cost-efficient manner possible. There are many forms of healthcare insurance plans, and the increasing cost of insurance has forced employers to absorb additional costs, pass more costs to employees, or find affordable alternatives.

- **Fee-for-service plans** allow employees to decide what services they need from any provider; fees are paid by both the employee and the employee's benefits plan through deductibles and coinsurance.
- **Preferred provider organization (PPO) plans** allow insurers to contract with providers of the employees' choosing, with lower fees and better coverage for providers within the organization; fees are paid by deductibles, coinsurance, and co-payments.
- **Health maintenance organization (HMO) plans** emphasize preventative care through fixed costs regardless of the number of visits, but primary care physicians (PCPs) must refer others, and no other providers are covered; fees are paid by deductibles, coinsurance, and co-payments.
- **Point of service (POS) plans** are similar to PPO plans, with certain elements (PCP referrals) of HMO plans; fees are paid by deductibles, coinsurance, and co-payments.
- **Exclusive provider organization (EPO)** is a plan whereby no payments or coverage will be made unless the individual uses a provider within the network of coverage.
- **Consumer-directed health plans** provide tax-favored accounts, such as a flexible spending account (FSA) or a health savings account (HSA), to pay for medical expenses and may allow employees to see any provider of their choosing. However, these plans carry high deductibles and may have low or no coinsurance after the deductible is reached.

Cafeteria Plans

Section 125 of the Internal Revenue Code defines a **cafeteria plan** as an employer plan providing participants the opportunity to receive certain benefits on a pretax basis. Funds allocated to these benefits are not included as wages for state or federal income tax purposes and are generally exempt from the Federal Insurance Contributions Act (FICA) and Federal Unemployment Tax Act (FUTA). Unused benefit credits can sometimes be reallocated by the employee to buy more benefits through pretax salary reductions, or the employee may end up losing the unused monies. An employer-sponsored cafeteria plan enables the employee to pick and choose benefits based on their preferences. (This idea of an employee choosing their benefits, like a customer choosing food at a cafeteria, gives cafeteria plans their name; they have nothing to do with actual cafeterias.)

Qualified benefits under these plans might include the following:

- **Medical healthcare coverage**—Plans may include some or all portions of physician services, office visits and exams, prescription drugs, hospital services, maternity services, mental health, physical therapy, and emergency services.
- **Dental coverage**—Plans may include some or all portions of routine exams, cleanings, x-rays, fluoride treatments, orthodontic services, fillings, crowns, and extractions.
- **Dependent care**—Plans may cover some or all portions of on-site childcare, allowances and flexible spending for childcare, daycare information, or flexible scheduling.

- **Short-term disability**—This provides partial income continuation to employees who are unable to work for a short period of time due to an accident or illness. "Short-term" is usually defined as three to six months.
- **Long-term disability**—This provides partial income continuation to employees who are unable to work for long periods of time due to an accident or illness. "Long-term" is usually defined as over six months.
- **Group-term life insurance and accidental death or dismemberment**—This provides financial assistance to an employee or their beneficiaries if the employee has an accident that results in loss of limbs, loss of eyesight, or death. The cost of group plans is frequently lower than individual plans, and payments are based upon the employee's age and annual salary.

Wellness Programs

Employer-sponsored **wellness programs** are implemented for three primary purposes: (1) to assist employees in improving their health in an effort to prevent serious health problems, (2) to help employers offset the expense of increasing healthcare costs, and (3) to improve employers' overall benefit offerings to remain competitive for attracting and retaining talent. Wellness programs indicate that employers are investing in their employees' health and well-being. Some companies create awareness about the available programs by encouraging employees to participate in a voluntary health assessment or screening as an impetus to encourage healthy lifestyle changes. Employers benefit from these changes through decreased absenteeism, decreased healthcare spending, higher employee morale, and improved productivity. Wellness programs can vary tremendously and may include personalized one-on-one health coaching, nutritional counseling, well-being workshops, healthy snacks at work, stress reduction programs, and fitness activities. Some employers will give monetary incentives to encourage participation in wellness programs.

Benefits Enrollment

Employers generally make their benefits packages available to full-time employees; some organizations also extend benefits eligibility to part-time employees.

- Some companies allow employees to enroll in benefits at the very beginning of their employment, while others require employees to work for a period of time, such as 30 or 60 days, before becoming eligible for benefits.
- Employees are able to change their benefits elections each year during annual enrollment, which is also referred to as open enrollment. Annual enrollment usually takes place in the fall, with new benefits elections taking effect on January 1.
- Employees who experience a qualifying event, such as losing eligibility for other coverage, getting married, or becoming a parent, may add or remove coverage or dependents outside of open enrollment.

In addition to providing access to group benefit plans, an employer may cover part or all of the cost of some benefits programs for employees; some companies offset the cost of benefits for dependents as well. Company contributions can add significantly to the value of a company's overall compensation, which is often referred to as total rewards.

Health Insurance

Health insurance is a very important aspect of a company's benefits package. Employers often pay a portion of employees' health insurance premiums. Some pay the full cost of employee coverage, as well as a portion of the cost for dependent coverage.

Employees don't all have the same needs when it comes to health insurance, so companies often offer multiple plans, with premiums at varying levels. This is to the advantage of the company and its employees alike.

- Employers with 50 or more employees should offer at least one health plan that meets the affordability requirement of the Patient Protection and Affordable Care Act (PPACA) in order to avoid costly penalties.
- Limiting health insurance options to only the plans that meet the affordability requirement of the PPACA would mean that employees wouldn't have access to health plans that offer higher levels of coverage.
- By offering varying levels of coverage at different price points, an employer is providing choices for employees. This helps employees find the right balance between services and cost, letting them get a level of coverage that meets their needs at a price they can pay. It also helps an employer compete for talent with other companies with robust health insurance offerings.

PREFERRED PROVIDER ORGANIZATIONS AND HIGH-DEDUCTIBLE HEALTH PLANS

It has become common practice for employers to offer both a **preferred provider organization (PPO)** plan and a **high-deductible health plan (HDHP)**.

Preferred Provider Organization (PPO)	High-Deductible Health Plan (HDHP)
Higher monthly premiums	Lower monthly premiums
Lower deductible	Higher deductible
Co-pay applies to office visits and prescriptions (rather than full fee) before deductible has been met	Individual pays 100% of costs until deductible has been met
Coinsurance percentage applies after deductible has been met (such as 80% paid by insurance, 20% paid by employee) until out-of-pocket maximum is met	Insurance policy pays all covered costs, once the deductible has been met
May require using an in-network provider or facility; if out-of-network is allowed, fees will be higher than in-network	May require using an in-network provider or facility; if out-of-network is allowed, fees will be higher than in-network
Generally best for people whose primary concern is to minimize out-of-pocket expenses for office visits or prescriptions while also having coverage for major medical events.	Generally best for healthy people who rarely seek medical care or for those who are likely to reach their deductible very early in the plan year, as the policy covers after that point.
Cannot be combined with a health savings account.	Can be combined with a health savings account.

LEAVE PLANS AND APPROACHES
PTO POLICIES

There are many different **paid time off (PTO)** policies across different businesses, industries, and geographic locations. Many of these all-encompassing PTO plans are available only to full-time employees. Whereas many companies recognize 8–10 fixed holidays, some companies have implemented policies that provide employees with floating holidays. Trends have shown an increase in organizations of all sizes adopting a collective in which vacation, personal, sick, and sometimes holiday days are kept in a **single pool** of PTO. Many employees and employers report that having flexibility in time-off plans leads to greater employee engagement and retention. However, as more states are imposing sick time regulations, recent trends reflect a number of organizations moving back to traditional buckets of separate vacation and sick time. Additional consideration should be given to state regulations for **termination payouts**. Some states do not require employers to pay out accrued sick time, but many consider PTO pools equivalent to vacation during terminations, so employers must pay out any accrued balances. Companies must also determine whether employees will be given a bank of time immediately or at a predetermined time versus **accrued**. Policies should provide details about carryover provisions and whether negative balances are allowed. Having an attractive and well-administered PTO policy can give employers an advantage against growing competition for talent, evolving legal regulations, and an increasingly diverse workforce.

Holidays and Other Pay for Time Not Worked

The average number of **paid holidays** is around eight per year, and most businesses will recognize the following six US holidays: New Year's Day, Memorial Day, Independence Day, Labor Day, Thanksgiving Day, and Christmas Day. Additionally, a majority of employers will pay a set number of days for bereavement and jury duty for eligible employees. However, employees may be required to provide documentation. Other instances in which employees might be paid for time not worked include reporting time guaranteed for minimal work, union activities, and time to vote.

Unpaid Leave

When an employee has exhausted all PTO options and needs to take time away from work, the employer may allow them to take an unpaid leave. This leave may be classified as a personal leave or a work sabbatical. Criteria to qualify and rules that govern the leave will depend on individual business policies. Policies will need to address items such as how to apply for the leave, length of leave allowed, benefits continuance, the employee's right to return to the same role, the process to return from a leave, and more.

Healthcare Accounts

Healthcare options offered by employers have shifted in recent years to a more "consumer-directed" initiative in order for employers to reduce costs and allow employees to choose or customize their healthcare spending. As a result of this shift, employer healthcare options tend to be high-deductible plans. For example, an individual employee could have a deductible of $3,000 and a family deductible of $6,000. This means that the employee must pay the deductible out of pocket before medical insurance begins to pay. This is frequently a burden for employees, so many employers have created and administer programs to help offset the employee expense.

Medical Costs and Contribution Limits

Eligible medical care expenses are defined by the IRS and include costs that relate to disease deterrence, diagnosis, or treatment. The costs of procedures undertaken for solely cosmetic reasons are generally not considered expenses for medical care and are not reimbursable. Expenses ineligible under an FSA include procedures and services such as liposuction, Botox treatments, contact lenses, and personal trainers. Eligible expenses do, however, include things like service or guide animals and acupuncture. Employees can also open dependent care FSAs, which allow them to use pretax dollars to pay for dependent care, like daycare.

The IRS determines FSA contribution limits annually. The main drawback to the FSA is that it requires careful budgeting because there is a use-it-or-lose-it provision attached to the benefit. If employees do not use the funds within an account during the given plan year, they may lose the money. Exceptions to this are when the employer opts to offer a grace period, granting an additional 2.5 months to use the funds, or a carryover provision, which is limited to $500. Employers are not required to offer either and can offer only one of the two. They may also offer a run-out period, which gives employees an additional 90 days to make claims for reimbursement.

Health Savings Account (HSA)	Health Reimbursement Account (HRA)	Flexible Spending Account (FSA)
Requires enrollment in a high-deductible health plan (HDHP)	Some HRAs require a health insurance plan; some do not	Does not require participation in a health insurance plan
Can be funded by employer and/or employee	Funded solely by the employer	Can be funded by employee and/or employer
Contribution can be changed at any time	Employer sets contribution rules	Contribution can be changed at annual enrollment or with a qualifying event
Employee owns the account	Employer owns the account	Employer owns the account
Account is portable; it will stay with the employee after separation of employment	Account is not portable; it will not follow the employee after separation of employment	Account is not portable; it will not follow the employee after separation of employment
Use for qualifying medical expenses	Use for qualifying medical expenses	Use for qualifying medical, vision, dental, and dependent care expenses
Funds do not expire	Employer sets rules for expiration/rollover	Funds expire if not used; limited rollover may be possible

Employees are generally eligible to enroll in an HSA, HRA, or FSA when they become eligible for benefits with their employer or during annual enrollment.

DISABILITY INSURANCE

Health coverage and healthcare accounts help offset the cost of seeking medical care, but they don't provide income replacement for employees who become unable to work due to illness or injury. That's why short-term disability and long-term disability insurance are often included in employee benefits packages.

Disability insurance policies don't provide full income replacement, but they do provide covered employees with a percentage of their ordinary income for a set period of time when they are unable to work due to illness, injury, or other disability.

In a few states, including (but not limited to) California, New Jersey, and New York, employers are required to provide short-term disability insurance to their employees. Most states don't require employers to provide—or even offer—disability insurance, but it is very common for employers to offer both types of coverage to employees.

Some employers pay for a level of coverage and allow employees to purchase additional protection if they want, while others do not offset the cost of disability insurance. Even in that case, it is usually more affordable for employees to sign up for disability coverage available via their employer than to purchase it on their own, because group plans tend to be less costly than individual coverage.

Short-Term Disability (STD)

Short-term disability (STD) insurance provides partial income for a short time, usually between three and six months (depending on the policy). Some STD policies provide coverage from the first day of disability, while others have an elimination period of a few weeks.

Long-Term Disability (LTD)

Long-term disability (LTD) is intended to extend income protection beyond the time covered by a company's STD policy, with the length of coverage varying greatly by policy. Most plans provide coverage for a set number of years; some may last until retirement age. This type of policy usually has an elimination period of at least 90 days, though it can be as long as six months.

Unemployment Compensation

Unemployment compensation is a national program that is regulated by the IRS as the **Federal Unemployment Tax Act (FUTA)** to provide workers with short-term sustenance while they are looking for new employment. Employers pay FUTA as a payroll tax at a rate of 6.2 percent. Although a majority of the administration is held at the state level, the federal government also administers the programs. FUTA applies to all employers who either employ one or more employees or pay wages greater than $1,500 in any quarter of a calendar year. Employees typically receive about half of their former weekly wages; however, each state regulates the amount and duration of benefits. Eligibility requirements require that individuals be available and readily seeking new employment opportunities, which they must record and present upon request. The company costs vary depending upon the employer's experience rating, which is based on prior claims receiving payments.

Workplace Flexibility Programs

There have been many benefits touted in favor of **workplace flexibility**, such as increased morale, better attendance, and higher productivity. Flexibility might involve either the **work location**, which is where work is performed, or the **work schedule**, which is when work is performed. However, the practice is gaining momentum slowly due to many employers embracing traditional viewpoints despite technological advances creating lower overhead costs for remote workers or greater employee engagement and satisfaction when they are allowed schedule flexibility to accommodate family or personal responsibilities. Workplace flexibility allows employees greater autonomy and empowerment as well. Flexibility can also be used to encourage brand recognition, attract talent, and support retention strategies.

Telecommuting

Employees may be able to perform their jobs outside of a traditional company office by **telecommuting** using tools such as email, phone, remote in, and video/chat apps. Telecommuting can be done on a full-time, part-time, or intermittent basis. Telecommuting offers increased flexibility and work-life balance, allowing employees a little more freedom in scheduling. Negative aspects of telecommuting include loss of professional direction or face-to-face interaction. Strong organizational skills, scheduling, and autonomy are beneficial skills for individuals who telecommute.

Alternative Work Schedules

Designed to provide an alternative to the "traditional" work week, **alternative work schedules** benefit individuals who need the flexibility that a standard schedule cannot offer. There are many options for alternative work schedules, such as a **compressed work schedule** of four 10-hour days or three 12-hour days. This allows the individual to work full-time hours in fewer days. **Flextime** is another type of alternative work schedule, where an employee is required work some of their hours during a specific designated time (for example from 9 a.m. to 12 p.m.) and their remaining hours on a flexible basis (for example, any time between 5 a.m. and 5 p.m.).

JOB SHARING

Two (or more) employees each working in a position part-time to fill a role that may have been filled by a single person working full-time is known as **job sharing**. The employees filling the shared role work together to accomplish the assigned tasks and duties. Job sharing allows increased flexibility, as the two part-time employees can tailor their shifts, hours, and duties. Employees that are sharing a job may both work the same hours and focus on different areas. Alternately, they may split a shift, working different hours in the same day. A third scheduling option is splitting the work week, so one employee works one day, and the other employee works the next day. A combination of each of these schedules can also be used.

SUPPLEMENTAL WELLNESS AND FRINGE BENEFITS

Many companies offer supplemental benefits beyond health and disability coverage. Most companies that offer employee benefits include standard offerings like dental and vision insurance, as well as at least a basic level of life insurance.

Recognizing that offering additional benefits can boost the value of their total rewards package, employers seeking to gain competitive advantage when it comes to recruiting and retaining employees often choose to go above and beyond standard supplemental benefits.

Popular supplemental benefits offerings include the following.

EMPLOYEE ASSISTANCE PROGRAMS (EAPS)

An **employee assistance program** (EAP) is a program sponsored by an employer that provides confidential counseling services to help employees manage all types of stressful life situations or problems. Because it is sponsored by the employer, an EAP is free to employees. The service is confidential, meaning the employer is not aware of the employee's usage. This confidentiality is primarily due to Health Insurance Portability and Accountability Act (HIPAA) regulations, meaning complete confidentiality is maintained with the third-party vendor contracted to provide the counseling.

An EAP is designed to help the employee, which in turn allows them to be more productive at work. EAP services can vary, but typically include mental health issues, family problems, financial concerns, legal issues, and substance abuse. Usually, the program provides guidance and professional referrals to resources that can help the employee on a short- or long-term basis.

GYM MEMBERSHIPS

Healthy employees tend to be productive employees who are less at risk for on-the-job injury than others, so it makes sense for a company to offer benefits that help employees get and stay as healthy as possible. That's why gym memberships are such a popular component of employee benefits programs.

Employers often sign up for corporate discount programs with local gyms or nationwide fitness networks, as doing so makes it possible for employees to join at a reduced rate and pay via payroll deduction. Some companies even cover all or part of the cost of gym memberships for employees who opt to participate.

Housing or Relocation Assistance

When an employer hires an employee for a job that requires the individual to relocate, the company may offer a relocation assistance program to the employee and their family. Relocation packages vary greatly, but usually include covering the cost of packing up and moving personal belongings and the cost of transporting the employee and their family to where they will be living.

Relocation benefits may also cover additional moving-related costs, such as fees associated with selling a house or breaking a lease, traveling to look for housing prior to the move, temporary housing assistance for a set time at the beginning of the individual's employment, and storage of personal items until a place of residence is secured.

Travel or Transportation Stipends

Recognizing that commuting and/or parking can be a significant expense for employees, some employers include benefits designed to help offset such costs in their benefits package. Some companies provide commuting stipends or reimbursement for parking expenses, the use of public transportation (such as subways or buses), or rideshare programs.

Additionally, some employers offer special travel/transportation stipends to employees who commute a long distance to work. For example, a company may provide a per diem to employees who drive more than a certain number of miles or who live outside the county where the company is located. This may be based on what county or state the employee drives in from, or the specific number of miles between an employee's home and the worksite.

US Federally Compliant Compensation and Benefit Programs

Methods of Ensuring Competitive and Fair Compensation

Compa-Ratio

A compa-ratio is a mathematical formula used to compare a specific employee's pay with the pay at the middle of the pay range. A **compa-ratio** is expressed as a percentage and can be determined by dividing the employee's base salary by the midpoint salary for the employee's pay range (*base salary/midpoint salary = compa-ratio*). For example, if an individual is in a pay grade that ranges from $25,000 to $45,000 a year and the individual receives $30,000 a year, the midpoint of the range is equal to ($25,000 + $45,000)/2 or $35,000, and the compa-ratio is $30,000/$35,000, which is equal to 0.857 or 85.7 percent. Compa-ratios are primarily used to compare an employee's current pay with the pay of other employees in similar positions to determine whether the individual is receiving a fair amount considering seniority, performance, and so on.

Using Benchmarking to Design Compensation Initiatives

When organizations and compensation professionals need to make pay decisions or determine whether internal rates are competitive with the industry, most will rely upon **benchmarking** against both internal and external peer groups. Benchmarking is a tool for measuring and comparing current practices or processes against **competition** so that any gaps may be addressed. For example, making changes to incentive plans may be a tough sell. If your business practice involves not providing employees with a bonus plan, benchmarking data might support new initiatives by showing that many in your industry do provide bonus incentives. Thus, not providing this incentive could jeopardize performance or risk losing top performers. However, it is important to consider organizational structure, size, location, industry, and other factors. Compensation rates in San Francisco will differ greatly from rates in Omaha, and smaller companies often pay less than large, national entities.

USING REMUNERATION SURVEYS TO ENSURE COMPETITIVENESS

Competitive compensation structures are not only equitable and motivating, but they should also be legal, be cost-benefit effective, and provide security. The most readily available **remuneration surveys** are those conducted by government agencies, such as the Bureau of Labor Statistics (BLS), and wage surveys conducted by private organizations. Government surveys may include local, state, or federal data. BLS regularly publishes reliable data findings on occupational earnings and benefits of blue- and white-collar jobs. Furthermore, professional organizations, journals, and associations may perform sophisticated surveys to obtain remuneration data of top managers, supervisors, and entry-level workers. Some popular publications are *Forbes*'s CEO compensation report and those compiled by wage survey companies like Payscale or Willis Towers Watson. Professionals should keep in mind that these surveys frequently consider varying components of compensation, such as base pay, incentives, and benefits.

FEDERAL LAWS AND REGULATIONS PERTAINING TO COMPENSATION AND BENEFITS
FLSA

The **Fair Labor Standards Act of 1938 (FLSA),** also known as the Wage Hour Bill, sets minimum wage standards, overtime pay standards, and child labor restrictions. The act is administered by the Wage and Hour Division of the Department of Labor. The FLSA carefully classifies employees as exempt or nonexempt from provisions, requires that employers calculate overtime for covered employees at one and one-half times the regular rate of pay for all hours worked in excess of 40 hours during a week, and defines how a work week should be measured. The purpose of minimum wage standards is to ensure a living wage and to reduce poverty for low-income families, minority workers, and women. The child labor provisions protect minors from positions that may be harmful to their health or well-being and regulates the hours minors can legally work. The act also outlines requirements for employers to keep records of hours, wages, and related payroll items.

MINIMUM WAGE

The FLSA established regulations designed to prevent employees from receiving substandard wages and established the federal minimum wage. The federal minimum wage is the lowest amount an employer can pay any nonexempt employee for each hour of work. An employee will be considered exempt from this provision if the individual receives a weekly salary of at least $455, if the employee works in a profession not covered by the FLSA or a profession identified as exempt from the minimum wage provision of the FLSA, or if the employer has received special permission to pay less than the minimum wage as part of a Department of Labor program.

There are two situations in which an organization may need to pay an employee more than the federal minimum wage. First, if the individual has worked more than 40 hours in a single week and is in a position covered by the FLSA, he or she is entitled to overtime pay for each additional hour over 40 hours. Second, when the minimum wage for the state in which the organization's employees are located is higher than the federal minimum wage, the employee is entitled to receive the state minimum wage. However, most states have their own list of exemptions and requirements, so that a particular organization may be part of an industry covered by the FLSA, but not by the regulations set by state law.

OVERTIME

The FLSA established regulations designed to prevent employees from receiving substandard wages, especially related to overtime pay. It defines overtime pay as $1\frac{1}{2}$ times the regular wage normally received and establishes that overtime pay must be paid to any nonexempt individual working more than 40 hours in a single week. The number of hours an individual has worked in a given week does not include hours paid for vacation time, sick leave, paid holidays, or similar pay received when work is not actually performed. Certain states may have overtime regulations in addition to those established by the FLSA.

ON-CALL

The FLSA established regulations designed to prevent employees from receiving substandard wages especially related to on-call pay. This regulation requires an employer to pay regular wages if the employee is required to wait at the job site ready to perform work as it becomes available. This must be paid to the employee even if the individual is not actually performing work as he or she waits. However, this regulation does not apply to individuals who are on-call at any location other than the job site.

CHILD LABOR

The Fair Labor Standards Act established child labor regulations designed to prevent children from entering the workforce before they are mature enough to do so, from working in hazardous environments, from working for long periods, and from working instead of attending school. These regulations prohibit employers from hiring anyone under the age of 14 unless the individual is working for a parent or for a farm and from hiring individuals under the age of 18 for any kind of work deemed hazardous by law. These regulations also prevent individuals under the age of 16 from working in any manufacturing or mining-related job, working during school hours, working more than 3 hours a day or 18 hours a week during a school week or 8 hours a day and 40 hours a week during a non-school week, and working before 7:00 a.m. or past 7:00 p.m. during the school year or working before 7:00 a.m. or past 9:00 p.m. during the summer.

EQUAL PAY ACT

The Equal Pay Act, which was passed in 1963, prevents wage discrimination based on gender. It requires an employer to provide equal pay to men and women performing similar tasks unless the employer can prove that there is an acceptable reason for the difference in pay, such as merit, seniority, or quantity or quality of work performed. This act also establishes the criteria that must be considered to determine whether a particular position is similar or not. This includes the effort necessary for the tasks related to the position, the level of responsibility associated with the position, the skills required to perform the position, and the working conditions associated with the position.

LILLY LEDBETTER FAIR PAY ACT OF 2009

The **Lilly Ledbetter Fair Pay Act** overturned the 2007 Supreme Court decision in the *Ledbetter v. Goodyear Tire & Rubber Company* case, which ruled that the statute of limitations to make a discriminatory pay claim was 180 days from the first discriminatory paycheck. Because of the Lilly Ledbetter Act, the statute of limitations now restarts with each discriminatory paycheck. The act applies to all protected classes and covers both wages and pensions. Due to the scope of the act, employers could face claims years after an employee has left the company. This act was designed to make employers more proactive in resolving pay inequities. Additionally, employers should review their compensation record retention procedures in case they need to produce any related documentation for potential pay disparities.

ERISA

ERISA was passed in 1974 to protect employees who are covered under private pensions and employee welfare benefit plans. ERISA ensures that employees receive promised benefits and are protected against early termination, mismanaged funds, or fraudulent activities. ERISA mandates that employers adhere to eligibility requirements, vesting requirements, portability practices,

funding requirements, fiduciary responsibilities, reporting and disclosure requirements, as well as compliance testing. Most employees who have at least 1,000 hours of work in 12 months for two consecutive years are eligible to participate in **private pension plans**. Employees have the right to receive some portion of employer contributions when their employment ends. Employees must be allowed to transfer pension funds from one retirement account to another. Sufficient funds must be available from the employer to cover future payments. Employers must appoint an individual to be responsible for seeking ideal portfolio options and administering pension funds. Employers must adhere to extensive reporting requirements, provide summary plan documents, and notify participants of any changes. Employers are required to complete annual minimum coverage, actual deferral percentage, actual contribution percentage, and top-heavy testing to prevent discrimination in favor of highly compensated employees.

FEDERAL WAGE GARNISHMENT LAW

The **Federal Wage Garnishment Law of 1968** imposes limitations on the amount of disposable earnings that may be withheld from an employee's income in a given pay period to satisfy a **wage garnishment order** for failure to pay a debt. The law restricts the amount that can be withheld to 25 percent of an employee's disposable weekly earnings or an amount that is 30 times the FLSA minimum wage, whichever is less. However, overdue payments to the IRS, child support in arrears, and alimony payments are a few exceptions that allow for more significant amounts to be withheld. Employers must immediately begin income withholdings upon receipt of a garnishment order, and funds must be sent to the respective agency within seven days. Failure to do so could impose hefty fines and penalties for the employer. There are certain protections for employees, whereby employers may not take disciplinary action or discriminate due to the receipt or obligation to comply with wage garnishment orders.

FMLA

The **Family and Medical Leave Act** (FMLA) of 1993 is a federal regulation that provides employees the right to take up to 12 weeks of unpaid leave in each 12-month period for the care of specified medical conditions that affect themselves or immediate family members. To be eligible for FMLA leave, an employee must have worked for a covered employer for the preceding 12 months and for a minimum of 1,250 hours during that time. All private employers, public or government agencies, and local schools with 50 or more employees within a 75-mile radius, must adhere to the regulations. Qualifying events covered under FMLA include the following:

- The birth or adoption of a new child within one year of birth or placement
- The employee's own serious health condition that involves a period of incapacity
- An ill or injured spouse, child, or parent who requires the employee's care
- Any qualifying exigency due to active-duty foreign deployment by an employee's spouse, child (or children), or parent. Exigencies may include arranging childcare, tending to legal matters, and attending military ceremonies.
- The care of an ill or injured covered service member, as long as the employee is a spouse, child, parent, or next of kin. In addition, time to care for military personnel or recent veterans has been expanded to 26 weeks in a 12-month period.

The FMLA has undergone some significant amendments, and HR practitioners should be aware of the following:

- If an organization fails to denote an employee's leave as FMLA leave, the employee may be eligible to receive compensation for any losses incurred.
- Prior to 2008, all FMLA disputes required Department of Labor or legal intervention. Now, employees and employers are encouraged to work out any issues in-house to avoid the cost of litigation.
- Light duty does not count toward FMLA taken.
- FMLA covers medical issues arising from preexisting conditions.
- Due to their unique scheduling, airline employees are eligible for FMLA after 504 or more hours worked during the preceding 12 months.

COBRA

The **Consolidated Omnibus Budget Reconciliation Act** (COBRA) of 1986 requires that all employers with 20 or more employees continue the availability of healthcare benefits coverage and protect employees from the potential economic hardship of losing these benefits when they are terminated, are working reduced hours, or quit. COBRA also provides coverage to the employee's spouse and dependents as qualified beneficiaries. Events that qualify for this continuation of coverage include the following:

- Voluntary or involuntary termination for any reason other than gross misconduct
- Reduction in hours that would otherwise result in loss of coverage
- Divorce or legal separation from the employee
- Death of the employee
- The employee becoming disabled and entitled to Medicare
- The dependent being over 26 and no longer a dependent child under plan rules

Typically, the employee and qualified beneficiaries are entitled to 18 months of continued coverage. There are some instances that will extend coverage for up to an additional 18 months. Coverage will be lost if the employer terminates group coverage, premium payments are not received, or new coverage becomes available. COBRA is a high-cost plan; typically the cost to the employee is the full cost that the employer pays for health coverage, plus an administrative fee that averages around 2 percent. Alternatives to COBRA are purchasing coverage through marketplace offerings, Medicaid coverage if applicable, or switching coverage through a spouse (again, if applicable) because a qualifying event entitles the spouse to special enrollment.

HIPAA

The **Health Insurance Portability and Accountability Act** (HIPAA) was passed in 1996 to provide greater protections and portability in healthcare coverage. Some individuals felt locked into current employer plans and feared that they would not be able to obtain coverage from a new employer plan due to preexisting conditions. As a result, some of the key HIPAA provisions are pre-existing condition exclusions, pregnancy, newborn and adopted children, credible coverage, renewal of coverage, medical savings accounts, tax benefits, and privacy provisions. Employees who have had another policy for the preceding 12 months cannot be excluded from coverage due to a pre-existing condition or pregnancy, and it must be applied to newborn or adopted children who are covered by credible coverage within 30 days of the event. **Credible coverage** involves being covered under typical group health plans, and this coverage must be renewable to most groups and individuals as long as premiums are paid. **Medical savings accounts** were created by Congress for those who are self-employed or otherwise not eligible for credible coverage. Individuals who are self-employed are also allowed to take 80 percent of health-related expenses as a deduction. Finally, HIPAA introduced a series of several regulations that impose **civil and criminal penalties** on employers who disclose personal health information without consent.

> **Review Video: HIPAA**
> Visit mometrix.com/academy and enter code: 412009

MHPA

The **Mental Health Parity and Addiction Equity Act** (MHPAEA), which was passed in 1996, is designed to prevent health plan providers from setting limits on mental health benefits that are stricter than the limits the provider has set for other health benefits. This act prohibits a health plan provider from setting a financial cap on the amount the health plan provider will pay for mental health benefits if that cap is lower than the cap the provider has set for other benefits. For example, if a medical or surgical lifetime cap is $8,000, then the cap on mental health benefits cannot be below $8,000. This act applies to any health plan provider providing coverage for an employer with at least 51 employees, but only if the regulations set by this act will not result in a 1 percent or greater increase in the costs of the provider. Also, health plan providers are not required to offer mental health benefits, and providers may set other limits related to mental health coverage as long as there is no specific payout limit.

PPACA

The **Patient Protection and Affordable Care Act** (PPACA) is a comprehensive healthcare law that was passed in 2010 to establish regulations on medical services, insurance coverage, preventative services, whistleblowing, and similar practices. A few key provisions of the PPACA include the following:

- **Individual mandate**—Requires all individuals to maintain health insurance or pay a penalty. It was removed from the statute effective tax year 2019. However, there are a few states that have an individual mandate.
- **State healthcare exchanges**—Provides individuals and families a portal in which they can shop through a variety of plans and purchase healthcare coverage.
- **Employer shared responsibility**—Requires that employers with more than 50 full-time employees provide affordable coverage to all employees that work 30 or more hours per week or pay a penalty.
- **Affordable coverage**—Does not allow employers to shift the burden of healthcare costs to employees and imposes a penalty on employers if their employees qualify to obtain government subsidies for coverage.
- **Flexible spending accounts (FSAs)**—Imposes a cap on pretax contributions to FSAs, health reimbursement arrangements (HRAs), and health savings accounts (HSAs).
- **Wellness incentives**—Allows employers to provide premium discounts for employees who meet wellness requirements.
- **Excise tax on "Cadillac" plans**—Imposes excise tax on employers that provide expensive coverage.
- **W-2 reporting requirements**—Requires employers to report the cost of coverage under employer-sponsored group health plans on each employee's W-2 form.
- **Summary of benefits coverage**—Requires insurance companies and employers to provide individuals with a summary of benefits coverage (SBC) using a standard form.
- **Whistleblower protections**—Amends the FLSA to prohibit employers from retaliating against an employee who applies for health benefit subsidies or tax credits.

NATIONAL FEDERATION OF INDEPENDENT BUSINESS V. SEBELIUS (2012)

Opponents of the PPACA argued that certain provisions of the law, such as the individual mandate, were unconstitutional. The court ultimately ruled that PPACA was constitutional, and it remained intact until President Trump reversed the individual mandate effective 2019. Other elements of the PPACA legislation are still currently in place.

OWBPA

The Older Worker Benefit Protection Act (OWBPA), which was passed in 1990, is an amendment to the Age Discrimination in Employment Act designed to prevent employers from unfairly refusing benefits to individuals over a certain age. This act prohibits an employer or benefit plan administrator from preventing participation or continuing to participate in a benefits program due to age if the individual is covered by the Age Discrimination in Employment Act. It establishes that an employer may only set a maximum age limit or reduce an individual's benefits due to age in situations in which the age limit or age-related reduction can be shown to significantly reduce the costs associated with implementing the benefit plan. The act also specifically establishes that an employer may implement a plan or system based on seniority as long as the plan does not require an individual to leave the program after a certain age.

REA

The **Retirement Equity Act** (REA), which was passed in 1984, is an amendment to ERISA designed to establish a number of benefit plan regulations in addition to those originally established by ERISA. These regulations are designed to protect spouses from losing their plan benefits after a plan participant's death or after a divorce, but they also include regulations to strengthen the protections offered by ERISA. Protections established by REA include:

- Regulations prohibiting benefit plan administrators from considering maternity/paternity leave as a break in service regarding the right to participate in a plan or become vested in a plan
- Regulations requiring pension plans to automatically provide benefits to a spouse in the event of the plan participant's death unless a waiver has been signed by both the spouse and the participant
- Regulations that lowered the age at which an employer had to allow an individual to participate in a pension plan

An employer not complying with this act could face severe criminal and civil penalties.

PENSION PROTECTION ACT

The Pension Protection Act, which was passed in 2006, is an amendment to the Employee Retirement Income Security Act (ERISA) designed to protect individuals from pension plans that do not have enough funding to pay out all of the retirement benefits promised to employees. This act requires any employer establishing a pension plan to make contributions in amounts large enough to ensure the plan is not underfunded and requires employers to offer at least three investment options in addition to the employer's own stock if the employer's stock is offered as part of a benefit plan. This act also allows employers to include employees in an organization's 401(k) program with or without the permission of the individual as long as the individual has the right to opt-out of the plan.

OASDI

The Old Age, Survivors, and Disability Insurance (OASDI) program, which was established by the Social Security Act (SSA) of 1935, offers benefits to employees that have retired or become disabled.

This program requires employees to pay a percentage of their income to the federal government and requires employers to match the contributions made by their employees. As employees contribute to the fund, they will accumulate Social Security credits and may receive up to four Social Security credits a year based on the amount paid into the fund. If an individual becomes completely disabled for a period of at least five consecutive months or retires at age 62 or older, he/she is entitled to receive a portion of previous earnings from the Social Security program. To receive retirement benefits from social security, the individual must have at least 40 credits before retiring.

> **Review Video: US Employment Compensation Laws**
> Visit mometrix.com/academy and enter code: 613448

Employee Engagement

Enhancing Employee Participation and Engagement

EMPLOYEE ENGAGEMENT

Employee engagement levels indicate the commitment employees have to the organization. Definitions of engagement vary, but according to Gallup, **engaged employees** are "involved in, enthusiastic about and committed to their work and workplace." An engaged employee will recognize work that needs to be done outside their role and proactively address the problem. Definitions of a disengaged employee vary as well. In general, a **disengaged employee** lacks commitment and is simply "putting in the time" without any extra effort or passion toward the job. At their worst, disengaged employees not only dislike their work and workplace, but also share that opinion with whoever will listen. Engagement levels can have a positive or negative impact on employee morale.

While there are some similarities between employee engagement and employee satisfaction, they are not the same thing. Both can be measured and provide valuable information to an employer. The difference is in terms of what is measured. Employee satisfaction measures the more objective factors of a job. It involves employee opinions about pay, benefits, workplace safety, and other things that the organization as a whole can control on a broad spectrum. On the other hand, employee engagement is more impacted by relationships. Engagement levels measure the emotional commitment employees have to the job. Often, engagement levels are impacted by the leadership practices of the department. This explains why there can be such a variance in engagement levels between departments.

Engagement levels have a direct correlation to business success. According to Gallup, a leading engagement consulting group, high engagement scores link to key business drivers. First and foremost, highly engaged teams report greater profitability compared to teams with lower engagement scores. Highly engaged teams also report lower absenteeism, fewer accidents, and lower turnover rates. It makes sense that an employee who is emotionally connected to their work would want to be at the workplace (lower absenteeism and turnover), would strive to stay safe (fewer accidents), and would go the extra mile to generate revenue or monitor expenses (higher profitability). All these factors affect the bottom line and should boost a leader's interest in improving employee engagement.

MEASURING ENGAGEMENT

Engagement levels can be monitored subjectively through conversations or observation. However, engagement levels are most often measured through anonymous surveys. True engagement surveys go beyond general job satisfaction questions (about pay, benefits, or work safety) and measure the emotional commitment to the team and organization. Engagement levels can vary a lot by business unit, as there are many mini-cultures within the larger organization. Therefore, engagement surveys are often administered at the business unit level, provided there are enough employees to allow for anonymity. Usually, five or more responses are needed for business unit survey results. Individual business unit results are combined to get the entire company's results. Engagement surveys can be administered internally, by a third party, or through a combination of both. Surveys are often administered on a recurring basis to monitor progress.

HR and management have overlapping but distinct roles related to employee engagement. Typically, HR is responsible for the selection or development of the engagement measurement tool.

It also has responsibility for administering the tool and communicating the need for managers to facilitate action plans to positively impact engagement. In addition, HR is responsible for developing employment policies and practices to encourage interest from the proper level of talent. While HR has broader engagement responsibilities, each manager sets the tone for their own department. The engagement level of the department is a direct indication of how well and how often communication is shared, how well expectations are set and communicated, and how much is shared about the company values and vision. Finally, senior leaders are responsible for supporting the process and modeling appropriate behaviors—both day-to-day and during the engagement survey administration. Active participation from employees is strongly impacted by the level of support shown by senior leaders.

EMPLOYEE PROBLEM-SOLVING

Part of an effective HR employee relations strategy is a formal problem-solving policy that outlines the avenues available to seek resolution, should a concern arise. Typically, the problem-solving policy specifies that the employee should address the concern with the supervisor first. After attempting to resolve the issue with the supervisor—or if the employee is uncomfortable going to the supervisor—the next-level manager is the outlet. The employee is directed to continue through the chain of command until the issue is resolved. If at any point the employee is uncomfortable with the chain of command process, HR is provided as an objective party to hear the concern. It is then HR's responsibility to assess when and where to bring management back into the problem-solving and to assist in facilitating the discussion. Having an internal problem-solving procedure helps prevent employees from taking their concerns outside the organization (or simply resigning).

OPEN-DOOR POLICY

An open-door policy communicates to employees that management is available to hear concerns or have conversations without hesitation. Open-door policies, in order to be effective, must go beyond the handbook policy. Such a policy means that any employee, at almost any time, can share ideas, concerns, or challenges with any level of management. If established correctly, employees will feel comfortable having candid conversations without fear of retaliation. This also requires managers to understand their role in creating a welcoming environment, which means encouraging frequent conversations before a concern occurs. Leaders who can build this level of trust help to improve employee/employer relations.

SPECIAL EVENTS

Company-sponsored special events can vary, but all serve as a way to leverage and promote employee engagement and build a positive company culture. Some special events can be recurring, such as holiday dinners, summer picnics, Friday social nights, or Tuesday tacos in the office. These events may be social outings with or without employee family members. However, they serve to build camaraderie among employee team members and give them opportunities to socialize with one another outside of the work environment. This may help build a stronger, more productive work team, as well as improve employee satisfaction. Events can also incorporate an element of community service, including serving food at a local soup kitchen, volunteering at an animal shelter, or building homes for those in need. Some special events might also include wellness-related campaigns, company walking or running teams, weight loss or healthy eating initiatives, or yoga classes at lunch. Special events demonstrate that the employer cares about the employees' health and well-being.

Methods for Assessing Employee Attitudes, Opinions, and Satisfaction

Employee Attitude Surveys

An employer would conduct an employee attitude survey to better understand what employees think about the company and its work environment. Employee attitude surveys can measure either employee satisfaction or opinions on specific issues. Some of the information that might be collected and evaluated includes workplace culture, communication effectiveness, management effectiveness, safety at work, and specialized initiatives in the organization. There are many advantages for an organization to conduct an employee attitude survey:

- Employees like to feel valued, so asking them their perspective on a number of key topics helps them feel their voices count while also helping employers adjust course if necessary. Also, it demonstrates the organization cares about their employees.
- Employee attitude surveys are anonymous, which encourages honesty. Employers gain the honest opinions of employees because of this format. It provides a better understanding of the organization's strengths and weaknesses as viewed by employees.
- New ideas resulting from the survey could lead to better development and training programs.
- These surveys boost employee engagement and two-way communications.

There are also some disadvantages an organization should consider before implementing an employee attitude survey:

- Surveys set the expectation that an employer will act upon its employees' responses. If the employer just wants to know employee thoughts and does not plan to implement changes or communicate rationales, then employee morale could drop.
- It could be time-consuming to design, implement, evaluate, and execute changes based on the survey.
- Completing a survey could be thought of as an annoyance, and employees may choose not to participate, resulting in a low response rate that may not be worth the effort.
- Employees may not give undivided attention to the survey and may concentrate only on areas they view negatively, which could be misleading for employers.

Pulse Surveys

A **pulse survey** is different from an employee attitude survey in that it is shorter in format, can measure anything, and can be administered more frequently. Hence, it gives an organization the ability to assess any specific topic on a more frequent basis. Pulse surveys can vary greatly, and they frequently track the same topic or item over time. These short, usually easier-to-administer surveys also enable an organization to evaluate and act upon the information quickly. Therefore, there is sentiment among employees that the organization is listening to them more and genuinely trying to implement changes that mutually benefit the employees and the organization. As a result, employees feel valued. Some of the topics or items a pulse survey might measure include effectiveness of business metrics, effectiveness of specific employer initiatives, and training effectiveness. A pulse survey is nimble, and its flexibility allows an organization to measure the effectiveness of a specific issue over time, allowing the organization to shift course if needed. Pulse survey results are sometimes viewed as a monitoring tool.

Focus Groups

Focus groups can be used to glean employee views and concerns. They may be used to assess a new benefit plan or organizational change. Most focus groups contain 5–12 voluntary participants, with 3–10 groups in total. Participants should be informed about the subject of the focus group and about who will benefit, and should be told that the information will be kept confidential. Participants may be selected at random or through the use of certain applicable filters. Focus group organizers should ensure that power differentials within the group are avoided. It is also important to involve participants from various levels of staff so they can fully represent the affected population. A neutral facilitator should be chosen to lead the discussion and ask open-ended, guided questions. Following the meeting, collected data should be analyzed and reported.

SUGGESTION BOXES

A suggestion box is a place, either physical or virtual, where employees can give their anonymous opinions about anything in the work environment, working conditions, or ways to improve efficiencies or profitability. A suggestion box is a tool to help employees feel more engaged and involved, as well as to help the organization become a better place to work. A suggestion box improves communication, increases innovative thinking to help solve organizational problems, and could improve employee morale.

If the organization is using a physical box, then the box should be placed in a location where all employees have access. A physical box should also be locked shut, with access limited to only those with keys. If a virtual box is being used, then IT needs to ensure suggestions are truly anonymous. Before implementing a suggestion box, an employer should be prepared to take it seriously by being welcoming of suggestions and eager to read and act upon them. A program, including guidelines, should be developed to administer and promote the suggestion box. Additionally, incentives could be offered for participating. Employers should read suggestions on a regular basis and be sure to thank employees for their input.

STAY INTERVIEWS

A **stay interview** is a discussion between a manager and an employee with the goal of the employer ascertaining why a valued employee continues to work for the organization and if there is anything the employer can do to make improvements. The goal is to retain top talent and have a better understanding of what the organization is doing poorly, as well as learn what the organization is doing well. While employee satisfaction and engagement can be measured in an attitude survey, a stay interview allows for an immediate two-way conversation, enabling the employer to ask follow-up questions. Generally, stay interviews are conducted by employers once or twice during the onboarding process, typically over a six-month period; and then annually, usually six months apart from an employee's annual performance appraisal. The following are some questions an employer might ask during the approximately 30-minute stay interview:

- What do you enjoy about working here?
- What are a few things you look forward to every day?
- What can we do to make your job more satisfying?
- Do you feel valued and utilized in your current position?

EXIT INTERVIEWS

Exit interviews are opportunities for organizations to gather honest feedback as to why an employee is choosing to leave the organization. Exit interviews are almost always encouraged because they yield information that may help the organization improve and retain employees in the future. In most organizations, a member of the HR team, acting as an impartial and neutral party (and not as the employee's direct supervisor), conducts the exit interview to put the employee at ease. The following are ways to make an exit interview as productive as possible:

- Try to make the employee feel comfortable. Remind them that their input is extremely valuable and thank them for their time and expertise.
- Ask open-ended questions and repeat responses to ensure understanding. Yes-or-no questions should be avoided, and notes should be taken about what the employee said and did not say.
- The most important question to ask is why the employee started to look for another job.

Typically, HR analyzes and summarizes the information obtained from an exit interview and shares the information with the organization's leadership team to examine areas for improvement.

Performance Management

PRINCIPLES OF EFFECTIVE PERFORMANCE APPRAISAL

Performance appraisals serve four main organizational functions:

- **Guide human resource decisions.** Performance data is required for supporting and justifying promotion or termination decisions.
- **Reward and motivate employees.** Pay rate, status, and recognition should be based on performance.
- **Promote personal development.** Performance feedback will help employees identify strengths and improve weaknesses.
- **Identify training needs.** A well-designed appraisal process establishes necessary skills and abilities for each role and identifies individuals, areas, or departments that could benefit from additional training.

Each employee's **performance** appraisal should assess the following:

- Progress toward goals set at the last appraisal meeting
- Completion of normal job duties
- Organizational behaviors such as cooperation, innovation, motivation, and attitude
- Any notable achievements

SETTING GOALS

Performance goals consist of both short- and long-term targets that individual employees or teams are expected to achieve. These goals serve as guidelines for what employees should achieve and accomplish to help further the broader strategic goals of their department or of the organization. Goals also help employees concentrate their efforts on professional development, skills improvement, and personal development. Setting goals is very important in establishing a sense of direction in what employees are expected to achieve, as well as which behaviors and activities will help them toward that target. Goals can be set by HR, department heads, managers, supervisors, and the employees themselves. Goals should be clearly defined, specific, and realistic. Goals should also include an expected completion timeframe, to make tracking progress easier. Setting performance goals helps both the individual and the company. Employees are motivated to achieve goals, which drives performance and productivity. When there are group goals, employees collaborate to ensure that those goals are met by improving and promoting teamwork. Goal-setting helps to clearly state the expectations of the employees and the organization alike.

Frequent Feedback

Feedback from leadership should not occur only during appraisal time. Employees should receive feedback from their supervisors and managers frequently throughout the year. Providing **frequent feedback** makes it clear whether an employee is meeting expectations, illustrates when an employee is doing something well, identifies an area that could use some improvement, discusses additional training opportunities, and demonstrates that leadership recognizes the employee and sees the work and development that the employee is putting in. Employees can ask their leaders for feedback, but feedback is something that leadership should provide on a regular basis even without being asked. This can be formal feedback such as a bi-weekly check-in, or informal such as through a simple affirmation about a certain item. Frequent feedback also ensures that employees and supervisors are aligned with one another, and there are no unexpected surprises during the annual appraisal process.

Performance Appraisal Methods

There are many different performance appraisal methods. Some involve feedback only from the immediate supervisor, and some involve the feedback of peers, clients, or subordinates. Many organizations begin the process with self-appraisals. **Self-appraisals** are most beneficial when used for personal development and identifying training needs, but less beneficial when they are used as a basis for the formal evaluation process. Good supervisors are able to evaluate performance and give meaningful feedback. Hence, it should not be surprising that **supervisor appraisals** are typically required as at least one major component of the overall performance appraisal process. One type of appraisal that considers feedback from multiple sources is a **360-degree appraisal**. These appraisals have rapidly grown in popularity and are expected to share a broader perspective of performance because they include feedback from everyone the employee interacts with—managers, peers, clients, and subordinates.

360-Degree Feedback

The **360-degree feedback performance assessment** is a multi-source performance feedback tool that derives its data from evaluations obtained by an employee's supervisor(s), peers, subordinates, and sometimes others outside the organization such as vendors and partners. The idea is that 360 degrees form a perfect circle, hence individuals with various roles can give comprehensive feedback based on their interactions with the employee. These directions include supervisors from above, subordinates from below, and peers along the sides. Peers may also be joined by employees from other organizations. This process captures information from a variety of viewpoints and perspectives. The majority of organizations utilize 360-degree feedback for developmental reasons. However, there are some organizations that use it as part of a performance evaluation, in which case it might be called a **360-degree review**.

There are advantages to using 360-degree feedback, such as providing a comprehensive perspective from multiple people who have interacted with the employee. If executed correctly, it can give a complete or holistic picture of the employee. Conversely, 360-degree feedback can render results that are misleading because people may have different ulterior motives or their own agenda when completing the form, and many people are untrained to give this type of feedback. Additionally, it can be a time-consuming process, as the form typically takes 45 minutes to one hour to complete. That means time away from work, which also comes at a certain price to an organization.

Ranking Techniques of Appraisal

Ranking procedures put employees in order from highest to lowest based upon evaluation characteristics such as performance. There are three main forms of ranking:

- **Straight ranking** involves listing all employees in order, with number one being the best, number two being second best, number three being third, and so on.
- **Alternate ranking** entails choosing the best and the worst from a list of all employees, removing these names from the list, and repeating until there are no names left.
- **Paired comparison** consists of evaluating only two employees at a time, deciding which is better, and continuing until each employee has been paired against every other employee.

Ranking procedures assist with distributing budgeted pay increases that are more clearly tied to performance, and they eliminate some of the biases found in traditional review criteria. The forced-distribution method, also known as **forced ranking**, uses a bell curve in which the majority of employees will receive an average score and a small group will receive extremely high or extremely low performance scores.

Rating Techniques of Appraisal

There are a variety of rating appraisal methods, but the two most common are the checklist method and the rating scale method. The **checklist method** is a series of statements describing a certain level of performance. The performance evaluator can then check a box next to the statement that best describes the individual's performance in each performance area. The **rating scale method** rates an individual's performance on a point scale, usually a 1–3, 1–4, 1–5, or 1–10 scale, with higher numbers representing better performance.

Behaviorally Based Techniques of Appraisal

Greater focus on accountability and results has led to new approaches for appraising performance. The three main **behaviorally based appraisal methods** are management by objectives, behaviorally anchored rating scales, and behavioral observation scales.

Management by objectives is proactive rather than reactive. It focuses on predicting and shaping the future of the company, accomplishing results rather than simply following directions, improving competence and effectiveness, and increasing the participation and engagement of employees.

Behaviorally anchored rating scales (BARS) assign numerical values to performance based on a given range, such as a five-star system or a scale from 1 to 10. The BARS method analyzes the job description for a particular position and identifies the tasks that must be performed for the organization to function effectively. Once the tasks are identified, a determination is made about the specific way the individual should behave to perform each task. For example, if communication is identified as a necessary skill for a management position, then an individual in that position must be able to keep others informed. A series of ranked statements are then designed to describe how effectively the individual performed. Performance appraisers can choose the statement that best describes the employee's behavior. The key benefits of BARS are that they create agreement by being less subjective and more based upon observations.

Behavioral observation scales are similar to BARS, but with greater focus on frequency of behavior than on quality of performance, such as a sliding scale of "always," "sometimes," and "never."

Narrative Techniques of Appraisal

The three most common narrative appraisal techniques are the critical incident method, the essay method, and the field review method.

The **critical incident method** documents each performance problem related to an employee occurring during a set period so that the evaluator can discuss problems with the employee at the end.

The **essay method** requires performance evaluators to write a short essay about each employee describing their performance during the period in question.

The **field review method** is a method in which an individual other than the employee's direct supervisor or manager performs the appraisal and writes down a series of assessments and observations about that employee's performance.

Common Performance Appraisal Problems

Performance evaluations are meant to measure performance of job objectives, but they can be tainted by a number of criterion problems. One dilemma is whether to focus evaluations on **outcomes and results** or **behaviors and activities**. Many will say that outcomes are more important than behaviors and will base performance on the measure of results. However, focusing only on outcomes can lure individuals to achieve results by unethical or adverse means. Evaluations should also measure performance results without contamination by factors that are beyond an individual's control, such as improper materials, poor equipment, or economic conditions. Furthermore, even performance evaluations that are consistent and reputable may be influenced by biases. The absence of standards to assist with grading performances can lead some evaluators to judge too harshly, some to inflate scores, and some to tend toward placing all performers in the middle. The best method ensures that group results form a **bell curve.**

Importance of Documenting Employee Performance

Up-to-date performance documentation is important to maintain in an employee's personnel file, as it frequently demonstrates the reasoning why decisions, both positive and negative, were made. This documentation is especially useful in an employee's performance appraisal because it demonstrates performance with examples. Some managers find it useful to keep a performance diary, documenting a record of key activities or tasks executed by the employee. Employee performance documentation is essential in the event of a lawsuit. Furthermore, the documentation must be accurate, objective, and specific. The following are some guidelines to maintain when documenting employee performance: document right away to avoid anything being forgotten, keep notes on all employees, separate fact from opinion, make sure notes are objective, remove emotion from documentation, and be respectful when writing. Performance documentation is not exclusively useful to avoid possible legal issues; it can be leveraged to improve an employee's performance and to create a professional development plan or possibly reward outstanding performance.

Performance Appraiser Training

It is important for an organization to train performance evaluators to use appropriate appraisal methods because a performance appraisal is useful to the organization only if it is fair and accurate. This is because an organization's performance management process relies heavily on the ability of the organization to identify and eliminate performance problems. As a result, a performance appraisal must offer an accurate view of an individual's performance so the organization can accurately identify problem areas or performance issues and then improve these problem areas or handle these issues appropriately. However, there are a number of different factors, such as the evaluator's own biases or the appraisal process that the evaluator uses, that can influence a performance appraisal, so it can often be extremely difficult for a manager or supervisor to conduct an appraisal that is completely fair and accurate. Therefore, to make sure that each manager or supervisor conducts each appraisal as effectively as possible, the organization must train each manager or supervisor to use the appropriate set of appraisal methods.

Performance Feedback Techniques

How performance feedback is delivered plays a vital role in how it is received and subsequent outcome(s). First, whenever possible, feedback should be given in private, and always in a respectful manner. It is important to remember that feedback is not negative. Rather, performance feedback is an opportunity for a supervisor to discuss information that should help make the employee more productive and provide clear direction and priorities moving forward. This should be a two-way discussion and not a supervisor speaking at length to a silent employee. It is important for a manager not to come across as overbearing or cruel, but rather to approach feedback in a manner that is sincerely helpful. The manager giving feedback should actively listen to the employee and recap or clarify what the employee is saying if needed, as well as empathize with the employee's point of view.

A manager should be cognizant that the words being used to describe an undesired behavior are factual, not judgmental. For example, "Ann, could you just stop making so many errors on the same XYZ activity? Try harder!" is judgmental. However, "Ann, it seems there are some issues doing XYZ. What are your thoughts?" is better. A manager should be specific when providing feedback, both positive and negative. For example, "Derrick, you are doing a good job!" isn't specific; instead, a manager should say something like, "Derrick, your closing numbers are great, 35 percent above the department average and 98 percent customer satisfaction ratings. That's awesome!"

Performance Management Software

The performance management process needs to be effective to be productive. If the process is too cumbersome, then there is the risk it becomes a "check-the-box" routine and not as productive as it could be. The end goal is to improve the performance of employees. Many companies utilize various forms and formats of performance management software, both web-based and mobile, to augment the process for efficiency. Software can vary, but most tools enable the manager to easily keep a record of all performance-related discussions, track progress against goals, and illustrate how progress against goals is linked to the company's strategic objectives. Most also provide a way of capturing skills for each employee, which in turn can assist with succession planning in case an employee leaves the organization. Many even have the capability to facilitate 360-degree feedback between managers, employees, and peers. Additionally, the majority of software packages are capable of producing helpful dashboards that illustrate progress, as well as standard and customized reports to assist management when evaluating performance. Performance management software can be a stand-alone product or part of a more integrated and robust HR system.

Approaches to Recognition

Almost all employees have an innate desire to be **valued and appreciated** for their contributions. **Employee recognition programs** vary from firm to firm. However, they are most often used to motivate and reward achievements. The most common types of recognition include verbal praise, performance acknowledgements, employee of the month awards, length of service awards, or certificates for other achievements. **Rewards** may include thank-you notes, business paraphernalia, spot bonuses, gift cards, or extra time off. A combination of **tangible and intangible incentives** ensure that the program is valuable to all participants. Employee recognition programs can also be used to reinforce organizational expectations, attract and retain talent, increase productivity, improve quality and safety, and reduce absenteeism and turnover. Regardless of the methods chosen by an employer, a **formal written policy** should be published to describe the rewards that will be given, how they can be earned, and when they will be doled out. This policy will ensure fairness and consistency and increase the likelihood of desired behaviors being repeated.

PERFORMANCE OR SERVICE AWARDS

A common form of employee recognition comes in the form of a **service award**, which is a special kind of recognition given to an employee who has worked with an organization for a specific length of time. These pre-determined lengths of times are called **milestones**. Service awards are also called milestone awards, years of service awards, or service anniversary awards. The type of recognition that comes with the awards tends to increase as the employee becomes more tenured in the organization. For example, a first-year service award may be a certificate or a card. A 15-year service award might be a certificate with a $150 gift card. Some companies offer branded items as service awards instead of a gift card. There are many ways to structure a service award program. Service awards are a great way to recognize the organizational loyalty and commitment of an individual employee.

Another common form of employee recognition is a **performance award** based on productivity and efficiency in the workplace. This type of award takes the employee's overall performance into consideration. This can be done on a monthly, quarterly, or annual schedule, depending on how the program is set up. "Employee of the month" and "most improved performer" are common examples of performance awards. Performance awards can come in many different formats through gifts, certificates, paid time off, or company swag. Performance awards are a great way to recognize individuals for their contributions to the organization and also a great way to create motivation for others to perform their best.

SPOT AWARDS

An employee can be given a **spot award** as a recognition or reward for his or her contribution as it happens. These awards are also called "on-the-spot" awards, because they happen immediately when an employee goes above and beyond or exceeds expectations in a particular area. Spot awards can be given as an immediate form of recognition for contributions by individuals or teams. These awards can come in the form of small bonuses or cash incentives, but may also have no cash value, like additional time off or experiential rewards. For example, Logan puts in additional hours to complete a presentation for an executive after a co-worker had to step away because of an emergency, so he is recognized by his manager with a gift card to a local coffee shop. Spot awards are a great form of recognition because they are totally customizable and can be tailored for the individual and the situation. The organization has considerable leeway when creating a spot recognition program because the options are almost limitless. Spot awards are an excellent form of immediate feedback and encouragement for employees. They boost morale and demonstrate to the employees that their efforts are recognized and appreciated.

POINTS-BASED SYSTEM

Another type of recognition that can be offered to employees is a points-based recognition system. A **points-based system** is one where employees decide which reward they really want. Employees are awarded points based on a variety of factors, which can include attendance, referrals, safety observations, performance, training, and many more. These points can then be cashed in to obtain a reward. Companies may offer gift cards, branded apparel, paid time off, charity donations, tickets to local events, and many more. A points-based system could be difficult to track and monitor without software, plus there are many factors to consider, such as who will be able to award points, whether recognition will be public, what rewards will be available, and what determines if a behavior is worthy of points. There are numerous companies that offer points-based platform implementation and administration. Points-based awards allow employees to choose a reward that is most meaningful to them, making the reward more impactful. Points-based systems increase engagement, boost morale, and decrease turnover.

PEER-TO-PEER RECOGNITION

When appreciation or commendation is expressed between two colleagues of equal status within an organization, the parties involved are on an equal footing, and one does not manage or supervise the other. This **peer-to-peer recognition**, or simply peer recognition, helps foster an environment of trust and support while also motivating high performance. Organizations with high levels of peer recognition will likely have increased levels of job satisfaction and strong teamwork. Peer recognition can occur formally (such as an announcement on a Slack channel or other platform) or informally (such as a verbal kudos or compliment). Both methods are effective, and peer recognition often grows organically.

PERSONALIZED REWARDS

Recognition matters more when it is meaningful. **Personalized rewards** are rewards given to employees that are tailored to their specific needs, interests, and motivations. With so many options for how to recognize and reward employees, it is easy to pick a wide variety of items that may never be used. Personalized rewards allow employees to choose things that hold value to them. Personalized rewards can be something as simple as a card with a handwritten note that recognizes an employee individually for a contribution he or she made. Employees feel valued when they are recognized on a personal level.

Performance and Employment Activities

PROGRESSIVE DISCIPLINARY PROCEDURES AND APPROACHES

Disciplinary procedures often consist of several consequences, including training, correction, evaluation, punishment, and termination. The objective of a disciplinary action is to remedy a problem, with the goal of helping employees achieve success. **Maintaining order** can be accomplished with an appropriate accepted standard of conduct, fair evaluation procedures, and an order of progressively severe consequences for violators. Many organizations have adopted a **series of consequences** that begins with a verbal warning, which is followed by a written warning that future violations may carry penalties up to and including termination. Strong disciplinary systems protect employee rights and preserve the interests of the organization. It is important that employees are provided with enough time and opportunities to correct their behavior if they desire but also rigorous enough to discharge previously warned yet unresponsive and problematic employees.

Choosing the correct vehicle with which to begin progressive disciplinary procedure depends on the severity of the infraction, the employee's existing record of behavior, the longevity of the employee's service, and the established practice within the company for dealing with similar issues. Consistency is very important to avoid claims of discriminatory, retaliatory, or otherwise unfair practices.

CORRECTIVE ACTIONS

While all managers and human resource (HR) employees would love for 100% of their employees to be productive, well-behaved, and happy, the reality is that there will be issues. Effective managers deal with issues promptly, fairly, and consistently. **Corrective actions** are any steps that an organization employs to improve behavior or performance and prevent reoccurrence of poor behavior. Organizations should have documented policies and procedures in place that identify the standard steps of corrective action, while reserving the right to combine or skip steps, if necessary, based on the nature of the infraction. Below are some of the types of corrective actions that an organization may incorporate in its progressive discipline policy.

Counseling

Talking to an employee to address a small problem or concern is always a good first approach. This **counseling** can be an informal session before any formal discipline procedures begin. This can often fix small problems right away, without escalating the issue. This gives the employee and the manager or HR representative an opportunity to speak more informally about the situation and can help improve mutual understanding. The manager should clearly inform the employee of the behavior in question and the expected conduct. The consequences of future infractions should be clearly articulated. Counseling is different from a verbal warning in that counseling is appropriate when the infraction is not severe and the behavior can be remediated before it becomes a serious problem. If the informal counseling session does not produce the desired effect, it should be followed by a written letter to clarify the discussion.

Verbal Warning

The second stage in a progressive approach to discipline is a **verbal warning**. This can be the first step in the process if the offense is more serious and requires something more official than an informal counseling session. When issuing a verbal warning, the manager must clearly articulate the infraction, the required remedy, and the consequences of failure to comply. A written record of the verbal warning should be maintained but does not need be given to the employee. The manager may need documented proof that the verbal warning occurred if the problem persists. While a conversation can occur in this setting, this should be regarded as more straightforward and direct than a counseling session. The manager should leave no doubt in the employee's mind as to the nature of the offense and the expected behavior going forward.

Written Warning

The next step in progressive discipline is a **written warning**. This is appropriate if the situation is escalating or if the first offense was serious enough to warrant going straight to documented discipline. The written warning can be appropriate for a continuation of previously addressed behavior, or if new unacceptable behavior occurs. As with counseling and verbal warnings, the manager should state the offense clearly, articulate the expected remedy, and outline the consequences of repeating the behavior. Dependent on the infraction, it may be necessary to give an employee time to remedy the situation. For example, if the infraction is tardiness because the employee's home day care provider is consistently late, it may take time for the employee to hire a new provider. If this is part of the discussion, management may state that the employee has a pre-determined amount of time to improve the situation and therefore the behavior. However, if the infraction is abuse of others or inappropriate language in the workplace, immediate change may be required. The written warning is documentation that should be placed in the employee's file. Management may require or request that the employee sign a copy of the warning. This can help the employee understand the seriousness of the infraction. A refusal to sign does not alter the memo or the inclusion of the memo in the employee's file. In some circumstances, a manager may choose to issue a second written warning if they see improvement but the behavior is still not at an acceptable level.

Performance Improvement Plan

When issues with an employee impact the quality of his or her work or the dynamics of the workplace, and counseling, verbal, or written warnings have not remedied the situation, the manager needs to consider implementing a **performance improvement plan**. Managers can address two issues with performance with a performance improvement plan:

- **Quality of work.** If the employee is failing to achieve the individual goals and objectives in his or her performance plan, this is a quality-of-work issue. Management should work with the employee to ascertain whether the employee has the right training, tools, and support to do the job effectively. If all of these elements have been provided and the employee still fails to achieve, a performance improvement plan may be the next step.
- **Behavioral issues impacting the work environment.** If the employee's behavior is causing workplace issues with team members, management, vendors, or others, management can incorporate these concerns in a performance evaluation, making clear that failure to improve performance may result in a performance improvement plan. As always, management should ensure that negative information in a performance evaluation is not the first time that the employee becomes aware of the issue. Feedback, counseling sessions, and verbal and written warnings should have already taken place.

A performance improvement plan should be viewed as an opportunity to give an employee a chance to succeed. While it is typically part of a progressive discipline system, a well-developed performance improvement plan can facilitate improvement by providing clarity on deficiencies and creating opportunities for the employees to succeed. However, the plan should be carefully crafted and reviewed, as it may also serve as documentation of failure to perform and a step toward termination proceedings.

Demotion

Depending on the nature of the concerns, **demotion** is a step that is reserved for situations where other forms of disciplinary action have failed to achieve the desired results. There are two primary reasons to demote an employee:

- **Correct fit.** If an employee's behavior is egregious, demotion does not serve the organization well. The employee should be terminated to protect the company. However, in some situations, an employee may have been moved into a management position or a similarly situated leadership position where he or she simply does not have the skills to do the job well. This can be evident with excellent individual performers who are promoted to leadership positions but fail to rise to the occasion. Demoting an employee back to a non-supervisory position may serve both the organization and the employee well by allowing the employee to succeed in a position he or she is qualified for.
- **Failure to perform.** This type of demotion might be appropriate if a manager has an employee who is not performing at an acceptable level in his or her current position. The manager should first try counseling, training, mentoring, or a performance improvement plan to give the employee an opportunity to succeed. If the employee cannot be successful but has skills that are valuable to the organization and otherwise fits well in the company, a demotion to a position with fewer responsibilities or a skill requirement that better matches the employee may be the right answer.

If handled correctly by the organization and with the employee involved agrees, demotion can benefit the company culture by demonstrating management's commitment to the employees and to the element of fairness.

EMPLOYEE DEPARTURES

INVOLUNTARY TERMINATION

An involuntary termination may occur "with cause," meaning the employee did something unacceptable. This could be a performance issue, meaning the employee failed to meet quality or quantity standards, or it could mean the employee violated a policy or rule. While the majority of workers are at-will employees—meaning that either the employer or employee can end the employment relationship at any time—employers are prudent to ensure that employment laws are not violated when termination decisions are made. A best practice is to document the reason for the termination, including specific dates of any performance deficiencies and notations of prior warnings from supervisors. Furthermore, supervisors are prudent to follow past precedent, meaning similar performance deficiencies from other employees were treated similarly.

An involuntary termination is difficult for all parties. Supervisors can reduce the stress of the situation by properly preparing for the termination meeting. Once the situation has been investigated and properly documented, the supervisor should feel confident in the decision. Prior to the termination, the supervisor should write a script for the conversation. A termination meeting can be stressful; therefore, having notes prepared is helpful. It is also wise to arrange for a witness to the discussion, preferably an HR representative or a member of management. Since the decision was thorough and properly documented, the meeting discussion should be fairly brief, sticking to the reason for the termination. Post-meeting arrangements should be made for the employee to collect any personal belongings and return company property.

VOLUNTARY TERMINATION

Voluntary terminations or resignations occur frequently in organizations. Employees may accept another job, go back to school, or simply resign for personal reasons. Best practices to facilitate a voluntary termination include:

- Accepting a written resignation letter: The letter should include the reason for the resignation and the expected last day of work. Having these items in writing from the employee are beneficial in case the resigning employee files an unemployment claim later on.
- Conducting an exit interview: Gathering information from an exiting employee can reveal previously unknown facts to an employer. It can also provide insight into what the employee found positive about the organization.
- Engaging the employee in the process: Asking the employee to assist with training others on any duties and asking the employee how the resignation information should be shared with others is beneficial.
- Using a checklist for administrative items: While gathering company property, removing computer access, and managing payroll and benefit details, it can be easy to forget something that could cost the company later. Creating and using a checklist is beneficial.

VOLUNTARY SEPARATION

Voluntary separations or voluntary layoffs are used when an employer decides that layoffs are pending. Voluntary separations allow employees to "raise their hands" and be included in the layoff in exchange for a severance payment. Voluntary separations can provide a win-win solution in an otherwise tense scenario. For example, voluntary separation reduces risk for the employer. Since the employee completes paperwork stating that the separation is voluntary, the risk of a lawsuit is significantly reduced. Moreover, the employer can save time by not having to document involuntary layoff decisions. The voluntary separation can be positive for the employee as well. Potentially, it may be good timing for an employee if they are planning to leave the organization to seek different work or planning to leave the workforce entirely. The severance payment could incentivize an employee to voluntarily separate, leaving jobs available for those intending to stay long-term with the employer.

SEVERANCE

Severance is sometimes described as providing an employee "a package" for leaving an organization. Severance can come in a lump sum or in continuous payments for a period of time. Typically, severance includes an agreement signed by the employee and the employer that outlines the severance package details, including a section indicating that the employee releases the employer from future legal claims, as well as confidentiality requirements for both sides. The employer often uses legal counsel to draft and consult on the agreement, and the severance document will usually recommend that the employee obtain their own counsel as well. Severance agreements include a timeframe during which the employee can revoke their decision to accept the severance (and in some cases the law specifies a timeframe as well). Due to the complexity of severance agreements, it is beneficial to engage counsel.

Some employers have severance policies, which outline how much severance an employee receives based on the employee's tenure. Other employers have ad hoc severance protocols, meaning the severance amount varies for each situation. Severance is often used in reduction-in-force or restructuring scenarios. In these cases, severance amounts are usually consistent (based on years of service) across employees that are chosen for severance. Offering severance packages in this scenario reduces the risk of broad litigation. Employers may offer one-off severance packages to senior leaders who are being terminated, or in cases where there is high risk of the employee pursuing legal action. In these situations, the employer believes the cost of the severance is worth mitigating the risk.

APPROACHES TO RESTRUCTURING

RESTRUCTURING DURING MERGERS AND ACQUISITIONS

Human resource (HR) and change management professionals are often called on for consultation during **mergers and acquisitions**. This involvement should start at the beginning of the process and carry through to full integration. HR experts ordinarily investigate factors like employee benefit plans, compensation programs, employment contracts, and organizational culture. Experience and many studies have shown that issues with people and culture are the most frequent cause of failure in most mergers and acquisitions. HR departments must play an active role in these transitions, and there should be a unified purpose and message from each of the previous units. These steps have been established for joining two companies:

1. Develop a workforce integration project plan.
2. Conduct an HR due diligence review.
3. Compare benefits programs.
4. Compare compensation structures.
5. Develop a compensation and benefits strategy for integrating the workforce. Any reduction in pay or benefits must be explained and justified relative to the strategy or economic conditions. It is best to minimize changes and act quickly.
6. Determine leadership assignments.
7. Eliminate redundant functions. The best people should be retained, and the remainder should be laid off, with careful consideration given to avoid adverse impact and Worker Adjustment and Retraining Notification (WARN) Act violations.

Restructuring Through Downsizing

A firm may need to reduce the number of layers of management to increase efficiency or respond to changes in corporate strategy. This **restructuring through downsizing** can occur via layoffs or early retirement agreements.

Conducting a Layoff or Reduction in Force

The following are the steps for conducting a **layoff or reduction in force**:

- Select employees for layoff using seniority, performance, job classification, location, or skill.
- Ensure that selected employees do not represent a protected class, to avoid adverse or disparate impact.
- Review compliance with federal and state WARN Act regulations, which require employers to provide 60 days' notice to affected employees while specifying whether the reduction in force is permanent or for a set amount of time.
- Review compliance with the Older Workers Benefit Protection Act, which provides workers over the age of 40 with an opportunity to review any severance agreements that require their waiver of discrimination claims. The act allows a consideration period of 21 days if only one older worker is being separated, or 45 days when two or more older workers are being separated. The affected workers also must receive a revocation period of seven days after signing the agreement. Additionally, they must be informed of the positions and ages of the other employees affected by the layoffs so that they can assess whether or not they feel age discrimination has taken place.
- Determine if severance packages, including salary continuation, vacation pay, employer-paid Consolidated Omnibus Budget Reconciliation Act (COBRA) insurance premiums, outplacement services, or counseling might be available to affected employees.
- Be empathetic, have tissues, ensure that all required documentation is available, and review all information in detail when conducting meetings with employees.
- Inform the current workforce by communicating sustainability concerns, methods used to determine who has been selected for the reduction in force, and commitment to meeting company goals and objectives to maintain morale and productivity.

Attrition

Attrition, or **restrictive hiring**, is the act of reducing the workforce by not replacing individuals who leave an organization. Only absolutely essential roles that are critical to strategic business success are filled. Typically, attrition is used to avoid layoffs during times of financial burden. A **hiring freeze** is the least painful way to reduce labor costs. A *"hard" freeze* means that all open positions will remain open indefinitely, whereas a *"soft" freeze* means that only nonessential roles will remain open.

Risks and Alternatives to a Layoff or Reduction in Force

It is of utmost importance to remember that it could be considered illegal retaliation to consider any past grievances, complaints, claims, or leave requests in the selection process if a reduction in force is necessary. To ensure fairness and avoid risk exposure, **selection criteria** should include measurable data such as seniority, merit or skill set, full- or part-time status, location, job category, or prior disciplinary actions. Reductions in force are commonly due to financial strains on the organization. Thus, the goal is to reduce human capital costs by a percentage or specified dollar amount. Some measures that can be introduced as an **alternative to a reduction in force** include eliminating overtime, freezing or reducing compensation, reducing work hours, cutting perks, increasing employees' share of benefit costs, and imposing a hiring freeze.

Furloughs

If an organization is restructuring and identified temporary constraints within the organization, **furloughs** can be used to temporarily reduce the size of the company while it completes the restructuring. Furloughed employees are typically put on unpaid leave on a temporary basis. In most cases, they will continue to receive benefits such as healthcare, but an organization can save the cost of salaries while they take the time to address the financial crisis. This reduces the company costs while keeping employees in their jobs.

However, this does not guarantee that employees will be available when the company is ready to bring them back. Unpaid employees will usually seek work elsewhere if they are uncomfortable with the stability of the organization. Therefore, furloughs should be used sparingly.

Offboarding

The terms "onboarding" and "offboarding" evoke images of getting on and off a vessel for an ocean voyage. Employment is being compared to a journey on the ocean. The complexity of the voyage dictates the steps needed for the onboarding and offboarding processes. The same holds true for employment. Every organization wants the beginning and ending of employment to be a good experience. **Offboarding** is a process that includes all decisions and steps that need to be completed when an employee separates from an organization. Offboarding is also an opportunity to talk with an exiting employee about ways to improve the organization. It is important to remember that, when an employee leaves an organization, he or she could be a loyal supporter of the organization, or could speak negatively about the employer. Offboarding gives an employer one final opportunity to influence how the employee feels when they leave. A good offboarding process can help minimize the chance that potential ill feelings might linger. Offboarding leaves a lasting impression in the minds of employees separating from an employer.

Steps Included in the Offboarding Process

Employers' offboarding processes can differ depending on the organization and functions of a job. The following are some of the items that might be included in the offboarding process:

- Planning for the transfer of knowledge from the departing employee to their replacement (if appropriate)
- Reviewing final pay, benefits, and financial information, including retirement options, unused vacation, health coverage, and COBRA (if applicable)
- Collecting all computer equipment, phone, and other technology-related items
- Collecting other employer-issued items, such as uniforms, credit card, and automobile
- Collecting physical keys and security badges
- Deactivating access to company intranet and other systems (email, databases, etc.), as well as related rights and passwords
- Verifying accurate contact information—mailing address, phone number, and email address
- Conducting an exit interview—Usually done by an HR representative to understand the employee's viewpoint on their overall work experience and other concerns that will enable the organization to improve going forward

Employee and Labor Relations

Outreach and Diversity, Equity, and Inclusion (DEI)

APPROACHES TO AN INCLUSIVE WORKPLACE

First, identify any areas of concern. An internal workforce should reflect the available labor market. Examine the corporate culture and communications to ensure that they advocate for a diverse and inclusive workplace. Review or amend policies and practices to support an inclusive culture. Focus on the behavioral aspects, how people communicate, and how people work together. Are all perspectives respected and input from all positions valued? Address any areas that might not welcome protected classes or disabilities. Then brainstorm approaches and ideas for an **inclusive workplace**. Once a **diverse culture** is established, target recruiting efforts to reach a broad audience. Some ideas may include college recruiting, training centers, career fairs, veteran's offices, and state unemployment offices or career centers. Set business objectives for areas that can be improved upon, document what changes will be implemented, and review progress.

DIVERSITY TRAINING

Although we most often think of diversity as inclusiveness toward minorities, diversity also includes a robust variety of traits such as generation, language, religious background, education, or life experiences. Diversity truly shines when we are able to consider and value the perspectives of all people. It is important for HR practitioners to recognize that everyone has both conscious and unconscious biases. **Diversity and inclusion training** supports establishing a nonjudgmental and collaborative workforce that is respectful and sensitive to differences among peers. Additionally, it can teach humility and self-awareness. Training program methods may be extensive or address specific gaps. Moreover, diversity and inclusion training may introduce new perspectives to the workforce, promoting creativity and innovation.

MANAGING A MULTIGENERATIONAL WORKFORCE

HR practitioners must learn how to manage a **multigenerational workforce**. We currently have baby boomers nearing retirement, Generation X gaining experience, and millennials becoming leaders in the workforce. Finally, Generation Z has started to join the workforce. How can employers address the management needs of this multigenerational workforce and their diverse sets of values? The most obvious change in values is the **loyalty factor** of each generation. Baby boomers began their careers believing they might have only a few employers over the course of their working years, whereas Generation X workers are more likely to change employers frequently to gain experience and better salaries. Millennial and Generation Z workers show the least amount of loyalty to their employers. Instead, they want to define their own careers and work their way. Millennial workers are more **entrepreneurial**, and Generation Z workers are anticipated to flood the **freelance markets**. Work-life balance and the chance to make a difference are valued more in the younger workforce. In return, they bring more tech savvy, social media awareness, and adaptability. Many millennial workers desire **feedback** more frequently than annual reviews can provide; weekly or even daily one-on-one meetings can help motivate millennial workers and provide them with inspiration and direction. Many millennials want plenty of learning opportunities and a manager who is concerned with their **career growth**. Coaching, mentoring, and on-the-job training are often attractive qualities for this generation. Millennials may flourish when they have freedom for creative expression and clear areas of responsibility.

Demographic Barriers Encountered in Today's Workplace

The Civil Rights Act prohibits **discrimination based on country of origin, race, sex, or religion** regarding any employment condition, including hiring, firing, promotional advancements, transfers, compensation, or admissions into training programs. In spite of this barriers exist throughout the workforce. For instance, many women experience subtle forms of discrimination that limit their career advancement (referred to as the *glass ceiling*). It encompasses a host of attitudinal and organizational barriers that prevent women from receiving information, training, encouragement, and other opportunities to assist in advancement.

The Civil Rights Act does not protect sexual orientation, but in recent years, other legal actions at the federal level have come to protect those attracted to or married to the same sex. The EEOC has ruled that **gender identity discrimination** can be asserted as claims of sex discrimination under existing law. Preferential treatment for any particular gender or religious quality is strictly prohibited unless there is a bona fide occupational qualification. Customer preference is not a valid defense of discrimination against appearance, such as a Muslim woman wearing a hijab (headscarf), Rastafarian dreadlocks, Jewish sidelocks, or a Sikh's turban and uncut hair.

Supporting an LGBTQ Workforce

There has been increased attention on the rights of the **lesbian, gay, bisexual, transgender, and queer (LGBTQ) community** in recent years. Many states have expanded civil rights to include **discrimination protection** for sexual orientation of employees and applicants. In most cases, gender identity is also protected. On a national level, all US presidents since Obama have enforced **workplace regulations** to protect the LGBTQ community from discrimination. Employers should remain vigilant in adhering to local regulations while accommodating employee needs.

Workplace Accommodations

Accommodations for Disabilities

If a job candidate or employee is disabled, but otherwise qualified, the employer must make reasonable workplace accommodations. For the accommodation to be reasonable, it must not cause the employer undue hardship. Some examples of disability accommodation include making the building more accessible (via ramps, elevators, redesigned restrooms, etc.); altering work duties, location, or schedule; ordering assistive equipment (like a screen magnifier or standing desk); and modifying policies, performance assessment tools, and training materials. HR should create a policy detailing how accommodation requests should be made, how they will be evaluated, and what appeals process exists if the request is denied.

Accommodations for Religion

Employers must accommodate job candidates' or employees' sincerely held religious beliefs so long as doing so doesn't cause the company undue hardship. Possible religious accommodations include allowing time off for religious holidays and having different dress and grooming rules. HR should create a policy detailing how accommodation requests should be made, how they will be evaluated, and what appeals process exists if the request is denied.

Accommodations for Veterans and Active Military

Employers must accommodate disabled veterans in the same manner as they would any other job candidate or employee. There are two main laws—the Family and Medical Leave Act (FMLA) and the Uniformed Services Employment and Reemployment Rights Act (USERRA)—that protect the employment of veterans and active-duty military. Employers may choose, however, to provide additional accommodation to service members. While the employee is away serving, the firm could decide to continue paying for medical coverage and make up the difference in compensation between the salary and military pay. HR should create a policy detailing how accommodation requests should be made, how they will be evaluated, and what appeals process exists if the request is denied.

> **Review Video: Diversity and Inclusion**
> Visit mometrix.com/academy and enter code: 990195

AFFIRMATIVE ACTION PLANS

Affirmative action plans (**AAPs**) require employers to implement timelines that correlate with measurable goals to prevent discrimination and enforce **Executive Order 11246**. This order prohibits employment discrimination by federal contractors and subcontractors whose contracts exceed $10,000 per year or first-tier subcontractors whose contracts exceed $50,000 and have 50 or more employees. **Executive Order 11478** extended the same anti-discrimination provisions to employees of the federal government. Executive Order 11246 also established the **Office of Federal Contract Compliance Programs (OFCCP)** to monitor AAPs. The OFCCP uses many tools and analysis techniques to investigate possible discrimination. Coverage was again extended in 2013 to include individuals with disabilities. It is important to note that the statute of limitations to file a complaint with the OFCCP is 180 days.

WORKFORCE ANALYSIS

A workforce analysis is required in most affirmative action plans. This analysis results in a **workforce profile** that conveys the talent, knowledge, and skills of the current workforce. The first step is conducting an examination of the **demographics** in the current workforce. Then, a **gap and risk analysis** can be performed to determine any vulnerability. Anticipated changes to how work is performed and how advances in technology can have an effect are documented. Finally, future talent needs can be forecasted. Workforce profile data can be obtained voluntarily or through publicly reported statistics and census results. Workforce profiles calculate employee traits such as age, experience level, average education in the field, as well as status changes as active, full time, part time, or temporary. These might be reported per department, salary band, or as a whole.

TECHNIQUES TO MEASURE AND INCREASE EQUITY
DIVERSITY OF EMPLOYEES AT ALL ORGANIZATIONAL LEVELS

The first step in acknowledging diversity within each organizational level is to measure the diversity across the organization's hierarchy. Human resource (HR) analytics and metrics are key tools in this step. Using gender as an example, if an organization is 50 percent women and 50 percent men at entry-level positions, 40 percent women and 60 percent men at frontline-level manager positions, and 20 percent women and 80 percent men at mid- and upper-level management positions, the organization needs to assess why women are no longer being promoted or participating at the same rate as their male counterparts.

When assessing diversity across organizational levels, it is important to remember that there is no one universal cause or reason for representation drop-off, and HR professionals must dive deeper into data and employee perspectives to better understand and address diversity across organizational levels. In the example of gender in the workplace, a drop-off may exist because of a lack of childcare options that fit the greater responsibilities of higher positions, so women are turning down promotions or leaving the workforce. Alternatively (or additionally), there may be historically based discrimination or microaggressions that emerge at a certain level of the organization so that women qualified for positions at higher levels choose to leave the organization for more-inclusive companies. Each of these possible reasons for drop-off requires a unique approach to address and correct it in order to improve diversity across an organization's hierarchy.

Pay Audits

A **pay audit** is a tool that can be used to promote a greater commitment to **pay equity** and fair compensation practices. Organizations use pay audits to assess current compensation practices. Pay audits can help to reveal discrepancies in pay practices across similar functions and positions and help to identify if and how discrimination may be causing these discrepancies. By identifying pay discrepancies, employers can get a head start in correcting discriminatory compensation practices, show initiative in offering back pay if appropriate, identify the factors or individuals responsible for the discriminatory decisions, and seek correction by means of education, discipline, or other actions.

Pay Equity Reports

When a company makes a commitment to pay equity, it is committing to compensation practices that reward similar work, knowledge, and experience at similar rates regardless of an individual employee's specific diversity dimensions. In addition to making a commitment to pay equity, an organization can support its words with actions by performing and publishing the results of pay audits, including providing **pay equity reports**, banning pay history inquiries, and practicing transparency in compensation practices. Pay equity practices can help to build an organizational culture based on trust, honesty, and fairness, and to build a culture that treats diversity as a valued means to improved work outcomes and not just a box to be checked.

Pay Transparency

It is important that organizations be aware of and follow all legal **pay transparency** regulations, regardless of their internal pay equity policies and practices. During the recruiting phase, transparency laws may require the job to be posted with the minimum and maximum pay range; these requirements vary from state to state, so organizations should be aware of the compensation laws of their home state as well as any state they aim to hire or recruit from. When addressing pay transparency among active employees, organizations also need to take note that discussing pay rates and practices is generally considered a **concerted activity** protected by the **National Labor Relations Act (NLRA)**. Companies are not permitted to prohibit employees from comparing salaries or discussing the details of their pay or compensation.

Employee Surveys

Performing employee surveys can be helpful for gauging employee support, opinions, and perceptions of an organization, including any diversity, equity, and inclusion (DEI) projects, stances, or events. **Employee satisfaction surveys** can help to gauge employee opinion and overall perception of the organization. These surveys are also referred to as "opinion surveys" or "climate surveys." **Employee culture surveys** seek to measure how employee perspectives line up with the organization's overarching mission and goals. **Employee engagement surveys** can be utilized to determine how committed employees feel to the organizational mission as well as how motivated and driven they feel in their day-to-day work. There are four key characteristics to consider when utilizing employee surveys: design, medium, frequency, and follow-up. Surveys should have a clear design (measurable data, questions that have been proofread for grammar and effectiveness, etc.), be given in an appropriate format (in-person, online, etc.), be given at a reasonable frequency (quarterly, annually, etc.) for their goals, and have resources designated to address survey follow-up (acknowledging or announcing results, laying out and seeing through plans for change or improvement, etc.). Survey follow-up and results transparency are critical to enacting actual organizational change. Employees are more likely to participate in surveys if they feel their voices are being heard.

EMPLOYEE RESOURCE GROUPS (ERG)

Voluntary employee-led groups known as **employee resource groups (ERGs)** come together based on a shared interest or background. They also sometimes form at the request of an employer. ERGs typically focus on creating a diverse and inclusive workspace. ERGs can form around gender, disability, religion, or race. For example, an interfaith ERG might work to spread awareness of norms and practices of various faiths and cultures. This group might celebrate all religious holidays and seek to respect cultural and religious sensitivities. ERGs benefit both employees and the organization by creating diverse and inclusive environments with resources for support and development.

CORPORATE SOCIAL RESPONSIBILITY STRATEGY
DEVELOPING A BUSINESS CASE

A **business case** defines the rationale for a corporate strategy. Created by and for executive management, a business case should define why a **corporate social responsibility (CSR)** strategy is an integral part of the overall corporate mission, vision, and strategy. The push for CSR strategies is both philosophical and pragmatic. Philosophically, a CSR strategy needs to evolve past pure economic interests and serve the relationship with its wide swath of stakeholders. Pragmatically, CSR strategies align with the push for organizations to benefit and improve society in a public-facing way.

The business case should cover the following elements:

- A clear link to corporate financial performance
- Cost and risk reductions of implementation and maintenance of a CSR strategy
- The competitive advantage that a CSR strategy would offer the company against competitors
- The benefit to the organization's reputation with customers
- A stewardship model that ties social values and financial goals, recognizing the interdependence between the business and society

There will be no single justification for a CSR strategy, and the business case should articulate how a CSR strategy will improve the bottom line.

OBTAINING EXECUTIVE APPROVAL

While most organizations understand and acknowledge the need and desire for a CSR strategy, it can still be viewed as a financial burden to the company, so securing **executive approval** is challenging but essential. There are four recommended approaches to obtaining buy-in and approval from the executive team:

- Use case studies to demonstrate the success that other organizations have achieved by implementing CSR strategies.
- Emphasize value beyond the financial data to highlight positive results that the CSR strategy will generate.
- Look within the organization to identify areas of improvement that the company can focus on while implementing the CSR strategy to create added value.
- Focus on the raw data using studies that both demonstrate the benefit a CSR strategy can bring and the detrimental effects of an organization that customers consider irresponsible or non-responsive to social responsibilities.

CSR is a business practice that is both ethical and strategic, and executives must buy in to both elements for success.

SELECTING PARTNERS

As organizations implement CSR programs, it is incumbent upon the team to first identify initiatives in areas of work that are congruent with the CSR strategy. Many companies look to opportunities in the sustainability market, such as water stewardship, social justice, environmental sustainability, alternative energy sourcing, and clean technology initiatives. Selection criteria should be created for assessing candidates. When the investment categories are defined, organizations need to do due diligence to identify the best **partners** with whom to work. Several factors should be reviewed and considered, including:

- The partner's mission and vision and how they align with those of the organization
- How the partner and organization can collaborate to meet the CSR strategy and goals in a way that is complementary to both the partner and the organization
- The partner's performance record
- Local partners that can demonstrate value to the communities where the organization is located
- The partner's ability to commit to a long-term relationship
- Partners that are meeting the needs of the local community

Partners should be rated against the established criteria and rank-ordered for selection.

IDENTIFYING AND ANALYZING PERFORMANCE INDICATORS

Overarching **performance indicators** should be designed and developed in the CSR strategy and more in-depth when partners are selected and onboarded. All performance indicators should start with strong and clear goals from the CSR strategy and the partnership agreements. Key criteria developed for each partner to measure the success of the partnership should include:

- **Key performance indicators (KPI)** to measure specific impacts and accomplishments in the environmental or social cause that was established in the plan. These KPIs can be established by:
    - Benchmarks against high performance in the industry
    - Employee perspectives on company performance
    - Adherence to social policies
    - Recognition achieved
    - Number of community members impacted positively
    - Satisfaction ratio (employees, partner, and community)
- Level of transparency on progress toward goals
- Ability to maintain close alignment with the organization's CSR strategy
- Assessment of performance by the community

Measuring CSR performance is critical and should be documented and disseminated both for future improvement and for efforts such as recruitment, investment, and reputational benefits.

RECRUITING AND ORGANIZING PARTICIPANTS

Setting a CSR strategy and even enlisting partners are not sufficient for success. Organizations need to recruit and involve employees and community members to implement the programs and to ensure that the desired impact is recognized by the community. To involve employees, an organization can:

- Implement surveys to ask for employee input on what efforts or partnerships the organization should commit to.
- Ensure that employees are fully informed about the selection of partners and the performance of the programs.
- Ask for donations to include automatic payroll deductions, letting employees select which efforts they would like to support.
- Encourage volunteerism by offering time off to volunteer or organizing corporate outings in support of an effort.
- Ensure management sets an example by personally participating in programs.
- Recognize high performers who work in and contribute to the CSR programs.

To involve the community, an organization can:

- Ask community members to share knowledge, information, and experiences with the company and its employees.
- Ask for contributions to the efforts which helps to increase buy-in and commitment.
- Request feedback on perceptions of performance and areas of improvement.

CSR programs are successful when the preponderance of stakeholders are involved and invested in the success of the program.

COMMUNITY INCLUSION AND ENGAGEMENT

Community engagement involves creating partnerships through dedication and community involvement. Both the internal organization and external community are strengthened through an exchange of responsibility, knowledge, and services. As they enter the workforce, members of Generation Z are changing the way businesses strategize to attract and retain younger workers. This group in particular is drawn to organizations that are active in philanthropy and community engagement. Although **community engagement programs** are designed to help the populations they serve, they may also be used to teach staff sensitivity, greater understanding, and leadership skills through employee volunteerism. Advocates of corporate community engagement programs also find that they achieve triple returns, providing benefits to the charity or nonprofit organization in the form of free services, to the employees in the form of useful experience, and to the employer in the form of a more-cognizant workforce. Community engagement can also provide advantages in recruitment, teamwork, morale, retention, corporate brand, reputation, and sales.

REPRESENTATION ON COMMUNITY BOARDS

When local companies contribute executives and specialists to the community within which it operates, it can forge relationships, offer expertise, create partnerships, and forge future plans that are jointly beneficial to the community and the corporation. **Community boards** are a fundamental way for members to govern their communities. Boards have three primary functions:

- Establish policy
- Make strategic decisions
- Oversee community activity

Corporate representatives on a community board should contribute (not run), advise (not manage), and contribute to (not dominate) the discussion and decision-making process. Representatives should be viewed as partners rather than overseers to foster strong relationships and add benefits to the community.

Joint Community Projects

Corporate involvement in the local community can be highly impactful and beneficial to both the community and the organization. There are many avenues that firms can take in establishing **joint projects** with the community. Organizations can identify local issues within the community where the company can advocate for policy change, program development, or resources such as drug treatment programs, after-school programs, or pregnancy crisis centers. Investing in its employees who live in the local community is a strong part of helping employee develop skills and qualifications that can be used outside of work. Companies can embed values of volunteerism in the organizational culture by allowing employees some paid time off to do volunteer work. Better yet, an organization can create group volunteer efforts and sponsor a team to do a community project. Firms can sponsor local events, such as science fairs, that align with the company mission. There are many options, and the organization must take care to be consistent and genuine in their efforts.

Employee Volunteerism

There are many companies that have implemented **volunteer programs** to encourage their employees to participate in charitable activities; some provide employees with supplemental time off during work hours. Employers may also set up community service days when the business closes or runs with a reduced crew and donates time to help the community. This could include stocking shelves in a food pantry, cleaning up a local park, or visiting sick children in the hospital. Leadership may also decide to join the board of directors for community organizations that matter to them. Whereas many companies will create **guidelines** of acceptable activities or reject things like hours spent participating on political campaigns, others might attempt to diversify local, national, and global support. The bottom line is that the firm must decide which causes and organizations to support. Some employers will also impose **exclusions**, such as limiting eligibility to employees with satisfactory performance, or requiring manager approval to ensure that time off will not conflict with scheduling or productivity.

These programs are intended to help the communities they serve, but they also help employees develop **soft skills**. Understanding, sensitivity, empathy, collaboration, communication, and leadership are some desirable workplace traits that are cultivated by volunteer activities. Moreover, organizations that are able to make a connection between volunteer programs and diversity will provide opportunities to build an inclusive workplace, cultural competence, and an ability to get along with individuals from diverse backgrounds. Information about volunteer programs, including how to sign up, and rules for scheduling time to participate in advance, should be clearly communicated. Although participation can be encouraged, human resources (HR) and leadership must keep these programs strictly voluntary and not pressure staff into taking part. The benefits of donating time or money are that it feels good, it puts the firm in a favorable light, and it helps others. Additionally, offering ways to give back can be a morale booster and a means to recruit and retain talent.

Corporate Philanthropy and Charitable Giving

The elements of **corporate social responsibility** differ greatly; some may emphasize philanthropy, donating a percentage of profits to charity, or volunteering activities. Organizations often find philanthropy and charitable work financially rewarding, especially when synchronizing business strategies to cause agendas. Not only can **corporate philanthropy** increase revenues, but it has also been known to boost morale and employee engagement. The corporate culture surrounding philanthropy and charitable giving should be covered during new-hire orientations. Employees should feel empowered to identify opportunities and explore creative ways to solve challenges efficiently. HR practitioners can support corporate philanthropy to demonstrate good values, build image, and foster a sense of efficiency. Volunteers serve as **philanthropic representatives of the company** in the community and can have a strong impact on the public. However, every company will need to determine the best approach for corporate philanthropy that aligns with organizational goals and values. Employers can set up payroll deductions so that employees can easily donate to causes that they support. The employer may also elect to match the employee's contributions.

US Federal Health, Safety, Security, and Privacy Laws

OSHA

The **Occupational Safety and Health Act** of 1970 mandates that it is the employer's responsibility to provide an environment that is free from known hazards that causes or may cause serious harm or death to employees. The only workers who are not protected by this act are those who are self-employed, family farms where only family members work, and workplaces that are covered by other federal statutes or state and local government. This act is monitored and enforced by the **Occupational Health and Safety Administration (OSHA)**. OSHA ensures that employees have a safe workplace free from recognized hazards. It also requires all employers and each employee to comply with occupational safety and health standards, rules, and regulations. Employers may be found in violation if they are aware or should have been aware of potential hazards that could cause injury or death.

Preventing workplace illness and injury includes training employees, following OSHA standards, and being mindful of and preparing for the potential hazards typically seen in the line of duty.

IDENTIFICATION OF HAZARDS

Every organization has an obligation to identify, inspect, and maintain **hazardous materials** in a way that prevents worker injury or death. OSHA recommends six steps to identify and assess hazardous materials:

1. Collect and maintain current information about all workplace hazards and materials.
2. Inspect the workplace regularly for any safety hazards, concerns, or potential risks.
3. Identify any materials that present a hazard to employee health.
4. Conduct immediate investigations into any incidents or accidents that occur.
5. Identify hazardous materials required for non-routine tasks or emergency situations.
6. Identify control measures and prioritize the hazardous materials for control.

Some hazardous materials, such as cleaning supplies or equipment, may be used on a daily basis. Other materials, such as fire extinguishers or chemicals for annual machine maintenance, may be used only infrequently or in emergency situations. All of these materials must be listed and inspected, and have control mechanisms in place for handling the material in use and handling the fallout of an accident or incident. Above all, the safety of the employees should be the primary concern.

REPORTING OCCUPATIONAL INJURIES

OSHA requires that any occupational injury or illness be **recorded** if it results in medical treatment that goes beyond first aid, restricted work activity or job transfer, time away from work, loss of consciousness, or death. An incident that results in an inpatient hospitalization must be reported within 24 hours, and any incident resulting in an employee's death must be reported to the nearest OSHA office within eight hours. For each recordable injury or illness, an **OSHA Form 301 Injury** and Illness Incident Report must be completed within seven calendar days. Employers are obligated to keep a log of all incidents on an **OSHA Form 300 Log of Work-Related Injuries and Illnesses**, and a concise report of annual incidents should be reported on an **OSHA Form 300A Summary of Work-Related Injuries and Illnesses** at the end of each year. Form 300A must be posted where all employees can find it on February 1 through April 30, and all documentation should be kept for five years so that it is available on request for examination. Any procedure or doctor's visit that can be labeled as first aid does not need to be recorded. However, any needle-stick injury, cut from a sharp object contaminated with another person's blood, or incision that requires stitches should be reported.

SAFETY TRAINING PROGRAMS

Most organizations can follow a series of basic steps to create an effective **safety training program**. First, a safety risk assessment is conducted to determine the safety hazards present in the workplace. Then each hazard is investigated to determine if training will help to eliminate the dangers associated with the hazard. If so, information that each employee needs to know about the hazard should be identified, and a series of training goals and objectives based on these needs can be established. Once training goals have been established, a training program can be created and implemented, and then the results can be evaluated.

WORKPLACE INJURY OR ILLNESS INVESTIGATION

When an employee is injured on the job or becomes ill as a result of completing work duties, the employer must **investigate** the incident to understand why it happened. This investigation should identify ways to prevent similar incidents from occurring in the future. An employer's internal investigation should entail interviewing the sick or injured employee, assessing that employee's immediate work environment, and interviewing other employees who may have witnessed the incident or worked under the same conditions. An **OSHA Form 301 Injury and Illness Incident Report** should be completed for all recordable incidents. In addition, employers may want to document the incident further for internal purposes. If that is the case, they should create a standardized form for collecting the details to ensure that each investigation is conducted in a similar fashion and that no important information gets overlooked. Sometimes, OSHA will investigate an employer. These investigations may occur either onsite or offsite.

WORKERS' COMPENSATION

Individuals who sustain work-related injuries are eligible for coverage of medical expenses and a continuation of income through the **workers' compensation** program. The program makes compensation and expenses the employer's responsibility without liability or fault to the employee, assuming that the employee has adhered to reasonable safety precautions. Each state administers its own workers' compensation program according to state and federal laws. There are three types of workers' compensation benefits awarded to employees: medical expenses, wage replacement payments, and death benefits. Wage replacement payments are often calculated based on an employee's average weekly wages and become available after a waiting period. Costs are determined by an experience rating based on an employer's claim history.

EMERGENCY RESPONSE

PREPARING FOR EMERGENCIES AND NATURAL DISASTERS

Because it is an employer's obligation to provide a safe and healthy work environment, many companies have begun to create **emergency and disaster plans** for handling situations such as fires, explosions, earthquakes, chemical spills, communicable disease outbreaks, and acts of terrorism. These plans should include the following steps:

1. Clarify the **chain of command**, and inform staff who to contact and who has authority.
2. Someone should be responsible for **accounting** for all employees when an emergency strikes.
3. A **command center** should be set up to coordinate communications.
4. Employees should be **trained annually** on what to do if an emergency strikes.
5. Businesses should have **first-aid kits and basic medical supplies** available. This includes water fountains and eye wash stations in areas where spills may occur.
6. An **emergency team of employees** should be named and trained for the following:
    a. Organizing evacuation procedures
    b. Initiating shutdown procedures
    c. Using fire extinguishers
    d. Using oxygen and respirators
    e. Searching for disabled or missing employees
    f. Assessing when it is safe to reenter the building

EMERGENCY ACTION PLANS

There is certain information that should be included in every organization's emergency action plan. All emergency action plans should explain the alarm system that will be used to inform employees and other individuals at the worksite that they need to evacuate. They should also include in-depth exit route plans that describe which routes employees should take to escape the building, and in-depth plans that describe what actions employees should take before evacuating: shutting down equipment, closing doors, and so on. All emergency action plans should also include detailed systems for handling different types of emergencies and a system that can be used to verify that all employees have escaped the worksite.

FIRE PREVENTION PLANS

The specific information included in a fire prevention plan will vary from organization to organization. However, certain information should be in every organization's fire prevention plan, including detailed descriptions of the following:

- The specific areas where employees can find fire extinguishers and other fire prevention equipment
- The types of fire hazards present in the workplace
- Appropriate procedures that should be followed to avoid these fire hazards
- Any hazardous waste that may be a fire hazard and the appropriate way to dispose of or store hazardous waste to avoid a fire

EMERGENCY RESPONSE PLANS

All emergency response plans should identify the records and resources essential to the organization, identify the individuals responsible for protecting those records and resources, and describe the procedures that individuals should follow to safeguard the records and resources essential for the organization to continue functioning. Emergency response plans must also establish a system the organization can use to continue communicating with vendors and the public during and after an emergency.

Disaster Recovery Plans

Certain information should be included in every organization's disaster recovery plan. The plan should identify equipment and locations that can be utilized temporarily in the event of an emergency. It should also identify agencies and personnel that may be able to help the organization continue functioning immediately after an emergency. It is also wise to establish a set of procedures the organization can use to bring the personnel and equipment together after an emergency. Additionally, disaster recovery plans should identify alternative sources the organization can use to receive supplies or products if the emergency disables the organization's normal supply chain.

Business Continuity Planning and Recovery

Business continuity planning is a process in which an organization attempts to ensure the organization will be able to continue functioning even after an emergency. This type of planning is important because there are a large number of emergencies that an organization can face, and each one may affect the ability of the organization to continue functioning normally. As a result, business continuity planning is a process that organizations use to create a plan or group of plans that will help the organization return to normal after a natural disaster or similar emergency occurs. The process of business continuity planning usually begins with an organization conducting a threat assessment such as a SWOT analysis. Once the organization has identified the threats that exist, the organization can rank those threats based on the risk associated with each threat. Finally, the organization can create a plan or set of plans that establish a system the organization can use to recover from emergencies, which the organization can continually update as threats to the organization change.

> **Review Video: Emergency Response, Business Continuity, and Disaster Planning**
> Visit mometrix.com/academy and enter code: 678024

Substance Abuse

Many employees may be involved in or suffering from **alcoholism and drug abuse**. These problems are long-term, and employees may need help correcting these behaviors. Alcoholism is now a **protected disability** under the American with Disabilities Act (ADA). The act does not protect employees who report to work under the influence, nor does it protect them from the consequences of their actions or blatant misconduct.

Problems caused by drug abuse are similar to those caused by alcoholism. However, additional problems associated with drug abuse are the likelihood of stealing due to the high cost of the employee's habit, and its illegal nature. The ADA does not protect current drug use as a disability.

Drug-Free Workplace Act

The **Drug-Free Workplace Act** of 1988 requires that government contractors make a good-faith effort to ensure a drug-free workplace. Employers must prohibit illegal substances in the workplace and must create drug awareness trainings for employees. Any federal contractor with contracts of

$100,000 or more must adhere to a set of mandates to show that they maintain a drug-free work environment. Employer responsibilities include:

- Develop a **written policy** prohibiting the production, distribution, use, or possession of any controlled substance by an employee while in the workplace.
- Develop **standards of enforcement**. All employees must receive a copy of the policy and understand the consequences of a violation.
- Implement **drug awareness trainings** to help employees understand the hazards and health risks of drug use.

Although drug testing is not required, employers should have some type of **screening** in place.

CAUTIONARY MEASURES WHEN DESIGNING DRUG TESTING PROGRAMS

Many employers utilize drug testing to screen applicants and, in some cases, current employees. Generally speaking, employers can legally require applicants to pass a **drug test** as a condition of employment or adopt programs that test active employees, as long as the programs are not discriminatory. Due to the controversial nature of drug-testing programs, employers must be meticulously cautious when designing these programs, to ensure that their practices will be upheld if brought to court. *Wilkinson v. Times Mirror Corporation* established the following elements for testing programs:

- Samples are collected at a medical facility by persons unrelated to the employer.
- Applicants are not observed by others when they furnish samples.
- Results are kept confidential.
- Employers are only informed by the medical lab whether the applicant passed or failed.
- Applicants are notified by the medical lab of any portion they failed—in some cases, applicants will haves an opportunity to present medical documentation prior to the employer receiving the results.
- There is a defined method for applicants to question or challenge test results.
- Applicants must be eligible to reapply after a reasonable time.

MEDICAL MARIJUANA

As with drug screening, there are no accommodations required by federal law to allow the use of **medical marijuana**, but some states do have laws in place protecting its use. Employers should review their policies to see if they violate any obligations under state disability accommodation or leave laws. The Americans with Disabilities Act (ADA) requires employers to enter into discussions about reasonable accommodations with workers with disabilities. The goal is to determine if a worker can perform the essential functions of his or her job. The Family and Medical Leave Act (FMLA) requires employers to allow time off for medical treatment for qualified employees. While medical marijuana use is not covered under either the ADA or FMLA and all marijuana use is still deemed illegal under federal law, courts have been reviewing the use of medical marijuana in some states. The initial set of cases have been ruled in favor of employers; however, employers must ensure that corporate drug-testing and screening policies are in line with emerging laws in the states in which they operate. Employers should identify if an employee has appropriate medical certification, if drug test results are tied to medicinal use, and if the use of medical marijuana will pose a risk in the workplace.

TREATMENT OF SUBSTANCE ABUSE

Employers are putting more and more effort into providing resources and other assistance to employees who are dealing with substance abuse problems. Substance abuse costs an organization time and money due to lost productivity, workplace violence, legal liability, and turnover. Some of the ways that employers have responded by expanding resources and services include:

- Expanding existing treatment options through Employee Assistance Programs to lower barriers to seeking care
- Offering telehealth services to ensure easier access to assistance
- Working with their insurance providers to offer physical therapy and chiropractic visits for employees to reduce dependency on pain medication
- Encouraging openness in the workplace to remove the stigma of substance abuse issues by having leaders share stories of past challenges
- Communicating more aggressively and visibly about the resources available to employees
- Working with the corporate health insurance organizations to ensure that there are providers for the employees who are available and seeing new patients
- Expanding coverage options for employees who work remotely to ensure adequate coverage

Substance abuse takes a big toll on the employee and the employer. Employers can create **Workplace Supported Recovery** programs to prevent substance abuse issues or assist employees with treatment. Support for treatment of substance abuse issues needs to be built into the culture of the organization.

INVESTIGATIONS

When an employee files a complaint, or when a manager has concerns about an employee, the human resources (HR) team should take immediate steps to begin an **investigation**, protect the parties involved, and address any conflict. These prompt investigations can help the organization identify internal issues, resolve conflict, and demonstrate its commitment to both the employees and the corporate goals and values.

CONSISTENCY

As soon as an investigation is initiated, a plan must be established to guarantee that all subsequent actions are effective and compliant with the organization's process for investigations. It is critical that the organization have a documented process for investigations to ensure that all steps are taken, properly documented, handled by the correct company representative, and, most critically, are **consistent** for all investigations. Using a **checklist** can be very effective in ensuring consistency. This will allow all investigations to be through and objective. HR should be able to demonstrate objectivity and unbiased actions in all investigations. Modifying the process, skipping steps, or otherwise adapting the process for any individual investigation could lead to complaints of biased behavior, which could taint the investigation.

INTERVIEW PLAN

The investigation interview process should be captured in an **interview plan**. The plan should include:

- **Questions.** Interview questions should be designed in advance of the session. Questions must be relevant to the issue and should be open-ended to elicit information. New questions may arise as new information is gathered during the process. These additional questions should be documented and added to the plan.
- **Confidentiality.** Confidentiality is of utmost importance to protect the rights of the employees involved. Interviewers and interviewees must be assured of confidentiality in the process.

- **Objectivity**. The interviewer must be impartial, gather data objectively, and be careful to not lead the interviewee. Results of the interviews should be captured per the plan and reported back to the lead investigator without the interviewer's opinions or viewpoints.

Creating and documenting a plan creates objectivity. Abiding by the plan adds credibility to the process.

Employee Misconduct Investigations

An **employee misconduct investigation** usually begins when a complaint is received or there is other reasonable cause to investigate an employee's conduct. The organization should identify exactly what is being investigated, what sort of evidence is needed to prove or disprove the misconduct, who should be interviewed during the investigation, and which questions need to be asked to gather the necessary evidence. Next, the organization needs to interview the person making the complaint, the individual the complaint is against, and any other employees who may have relevant information. Finally, the organization should come to a decision and take the appropriate action.

Weingarten Rights

In *NLRB v. Weingarten*, the Supreme Court established the right of employees to have **union representation** at investigatory interviews in which the employee must defend conduct or behavior. If an employee believes that discipline or other consequences might follow, he or she has the right to request union representation. However, management does not need to inform an employee of their **Weingarten rights**. It is the employee's own responsibility to know and request representation. When an employee requests representation, management can a) stop questioning until a representative arrives, b) terminate the interview, or c) ask the employee to voluntarily relinquish his or her rights to representation. The company does need to inform the representative of the subject of the interview, and the representative does have the right to counsel the employee in private and advise him or her on what to say.

Summary Report

When the investigation is completed, the investigator should prepare a final **summary report**, including an executive summary to capture the findings. A summary report should identify the following:

- The incident or event, including relevant dates, times, and locations
- The names, titles, and contact information of the employees or outside parties involved, if the investigation extended beyond the company
- The key facts and findings that were deemed credible and relevant to the investigation, with sources identified where appropriate
- Any company policies or procedures that were applicable to the situation
- The conclusions of the lead investigator, with objective language
- The names, titles, and contact information for the corporate leadership who were the final decision-makers on the outcome of the investigation
- If the situation was not resolved, the reasons for the lack of resolution
- Any actions taken by the employer that resolved the situation, held an employee accountable, or otherwise disciplined an employee

Ultimately, any documentation could potentially be referenced in any court proceeding that might occur because of the investigation. Investigators should present their findings in the report in an objective manner.

COMPLIANCE AND ETHICS PROGRAMS

Companies should design **compliance and ethics programs** to prevent and detect illegal and unethical conduct within an organization. Programs developed for training and development should be designed and implemented by professionals trained in the subject matter. The features below should all be addressed when planning programs for compliance and ethics training.

DESIGN

Programs to address compliance and ethics are more than just training. While training the employees is a critical element, the overall program must be more comprehensive. A strong compliance and ethics program should include the following elements:

- **Written standards of conduct.** The organization must publish standards for employee actions and behaviors. Without these, the company cannot ask its employees to adhere to ethical conduct.
- **Training on the standards of conduct.** Having written standards is good but not enough. The company must actively train employees, and document the training, to ensure that employees know and understand the standards and see the company's commitment to upholding the standards.
- **Company resources for advice on ethics issues.** Most organizations provide hotlines or other methods for employees to anonymously ask sensitive questions or report concerns or issues. These resources should be publicized so that all employees know where to go if they have a concern.
- **A process to report potential violations confidentially or anonymously.** Not only should there be a vehicle for employees to ask for advice or report issues, but there must also be a process by which an employee can appropriately escalate issues. **Whistleblower** programs can guide an employee through specific steps to receive legal whistleblower protections.
- **Performance evaluation requirements for ethical conduct.** If ethics are critical to an organization and an essential component of the culture and behavior, then employees should be evaluated on their commitment to ethical behavior. There should be a measurable goal for ethical conduct on every employee performance evaluation.
- **A system for disciplining violations.** If ethical conduct is evaluated, there must be consequences or ramifications for not meeting the organizational standards.

IMPLEMENTATION

A training plan must be **implemented** to be effective. Training is typically part of a new hire orientation program to ensure that all new hires are fully versed in the standards of conduct, the process and system for reporting issues or concerns, and the ramifications for failing to live up to the company conduct standards. Depending on the size and complexity of the organization, new hire orientation may be done in person or online, but each employee should be required to sign a document to verify that they have received the training.

Training should be repeated on an annual basis to remind employees of the content or update them on changes to the program. Again, dependent on the size and complexity of the organization, this can be done in-person or online, with a record of compliance with the training. The employee should walk away from the training with a full understanding of the company's commitment to compliance and ethics.

REQUIRED POSTERS

The US Department of Labor requires workplaces to post certain information in an area that is open and visible to employees There are both federal and state requirements, and it is the responsibility of the organization to know and comply with the posting requirements. Some of the **required posters** are:

- Job Safety and Health
- Employee Rights and Responsibilities under the Family and Medical Leave Act
- Know Your Rights
- Pay Transparency Nondiscrimination Provision
- Employee Rights Under the Fair Labor Standards Act

MEASURES OF PERFORMANCE

As with training, a compliance program is only as good as its enforcement, which includes **measures of performance**. Measuring performance in compliance is straightforward: organizations must comply with federal, state, and local requirements. These requirements can be itemized and reviewed for compliance. For example, human resources (HR) must post certain workplace posters, and a quick physical review can assess if they have complied.

Ethics is a more difficult area in which to measure performance and rate compliance. One of the most effective ways to do this is to have ethics as a stated goal on performance reviews. There should be a statement that lays out what compliance with the ethics program looks like, and managers should observe and assess compliance. Additionally, HR can provide input if employees have been confidentially coached or counseled about an ethics-related situation. It is critical to keep ethics concerns or complaints against specific employees confidential.

Organizations must have a dedicated department or, at a minimum, compliance and ethics performance officials whose responsibility it is to measure and report compliance.

Organizational Policies and Procedures

IMPORTANCE OF HR POLICIES AND PROCEDURES

An **HR policy** is a set of rules that all members of an organization are required to follow, whereas an **HR procedure** covers the steps necessary to implement a policy. Basically, policy states what rules must be followed in an organization, while procedures detail in writing how to adhere to organizational policies. For an organization to be successful, HR policies and procedures should contain the following core elements:

- Employee role descriptions that detail employee expectations specific to each position in an organization
- Rules and regulations that specify what employees can or cannot do, as well as behavior that is or is not acceptable
- A clear description of consequences for unethical or inappropriate behavior or actions

There are many reasons why an organization needs to have HR policies: (1) They give people defined rules to achieve a respectful environment, (2) they reduce conflict and provide an organization with a certain standard to guide acceptable behavior, and (3) they assist an organization in forming an image in the community that is also helpful for recruiting.

Communicating Human Resource Programs, Practices, and Policies to Employees

Human resources (HR) will not achieve much success in initiatives, policies, and programs if they are not properly communicated. Policies should be communicated throughout the onboarding process, whenever changes occur, and as often as the organization believes a revisit is necessary. Employees should be given access to updated copies of policies when changes are made. Compliance items or employment-contingent items should require a signature and be kept on file. HR programs should be advertised. This can be through Slack channels, on the organization's intranet, or even posted on a bulletin board. HR should send out regular communications on policy or program changes. Keeping employees informed about HR-driven material helps build an informed, engaged, and compliant workforce.

Opt-In/Opt-Out Policies

Opt-in and opt-out are both ways to gain consent for a particular policy. To **opt-in** requires a positive action to confirm consent, participation, or agreement. For example, an opt-in policy might require checking a box to acknowledge consent to a policy or procedure during digital onboarding. An **opt-out** policy requires an action to withdraw consent, participation, or agreement. An example of an opt-out policy is requiring employees to fill out a waiver when declining benefits coverage.

Distribution and Collection of Company-Mandated Documents

A company should distribute company-mandated documents to new hires on their first day of employment. Employees should be required to sign off indicating that they have received, read, and understood each document.

Employee Handbook and Policy Acknowledgements

A company should distribute an employee handbook or policy manual to new employees at the beginning of employee orientation so that new hires can become familiar with company policies and procedures right away.

The handbook can be printed, emailed, or posted to the company intranet in a manner that all employees can access. Employees should be provided with time to review each document and ask questions before signing an acknowledgement that will be stored in their personnel file.

Nondisclosure or Other Agreements

An employee handbook isn't a contract and doesn't extend to former employees. Any policy that needs to extend beyond an individual's employment and/or be legally binding should be presented to employees as a formal agreement that they're required to sign, separate from the employee handbook or policy manual.

A nondisclosure agreement (NDA) is an example of a document that companies often require employees to sign separate from the handbook or policy manual. The purpose of an NDA is to protect the confidentiality of important company information, such as client lists, marketing strategies, and product formulations. This type of document is particularly important for employees with access to proprietary information.

Other documents that employers often require employees to sign as standalone agreements may include, but are not limited to, a noncompete agreement, privacy policy, anti-harassment policy, or code of ethics. Signed agreements should be kept in each employee's personnel file.

BENEFITS PAPERWORK

New employees should be provided with benefits paperwork on the first day of orientation, including details about each plan. Depending on what the company offers, this may include information about the company's health insurance, retirement plan, life insurance, dental plan, vision coverage, cafeteria plan for health and dependent care expenses, and available supplemental group benefits.

Benefits paperwork may be distributed in print or digital form. It should include:

- Plan details
- Cost
- Eligibility
- Enrollment forms

New employees should be given a few days to review the information so they can make an informed decision on which benefits they want. They should also be informed of the company's open enrollment date, so they'll know how long they'll have to wait to opt in on any benefits that they decline at this time. The company should collect their benefits enrollment paperwork, along with documentation that specifies any benefits they are declining.

SOPs

A **standard operating procedure (SOP)** is a collection of step-by-step instructions put together by an organization to help employees perform routine tasks and duties. **SOPs** aid in quality assurance, consistency, efficiency, and uniformity of output from employees. The use of this tool helps to minimize miscommunication and errors. Internal processes and procedures are clearly outlined to keep all employees and stakeholders on the same page. **SOPs** improve employee training and onboarding because key tasks are clearly defined with work instructions, eliminating guesswork and uncertainty. They also help maintain organizational knowledge as turnover and promotions occur. These instructions are documented so that there is no confusion or loss of understanding as people move in and out of a department or company.

Employee Complaints, Concerns, and Conflicts

ELEMENTS OF COMMUNICATION

Communication is defined as the practice of exchanging information, data, ideas, and opinions. There are many models that depict complex **communication processes**. However, almost all communications will include some variety of these fundamentals: source, sender, encoding, message, channel, receiver, decoding, and feedback. The **sender or source** chooses, creates, and encodes the message. The **receiver** decodes and interprets the message. In between, the message must be **transmitted** through some communication channel or medium like phone, text, email, video, or broadcast. Communication messages often pass through **noise barriers** such as environmental sounds, people speaking, traffic, and construction. Removing these barriers can decrease instances of misunderstanding and confusion. **Feedback** allows the model to be interchangeable, allowing for communication to flow both ways.

GENERAL COMMUNICATION TECHNIQUES
PLANNING COMMUNICATIONS

Delivering messages can be difficult, especially if the context is serious. The message content should be tailored to fit the audience. This requires understanding the roles, expectations, and perspective of recipients. First, focus on eliminating any barriers or vague wording that may interfere with interpreting the message. Once the proper channel for delivery is selected, it may be important to focus on nonverbal signals and ensure that they coincide with the mood of the message content. Finally, messages should allow for feedback that will lead to follow-up discussions. If a message is complex, such as a business change or new benefits offering, it may be critical to share repeated reminders and have open lines of communication to reduce confusion and ensure success.

ACTIVE LISTENING

Active listening is an important component of communication that requires paying close attention to what is being said. It often involves making eye contact and appropriately nodding to show engagement. To gain a better understanding, listeners should try to understand things from the speaker's point of view, or visualize what they are saying. It is important to be considerate, avoid distractions or interruptions, and respond appropriately. Additionally, listeners should try to pick up on emotional cues beyond the literal words that are used. Even if the message differs from the active listener's own opinion, the listener will try to focus on accepting what the other person has to say rather than being critical. Active listeners should make sure to fully hear what the other person is saying before formulating their own response. When compared to passive listeners, active listeners are more connected and conscientious.

COMMUNICATION TECHNIQUES FOR SPECIALIZED SITUATIONS

GIVING FEEDBACK

Feedback can be written or verbal and should be based upon factual data. Although the process can be emotional, it's important that feedback be constructive in nature, detailing the quality of someone's performance or conduct without judging on a personal level. Effective feedback should be delivered in a timely, consistent, and positively framed manner. If informal, feedback can be used to give advice or to provide clarity. If disciplinary, the feedback should also include required improvements to be made and potential consequences for not meeting the standard. When receiving feedback, take the time to carefully consider it and implement it as appropriate. The most important thing to remember about feedback is why it's being given: to facilitate an improvement.

FACILITATING FOCUS GROUPS

Focus groups can be used to investigate ideas, opinions, and concerns. **Focus groups** can be beneficial for clarifying supplemental research because they are relatively timely and inexpensive. The topic and objectives of the group should be clearly defined before potential participants are identified. Participants should be notified that their identities will be anonymous and that all information will be confidential. Once a **pool of participants** has been selected and separated into groups, a trained **facilitator** should be chosen, and a guide with discussion questions should be constructed. Most studies will contain 3–10 focus groups, each with 5–12 voluntary participants. A private location is ideal, and many discussions will last approximately 90 minutes. Finally, all collected information will be analyzed and reported.

FACILITATING STAFF MEETINGS

There are three core elements to a successful **staff meeting**: 1) invite all attendees to share a little, 2) focus on the group and any outcomes that might need adjustment or improvement, and 3) allow time for feedback in the decision-making process. Staff meetings are an excellent way to increase organizational communication and alignment, offering an open floor for staff to give feedback on recent messages or events. They are also a low-budget way to promote staff recognition, wellness programs, employee referral programs, and employee surveys. Moreover, staff meetings have a history of improving productivity, workplace conflicts, team synergy, and employee relations. It is important to consider religious holidays when scheduling staff meetings, seminars, or training events. For example, staff meetings scheduled on Ash Wednesday, Good Friday, Passover, Rosh Hashanah, or Yom Kippur might have low attendance.

COMMUNICATIONS MEDIA

Communication can be transmitted through a wide variety of channels or media, such as phone, email, face to face, reports, presentations, or social media. The chosen method should fit both the audience and the type of communication. **Information-rich communication channels** include phone, videoconferencing, and face-to-face meetings or presentations. **Information-lean communication channels** include email, fliers, newsletters, and reports. When trying to sell a product or service, a salesman might use a series of phone calls, face-to-face meetings, and presentations. This is because information-rich media are more interactive, which is more appropriate for complex messages that may need clarification. Rich and verbal communications should be used when there is time urgency, immediate feedback is required, ideas can be simplified with explanations, or emotions may be affected. Lean and written communications should be used when the communicator is simply stating facts or needs information permanently recorded.

METHODS FOR INVESTIGATING COMPLAINTS OR GRIEVANCES
GRIEVANCES

A **grievance** is a work-related complaint or formal dispute that is brought to the attention of management. However, in nonunion environments, grievances may encompass any discontent or sense of injustice. Grievance procedures provide an orderly and methodical process for hearing and evaluating employee complaints, and they tend to be more developed in unionized companies than in nonunionized companies as a result of labor agreement specifications. These procedures protect employee rights and eliminate the need for strikes or slowdowns every time there is a disagreement.

Disagreements may be unavoidable in situations where the labor contract is open to interpretation because negotiators cannot anticipate all potential conflicts. Formal grievance procedures increase upward communication in organizations and make top management decisions more sensitive to employee emotions. The first step to resolving grievances is for a complaint to be submitted to the supervisor or written and submitted to the union steward.

If these parties cannot find a resolution from there, the complaint may be heard by the superintendent or plant manager and the industrial relations manager. If the union is still unsatisfied, the grievance can be appealed to the next step, which may be arbitration if the company is small. Large corporations may have grievance committees, corporate officers, and/or international union representatives who will meet and hear grievances. However, the final step of an unresolved dispute will be binding arbitration by an outside third party, where both parties come to an acceptable agreement.

RESOLVING DISCRIMINATION COMPLAINTS

Resolving discrimination complaints requires an employer to decide between two different paths:

- An employer can follow the process defined by the Equal Employment Opportunity Commission (EEOC) and thus be subject to further investigation by the state or local Fair Employment Practice Agency (FEPA). An employee has 180 days from the date of the incident to file a discrimination complaint with the EEOC. After an investigation, probable cause will or will not be found, and the process can go one of two ways:
    - Probable cause found—The EEOC will try conciliation, and the employer can agree to settle, or litigation could be pursued with the EEOC or private court.

- o Probable cause not found—After the 180-day period is over, the employee can ask for a right-to-sue letter, and then has 90 days to file in court. At this point, the EEOC's involvement with the matter ends.
- An employer can make the decision to settle the alleged charges instead of facing an investigation by FEPA.

An employer must contemplate a number of issues before deciding which path is best. Typically, employers will weigh the costs involved in a one-time settlement versus a possibly extended period of legal disruption that could cost both time and money. An open investigation could harm a company's reputation whether the allegations are true or not. Also, if a company believes the claim of discrimination might be truthful, the one-time settlement might make sense in order to quickly pivot, address, and rectify any possible systemic discriminatory practices within the company.

FRONT PAY

When an employer is found guilty of discrimination, the employee who brought forth the complaint is usually permitted to return to their position in the organization. However, the court will sometimes instead rule for front pay. **Front pay** is money awarded to the employee from the employer in a discrimination situation. Generally, the amount awarded is equal to lost wages. There are three situations in which front pay is required from the employer:

- The position left vacant by the employee discriminated against is no longer available.
- The employer has taken no action to rectify the discriminatory practice(s) occurring within the organization.
- The returning employee could be facing an unreasonable, possibly hostile, work environment if he or she were to return to the prior position.

MEDIATION PROCESS

The goal of the **mediation process** is to solve a dispute without having to take more aggressive legal steps. A mediator is specially trained to work with two or more disagreeing parties to reach an agreeable resolution. There is a difference between mediation and arbitration. Arbitration can be the final judgment for a dispute, meaning that if mediation doesn't work, the parties involved can move to arbitration or litigation. Mediation is considered non-binding.

Typically, both parties must mutually agree on a mediator to start the process. A mediator speaks with both parties and there are agreed-upon ground rules, such as logistics, when the negotiation will occur, what specifically will be discussed, who should be involved, and protocol or procedures for discussion. During the agreed-upon negotiations, the mediator will work with both parties to problem-solve and create a reasonable solution to move forward. Frequently, this requires compromise on both sides. If a resolution or compromise is agreed upon, both parties must sign documentation stating they will abide by the agreed-upon plan. If a resolution is not reached during the mediation process, then the parties can either pursue arbitration or litigation to resolve the dispute.

TYPES OF ARBITRATION

Arbitration is a formal way to settle disputes outside of court. Frequently, parties in a dispute try arbitration if mediation does not work. Parties must agree on a neutral, third-party arbitrator, who listens and makes decisions based on the information and facts presented during the questioning and subsequent discussions. There are many types of arbitration:

- **Binding** arbitration—During this type of arbitration, both parties are required to abide by the final judgment. In other words, the party that "loses" the arbitration must carry out the final judgment. Also, in binding arbitration, this is the end of the legal process: both parties have no other legal recourse with regard to the dispute after a decision is rendered in binding arbitration.
- **Non-binding** arbitration—This type follows the same process as binding arbitration, except the decision rendered does not have to be followed and cannot legally be enforced. Additionally, if either party chooses, they can pursue further legal action.
- **Compulsory** arbitration—In this situation, both parties are required by law to enter into the arbitration process. Generally, this occurs due to one of two reasons: (1) a court order dictated that compulsory arbitration is mandatory, or (2) an agreed-upon contract states that disputes require compulsory arbitration to be resolved.
- **Voluntary** arbitration—The parties in dispute mutually agree to willingly participate in the arbitration process in the hopes of avoiding potentially expensive and time-consuming legal alternatives.

TYPES OF ARBITRATORS

There are three different types of arbitrators that could lead the resolution of a dispute. Which type of arbitrator an organization chooses is dependent on the circumstances and previously agreed-upon contracts, if applicable.

- **Permanent** arbitrator—This type of arbitrator usually judges cases for a particular organization or during the life of a contract. In either case, the arbitrator has intimate knowledge of the organization and material being discussed. This knowledge makes arbitration highly efficient, but it is important that both parties continue to believe the arbitrator is unbiased.
- **Ad hoc** arbitrator—In this situation, an arbitrator is mutually agreed upon by both parties, but the arbitrator does not have a previously established relationship with either party. Usually, an ad hoc arbitrator is chosen in one-time situations.
- Arbitrator **panel**—This group of arbitrators, usually three, is similar to ad hoc arbitrators in that they do not have a previously established relationship with the parties involved. This type of panel is sometimes referred to as an arbitral tribunal or a tripartite panel. In the case of a tripartite arbitration panel, the representation is as follows: one arbitrator represents the management, one arbitrator represents the union, and one is neutral. In most cases, the neutral arbitrator is the one who makes the deciding vote.

EMPLOYEE CONFLICT

Employee conflict, or disagreement among employees, will occur. Not all conflict is unproductive. Many times, employee disagreement or conflict that occurs in a constructive, respectful manner leads to innovation, increased creativity, and ultimately improvements. However, there are times when the opposite occurs and employee conflict is a negative experience for all involved. The following are some strategies for an organization to address negative employee conflict:

- Ask questions and gain a complete understanding of the problem. First, evaluate whether the conflict involves any EEOC violations, such as discrimination or harassment. Assuming no EEOC violations, gain an understanding of the root cause of the problem, not the fallout. Depending on the situation, encourage employees to work it out on their own, if possible. This is a judgment call.
- If intervention becomes necessary to prevent escalation, do so immediately. Listen to both sides, ask questions, and restate issues for clarification. Make sure both parties understand that they must let each other speak uninterrupted and address each other with respect. Encourage both parties to devise a way to manage going forward, and assist in devising a written plan that both agree to follow. Reference the employee handbook for behavioral expectations.
- Offer training or personality assessments to help conflicted employees improve their communication style, and encourage managers to lead by example.

ESCALATION

Employees need to know what to do when discrimination, harassment, or bullying occurs in the workplace. There are several ways to address these types of issues. If the employee is comfortable, he or she can confront the perpetrator of the behavior directly. The employee can talk with the perpetrator and let that individual know which behaviors, language, or actions are causing the issue. Individuals can be less defensive when addressed about a possible issue privately.

If the concerning behavior, commentary, or actions continue, escalation will be required. Escalation involves bringing the complaint or issue to the next level up. If confronting the perpetrator directly is not successful, the individual can bring the complaint to a team lead, supervisor, or manager. This allows an outside party with a particular level of authority the opportunity to help work through the issue. The leader can mediate between the two parties or address the perpetrator directly.

If the behavior persists after escalating to a leader within the organization, or the leader fails to address the complaint satisfactorily, the individual can then escalate the complaint to HR. HR is required to address and investigate complaints of harassment, bullying, or discrimination. HR should meet with the individual raising the complaint to get as much information as possible. HR should also meet with anyone who may have seen or overheard, or has knowledge of, the concerns raised. The person responsible for the areas of concern should also be interviewed. Once the interviews or conversations are complete, the HR department should review all company policies and regulations, as well as employment laws, to determine whether a violation has taken place. If a violation is found, it should be handled according to policy and law. If the concerning behavior persists after HR intervention, if retaliation occurs, or if HR fails to adequately address the issue, the next step in escalation is to lodge a complaint with the EEOC and allow that process to begin.

Organizational policies surrounding harassment, bullying, and discrimination should clearly state the levels of escalation so that all employees know what to do should they find themselves in that situation.

RETALIATION

Within an organizational setting, retaliation can take place when an employer takes adverse action against advocation of protected rights. Retaliation is usually seen on an individual level. The action taken by the employer could come from an administrator, team lead, supervisor, or manager.

Adverse actions can include demoting the employee, passing him or her over for a promotion, excluding that employee from meetings or events, giving unwarranted and excessive negative reviews, transferring the employee to a lesser position, harassing the employee, or even terminating the employee.

Retaliation in the form of adverse actions can result when an employee communicates with an individual of authority within the organization about harassment or discrimination, resists sexual advances, requests a religious or disability accommodation, or refuses to follow directives that could result in some type of discrimination. Retaliation stemming from an employee exercising his or her rights within the workplace is prohibited under law.

When an employee feels that the employer utilized retaliatory acts, he or she can file a charge with the EEOC for investigation. Should the EEOC validate the charge, the employee may receive money for damages (such as a settlement, backpay, or reinstatement to a position) from the employer. Additionally, the employer might be required to change policies and procedures, to complete training, or to take other measures to prevent further issues.

PREVENTING RETALIATION CLAIMS

To prevent retaliation, employees must believe that a) complaints can be easily presented without a lot of hassle, embarrassment, or paperwork; b) complaints will be assessed by a fair and impartial third party; and c) they will not be mistreated or terminated for submitting complaints or pressing for resolution. The final protection is necessary for the success of both union and nonunion **grievance procedures**, although union employees typically have more protections than nonunion employees because their labor agreement is written and enforceable by collective action. However, federal regulations such as the Sarbanes-Oxley Act and Whistleblower Protection Act now include safeguards for employees who have witnessed or stumbled upon illegal or immoral actions and make the information known to the public. Employers can also follow a number of best practices to **avoid retaliation**, such as these:

- Treat all complaints seriously and similarly.
- Allow the employee a chance to be heard, investigate the claim, collect evidence or witness statements, and treat all cases as though they might result in arbitration.
- Review the labor agreement carefully, and follow any required procedures.
- Examine all information prior to making a final determination.
- Avoid any unnecessary delays, and clearly communicate the conclusion.
- Correct the problem if the company is in the wrong.

DOCUMENTATION

Documentation in HR is critical, as proper and detailed documentation keeps the organization compliant and protected from questionable lawsuits and legal actions. There must be a clear and consistent documentation process for all HR departments. In the event of official complaints and allegations, those interactions must be written down. Official conversations or interviews related to the complaints must also be documented. When complaints are substantiated, those results need to be written down as well, along with which regulations, policies, or laws were violated. Official counseling, warnings, or disciplinary actions stemming from complaints or concerns should also be recorded. All documents surrounding the complaint should be stored in a central location. This could be in the personnel file or in a separate area for complaints. There are many different templates for investigations, complaints, and employee contact available for use. Thorough documentation illustrates the process and intent behind different actions and can be used to provide evidence for both progressive discipline and termination actions.

IMPORTANCE OF CONFIDENTIALITY IN THE WORKPLACE

Confidentiality is vital in HR practices. Maintaining the confidentiality of all employee records is imperative. Information to be safeguarded includes, but is not limited to, Social Security numbers, birth dates, addresses, phone numbers, personal emails, benefits enrollments, medical or other leave details, garnishments, bank account information, disciplinary actions, grievances, and employment eligibility data. When employee record information is requested for legitimate purposes, a written release signed by the employee should be obtained and kept on file. Examples of these requests include employment verification for bank loans and mortgage applications.

Further, HR should internally disclose this sensitive data only to those who are authorized and have a need to know based on the scenario at hand. For example, a supervisor should know employees' disciplinary histories so that they can manage them more effectively. But that supervisor doesn't need to know what benefit plan the employee chose, or that the employee has a tax lien.

However, HR cannot always promise complete confidentiality. For example, if an employee makes a harassment allegation, HR will move to investigate immediately. HR should inform the complainant, and anyone involved in the investigation, that the situation will be handled as discreetly as possible; the nature of an investigation dictates that information obtained during the process may be shared with those who need to know, including the accused.

Employee and Labor Relations

NLRA

The **National Labor Relations Act** (NLRA) was passed by Congress in 1935 after a long period of conflict in labor relations. Also known as the Wagner Act, after New York Senator Robert Wagner, it was intended to be an economic stabilizer and to establish collective bargaining in industrial relations. Section 7 of the NLRA provides employees with the right to form, join, or assist **labor organizations**, as well as the right to engage in **concerted activities** such as collective bargaining through representatives or other mutual aid. Section 8 of the NLRA also identifies five **unfair labor practices**:

1. Employers shall not interfere with or coerce employees from the rights outlined in Section 7.
2. Employers shall not dominate or disrupt the formation of a labor union.
3. Employers shall not allow union membership or activity to influence hiring, firing, promotion, or related employment decisions.
4. Employers shall not discriminate against or discharge an employee who has given testimony or filed a charge with the NLRA.
5. Employers cannot refuse bargaining in good faith with employee representatives.

TAFT-HARTLEY ACT

Because many employers felt that the NLRA gave too much power to unions, Congress passed the Labor Management Relations Act in 1947. More commonly known as the **Taft-Hartley Act**, it sought to avoid unnecessary strikes and impose certain restrictions over union activities. The act addresses **four basic issues**: unfair labor practices by unions, the rights of employees, the rights of employers, and national emergency strikes. Moreover, the act prohibits unions from the following:

- Restraining or coercing employees from their right to not engage in union activities
- Forcing an employer to discriminate in any way against an employee to encourage or discourage union membership

- Forcing an employer to pay for work or services that are not needed or not performed
- Conducting certain types of strikes or boycotts
- Charging excessive initiation fees or membership dues when employees are required to join a union shop

LANDRUM-GRIFFIN ACT

The government exercised further control over union activities in 1959 by the passage of the Labor Management Reporting and Disclosure Act. More commonly known as the **Landrum-Griffin Act**, this law regulates the **internal conduct of labor unions** to reduce the likelihood of fraud and improper actions. The act imposes controls on five major areas: reports to the secretary of labor, a bill of rights for union members, union trusteeships, conduct of union elections, and financial safeguards. Some key provisions include the following:

- Granting equal rights to every union member with regard to nominations, attending meetings, and voting
- Requiring unions to submit and make available to the public a copy of its constitution, bylaws, and annual financial reports
- Requiring unions to hold regular elections every five years for national and every three years for local organizations
- Monitoring the management and investment of union funds, making embezzlement a federal crime

> **Review Video: US Employment Compensation Laws**
> Visit mometrix.com/academy and enter code: 972790

NORRIS-LAGUARDIA ACT

The **Norris-LaGuardia Act**, which was passed in 1932, protects the right to unionize. This act grants employees the right to form unions and initiate strikes. In addition to granting the right to unionize, this act also prohibits the court system from using injunctions to interfere with any nonviolent union activity and prohibits employers from forcing employees to sign "yellow-dog" contracts. A **yellow-dog contract** refers to any contract that prohibits an employee from joining a union, or any contract that requires an employee to agree to be terminated if it is discovered that they are a member of a union or intend to become a member of a union. The act stated that members belonging to a union have "full freedom of association," meaning they are free to strike, picket, or initiate boycotts without legal penalty.

EMPLOYMENT RIGHTS, STANDARDS, AND CONCEPTS
LABOR RIGHTS

Before **labor rights** can be discussed, terminology must be defined clearly, as the understanding and application of legal definitions can drive how decisions are made:

- **Employees** are persons who exchange work for wages.
- **Employers** are the entities that are responsible for the health and welfare of employees.

The relationship between the employer and the employee regarding terms and conditions of employment is defined by the rights of the employee and the employer. Labor rights are driven by the **Fair Labor Standards Act (FLSA)**, which was designed to protect workers against unfair employment practices. The FLSA has three main components:

- Minimum wage and overtime, with qualifications of exempt and non-exempt, which drive eligibility for overtime pay
- Accurate recordkeeping, consisting of hours worked and wages earned and paid
- Youth employment standards, including child labor laws to protect underage employees from harsh or damaging work conditions

Employers are bound to ensure that all applicable laws and regulations are implemented, documented, and adhered to.

THE INTERNATIONAL LABOUR ORGANIZATION

The **International Labour Organization (ILO)** was founded in 1919 to address global working conditions. A part of the United Nations, the ILO is made up of 187 member states. Its mission is to promote decent working conditions, including eliminating child labor, ending unlawful discrimination, protecting human rights, and supporting worker rights to organize. The ILO extensively researches compensation practices and advocates for a living wage for all. A living wage is pay that can cover a decent standard of living for the worker's household. Going a step further, the ILO also pushes for a fair wage, which uses the living wage as the foundation but is adjusted for a given country's pay laws (such as overtime), any collective bargaining involved, and an individual worker's skills and performance. The ILO has also championed the standard eight-hour workday, recognizing that overworked employees can experience negative health and safety outcomes. Although not every country adopts every ILO standard and practice, research from the ILO sets the tone for the discussion and aims to keep advancing working conditions for the world's employees.

THE NATIONAL LABOR RELATIONS BOARD

Unfair labor practices are actions taken by either the union or management that are prohibited by law or **National Labor Relations Board (NLRB)** rulings. Charges of unfair labor practices must be filed with the NLRB within six months of the alleged practice, and can be submitted in person or via mail. Then, a preliminary NLRB investigation will be assigned to a field examiner or attorney through a regional office. After the investigation, a formal complaint may be issued to the general counsel, or the case may be disposed of through withdrawal, settlement, or dismissal. A complaint issued to the general counsel may be either dismissed or moved forward to a formal hearing. After the NLRB issues a decision, dissatisfied parties may appeal; however, this process can be lengthy and take many years.

MINIMUM WAGE, LIVING WAGE, AND FAIR WAGE CONCEPTS

The **minimum wage** is the minimum amount that employers in the United States are required by federal regulation to pay employees; many states have higher minimum wages. The federal minimum wage is currently $7.25/hour. Poverty guidelines indicate that an individual needs to earn $14,580 to be at poverty level, which would be $7.00 per hour for a full-time employee. All employers that have annual gross sales or business of at least $500,000 must pay at least minimum wage, other than some specific categories that have been exempted, including:

- Farm workers and other seasonal workers
- Tipped employees
- Minors and young workers
- Full-time and vocational students

- Employees with disabilities
- Employees of organizations exempt from minimum wage requirements (some colleges, universities, and non-profits)

A **living wage** is the amount an individual needs to be paid to afford a decent standard of living including food and water, basic nonfood items (housing, education, healthcare, transportation, clothing, etc.), and other discretionary expenditures.

A **fair wage** is defined as a wage that is fairly and reasonably commensurate with the value of the services or class of services rendered. Components that can influence a determination of fair pay include:

- The market rate for a particular position
- Employee experience level, skill, and location
- Pay transparency and anti-discrimination laws

Organizations must comply with minimum wage requirements and should consider fair pay requirements when recruiting for positions and candidates.

STANDARD WORKDAY

A **standard workday** is defined as an eight-hour day for a full-time employee who is normally scheduled to work eight or more hours a day, 5 days a week, for a total of 40 hours a week. Standard hours are typically considered to be 9:00 a.m. to 5:00 p.m. A standard workday for employees who are scheduled for less than eight hours a day is defined as the average number of hours per workday in the preceding month.

Standard workdays of 9-to-5 were established in the 1800s through efforts by the National Labor Union to protect workers' rights. With manufacturing jobs predominant at the time, the average worker could be expected to work up to 100 hours a week. In the 1920s, Henry Ford introduced the 40-hour workweek at his Ford Motor Company.

The standard workday has been strongly affected by the adoption of electronic methods of communication that allow for instant access at all times of the day and night, and flexible, remote working options that blur the lines of a standard workday.

HARASSMENT AND DISCRIMINATION PREVENTION

Companies should complete regular **harassment training** because employers must exercise reasonable care to avoid and prevent harassment. Otherwise, employers may be found liable for the harassing behaviors of vendors, clients, coworkers, and supervisors. Harassment is defined as any demeaning or degrading comments, jokes, name-calling, actions, graffiti, or other belittling conduct that may be found offensive. Any form of **derogatory speech** can be considered harassment, including neutral words that may be perceived in a vulgar or intimidating way. Furthermore, the Civil Rights Act of 1964 protects individuals from harassment on the basis of race, color, religion, sex, or national origin. Damages awarded under Title VII can total anywhere from $50,000 to $300,000, depending upon the size of the employer.

Sexual Harassment

The Civil Rights Act of 1964 bans **sexual harassment** and makes it an employer's responsibility to prevent it. Sexual harassment can be defined as unsolicited sexual advances, requests for sexual favors, and any other conduct of a sexual nature that meets any of the following conditions:

- Obedience to such conduct is a condition of employment, either explicitly or implicitly.
- Obedience to or rejection of such conduct is used as the basis for employment decisions affecting an individual.
- Such conduct produces an intimidating, hostile, or offensive working environment or otherwise has the effect of interfering with an individual's work performance.

Sexual harassment is separated into two types: **quid pro quo (this for that) cases** and **hostile environment cases**. Victims do not need to suffer loss, but the harassment needs to be pervasive or severe. Employees may be offended by any sexual conduct in the workplace, such as lewd comments, jokes, pornographic pictures, or touching. Employees who voice discomfort may request that the environment be changed. If an employer fails to correct the offensive environment, employees may press charges without needing to demonstrate physical or psychological damage.

Other Illegal Harassment

Harassment usually involves unwelcome verbal exchanges, unwelcome physical contact, or unwelcome actions that are based on a person's race, religion, gender, sexual orientation, national origin, age, disability, genetic information, military membership, or veteran status. The action(s) taken must meet the threshold of a "severe and pervasive" work environment, characterized as hostile, abusive, or intimidating for "a reasonable person." If this type of harassment is present, it could be a violation of the following federal regulations: Title VII of the Civil Rights Act of 1964, the Americans with Disabilities Act (ADA), the Age Discrimination in Employment Act (ADEA), the Genetic Information Nondiscrimination Act (GINA), or the Uniformed Services Employment and Reemployment Rights Act (USERRA). Additionally, many states and local laws provide even more enhanced legal protections against harassment. Harassment interferes with an employee's ability to accomplish their work. All allegations of harassment should be reported, investigated immediately, and acted upon appropriately by the employer.

Conducting Harassment Training

Companies should conduct regular harassment training because employers must exercise reasonable care to avoid and prevent harassment. Several states have mandatory harassment training for certain types of employees. Otherwise, employers may be found liable for the harassing behaviors of vendors, clients, coworkers, and supervisors. **Harassment** is defined as any demeaning or degrading comments, jokes, name-calling, actions, graffiti, or other belittling conduct that may be found offensive. Any form of derogatory speech can be considered harassment, including neutral words that may be perceived in a vulgar or intimidating way. Furthermore, the Civil Rights Act of 1964 protects individuals from harassment on the basis of race, color, religion, gender, or national origin. Damages awarded under Title VII can total anywhere from $50,000 to $300,000, depending upon the size of the employer.

Bullying in the Workplace

Bullying is a form of aggressive behavior in the workplace that includes numerous forms of mistreatment that allow the bully to assert control and attack another person's self-confidence or self-esteem. Bullying can be overt, such as yelling, obscene language, and public humiliation. However, bullying can also be much more subtle, such as failing to invite a targeted employee to an essential meeting, withholding needed resources, sabotage, micromanagement, and inequitable treatment. In either case, while bullying is obviously detrimental to the victim, it may also damage the business by harming productivity or incurring legal costs. Many organizations have modified their harassment policies to specifically address bullying. Changing the policy needs to be combined with an awareness campaign so that employees understand what bullying is, what its consequences are, and how to report it. There should be a process for reporting claims of bullying—such as a contact in HR—so that the victim feels comfortable. All reported bullying incidents should be investigated immediately and, if necessary, met with action. Also, Title VII of the Civil Rights Act of 1964 and the EEOC could offer protections against harassment in the form of bullying, depending on the circumstances and investigative findings.

HR Information Management

HR Database Content and Technologies

HUMAN RESOURCE INFORMATION SYSTEMS (HRIS)

A **human resource information system** (HRIS) is a computer system designed to help HR professionals carry out the day-to-day HR functions necessary for an organization to continue functioning normally. Most HRISs are designed to collect and store data related to the use of employee benefits, hiring, placement, training and evaluations of employees, payroll, and information about the work performed by employees during a given period of time. An HRIS is designed to help an HR professional carry out all primary functions associated with HR needs, which include benefits administration, payroll, time and labor management, and human resources management. An HRIS not only aids the HR department, but also helps the entire organization function effectively. Some HRIS functions could include the following:

- **Tracking basic employee information**—May include name, address, salary, and emergency contact information.
- **Keeping company documentation**—May include items such as employee handbooks, emergency procedures, and safety guidelines.
- **Benefit administration**—Could include enrollment capabilities, insurance changes, attendance and time off, and the ability for employees to look up and track information.
- **Payroll integration**—Reduces duplication of efforts with payroll and increases efficiencies.
- **Applicant tracking**—Allows recruiters to manage an applicant's information, then move the applicant to employee status and retain information.
- **Performance management**—Could include performance evaluations; possible improvement plans can follow the employee throughout the organization.
- **Tracking disciplinary issues**—May include the recording of demotions, suspensions, or other negative actions taken, all of which may be important to retain even after an employee leaves the organization.
- **Training**—Retains records of required certifications, licenses, and/or other compliance training.

APPLICANT TRACKING SYSTEMS

An **applicant tracking system (ATS)** can be particularly useful for organizations that perform high-volume recruiting on a consistent basis, but they can be valuable to businesses of all sizes. Despite the initial cost, most medium to large businesses use an ATS due to the time it can save by scanning thousands of resumes or automating new-hire paperwork. New, cloud-based systems may integrate with social media or popular job boards and receive automatic updates that eliminate the need for pricy servers and onsite specialists. Additionally, an ATS is a positive first impression for applicants because it can make the process easier and save time on their end.

In addition, an ATS can allow you to do the following:

- Brand your company with a career page
- Modify or set up standard templates
- Save forms for compliance or reporting

- Push employee information to a payroll or HR module
- Collect data and metrics for reporting and strategic review

> **Review Video: Applicant Tracking System**
> Visit mometrix.com/academy and enter code: 532324

PERFORMANCE MANAGEMENT SYSTEMS

Just as a learning management system can deliver, monitor, and track learning and development content, a **performance management system (PMS)** is a software system that can track and monitor employee performance in a consistent and measurable way. A PMS allows collaboration between the employee and the supervisor or manager to identify expectations, set goals, recognize achievement, provide regular feedback, and discuss performance reviews. A PMS allows clear expectations to be established and communicated across the workforce while emphasizing individual accountability for meeting goals and objectives. PMSs can be administered in-house, through a cloud-based provider, or a hybrid of the two. It is important that a well-developed and properly implemented PMS includes information about previous performance (achievements, reviews, and discipline), a way to provide feedback, a score or rating for performance, and a way to detail future development plans for the employee. Performance should be both tracked and reviewed on a consistent and ongoing basis.

BIG DATA ANALYTICS SOFTWARE

Companies can use **big data analytics software** to examine and analyze large data sets to reveal information such as correlations, customer preferences, and various market trends. This is used to help make data-driven decisions in areas such as marketing campaigns, increased operational efficiencies, and increased personalization for individual customers.

In HR, big data analytics software is more often used to analyze people. Big data analytics can be used to refine the hiring process, helping an organization avoid making bad hires. Big data analytics can also be used to examine and map out retention and potential turnover. Big data analytics software can determine the efficacy of current training programs, and identify areas where improvements can be made. Big data analytics software can include programs such as Microsoft Excel for forecasting, and projections can be made using existing data. Big data analytics can also be compiled using various HRIS, as many offer numerous types of data analysis. Big data analytics software, when implemented and utilized correctly, can save the organization time, resources, and efficiency throughout any department or opening.

EMPLOYEE RECORDS MANAGEMENT

Workplace employee-related records should have organizational policies that might be regulated by federal, state, and local laws as well as operational necessity. It is sometimes easier to think of a record as the complete, final version of a document so that there is no need to keep every draft or note. The following are key elements of workplace records retention management and access:

- How long to **retain** records—First, all records that are regulated by law should be kept for the prescribed time period according to federal, state, and/or local laws. This can be confusing because certain records might be regulated by more than one law, or the time period may vary. In these cases, records should be kept for the longest period required.
- Who should have **access** to records—Access should be provided (1) only to those people with a legitimate business need, and (2) only where federal, state, and local laws permit such access. For example, HIPAA and many data privacy regulations specify not only who may have access, but how the information may be used.

Storage of Records and Security Needed

Workplace policy should describe specifically where records will be stored and in what format—paper or electronic. Records should be held in a secure, locked location or electronically maintained with necessary technological protections. There is no specific law that dictates how records must be stored, whether paper or electronic, but the law does dictate that an organization must have the ability to quickly retrieve information and supply paper copies if necessary.

It is imperative for HR to always protect employee records and the privacy of the information, regardless of the format. Frequently, an organization will have a documented employee records confidentiality policy to protect all employee information and maintain confidentiality. Furthermore, if an employee feels there has been a breach in confidentiality, then HR needs to investigate the allegation immediately. Alternatively, if an organization feels there was a breach in confidentiality, regardless of how it occurred, the organization usually has an obligation to share the breach and offer corrective actions.

Concerns Before Destruction of HR Records

Employee records management is critical to comply with federal, state, and local requirements and to reduce legal liabilities. If an organization prematurely destroys HR records, that organization could face criminal liabilities and possible legal penalties or litigation. Additionally, the organization may not be able to adequately defend itself in employment-related litigation due to spoliation of evidence. An organization should only retain the legal HR records that are required to comply with federal, state, and local laws or operational necessity. For example, holding on to every scrap of paper an employee writes on is not necessary; only legally mandated documents are necessary. In some cases, keeping every scrap could turn into a liability for the organization.

The end goal for HR is to keep what is legally mandated and to properly, legally dispose of the rest. Disposal of confidential, personal, or financial information after the legally dictated retention period is over should comply with all federal, state, and local regulations. For example, the Fair and Accurate Credit Transactions Act (FACTA) has specific rules for how to dispose of background check documentation. Usually, if it is paper, this means shredding on-site or hiring a professional vendor that specializes in shredding. In the case of electronic records, the organization must follow protocols so that the information is erased and cannot be read or reconstructed.

Pre-Employment Records Retention

The pre-employment phase of a job comprises activities that occur before a candidate is chosen for and has accepted a position at an organization. During this phase, HR posts a job, resumes are submitted, applications are completed, reference checks and/or background checks may be conducted, and interviews may be held. All of these documents should be retained for EEO purposes demonstrating nondiscriminatory hiring, equal opportunity, and overall fairness and equity.

Organizations must retain the following information for all applicants: job posting; resumes; and completed applications, including interview notes related to the decision to hire or not hire an applicant. Based on federal regulations in the Age Discrimination in Employment Act (ADEA), Americans with Disabilities Act (ADA), and Civil Rights Act of 1964 (Title VII), these documents are retained one year after creation of the documents or hire/no-hire decision, whichever is later. In the case of federal contractors, document retention is two years. If the contractor has less than 150 employees or a government contract is less than $150,000, then the retention is, again, one year. These are the federal retention regulations, but retention rates could vary slightly depending on state and local laws.

EMPLOYMENT RECORDS RETENTION

Employee records, whether they are paper or electronic, have specific retention requirements. Retention of employee records could vary according to federal, state, and local laws. Therefore, it is important to understand the legal requirements as well as the system that an organization utilizes. The following is a summary of federal guidelines for the most common HR records.

- **I-9 forms**—Securely retained for three years beginning from the hire date, or one year after separation of employment.
- **Payroll records**—These records, which contain personal information such as name, address, Social Security number, and compensation, should be retained for three years according to federal laws. There are many federal laws that regulate payroll records, including the Age Discrimination Employment Act (ADEA), Fair Labor Standards Act (FLSA), Service Contract Act, Davis-Bacon Act, Walsh-Healey Act (for federal contractors), and Family and Medical Leave Act (FMLA). However, it is recommended for the purposes of the Lilly Ledbetter Fair Pay Act to retain these documents for at least five years after the end of employment. Additionally, under the Equal Pay Act (EPA), employers must retain two years of all payroll records in case they need to justify the pay wage differential between different sexes.
- **Employment benefits**—These records should be retained for six years and are carefully regulated, requiring employer reporting based on the Employee Retirement Income Security Act (ERISA).
- **Background checks**—These are retained for a minimum of one year based on the Equal Employment Opportunity Commission (EEOC) requirements and Title VII of the Civil Rights Act of 1964 to possibly report hiring and selection records. However, it is often recommended to save background check documents for five years after the date the consumer report is accessed because the statute of limitations in the Fair Credit Reporting Act is five years.
- **Tax records**—All related tax records should be retained by the employer for four years after the fourth quarter of the year in order to be in compliance with the Federal Insurance Contributions Act (FICA), Federal Unemployment Tax Act, and Internal Revenue Code.
- **Safety records**—This data, and related reports, should be retained for five years after the year that the record pertains to, based on the Occupational Safety and Health Act (OSHA) and the Walsh-Healey Act (for federal contractors).
- **Family and Medical Leave Act (FMLA) records**—Based on the requirements in the FMLA, these records should be retained for three years.
- **Disability accommodations**—All employee disability and accommodations documentation should be retained for one year from the date of the record or last date of an action. However, for contractors and public employees, the records should be retained for two years. There are many laws that require compliance with disability issues, such as the American Disabilities Act as Amended (ADAAA), Executive Order 11246, and the Vietnam Era Veterans' Readjustment Assistance Act (VEVRAA).

Records retention can be a complex process. However, it is a critical HR function to support and protect an organization.

Separating Personnel Files into Two Categories

Not every record in a personnel file should be treated the same. Specific records regarding an employee and their employment history should be kept in their personnel file, while other documents, because of their confidential nature, might need to be protected differently.

- **Personnel file**—This file should include the job description, application resume, offer letter, acknowledgement of organization handbook, emergency contact information, job performance, promotions, transfers, appraisals, awards, training, any disciplinary actions, and all documents related to separation from the organization.
- **Confidential personnel information**—These records should have an added layer of protection because of the employee's privacy rights and, if these rights are breached, to protect the employer from liability. These records usually include any medical information such as ADA accommodations, workers' compensation, drug tests, disability information, Family and Medical Leave Act (FMLA) information, health insurance, COBRA information, all employee credit information, I-9 form, and any documents related to a complaint or investigation.

Using Information Obtained from HR Databases

Business Intelligence Tools and Techniques

Businesses are constantly generating data, and they need an effective way to utilize this data to become and stay competitive. Previously, businesses would simply construct reports with their data and use the reports for decision-making. Although that still happens every day, data is now also being used in more advanced ways.

Online Analytical Processing (OLAP)

An on-demand method of processing data that facilitates decision-making, **online analytical processing (OLAP)** is capable of reporting, what-if planning, and trend spotting, to name a few of its uses. OLAP also allows the user to view data from different perspectives, which provides a deeper understanding of the subject at hand.

Business Intelligence Portals

A **business intelligence portal** is a centrally stored collection of firm data that is accessible on demand across the organization. This type of portal has a user interface that allows employees to run a number of analytical processes. It shows the results of queries in a visual format, making it easier to spot trends and answer business questions.

Advanced Analytics

Although **advanced analytics** includes reporting data, it goes way beyond that. By way of data mining, formulas, and algorithms, advanced analytics can be used for forecasting, detecting patterns, and revealing correlations. Advanced analytics is also a part of keeping up with technology, including machine learning and artificial intelligence. Although advanced analytics is a powerful business intelligence tool, there is a caveat. Using data for reporting produces straightforward, typically accurate results. Analyzing the data, however, requires interpretation. Those handling the task should be trained to do so and prepared to continuously refine their approach.

PREDICTIVE ANALYTICS

The use of statistics, historical data, and modeling techniques to make predictions about outcomes and performance in the future is called **predictive analytics**. This type of analysis looks at current and past data patterns to establish whether those patterns are likely to appear again. These techniques can help the organization determine what resources need to be adjusted to be best prepared for future events. Numerous industries rely on predictive analytics as one of many decision-making tools. Human resources uses predictive analytics to determine staffing needs, determine the causation behind high turnover, and for diversity and inclusion initiatives. Supply chain uses predictive analytics for managing inventory levels, downtime, and demand. Marketing uses predictive analytics for targeted campaigns, looking at content and strategies that appeal to specific demographics. The benefits of using this technique are plentiful and can help reduce risk to the organization and allow better positioning for future growth.

TREND ANALYSIS

Using a company's financial statements to identify and recognize patterns within the market and to forecast future performance, in an attempt to make the best decisions based on the results of the completed analysis, is called **trend analysis**. Trend analysis is performed by collecting data from records and plotting that information on a chart, with time on the horizontal axis, to define patterns from the information provided. There are three primary types of trends to understand:

- **Downtrends** indicate that the market is moving downward. The value of stocks and assets may decrease. The size of the economy may decrease. Businesses may need to seek new and innovative ways to stay competitive. Job loss and production decreases may occur. This may also indicate that the market is not favorable for further investment.
- **Uptrends** indicate that the market is moving upward. This can mean that the price of stock or the number of jobs available is increasing. This can also indicate a period of economic growth, that the economy is moving into a positive market, and that the investment cycle has begun.
- **Horizontal trends** indicate that the prices of shares and assets are staying relatively consistent and are not moving noticeably upward or downward. It can be difficult to determine the direction of this trend and whether it is a good time to invest. Forecasting may be challenging. The government will often attempt to push the economy toward an upward trend.

Trend analysis is used in sales patterns, budget forecasting, and expense reporting. When using this technique, the goal is to determine the change within the market from one period to another to make more informed business decisions.

DATA GATHERING
APPROPRIATE METHODS OF GATHERING DATA

Collecting data to assist in creating organizational solutions is a key business function. There is an abundance of data collection methods that can be utilized. When determining how to gather the data there is a lot to consider. The individual in charge of **gathering data** needs to determine if primary or secondary data collection will be used. **Primary data** comes directly from the source or through interacting with respondents. Primary data gathering can occur through surveys, interviews, observations, and focus groups. **Secondary data** comes from using data that was previously collected for a purpose other than its original intention; this data is analyzed with the new purpose in mind and relevant information is drawn out. Secondary data can come from online databases, previous research, public data, government records, and published materials. The correct method may depend on what information is being sought. When evaluating a policy change, a focus group or survey might be the best method. Using previous research studies would not provide relevant or accurate information, so it would be a poor choice at that stage. Before gathering data, it is also key to understand if qualitative, quantitative, or a combination of both types of data will be needed to meet the investigative goal.

SCANNING EXTERNAL SOURCES FOR DATA RELEVANT TO THE ORGANIZATION

Organizations can easily identify **internal factors** that may affect the business such as staffing, finances, and procedures. **External factors** that may affect the business, such as inflation, scarcity of resources, or changes to regulations, are a little more difficult to identify and analyze. A SWOT (strengths, weaknesses, opportunities, and threats) analysis can help identify some of those factors, particularly in the "threats" category, but that analysis is still largely focused internally. A highly successful environmental or external scan that can be used by organizations is the PESTLE (political, economic, social, technological, legal, and environmental) analysis. Conducting a PESTLE analysis can better prepare an organization to understand which external factors may impact business operations and success.

USING DATA TO SUPPORT A BUSINESS CASE

When human resource (HR) professionals present a business case to senior leadership, they must show a compelling need for the resources that they are requesting. They can accomplish this by incorporating relevant data into their business case. For example, if HR wants to hire an additional maintenance technician on each shift, they should include things like the average machine downtime (and the resulting cost of lost productivity) and how long the average repair ticket stays open. Additionally, HR could add descriptive data in the form of complaints from production management and current maintenance staff, who are experiencing major disruptions in productivity or are feeling overworked, respectively.

INTERPRETATION OF DATA

Presenting a business case involves drawing conclusions from data sets with the goal of answering a question and spurring meaningful action. There are two categories of data, qualitative and quantitative. **Qualitative data** is descriptive and focuses on categorizing concepts based on making observations, conducting interviews, or reviewing documents. **Quantitative data**, on the other hand, involves a numerical, statistics-driven approach, in which data is derived from surveys and other quantifiable media.

Data **interpretation** refers to the process of reviewing data to draw meaningful conclusions from the material using a variety of analytical methods. Interpreting data aids researchers or presenters in categorizing and summarizing information to illustrate a point, trend, or need. Data interpretation can be used to answer critical questions and to help make solid business decisions. When used appropriately, data interpretation can help provide factual evidence for proposed initiatives or utilization of resources. Data interpretation is a critical component of presenting a business case, as it highlights statistical or numerical proof for a statement or problem.

GRAPHICAL REPRESENTATION

The use of graphs and/or charts to visually display numerical data, **graphical representation** helps with data analysis, interpretation, and clarification, and illustrating the relationship between data points. Data is entered and then a graph type, such as a bar graph, pie chart, scatter plot, or frequency table, is selected. Graphical representations allow viewers to quickly draw conclusions from data, like trends, relationships, and correlations. When presenting a business case, graphical representation provides solid visual evidence, which is helpful when seeking buy-in from key stakeholders.

Data Visualization

An extension of graphical representation, **data visualization** is when data is represented through visual elements such as infographics, and pictures. Visualization is an effective way to translate complex or detailed data into an image that is easier to process, understand, and follow. Visualization is an excellent aid in supporting a business case because listing statistics, numerical values, and data can cause the audience to become overwhelmed or lose sight of the overall intention. Displaying data in a visual format can add emphasis to the data without going too far into the weeds.

Storytelling

The art of **storytelling** involves translating data analysis into a narrative that helps illustrate the data and both influences and informs an audience. Storytelling can add significant value to a business case, as it highlights key points to the audience while adding a human touch. A recitation of hard data can be difficult to digest, but when a story is crafted around the information, the audience is more engaged and drawn into the presentation. Storytelling also allows the presenter to alter the presentation based on the audience, and can therefore reach a variety of listeners. Storytelling can also add value to the data by making it more relatable. Data visualization or graphical representation can be included in storytelling to create a compelling presentation. Using this method can help turn analysis into action.

Identifying Decision Points That Can Be Informed by Data and Evidence

Every issue, opportunity, trend, or initiative has at least one **decision point**. Being able to accurately identify such decision points and then supporting those decision points with evidence and data is critical to moving forward with a solution or implementation. For example, if an organization is experiencing low morale or decreased employee engagement, there is likely a reason. Data resources such as satisfaction surveys, exit interviews, and employee interviews can be used to identify the cause, or the decision point. Once the cause has been identified, it can be backed up with evidence. A solution can be proposed. Understanding the culture and atmosphere of an organization will help leaders and stakeholders identify areas where improvement or changes may be needed.

Data Analysis
Identifying Potentially Misleading or Flawed Data

Misleading or flawed data contains faulty or inaccurate information from the data gathering, processing, or presentation. This fault or inaccuracy could be purposeful or unintentional. There are several ways that flawed or misleading data can be identified. In a visual representation, if the baseline is missing or begins with a specific number, this data could be skewed to show a favorable result. If the axes of a graph are manipulated (such as using different scales), the graph can be hard to read and interpret without getting into the raw data. Incomplete data is difficult to validate, and some visual representations will only illustrate some of the data to create a larger impact. Selecting data that only presents a favorable time period also causes issues, because the data for the full time period is incomplete. When reviewing and analyzing data, it is critical to check sources. Know who conducted the research and where the data was derived from. Data should be objective, but research funded by a vested party can often be subjective. The length of the study and the size of the sample being presented are also important to know, as is the framing of the research questions. Some research questions are misleading and manipulate respondents. If an individual is conducting his or her own research, the analysis should be done by a third party in order to limit potential bias.

IDENTIFYING DATA GAPS BASED ON ANALYSIS

It can be difficult to identify **data gaps**, particularly for the individuals collecting the data. However, missing data leads to an incomplete and inaccurate analysis. There are several areas researchers or analysts can examine when reviewing data to check for gaps. The first area to examine is time-related gaps: the time of year could impact data collection, weekends and holidays might cause missing data, or changing data collection methods could cause gaps during transition periods. Examining the data looking at these key points can help determine if time-related gaps exist. Another key area to examine is the aggregation of the data. Would the information look different if grouped using different methods such as by city, or is the data being sampled at a consistent interval that may miss oddball occurrences, or is the correct sampling method being used, such as groups of five versus ten? Examining if human bias has created a gap is important as well.

Once any gaps in the data have been identified, the individual analyzing the data needs to determine what to do next. There are several options. With statistical data, the missing data can be replaced using **imputation**, which is estimating value based on available data. Alternatively, the set of data with a gap can be deleted. This can shrink the sample size and impact the validity of the data, so this is not always the best solution. For other types of data analysis, similar research can be analyzed to provide additional insight into the missing data. If the missing data comes from internal content, data gathering can be resumed in order to pick up the missing data. Surveys, interviews, and questionnaires can be collected to address the gap.

Security Best Practices

DATA SECURITY

Data security is important to all employers, as data security laws require organizations to notify those who have been subject to a breach. A breach is an unauthorized release of an individual's or group's personally identifiable information (PII). Healthcare organizations are subject to a whole other set of regulations related to personal health information (PHI). Not all information held by an organization is PII. Specifically, PII is valuable information that is linked to a person's name—such as a Social Security number, mailing address, or email address. This information can be compromised intentionally by external hackers who wish to damage an organization on a large scale. Such breaches may come with ransom requests from the hackers. However, the majority of breaches are on a smaller scale and come from inside the organization. Such a breach could be an intentional action by a disgruntled employee, or it could be the result of an error made by an employee.

Companies have a responsibility to communicate the importance of data security and establish policies and practices to reduce the risk of a data breach. Likely the most important step is to make data security a responsibility of all team members. This starts with training so that employees understand the risks and responsibilities. Training should occur for new hires and on a recurring basis for all staff since data breach risks change continuously. Background checks are also recommended for new hires to avoid hiring someone with a concerning criminal background. Moreover, data security policies should encompass all employees and not just impact the IT department. These policies can be standalone or part of the employee handbook. Regardless, it is recommended to have employees sign an acknowledgement of understanding. Finally, companies should have an inventory system to track system access and equipment assigned to employees. This makes it easier to ensure system access removal and equipment collection when an employee leaves the organization.

DATA PRIVACY

Data privacy consists of keeping confidential information secure. While people often think of the digital aspect of data privacy, data privacy includes keeping hard-copy documents secure as well. Individuals have long kept documents in safes or locked in file cabinets; the same level of security is needed electronically as more and more information is in electronic form. These steps are taken because if information falls into the wrong hands, data privacy is compromised and the organization could face financial or credibility problems. Therefore, companies are wise to have a data privacy plan and data privacy policies. At their most basic, these plans and policies should expect employees to secure confidential documents and maintain "need to know" practices regarding customer and employee information and conversations. On a broader scale, companies that maintain customer information electronically should have a digital data security plan and policies to mitigate the risk of private information being subject to an electronic breach.

DATA INTEGRITY

Data integrity involves maintaining and protecting data content to ensure that it is complete, accurate, and reliable. The design, implementation, and usage throughout the **data life cycle** is critical to any system that stores or processes data. Individual users, management, culture, training, controls, and audits can all affect **data integrity**. Poor configuration and inaccurate data entry can corrupt data. Therefore, thorough testing and safeguarding of data is required to avoid spending many hours debugging and reconciling information. Moreover, policies and training on what to do in the event of a breach can help mitigate risk by increasing staff awareness and ability to fight off breaches.

CONFIDENTIALITY DISCLOSURES

Confidentiality disclosures should include definitions and exclusions of confidential information while outlining individual responsibilities. **Confidentiality disclosures** are used to keep private or secure information available only to those who are authorized to access it. It is important to ensure that only the proper individuals have access to the information needed to perform their jobs. Moreover, legislation mandates **due diligence** to protect the confidential information of employees and customers. **Technology breaches** in confidentiality could happen via phone, fax, computer, email, and electronic records. For this reason, some businesses might utilize encryption software, limit the communications that can be sent via email, and include a statement notifying the reader what to do if it is inadvertently sent to the wrong person.

IMPORTANCE OF IT SECURITY

IT security is becoming a more serious topic and rapidly gaining more attention. It is important for HR practitioners to be conscientious of controls to mitigate organizational exposure and risk. Some companies may have **IT security policies and acknowledgements** in place to reduce liability and identify and document compliance and security controls. Multiple layers of corporate IT security might include the encryption of data files, firewalls, access controls or logins, systems monitoring, detection processes, antivirus software, and cyber insurance. Implementing stronger IT security can provide companies with benefits such as mitigating lost revenue, protecting brand reputation, and supporting mobilization.

CYBERCRIMES

Cybercrime is when a computer or element of technology is used to commit an illegal act such as violating privacy or stealing data, money, intellectual property, or identities. Cybercrime is a criminal activity even if the activity is not specifically monetary, such as spreading viruses or causing other forms of technological harm. In fact, companies could be held liable if they do not impose actions or precautions to prevent cybercrimes from occurring. Furthermore, the financial cost of cybercrime to a business can be astronomical. The reality is that a large majority of work done by employees involves inputting, analyzing, and transferring highly sensitive data. Therefore, it is extremely important for organizations to conduct background checks that include a criminal history of malicious hacking.

Employers should take steps to allow and promote open communication and report any suspected cybercrime the moment there is an indication that something might be wrong. Employers should communicate the importance of not opening anything via email (or any other form of technology or software) that could be linked to scams, hacking, or phishing. Companies should make every effort possible to protect their data, including not transferring data on unsecured or unencrypted servers, not posting company information on public social media sites, and updating antivirus protection software. An organization's best defense against cybercrime is vigilance in monitoring and taking every possible systemic precaution to protect its data.

Minimizing Password Breach Risks

Passwords are needed for almost every program that is opened on a computer, and it is critical to develop and maintain them in such a way as to minimize risk to the company. Many companies have developed password polices to help manage the process and ensure it is being monitored and enforced with regularity. Most password policies are developed with the whole lifecycle of the password in mind—for example, the creation of passwords, the times when they are changed, and guidelines for the prevention of password theft. Research indicates data breaches involving passwords are more likely to occur with a phishing attack or someone inside the company getting knowledge about passwords (as when passwords are left out on a drawer or written on a piece of paper) than by outside hacking. The following are some guidelines that could be adopted while drafting a password policy:

- Passwords should be strong, complex, and challenging for someone to guess—typically they should be combinations of uppercase letters, lowercase letters, numbers, punctuation marks, and special characters. Preferably, they should be over 8 characters long. Passwords should not be obvious or easy to determine. For instance, "Password123!" would be a poor password.
- Default passwords, such as those given by IT for various reasons, should be changed immediately after logging in.
- Passwords should not be shared with anyone. If this occurs, then the employee should change the password immediately.
- Employers should educate employees on ways to avoid phishing scams that might be used to steal passwords.
- To prevent discovery, passwords should not be written down or stored in an employee's workspace.

PHR Practice Test #1

Want to take this practice test in an online interactive format?
Check out the bonus page, which includes interactive practice questions and much more: **mometrix.com/bonus948/phr**

1. Which of the following individuals is MOST appropriate to conduct exit interviews?
   a. Direct supervisors
   b. Senior executives
   c. A third party
   d. Departmental managers

2. Sandra is the head of a small human resources department. She wants to implement a human resource information system, so she begins by commissioning a needs analysis. What is her next step?
   a. Researching possible systems
   b. Asking for permission to implement the system
   c. Identifying possible conflicts with other organizational systems
   d. Creating a timeline for implementation

3. Which of the following types of employee rating systems is usually better for a smaller group of employees but can be difficult to organize with a larger group?
   a. Behaviorally anchored rating scales
   b. Forced distribution
   c. Ranking
   d. Competency-based

Refer to the following for questions 4 - 5:

> You are a human resources manager for a midsized technology company with a diverse employee group—there are many employees from India, some are from Russia, and others are American. Employees tend to stay within their own cultural groups for socializing and even for project collaboration. This has created a siloed work environment, resulting in minimal communication and inefficient work processes.

4. What would be a creative and effective way to improve communication across the organization?
   a. Pair up individuals from different cultures on specific work assignments.
   b. Require language classes for each of the dialects spoken in the organization.
   c. Offer cultural sensitivity training for the entire organization.
   d. Organize on-site social activities to take place during work hours.

5. What guidance would you give to supervisors/managers for managing teams from different backgrounds?
   a. Consider employees' cultural preferences before assigning work tasks.
   b. Have weekly team meetings and ask employees to share what they're working on for the week.
   c. Get to know each team member and their background to build trust and establish the relationship first.
   d. Facilitate face-to-face discussions among team members during times of conflict.

6. The Fair Labor Standards Act (FLSA) mandates that most employees be paid overtime for more than 40 hours in a week unless they fall under certain criteria. Which is NOT an FLSA exemption?
   a. Outside sales exemption
   b. Computer employee exemption
   c. Creative professional exemption
   d. Advanced engineer exemption

7. Which of the following elements is the most critical when establishing an organizational diversity, equity, and inclusion (DE&I) strategy?
   a. Employee survey data
   b. Leadership buy-in
   c. Budgetary allocations
   d. Training and development

8. Return-to-work (RTW) programs are an effective tool to help transition employees back to full duty. When are they used?
   a. An employee experiences an on-the-job injury.
   b. An employee experiences an injury, whether on the job or off duty.
   c. Family and Medical Leave Act (FMLA)-protected leave is denied for the employee.
   d. An employee's physician will not give a medical release.

9. One kind of bias that can occur during an interview is a halo bias. What is a halo bias?
   a. Interviewers tend to rank candidates higher when they are similar to themselves.
   b. An interviewer observes one negative trait in a candidate, and it negatively influences the perception of other traits.
   c. An interviewer observes one positive trait in a candidate, and it positively influences the perception of other traits.
   d. Interviewers base a hiring decision immediately upon their first impression of the candidate.

10. There are many critics of using personality assessments as part of the hiring process. Which of the following is the MOST valid concern that critics have expressed?
   a. Assessments can pigeonhole applicants based solely on personality traits.
   b. Applicants can usually manipulate the results—they choose the option that the organization wants to hear rather than how they feel.
   c. Assessments may ask questions that would identify and exclude disabled individuals.
   d. Disparate impact—protected groups of people may be excluded from consideration based on their responses.

Refer to the following for questions 11 - 12:

> Human resources has been tasked with creating a comprehensive and consistent training program in an organization that has never had a structured program in the past. Previously, training was administered and tracked differently across departments according to their specific needs and requirements.

11. What should be the first task of human resources in creating the program?
   a. Taking inventory of each department's training needs and current processes
   b. Researching learning management systems—obtaining quotes, checking references, and so on
   c. Becoming familiar with the legal requirements and best practices of training programs in the industry
   d. Creating an organization-wide training calendar with scheduled training assignments and due dates

12. Which criterion is the LEAST important to consider when deciding on training delivery methods and course durations for the new program?
   a. Legal obligations to remain compliant
   b. Current training delivery methods and course durations
   c. Workplace logistics and preferred learning styles of employees—that is, whether there are field-based employees who may not have easy access to a learning management system, or perhaps employees who aren't able to step away from their desks for long durations
   d. The content of the training being delivered

13. In assessing HR technology programs, what is an example of a "best of breed" concept?
   a. Selecting an HR/payroll system and a separate third-party learning management system (LMS) with better features
   b. Performing a needs analysis internally to determine the optimal system to streamline current processes
   c. Selecting an all-in-one, integrated solution with HR, payroll, performance management, and learning management capabilities.
   d. Selecting an HR/payroll system that requires the least amount of customization to ensure a fast implementation and simpler future upgrades.

Refer to the following for questions 14 - 15:

> A long-tenured and valued employee has recently been coming to work late, calling in sick on Mondays, and his overall appearance is messy and disheveled. He has also been behaving strangely and getting agitated more easily than usual. His supervisor suspects that he has a drug problem.

14. How would you approach the situation as a human resource representative?
   a. Call the employee's emergency contact on file, and inquire if something has changed with the employee recently.
   b. Pull the employee into a private conference room along with the supervisor. Explain the strange behavior that you and the supervisor have witnessed, and ask for an explanation.
   c. Coach the supervisor to have a conversation with the employee privately.
   d. Require that the employee complete a drug test before any conversation occurs.

15. Assume the employee admitted that he began using cocaine about six months ago. He says that he started using casually, but recently it's gotten out of control, and he needs help. What would be your next course of action?
    a. Explain that despite the substance abuse problem, he will be held to the same performance standards as any other employee.
    b. Your company has a zero-tolerance policy, so his employment should be terminated immediately.
    c. As an active drug addict, he is protected under the Americans with Disabilities Act, so work with him to find a reasonable accommodation to help him get clean.
    d. Offer the employee Family and Medical Leave Act (FMLA)-protected leave to enroll in and attend a rehab program.

16. How would you describe an engaged employee?
    a. An employee who is satisfied with his or her job
    b. An employee with commitment to the organization and motivation to perform well
    c. An employee with high motivation for the first 30 days after hire but that fades
    d. An employee who is ambitious and works hard but is always looking outside the organization for new opportunity

Refer to the following for questions 17 - 18:

> Late in the afternoon an account manager, Sharon, knocks on your door and asks to come in. It's clear she's been crying: her face is red and her eyes are swollen. She sits down in your office chair and begins sobbing. Through her sobs she explains that she put a lot of work into building a client relationship within a shared account, but her colleague just took all the credit in a team meeting.

17. What would be the most effective way to calm Sharon down?
    a. Say, "She should not have taken credit. I'm sorry you had to go through that."
    b. Suggest that she talk to her supervisor about it.
    c. Suggest that she take some time to calm down, then speak directly with her colleague, and explain how it made her feel.
    d. Guess Sharon's feelings and ask if you're correct. For example, "It sounds like you're feeling a lack of recognition and maybe disrespected by your colleague. Do I have that right?"

18. Sharon has calmed down and says, "Thanks. I feel a lot better. I just needed to vent to someone. Now I can go on about my day and put this behind me." What would you do next?
    a. Give a warm smile to Sharon, and say, "My door is open any time." Consider it "case closed." Sharon clearly didn't want this conflict to progress into anything more.
    b. Give a warm smile to Sharon, and say, "My door is open any time"; however, after she leaves your office, give her supervisor a call and explain what just happened and that she should keep an eye on things between the two.
    c. Thank Sharon for confiding in you, but diplomatically explain that it is not HR's role to be a therapist.
    d. Explain to Sharon that anything she says in your office is not confidential and that you may be looking into this further.

Refer to the following for questions 19 - 22:

> In response to a rise in turnover rates across the labor market, the executive team of a large nonprofit decided to raise the wages of all hourly employees by 3%.
>
> Despite the increase in pay, turnover rates remained higher than usual for the company, so the HR team reviewed recent exit interview responses to better understand why employees were leaving. Overall, the interview data was mixed. The company received, in general, high praise for "corporate vision" and "workspace amenities," but it was criticized for "untrustworthy leadership" and "compensation dissatisfaction." Additionally, these were some of the recurring remarks that were mentioned:
>
> - Belief in mission and doing good for others
> - Lack of opportunity for advancement due to favoritism

19. What would be the most effective first step for the HR team following the exit interview review?

a. Review performance management practices to assess effectiveness of promotion procedures.
b. Launch an internal investigation into all managers to identify toxic leaders.
c. Conduct stay interviews to better understand why current employees have chosen not to leave.
d. Recommend an additional 5% salary increase for all employees.

20. Reviewing the performance management reports has revealed managers selecting candidates for promotions based on personal similarities instead of on actual performance outcomes. Which of the following tools would be most helpful for tackling performance assessment criteria?

a. Job analysis
b. Workplace observations
c. Job evaluation
d. Employee survey

21. Before recommending an additional round of companywide raises, which of the following steps would be most effective at addressing compensation criticisms and the lack of trust in company leadership?

a. Propose an expanded C-suite to include a chief human resources officer who is best suited to build the trust of the workforce.
b. Design a pay-for-performance model of compensation to improve the work-to-reward visibility.
c. Review benefits and how they compare to market standards in relation to what the workforce actually uses.
d. Conduct a pay audit and publicize the results and any proposed follow-up action.

22. Many of the exit interviews mentioned employees seeking leadership positions outside of the company because they did not possess the education standards required to advance and their hands-on experience was not recognized as an equivalency. What barrier to diversity is most likely at play in these instances?
    a. Disparate treatment
    b. Systemic inequality
    c. Ableist standards
    d. Stereotyping

23. What is a performance improvement plan (PIP) best suited for?
    a. Documentation prior to a termination action
    b. Insubordinate behavior
    c. Quantifiable performance deficiencies with potential for improvement
    d. Unionized workplaces

24. Why are human resource representatives generally excluded from bargaining unit representation?
    a. They often oversee the work of others in a supervisory capacity.
    b. They act as an advisor and/or representative of management during collective bargaining.
    c. They are responsible for defining organizational policies that may conflict with collective bargaining agreements (CBAs).
    d. They are responsible for enforcing the provisions of the CBAs and policies.

25. Focus groups are an effective means to gather employee feedback. For what are they best suited?
    a. Employees in the same division or department
    b. Specific subjects of discussion
    c. Fewer than five participants
    d. Unstructured brainstorming sessions

26. If a rejected candidate asks for feedback from the employer on how he or she might improve, what is the MOST appropriate response?
    a. A non-specific response like "You just weren't the right fit for our team."
    b. Honest and direct feedback with a list of areas to improve upon
    c. A standard, generic response, which is given to all candidates: "We decided to move forward with another candidate."
    d. A customized response based on several factors from the level of position, number of candidates interviewed, and whether the candidate is internal or external

27. What is the primary difference between coaching and mentoring?
    a. Coaching is generally used for a specific reason—either to prepare an individual for a new challenge or to change a specific work behavior.
    b. Coaching is generally conducted in a one-on-one setting.
    c. Coaching is usually used in the case of pending, or as a result of, disciplinary action.
    d. Coaching is more instructional and includes job-related training.

28. Under the Patient Protection and Affordable Care Act (PPACA), an employer may utilize the look-back measurement method to determine _____
   a. if an employee will be expected to work more than 30 hours per week.
   b. if an employee has received health insurance coverage over the past year.
   c. if an employee has worked more than 130 hours in a month.
   d. if an employee's pay is low enough that he or she qualifies for a subsidy.

Refer to the following for questions 29 - 30:

> A supervisor reports to you that she is having some personality clashes on her team. Specifically, there is one employee who is particularly forceful in his opinion and tends to dominate the weekly team meetings. He openly complains about routine tasks that all human resource team members have to complete because he feels that they're "beneath" him. Other employees have expressed frustration when working with this individual.

29. What advice would you give to this supervisor?
   a. Have a direct conversation with the employee. Explain how this behavior has been putting off others on the team.
   b. Be specific in the feedback—explain how talking over others in a meeting makes others feel like they don't have a voice.
   c. Tailor the employee's work assignments so that they're more challenging and complex.
   d. Provide conflict resolution training to the employee and others on the team.

30. Another employee on the team has poor attendance. He always seems to be having one personal crisis after another, from personal medical conditions to taking care of family members to a sick dog. He is not private about any of these details and will share these ailments with anyone who will listen. How would you guide the supervisor to handle this employee?
   a. Meet with the employee privately and hear him out. Understand the issues he is facing, and remain empathetic.
   b. Try your best to avoid discussing any personal issues in the workplace. Change the subject when the employee begins to overshare about his personal life and stick to talk about work.
   c. Focus on the attendance issue. Hold the employee accountable for being late, and request a doctor's note the next time he calls in sick.
   d. Facilitate a 360-degree performance evaluation for the entire team in hopes that feedback from others on the team will help give the employee some self-awareness.

31. Under the United States-Mexico-Canada Agreement (USMCA), what do Canadian professionals need to work in the United States?
   a. A TN visa
   b. An H-1B visa
   c. The appropriate documentation (i.e., offer letter, proof of Canadian citizenship, proof of qualification) presented at the U.S. border
   d. U.S. permanent residency (green card)

32. Currently, 28 states in the United States are considered "right-to-work" states. What are right-to-work laws?
   a. Legislation that forbids unionizing among employees
   b. Legislation that allows for an employee to be terminated for any reason as long as it is not illegal
   c. Legislation that provides a choice to employees with respect to union membership
   d. Legislation that ensures employment opportunities for permanent resident aliens

33. An employee emails you, as a designated human resources (HR) representative, with a complex explanation of his medical history and explains that he has an upcoming surgery. It's clear from the tenor of the email that he is stressed about missing work time. He wants to know what the next steps are to prepare for the upcoming leave. You don't know the answer to the question off the top of your head, and the HR person who specializes in leaves is out of the office for a week. How should you respond to the email?
   a. First, explain that the employee should not send any protected health information over an unsecure network. Request that he come into the office and meet with the human resource (HR) specialist face-to-face upon her return from vacation.
   b. Thank the employee for the email, and explain that the HR specialist who is the point of contact is out of the office. Offer to explain the situation to her when she is back and have her touch base with the employee at that point.
   c. Research the information he is seeking on your own, and respond back to the employee within the day.
   d. Reply to the employee with a CC to the HR leave specialist, explaining that the HR specialist will reach out to the employee upon her return to the office.

34. Critics of utilizing key performance indicators (KPIs) to measure goal attainment say that instead of fostering collaboration, they often promote _____
   a. competition.
   b. micromanagement.
   c. slow progress.
   d. unachievable standards.

35. How would you handle this complaint?

   A supervisor, John, gives you a call and says, "I have an issue. Another supervisor, Steve, made a joke to one of my employees that made her feel uncomfortable." John goes on to describe the insensitive joke about a "black Santa" that Steve told to the African American employee, Karen. John finishes with, "So what do I do?" Steve is a well-liked supervisor who has never crossed the line before. According to John, Karen and Steve are friends, and she doesn't want him to "get into trouble," but she thought she should at least mention it.

   a. Thank John for bringing this to your attention, and ask that he let you know if it ever happens again. Take no further action because this was an isolated incident with Steve
   b. Document the interaction between Steve and Karen based on the facts presented by John. Save it in case another questionable scenario with Steve ever comes up.
   c. Speak with Karen directly, and document the conversation. Ask her how she wants you to proceed.
   d. Have an informal but stern conversation with Steve. Explain that his joke was inappropriate and should never happen again.

36. When an employee is injured on the job, what is the first thing supervisors and managers should be instructed to do after stabilizing the employee?
   a. Draft a statement of what happened.
   b. Contact human resources.
   c. Collect witness statements.
   d. Address the cause of the injury, and fix it if possible.

37. A job hazard analysis is a tool that the Occupational Safety and Health Administration (OSHA) recommends to prevent workplace injury, illnesses, or accidents. When performing a job hazard analysis, who is it most important to consult with?
   a. The employees who are performing the work
   b. The supervisor of the employees who perform the work
   c. OSHA
   d. The organization's safety officer

Refer to the following for questions 38 - 39:

> A team of five customer service representatives (CSRs) works in a call center. They usually sit for the entirety of their eight-hour shifts, answering calls and speaking to customers with a headset. One CSR has severe back issues, so he has requested a stand-up desk to help with back pain.

38. How would you handle this request?
   a. Provide the stand-up desk to the employee, as it's a reasonable request.
   b. Perform an ergonomic assessment of the workstation before determining whether a modification is needed.
   c. Ask for a doctor's note. If the doctor states that the CSR requires a stand-up desk to perform the essential functions of the job, provide it.
   d. Back pain does not qualify as "disability" under the Americans with Disabilities Act, so no accommodation needs to be made.

39. After you provide the stand-up desk to the CSR, another employee complains about unfair treatment. She would like a stand-up desk as well. However, she is not requesting the desk due to a disability, as she is requesting it for health and wellness purposes. There may be room in the budget to purchase two to three more stand-up desks, but there is not enough for all five CSRs. How would you handle this request?
   a. Explain that the reason the other CSR was given a stand-up desk was for a disability, and this was an accommodation under the Americans with Disabilities Act. For that reason, she will not be given one unless she too has a doctor's note.
   b. Purchase the stand-up desk. If anyone else asks for one, provide it as well until the budget is exhausted. Work to obtain more budget the following year to provide the desks to all five CSRs.
   c. Set up a program in which the highest-performing CSR of the quarter is awarded with a stand-up desk until the budget is exhausted.
   d. Offer to help set it up if she purchases the equipment using her own money.

40. What is a "top-heavy" 401(k) plan?
    a. A plan with an average deferral by highly compensated employees at 2% greater than non-highly compensated employees
    b. A plan with more than 60% participation by executives
    c. A plan with greater than 60% of its total value in the accounts of "key" employees
    d. A plan with less than 60% participation by non-highly compensated employees

41. Which is NOT a best practice for Form I-9 retention?
    a. Retain the form three years after hire date or one year after termination date, whichever is later.
    b. Restrict Form I-9 access to supervisors and managers.
    c. Shred the forms once an employee reaches the three-year employment anniversary.
    d. File terminated employees' forms separately from active employees' forms.

42. For an employer to hire an unpaid intern, the internship must meet several criteria. Which option is NOT a criterion to qualify for an unpaid internship?
    a. The intern receives academic credit for completion of the internship.
    b. The intern's work does not take away work from another paid employee.
    c. The intern must work less than 20 hours per week.
    d. The intern receives relevant and valuable on-the-job training.

43. What is the style of negotiation that aims to meet the needs of both parties and leverage collaboration to come to an agreement?
    a. Principled bargaining
    b. Positional bargaining
    c. Distributive bargaining
    d. Composite bargaining

44. Which type of employee must be excluded from bargaining units as per the National Labor Relations Act (NLRA)?
    a. Supervisors
    b. Employees who work in the private sector
    c. Part-time employees
    d. Seasonal employees

45. Which is the provision that does NOT typically describe a health savings account (HSA)?
    a. "Use it or lose it"—funds expire at the end of the plan year.
    b. Both employees and employers may contribute to the account on the employee's behalf.
    c. Employees may reduce their taxable income by contributing funds to an HSA.
    d. HSA funds are portable—if an employee leaves the organization, he or she can take the funds.

46. Under "coordination of benefits" rules, how are insurance claims processed?
   a. Charges are first allocated to the primary payer, and then residual charges are submitted to a secondary payer.
   b. Claims are processed only at an "allowable amount" as determined by the insurance company, and any residual cost is an out-of-pocket charge to the employee.
   c. Out-of-pocket expenses are deducted directly from the employee's flexible spending account.
   d. Charges are split evenly between the primary and secondary payers.

47. What would be the next course of action for you to get this position filled?

   As a recruiter, you are having a difficult time filling a civil engineer position that has been open for a few months. Few qualified individuals have applied, and the passive candidates who you've contacted haven't returned your calls. You've been aggressive in your advertising approach (in fact you've exceeded your advertising budget), but it's proving to be difficult to find quality candidates in this competitive market.

   a. Re-assess the salary and benefit package for the position.
   b. Work on obtaining additional budget, and post more job advertisements.
   c. Have a brainstorming session with the hiring manager, and ask for ideas and suggestions.
   d. Change the requirements for the job; it could be that they are hindering potential applicants from applying.

48. What is the practice of storing, managing, and processing data in remote, internet-based servers commonly called?
   a. Cloud computing
   b. Locally hosted computing
   c. Software as a service (SaaS)
   d. E-commerce

Refer to the following for questions 49 - 50:

   Acme Corp is experiencing a rapid increase in new projects and, in turn, revenue. Because of this influx of new work, the hiring pace has quickened as well. The employee headcount is projected to grow from 500 employees to 600 over the course of the year. Unfortunately, turnover seems to be increasing at the same rate, and it seems to be mostly newer employees leaving the organization.

49. What would be the most impactful action human resources could take to identify the cause of this increase in turnover?
   a. Conduct exit interviews with each employee who leaves the organization. Identify trends in the reasons mentioned.
   b. Speak with the managers of each exiting employee. Ask if they have any insight on why the individuals are choosing to leave the organization.
   c. Analyze the recruitment strategy and interview notes when the employee was hired. Because they're often new employees who leave quickly, it's likely that the wrong hiring decision was made.
   d. Send out an employee satisfaction survey to all employees. Identify areas of discontent among current employees.

50. The exit interview comments have shown that employees feel overwhelmed and burnt out—this is causing employees to quit within their 90-day probationary period. What would be a possible solution human resources could take to reduce turnover?
   a. Speak with managers and supervisors, relay this information, and request that they lighten the workload for all employees.
   b. Introduce every Friday as a work-from-home day to improve work-life balance.
   c. Implement realistic job previews during the interview process to give candidates a better idea of what will be expected of them.
   d. Improve new hire orientation and training, ensuring that new hires are able to get up to speed quickly.

Refer to the following for questions 51 - 52:

> You are the vice president of human resources for a small start-up software company. The bulk of your employees are young, highly educated hard workers and smart when it comes to technology but not so much when it comes to healthcare benefits, retirement, and other employment-related details. For most, this is their first job out of college. The CEO is a visionary and has expressed that she wants the company to always be cutting edge and a desirable place to work to attract only the best software developers in the country.

51. Given the information in the scenario, what proposed initiative or program would you include in your annual strategic human resources plan?
   a. Unlimited paid time off (PTO)
   b. An on-site health clinic for employees and their dependents
   c. An employee recognition program with cutting-edge technology as rewards
   d. A structured career path program with learning and development opportunities

52. The career path program was a hit with the software developers. The next step in creating that cutting-edge workplace reputation is embracing flexible/remote work opportunities. Your CEO doesn't like the idea and thinks it would negatively impact productivity. However, you're confident that it's the way of the future. How would you sell the idea to the CEO?
   a. Provide positive case studies from other organizations that have embraced remote assignments.
   b. Suggest that you allow it for a maximum of once per week as a trial. Monitor the remote work output, and expand the program if successful.
   c. Remind the CEO that remote work assignments would expand your recruitment reach into other hot technology markets, not just local to your headquarters office.
   d. Remind the CEO that not only is telecommuting cutting edge, but it allows software developers to focus better and in turn produce higher-quality work.

53. How would you deliver the feedback to this employee?

You are a supervisor who manages a small team of three professionals. One in particular is a high performer with a great attitude. Unfortunately, he made a huge error on his most recent client report, which ended up costing the organization a significant amount of money. It is an error that you need to address, but you don't want to dampen his spirits, as he tends to be sensitive to negative feedback.

a. Remain neutral and state the facts of the mistake in the report. Ask for feedback on how to avoid these mistakes in the future.
b. Send an email with the details of the mistake to be less confrontational.
c. Explain the mistake and the impact it had on the company. Warn him that if it happens again, he might be disciplined.
d. Document the event in the details of his next performance review.

54. To meet eligibility for Family and Medical Leave Act (FMLA)-protected leave, an employee and employer must meet specified criteria. Which criterion is NOT an FMLA qualifier?

a. The employee must have worked for the employer for at least 12 months.
b. The employee must have worked at least 1,250 hours in the past 12 months.
c. The employer must employ at least 50 employees within a 75-mile radius.
d. The employee must give the employer at least 30 days' notice of an upcoming leave.

55. Which is NOT an example of an unfair labor practice?

a. An employer declining to participate in collective bargaining
b. An employer not making concessions during collective bargaining
c. An employer offering benefits to employees who decline participation in a union
d. An employer closing down a location upon unionizing activity by employees

56. What does the Worker Adjustment and Retraining Notification (WARN) Act require?

a. An employer must provide affected employees with 60 days' notice of an impending layoff of more than 50 employees.
b. An employer must provide employees who are over the age of 40 with a revocation period after signing a severance agreement.
c. An employer must provide affected employees with 60 days' notice of an impending layoff of any size.
d. An employer must publicly release the names of each person affected by a layoff.

57. What types of organizations are required to maintain an affirmative action program (AAP)?

a. Federal government contractors or subcontractors, as mandated by the Office of Federal Contract Compliance Programs (OFCCP)
b. All organizations with more than 50 employees, as mandated by the Equal Employment Opportunity Commission (EEOC)
c. None, rather it is best practice for all organizations to remain informed of minority and female representation
d. All federal, state, and local government agencies

58. What is the most important action to take before initiating recruitment efforts to fill an open position?
   a. Determine where the position will be advertised.
   b. Build a candidate pipeline.
   c. Define the skills needed for the position.
   d. Determine the appropriate compensation level for the position.

59. Which of the following does NOT describe unlawful harassment?
   a. Unwelcome conduct that is based upon the victim's protected status
   b. Behavior that is severe and pervasive enough that a reasonable person would find it hostile or abusive
   c. Enduring offensive conduct becomes a condition of employment
   d. Any type of bullying or unwelcome conduct from a supervisor

60. After a lengthy investigation concludes, a sexual harassment complaint is determined to be unfounded. What is the most appropriate course of action?
   a. Disciplinary action for the complainant—there were no grounds for the complaint.
   b. Disciplinary action should be taken only if the reason was malicious.
   c. Disciplinary action would be considered retaliation if the complainant were to be disciplined for making a complaint.
   d. Initiate a gentle conversation with the complainant and subject together to describe the results of the investigation.

61. In selecting a new human resource information system (HRIS), what is the first step in the process?
   a. Determine the available budget.
   b. Define organizational needs versus wants in a new system.
   c. Determine if the selection process will be conducted by a consultant or internal resources.
   d. Collect quotes and proposals from prospective HRIS vendors.

62. When conducting a strengths, weaknesses, opportunities, and threats (SWOT) analysis, what portion may be accomplished by a political, economic, social, and technological (PEST) analysis?
   a. Weaknesses and threats
   b. Strengths and weaknesses
   c. Strengths and opportunities
   d. Opportunities and threats

63. When conducting market research for compensation studies, which is a best practice?
   a. Consider the job title and level of the position at other organizations.
   b. Contact other organizations directly for pay information, as the information is more accurate.
   c. Leverage employee-reported salary figures through online tools.
   d. Utilize at least one market survey with aggregated salary information.

64. What is an advantage of hiring externally rather than from inside the organization?
   a. It brings a fresh perspective and creativity to the organization.
   b. It can be less expensive for recruitment efforts.
   c. It causes less conflict among coworkers.
   d. External candidates are likely to be more competent.

Refer to the following for questions 65 - 68:

> A small marketing firm within a niche tech industry is facing some growing pains following its initial business successes.
>
> The organization's initial achievements were attributed to the cooperative culture among its team members and the high transparency practiced by company leadership in decisions and operations. As a result of the early successes, the company began to experience substantial growth; after a series of acquisitions and expansions, it now has several hundred employees in both domestic and international offices.
>
> In an attempt to harness the people power of a diverse employee base, the chief operations officer tasks the division leaders with creating virtual teams of employees who specialize in specific skills or knowledge to help solve pervasive operational challenges. These focus teams consist of employees across a wide range of geographical regions, and they are tasked with discussing and proposing solutions for several operational, strategic, financial, and systematic challenges facing the growing organization.
>
> Six months after tasking the division leaders, the COO checks in with each of the focus teams to gauge their progress and gather feedback; however, the COO is disappointed to learn that the majority of groups fail to meet on a regular basis and that, even when they do, they struggle to agree on a focus or direction for which challenges to address or what possible solutions might look like.
>
> In response to the follow-up meetings, the COO seeks the guidance of the organization's HR director for assistance in improving the efficacy of the focus teams.

65. After the focus teams are up and running with renewed leadership buy-in and clearly defined timelines and goals, the HR director checks in with the COO to see how his vision is playing out. The COO is grateful for the director's initial observations and course correction suggestions but observes that since the teams have been working more closely together, there has been a rise in conflicts due to misunderstandings between team members from different regions and cultures. Which of the following actions that the HR director could recommend would be most effective?
   a. Issue a "celebrate diversity" online training for all team members to take.
   b. Design a team-building activity that connects members to common work goals and values.
   c. Let the misunderstandings play out naturally to encourage the evolution from conflict to collaboration.
   d. Assign conflicting team members to different teams or projects to ease the tension.

66. After collecting data from the focus teams, the HR director discovers one of the major obstacles to consistent meetings is the time zone differences. Which of the following solutions would be most effective to suggest?
   a. Team meetings should be scheduled several months out in advance to enable team members to plan accordingly.
   b. The teams should only use collaborative technologies that allow them to discuss and contribute in a running thread.
   c. Teams should be redistributed to keep all group members within no more than two time zones of each other.
   d. Team members who are unable to participate in the meetings should be removed from the project.

67. Which of the following action steps should the HR director take first in assisting the COO?
   a. Sit in on the next focus teams' meetings to observe discussions and interactions.
   b. Design an employee feedback survey to better understand the perspectives of the focus teams.
   c. Facilitate a meeting between the COO and the division leaders to discuss obstacles and future timelines.
   d. Meet with the division leaders to gauge their understanding of the focus teams and challenges they have experienced.

68. During the HR director's initial meeting with the COO, which of the following questions would be most effective in helping the director determine possible root causes for the initial shortcomings of the focus teams?
   a. How many focus teams were created?
   b. What type of timeline was provided to the division leaders for this project?
   c. Where would you like the focus groups to be in six months?
   d. How often and for how long do the focus teams meet?

Refer to the following for questions 69 - 70:

   A CEO of a midsized technology company has gained a reputation for berating others in meetings, firing employees who make minor mistakes, and micromanaging his senior leadership team.

69. How would you describe the likely culture of the company and its employees?
   a. Fear based with minimal contribution from employees
   b. Competitive among employees with a cutthroat mentality
   c. Tight-knit—employees commiserate about their experiences with the CEO
   d. High performing—employees wanting to prove the CEO wrong by doing their best work

70. As an HR leader in this organization reporting to the CEO, how would you propose fixing this leadership challenge?
   a. Clearly communicate with your own HR staff and other employees in the organization that you're aware of the issue and are working to resolve it. Offer an open door to anyone who needs to talk about their challenges.
   b. Hire a third-party consultant to conduct a leadership assessment with the entire executive team, including the CEO.
   c. Launch an internal investigation into inappropriate behaviors by the CEO. Interview multiple employees across the organization about their unpleasant interactions.
   d. Begin looking for another job. The CEO runs the company how he wishes and will likely not be receptive to feedback or any attempts to correct behavior. It's best to begin looking for a better work environment elsewhere.

71. What does Title II of the Genetic Information Nondiscrimination Act (GINA) prohibit?
   a. Discrimination against employees or applicants based on genetic information
   b. Discrimination against employees or applicants based on gender identity
   c. Unauthorized sharing of protected health information
   d. Discrimination against applicants based on disability status

72. Which of the following actions would be the most helpful in determining the cause of employee turnover?
   a. Separate out involuntary terminations from voluntary terminations.
   b. Include both voluntary and involuntary terminations in the calculation.
   c. Consider the prior year's headcount when dividing by the number of employee exits.
   d. Consider the prior year's total number of employee exits when dividing by average headcount.

Refer to the following for questions 73 - 74:

> Your organization is opening its first international office in Chennai, India. It will start as a relatively small office with mostly software developers, but there is a need to have an HR person located there. You will oversee the work of this India-based HR manager in addition to your U.S.-based team of five.

73. What would be your first step in helping open the India office?
   a. Conduct a political, economic, social, and technological (PEST) analysis through an HR lens.
   b. Travel to Chennai, see the landscape, meet the location contacts, and begin recruiting for the HR manager.
   c. Conduct a strengths, weaknesses, opportunities, and threats (SWOT) analysis through an HR lens.
   d. Begin collecting sample employee handbooks, forms, and policies from India companies.

74. Six months later, you have a promising human resources manager on board, and the India office seems to be running smoothly. However, as expected, there are some minor challenges with communication between the two offices. What would be the most effective practice to adopt to improve daily communications?

    a. Regular video conference calls for all virtual meetings
    b. A reminder to the U.S. location to use clear language in emails and eliminate the use of slang
    c. A daily 15-minute status call at a time that is convenient for both time zones
    d. Training provided at both locations regarding customs of the other culture—India culture training at the U.S. location and American culture training at the Chennai location

Refer to the following for questions 75 - 76:

> ABC Corp has a large number of millennial employees joining the company in entry-level positions. Most of these individuals show great promise and ambition upon hire, but after a few months, they struggle with the steep learning curve of ABC's complicated product lineup and proprietary sales techniques. They become frustrated and are leaving the organization at a high rate. Because of this, human resources has decided to implement a mentoring program in the hopes that pairing more senior sales leaders and executives with these entry-level employees will help retain millennials. The problem is that a good mentoring program needs a budget, and ABC is conservative with nonessential spending.

75. How would you appeal to senior finance leadership and convince them of the importance of this program?

    a. Put together a comprehensive document that defines eligibility requirements, high-potential employees who may participate, a timeline, marketing material, and a communication plan.
    b. Put together a succinct, finance-centered document with the total budget needed, how the budget will be spent, the expected impacts on employee retention, and in turn, cost savings.
    c. Start a six-month pilot program, which costs much less than the full program, and hope that its success will justify the money spent thus far.
    d. Give a presentation to the senior finance leadership, and give several case studies of other organizations that had success with mentoring programs. Explain the employee morale-boosting benefits, and answer any questions they have.

76. Assuming you were given the budget for the mentoring program, you finalize the details and launch the program. So far, you've had plenty of mentors and mentees who are eager participants. What is the LEAST important consideration when pairing mentors and mentees?

    a. Similar goals for the mentoring relationship
    b. Similar career aspirations and field of work
    c. The seniority and experience level of the mentor
    d. The mentor and mentee's preference of match

77. What happens if an employee on leave submits a medical certification and human resources questions the validity of diagnosis and the professional's credentials?
    a. HR should contact the medical professional for more information about the employee's medical condition.
    b. HR must make the best determination of its validity based on the information provided to maintain the employee's privacy.
    c. HR may require a second opinion from another healthcare provider.
    d. HR may not contact the medical professional but should contact the employee for more information on the health condition.

78. What does PEST stand for in relation to analysis framework?
    a. Political, electronic, social, taxation
    b. Political, economic, social, technological
    c. Pop culture, economy, strategy, technology
    d. Political, environmental, social, technological

79. Which of the following is true regarding 401(k) plan auto-enrollment for new hires?
    a. It is a great strategy to boost participation and encourage financial responsibility among employees.
    b. It is not legal.
    c. It is not advisable from an employee relations standpoint; employees tend to feel deceived.
    d. It is a requirement of most retirement plans.

80. A nine-box grid is an effective tool that compares an employee's performance with his or her potential for advancement. What is it most commonly used for?
    a. Disciplinary documentation
    b. Succession planning
    c. Talent acquisition
    d. Compensation planning

81. To comply with the Age Discrimination in Employment Act (ADEA), what should severance agreements include for employees over age 40?
    a. A 21-day consideration period plus a seven-day revocation period after signing
    b. A seven-day consideration period plus a 21-day revocation period after signing
    c. A waiver of any type of complaint to the Equal Employment Opportunity Commission (EEOC)
    d. A minimum of 30 days' health insurance coverage

82. How would you describe the most effective approach to diversity recruitment?
    a. Hire more diverse employees into the workplace.
    b. Alter workplace practices to appeal to multiple generations of employees—leverage technology where appropriate, and train older workers on this technology.
    c. Train hiring managers and other interviewers on appropriate, and inappropriate, questions to ask during an interview.
    d. Expand advertising sources to include diversity-focused professional organizations and websites.

83. Under the Patient Protection and Affordable Care Act (PPACA), what is the period of time during which an employer must offer coverage to those employees who are considered full time?
   a. The measurement period
   b. The stability period
   c. The administrative period
   d. The standard measurement period

84. How would you handle this situation?

   A new father, who has not exhausted his Family and Medical Leave Act (FMLA) leave for the year, has requested the next 12 Fridays off to care for his new baby. He cites "baby bonding time" under the FMLA law and feels that this intermittent leave qualifies. His supervisor has expressed the challenge this will present to his department, as they usually have a time-sensitive report to submit each Friday.

   a. Decline the employee's request, as this would clearly present a hardship on his department.
   b. Approve the employee's request, as he still has Family and Medical Leave Act (FMLA) leave available.
   c. Speak with the supervisor to see if other employees in the department would be able to work overtime on Fridays to cover the absence of this employee. If so, allow the request.
   d. Require that the employee use vacation time or paid time off, as this would not qualify for FMLA.

Refer to the following for questions 85 - 87:

   You are the project manager of a large human resources/payroll system implementation at your organization, which is a high-tech digital marketing firm. The implementation is not underway just yet, but you have sent out several requests for proposal, and the responses are coming in from vendors. As part of your role, you must keep the entire organization informed.

85. What type of initial message would you convey to the organization regarding this project to gain buy-in?
   a. That a new system will improve efficiencies and ultimately save the company money
   b. That there will be lots of training on the new system once it is in place
   c. That the executive team is fully committed to replacing the system
   d. That the current system is obsolete, and it is a risk to continue to rely on it for human resource and payroll functions

86. To convey the initial message and all subsequent communication, your plan is to issue updates through a variety of mediums. What technique would likely be the LEAST effective method of relaying important information to employees?
   a. Sending emails
   b. Attending department-wide meetings and giving verbal updates
   c. Mailing out a printed newsletter to employees' homes
   d. Posting updates on an electronic bulletin board

87. In this organization, employee career levels range from entry-level to advanced software engineers, with several employees fresh out of college and a few gearing up for retirement. Given this wide range in employee demographics, which communication technique should you utilize when giving your next departmental presentation?
   a. Tailor the message based on the group you're presenting to.
   b. Use stories and real-life examples to be more relatable.
   c. Describe the human resource information system project and its intricacies in lay terms.
   d. Provide a visual presentation with graphics and charts.

88. What is an important criterion in defining an employee's behavior as insubordination?
   a. The threat of discipline up to and including termination
   b. The employee yelling or being generally disrespectful toward a direct supervisor
   c. The employer making a clear directive to the employee
   d. The employee being represented by a bargaining unit

89. In the six stages of change readiness, what is the optimal stage for employees during a large organizational change?
   a. Indifference
   b. Experimentation
   c. Neutrality
   d. Commitment

90. When a company uses a matrix organizational structure, what does it mean?
   a. The functions of the company are separated into autonomous divisions.
   b. There are several layers of authority, and each manager has only one or two direct reports.
   c. Employees generally report to more than one supervisor or manager.
   d. There are minimal layers of reporting relationships, resulting in the need for more cross-functional teams.

91. What guideline should an organization follow when it keeps employment records electronically?
   a. Files must be able to be converted into a paper version.
   b. Files must be audited at regular time intervals.
   c. Files must be organized alphabetically and chronologically.
   d. Files must be made available to employees upon request.

92. When a company decides to review information it has gathered related to success rates achieved from recruiting from different schools to ensure there were no duplicate applications, this process is called:
   a. Data mining
   b. Data cleansing
   c. Statistical analysis
   d. Visualization

93. If a manager issues a written warning to an employee who comes in late to work because he concludes that the employee just wants to exert the least amount of effort to remain employed, which theory of motivation is he is utilizing?
   a. Attribution theory
   b. Self-determination theory
   c. Trait theory
   d. Contingency theory

94. If you are reviewing the three levels of needs for your department (organizational, task, and individual) then you are in which stage of the ADDIE process?
   a. Design phase
   b. Evaluation phase
   c. Implementation phase
   d. Analysis phase

95. If the salary range for a role is between $26 and $32, and an employee earns $31 an hour, what is the compa-ratio?
   a. 26/31
   b. 32/31
   c. 29/31
   d. 31/29

96. If an employer has 100 employees, 15 employees leave, and each of them is replaced, what is the retention rate?
   a. 85%
   b. 15%
   c. 100%
   d. 0%

97. What is the purpose of an ATS?
   a. Automate payroll processing to ensure that nonexempt employees are paid overtime at the correct rate
   b. Automate employee leave records to ensure that all leaves are coordinated (i.e., vacation leave, sick leave, FMLA, disability leave)
   c. Automate payment of vendor contracts that are paid in monthly installments
   d. Automate part of the recruiting process such as receipt of applications and completion of screening interviews

98. Which of the following is a true statement?
   a. Compliance and ethics are the same organizational principles.
   b. Compliance and ethics are two non-overlapping organizational principles that are separate and distinct from one another.
   c. Compliance refers to whether a company's actions are aligned with the law, while ethics refers to whether a company's leaders follow a set of established guidelines related to morals and ethics.
   d. Ethics refers to whether a company's actions are aligned with the law, while compliance refers to whether a company's leaders follow a set of established guidelines related to morals and ethics.

99. How is a furlough different than a layoff?
   a. An employee usually still receives a salary during a furlough period, even when no work is performed.
   b. An employee who is furloughed never has the opportunity to return to the role.
   c. A furloughed employee is viewed as being on an extended leave.
   d. A laid off employee is viewed as being on an extended leave.

100. When considering upgrades or accommodations to create more inclusive workspaces, which of the following steps in the process should come first?
   a. Confirm budgetary resources
   b. Determine legal requirements
   c. Collect employee needs data
   d. Secure building permits

101. If an organization uses a comparable worth approach to its compensation policy, then:
   a. Individuals are paid based upon their sex.
   b. Individuals that work in roles that have the same value to the company are paid the same.
   c. Individuals are paid based upon rigid pay bands.
   d. Individuals are paid based upon their seniority.

Refer to the following for questions 102 - 103:

> A common recruitment practice of your organization is to attend career fairs to attract a variety of different candidates for multiple open positions. You usually attend the fairs, as well as two to three other recruiters. You enjoy speaking with attendees and sometimes find some quality candidates. The CFO (your boss) has come to you and expressed his concern that the career fairs are very costly, and he's not sure if they're worth it.

102. What metric would you use to either verify the CFO's concerns or prove that the career fairs are worth the expense?
   a. Cost per hire
   b. Cost per candidate by source
   c. Applicants per opening
   d. Source of hire

103. Assume you've crunched the numbers and discovered that the career fairs are producing more candidates than other sources such as online job postings or employee referrals. How would you convey to the CFO that he was wrong?
   a. Choose your battle. Don't tell the CFO that he was incorrect, but simply stop registering for career fairs and instead focus on improving other recruitment methods.
   b. Casually mention it at the next regularly scheduled team meeting when the topic of recruitment comes up.
   c. Schedule a meeting with him and bring a print-out showing the data. Ask him what he'd like you to do, given this information.
   d. Schedule a meeting with him, and bring a print-out showing the data. Suggest that you continue attending but perhaps reduce the number of other company representatives to reduce the cost.

104. If a company is reviewing a remuneration survey they are reviewing:
   a. Compensation plans
   b. Vendor agreements
   c. Compliance audits
   d. Debt agreements

105. The process of using escalating levels of discipline as a way to identify and correct problematic workplace behavior is called:
   a. Progressive termination
   b. Progressive discipline
   c. Just cause
   d. A counseling session

106. An employee is having trouble assimilating to a workplace culture and HR asks the individual whether they would be open to the idea of a reverse mentorship. How does a reverse mentorship differ from a traditional mentorship?
   a. Reverse mentorship includes a significant age difference between the mentor and the mentee.
   b. In a reverse mentorship situation, the mentee selects the mentor.
   c. In a reverse mentorship situation, both parties generally learn from one another.
   d. There is no significant difference between reverse mentorship and traditional mentorship.

107. Consider the following employee roll call data. If a human resources professional were researching the workplace environment and employee benefits to inspire diversity among leadership, at what level would he or she begin the data collection?

	Entry-Level Workers	Front-End Managers	Store Managers	Department Heads	Associate VPs	C-Suite Executives
Total Number of Employees	3,655	189	62	18	10	5
Male Employees	1,663	96	47	13	8	4
Female Employees	1,992	93	15	5	2	1

   a. Entry-level workers
   b. Front-end managers
   c. Store managers
   d. C-suite executives

108. Which of the following is not an example of a calculation used to evaluate the effectiveness of a talent acquisition process?
   a. Time to fill
   b. Cost per hire
   c. Applicant to interview to offer ratio
   d. ATS

109. An individual who has full discretion as to how their work is completed and where their work is completed, and is paid on a 1099 form upon completion of each specific project is classified as:
   a. An independent contractor
   b. A regular employee
   c. A non-traditional employee
   d. A temporary employee

110. An employee is told that they will be spending one day per week working in a different role as a way to expand their skills. This is an example of:
   a. Job enlargement
   b. Job enrichment
   c. Job rotation
   d. Career succession planning

111. When an employee submits their resignation, what tool does an HR professional have at their disposal to seek to gain information about how the departing employee viewed the workplace culture?
   a. An employment engagement survey
   b. An exit interview
   c. A focus group
   d. An ERG group

112. If a female patient requests that a female nurse assist her in the shower, the employer agrees to the request, and the male nurse files a claim for employment discrimination because the shift change resulted in loss of overtime hours, the employer would likely have a defense under what legal theory?
   a. The customer requested the change
   b. The BFOQ defense
   c. A reasonable accommodation was requested
   d. There is no defense and the employer will likely be held liable for sex discrimination under Title VII

113. If the CEO indicates she is going to retire within the next 3-5 years and the company develops a strategic plan to fill the role this is called:
   a. A pipeline review
   b. Succession planning
   c. Balance scorecard review
   d. Managerial matrix

114. An example of an insider threat that may result in loss of sensitive workplace data may be:
   a. Phishing
   b. Catfishing
   c. Spearing
   d. A departing employee

115. Angela, an operations manager, is interviewing candidates for an open position and is considering selecting Melanie, who, like Angela, recently earned her master's degree after taking time away from her career to raise her family. Which of the following biases might be affecting Angela's decision?
   a. Extroversion bias
   b. Social comparison bias
   c. Affinity bias
   d. In-group bias

Answer Key and Explanations for Test #1

1. C: Exit interviews should be conducted by a third party. In many cases, employees will leave an organization because they are not satisfied with it or with the work environment. However, an employee may not feel comfortable sharing these complaints with current members of the organization. Indeed, this reticence may be a result of why they are leaving the organization in the first place. Having exit interviews conducted by a third party ensures that the process will yield more useful information for the organization.

2. A: Sandra's next step is to research possible systems. Since she has obtained a needs analysis, she should have a good idea of the appropriate system for her business. However, her business may not be able to afford the best possible human resources information system. Sandra's next step will be to shop around for the best value. Answer choices B, C, and D represent steps that she will need to take later in the process.

3. C: A ranking system is usually better for a smaller group of employees but can be difficult to organize with a larger group when multiple departments, positions, and supervisors come into play. Behaviorally anchored rating scales and competency-based ratings set clear parameters for assessing performance based on an employee's behaviors or the job's required competencies and can be applied uniformly across individuals within a position. Forced distribution ranking is more effective for larger groups of data and is, therefore, the incorrect answer here.

4. D: Encouraging social connections will help work interactions as well. If the social activities occur on-site during work hours, employees are more likely to attend than if they are off-site or on employees' own time.

5. C: Direct confrontations and group meetings where people are expected to share updates can be uncomfortable for some cultures. Supervisors and managers should focus their time and energy on establishing trust with each individual on their team.

6. D: There is no specific advanced engineer exemption. The Fair Labor Standards Act (FLSA) exemptions apply only to white-collar-type employees who fall under the salary and duties test; these include executive, administrative, professional (learned and creative), computer, outside sales, and highly compensated employees.

7. B: Each of the listed elements is important to a successful DE&I strategy, but leadership buy-in is one of the essential first steps. It will lead to the effective collection and use of employee survey data (A), appropriate financial resources to fund action steps (C), and impactful training and development (D) opportunities. Leadership buy-in serves as both a practical step to secure tangible support for financial and personnel-driven resources and as a cornerstone for the more intangible support elements such as trust-building and role modeling across an organization.

8. B: Return-to-work (RTW) programs can be used for on-the-job injuries or off-duty injuries as well.

9. C: A halo bias is when interviewers or recruiters base their assessment of a candidate solely on one positive characteristic. A horns bias is the opposite: one perceived negative trait sours the entire interaction. A similarity bias is when interviewers are drawn to a candidate who is similar to themselves, and a first-impression bias is when interviewers make a hiring decision based solely on their initial thoughts and feelings of the person.

10. A: The other concerns listed can usually be assuaged with a legitimate assessment provider. But no matter how buttoned up the assessment tool is, great applicants might be eliminated from the process based solely on their personality type.

11. A: Understanding the current state of training and the needs for each department will help HR determine where the gaps are and what training needs to be eliminated, added, changed, or maintained. At that point, HR can verify that legal obligations are being met and best practices are being followed, and a plan can begin to take place.

12. B: Current training delivery methods and course durations should not be an important factor in deciding how to structure the new training program. Human resources should factor in legal obligations and logistical requirements. In addition, some training content is best delivered in person rather than online—for instance, training that needs discussion or opportunities for learners to ask questions.

13. A: "Best of breed" is a term used to describe the process of selecting only the best software system for a specific need of the organization, which often means not choosing an all-in-one system, which may have system limitations in various areas.

14. B: Suspected drug users who are acting erratically should never be confronted alone. Also, supervisors are often not trained to handle a conversation of this magnitude, so it is best to have both a human resource representative and the supervisor present. Also, presenting the employee with a drug test prior to any conversations could cause the employee to panic and risk a negative outcome for the situation.

15. D: The most appropriate course of action would be to offer Family and Medical Leave Act (FMLA)-protected leave so the employee can attend rehab. You might also verify with your insurance to see if, and how, it is covered. Although it is true that he could be held to the same standards as other employees, it is important to first provide the tools for the employee to get clean. Once he is recovered, you may hold him to that standard. Additionally, current drug users are not protected under the Americans with Disabilities Act, but recovered addicts are.

16. B: An engaged employee is one who is loyal to the organization, speaks highly of the organization to friends and family, knows what work needs to be done to make a positive impact, and does it. Job satisfaction and employee engagement are not the same thing; job satisfaction is usually driven by extrinsic factors such as pay, benefits, and time off, whereas intrinsic motivators and strong leadership drive engagement.

17. D: When an individual is in the "red zone," an effective technique is to guess an employee's feelings and/or needs that aren't being met. This can help the employee articulate his or her feelings while focusing on the facts. Advice in any form to an individual in this state is usually not well received. Once he or she has calmed down, you might ask if you can give him or her some advice.

18. B: This conflict does not rise to the level of any type of harassment or even bullying; it sounds like normal workplace conflict between two colleagues. For this reason, there is no need for a formal investigation; however, the supervisor should be made aware of the situation so that the conflict does not escalate.

19. A: By reviewing the performance management processes, measurable work outcomes are set as the center of the investigation. While this review may lead to eventual investigations of certain managers for unethical practices (B), putting the work outcomes as the focus clearly communicates the ultimate goals of the review and any follow-up actions. Stay interviews (C) can be useful to recognize what the company does well and what it should continue to do with respect to retention; however, getting to the root of any possible favoritism or discrimination is of a higher priority when data from the exit interviews can serve as a starting point for key retention factors. Recommending an additional salary increase (D) may eventually be part of the solution but increasing salaries without additional data about compensation decisions like starting rates, compensable factors, bonuses, and merit increases may lead to inefficient spending.

20. C: A job evaluation is used for assessing each position's relative worth to organizational outcomes. Job evaluations are critical tools to define what roles and responsibilities are of highest value to the organization. This data can then be utilized to design performance management processes and outcomes that are based on quality of work rather than personal similarities. Job analysis tools (A) can be useful for more accurately defining what a job actually does and how it functions within a team or organization but do not necessarily get to the root of responsibility value within the context of performance management. Workplace observations (B) and employee surveys (D) can be useful tools to better understand performance review priorities but are typically used within the job evaluation process rather than on their own as standalone tools.

21. D: Pay audits assess the actual compensation rates of employees in comparison to each other and to their worth to the company. Pay audits can be an incredibly useful tool to root out disparate treatment or disparate impact in compensation practices. This data can then be used to right any wrongs that may be occurring across the organization rather than raising pay rates across-the-board. By publicizing the data, the company is displaying the transparency in operations that is critical when building trust with the workforce. A benefits review (C) or performance-pay adjustments (B) may end up being productive steps forward, but conducting a pay audit first will more directly address the root of complaints about compensation practices. Expanding the C-suite to include the HR function (A) at the top levels of leadership may assist in long-term human management operations; however, this could also cause tension in the short term if the company is trying to expand the reach of leadership while the leadership is already considered untrustworthy.

22. B: Systemic inequality (oftentimes manifested as systemic racism and/or systemic classism) refers to the societal histories, policies, and disenfranchisement that can lead to disadvantages for certain dimensions of people. Lack of access to affordable higher education can force those who grew up in less economically stable communities to seek employment instead of a college education; this lack of formal schooling can be a barrier even in situations where the experience in the field may be more valuable than the diplomas their more privileged peers have earned. It is essential for companies to review and assess the job descriptions and promotion specifications to ensure that the job requirements are truly required and not just preferred. Unintentional discrimination in the job descriptions like this situation is likely to amount to disparate impact as opposed to disparate treatment (A). Ableist standards (C) may be at play in the event that an employee was not physically or mentally able to complete a college education; however, this explanation is less likely to affect many experienced individuals at once. Stereotyping (D) is a barrier to diversity but is not overtly present in this scenario.

23. C: PIPs are best for specific and measurable problems with an employee's performance that may be turned around with guidance and training. Insubordinate behavior is not generally resolved with a PIP. And last, although PIPs are sometimes the final step before a termination, it is best for managers and supervisors to issue a PIP with the intent that the behavior can be improved.

24. B: Human resources is usually in the role of preparing for, and participating in, collective bargaining. This falls under the "confidential employee" exemption with the National Labor Relations Act (NLRA).

25. B: Focus groups with employees are optimal when they pertain to specific topics, such as feedback on the benefit plan or succession planning. Around eight to 10 participants are best, and they should be a diverse group of employees to more accurately represent opinions across the organization. Although employees should feel free to voice their opinions openly, the facilitator should bring some semblance of structure to the focus group. He or she should give an introduction, ask open-ended questions to participants, and be prepared to summarize the discussion at the conclusion.

26. D: A response to a candidate asking for feedback on how to improve can vary based on multiple factors. If there is a reason to foster a relationship with a candidate, it can be worthwhile to provide constructive but carefully worded and concise feedback.

27. A: Coaching is used in specific instances for individuals—to help them prepare for a leadership role or an upcoming assignment or to help them develop a specific skill or stop exhibiting a certain behavior. Mentoring is usually in the case of a formal or informal program and can help individuals pursue their personal or professional goals.

28. A: The look-back measurement period is a method of determining eligibility for coverage. The employer looks at a defined period of time that the employee has worked and averages the weekly hours. If the average is 30 hours or more per week, the employee would likely be eligible for coverage.

29. B: Feedback is best delivered using specific details. Describe the exact behavior that needs to stop and what needs to start happening. In this case, the employee needs to stop talking over people in meetings. Providing more complex work assignments to the employee may further alienate others on the team, as they'd see the poor behavior rewarded with more advanced assignments.

30. C: Although this employee may be going through a series of personal crises, it's important to focus on his work performance and attendance issues. If the attendance issues are not addressed, they can have a negative impact on the others on the team.

31. C: Canadian citizens, unlike Mexican citizens, do not need a TN visa to work in the United States. At the U.S. border, they need only present proof of Canadian citizenship, a written job offer from the prospective employer, and proof of qualification for the position. They are generally then admitted as a TN nonimmigrant.

32. C: In a right-to-work state, employees are able to decline union membership if they choose.

33. C: As the employee is noticeably anxious about the health condition and missing work, it is best to respond to the email as soon as possible rather than deferring to the HR specialist, who is not in the office.

34. A: Key performance indicators (KPIs) are relatively controversial, with some experts claiming they foster competition rather than collaboration.

35. C: Based on the facts that Karen and Steve are friends, Steve is in good standing with the company and has never been in trouble before, and Karen clearly has a desire to maintain the friendship, it would be best to let her make the decision on the next course of action.

36. B: Once the injured employee is helped and stabilized, the first call should be to HR before taking any witness statements or writing up a summary of events. It could be dangerous to fix the cause of the injury, so again, it is best for supervisors to consult with HR before handling anything themselves.

37. A: Although a supervisor may also be a good resource in assessing the dangers of the job, employees have the best familiarity with the potential hazards of their everyday responsibilities.

38. C: The CSR's medical professional should make the determination of the need for the stand-up desk. You should not try to determine the legitimacy or severity of a disability; rather, focus on the reasonableness of the accommodation request. And in this case, the request is reasonable.

39. B: Employers should never divulge another employee's personal health information, even to justify the reason for an accommodation. Although the performance-based program is creative, an employee's comfort should not be dependent on how well he or she performs on the job. The best course of action in this case is to work to obtain a budget to eventually offer stand-up desks to all employees who sit for extended periods of time. This can be treated as a perk of the job and may end up preventing future health issues for employees.

40. C: A "top-heavy" 401(k) plan is one in which more than 60% of the entire plan's value resides in the accounts of "key" employees. A key employee is defined as an employee with major ownership of the company and/or in a decision-making role.

41. C: Forms for active employees should never be destroyed. The retention requirement is three years after hire date or one year after termination date, whichever is later.

42. C: The Department of Labor has issued seven criteria that qualify an internship to be unpaid. There are no restrictions for weekly hours.

43. A: The principled negotiation style is an interest-based bargaining technique that aims to identify a mutually beneficial agreement, also known as "win-win."

44. A: Supervisors are to be excluded from bargaining units under the National Labor Relations Act (NLRA) if they have independent judgment to make personnel decisions such as hiring, terminating, or promoting.

45. A: HSA funds never expire, and employees who leave the organization do not lose access to the funds.

46. A: Coordination of benefits rules require that the insurance plan listed as primary will be charged first, and any residual charges will be processed by the secondary payer.

47. C: The hiring manager knows the position and the industry best. He or she can give expert insight into the next steps in the recruitment strategy.

48. A: Cloud computing is a practice of storing, managing, and processing data in remote servers rather than a locally hosted server.

49. A: Although each option presented could help identify different causes of turnover, the best way to pinpoint the top reason would be to conduct exit interviews with each exiting employee and identify trends.

50. C: Realistic job previews would give candidates a realistic glimpse into what the job would entail on a daily basis. It would encourage them to self-select out of the hiring process if they aren't a good fit rather than waiting until after they're hired.

51. D: The software developers in this scenario are young and hardworking, so unlimited paid time off (PTO) may not resonate with them as much as other perks. Additionally, unlimited PTO has plenty of pitfalls and risks, so ultimately it may not be worth the potential issues. These employees also seem to have minimal interest in anything related to health care or insurance benefits. Millennials typically have a strong desire to remain challenged and advance quickly in their careers—a career path program would allow them to constantly learn, evolve, and move to the next level when the time is right.

52. B: The most effective method of gaining leadership buy-in is to show, rather than tell. If the CEO is willing to agree to a trial period, she will see the intangible benefits of allowing employees to work from home. Trial periods are effective methods of testing out a workplace program without a full commitment. The CEO is more likely to agree to this.

53. A: Direct, timely feedback is always the best approach with employees. Asking for feedback on how to avoid mistakes in the future makes him feel invested in the solution.

54. D: Although 30 days' advance notice of an upcoming leave is ideal, in many instances it will not be feasible for an employee to give any advance notice. If no advance notice is given, it is not an adequate reason to deny Family and Medical Leave Act (FMLA) leave.

55. B: Both the employer and the union must participate in the collective bargaining process and display good-faith bargaining efforts; however, neither party is required to make concessions.

56. A: The Worker Adjustment and Retraining Notification (WARN) Act requires that for a layoff affecting 50 or more employees at one location, employees must be given 60 days' notice prior to their employment ending.

57. A: Federal contractors and subcontractors are required by the OFCCP to annually review and update their AAPs, which include a report and documentation of affirmative actions such as outreach efforts and training programs.

58. C: The most important first step before beginning a recruitment process is defining the needed skills an incumbent should have to be successful in the role. Once this list is established, that will help define compensation, optimal advertising sources, and finally, qualified candidates.

59. D: According to the Equal Employment Opportunity Commission (EEOC), petty slights, annoyances, and isolated incidents will not rise to the level of illegality.

60. B: A harassment claim that is found to be malicious should result in discipline for the complainant. It is never a good idea to discuss an investigation and its results with the complainant and subject in the same room.

61. C: The first step in the process of selecting a new human resource information system (HRIS) is to determine if the organization will conduct the vendor selection process internally or if a third-party consultant will be hired to perform the search. Once that decision is made, the other steps will follow.

62. D: A political, economic, social, and technological (PEST) analysis is a method of obtaining and reviewing data from external influences to the organization.

63. D: Organizations should not contact other organizations directly for specific compensation amounts, as this may lead to antitrust violations. Also, job titles and levels can vary across organizations; the actual duties and responsibilities should be taken into account when determining the similarity of positions. Last, employee-reported salary amounts are not always accurate.

64. A: External candidates can bring new ideas and approaches to an organization, whereas an internal candidate is influenced by the current organizational mindset.

65. B: Misunderstandings and conflict are to be expected on newly formed global teams due to clashes between the external cultures and beliefs that each member brings to the team. Team building intent on highlighting the common ground of skills and organizational goals and values can help to build an internal team culture. A strong internal team culture uses trust and mutual respect to turn conflict into collaboration and takes advantages of the individual differences of its members. Online trainings (A) can be a useful part of the puzzle when managing a diverse team, but they are not as effective as interactive, values-based activities. Allowing conflict to play out (C) without intervention may work but may also cause resentment and mistrust. Automatically assigning conflicting team members elsewhere (D) does not get to the root of the challenges and weakens the teams, as members were initially chosen for their specialty knowledge, which may not translate as well to different teams.

66. A: Scheduling meetings in advance enables the groups to rotate the days and times of the meetings so that group members can share the burden of inconvenient time zones. In addition, scheduling meetings in advance can give group members an adequate amount of time to schedule their professional and personal responsibilities accordingly so they will be able to participate. Collaborative technologies that allow for passive discussion and group work (B) are great as a supplemental component to global teams but can negatively impact group progress when decisions must be made or discussions require real-time feedback or consensus. Redistributing teams according to the members' respective time zones (C) would take away from the project's initial vision to take advantage of the combination of specific skills and global perspectives to solve challenges. Eliminating a team member solely due to lack of meeting participation (D) is an extreme reaction if the rest of his or her contributions are of high quality, and he or she is otherwise communicative and responsive. Before eliminating a team member, the team and its leaders should first seek feedback from that member to learn what his or her desire to take part in the team is and what individual barriers he or she may experience in attending the meetings.

67. D: The division leaders are the linchpin between the COO's vision and the focus groups themselves and will provide the most insight on the practical side of the project's launch and progress. By targeting the division leaders for data collection, the HR director will better understand the progression from executive idea to leadership design to ground-level execution. With the information from the division leaders, the HR director will be better equipped to then observe the focus groups (A), collect data from group members (B), and facilitate future meetings or plans of action to improve focus group outcomes (C). Additionally, data collection at the division leaders' level may help to uncover other tensions or misunderstandings that could have developed as a result of recent organizational globalization.

68. B: Leadership buy-in is one of the most critical elements of any successful diversity, equity, and inclusion (DE&I) project or initiative. Leadership buy-in must be more than a one-time occurrence, and it must be highly visible and consistent. It is important for the HR director to dig further into why and how the first project check-in by the COO occurred a full six months after its launch. By establishing timelines with clear deadlines for goals and objectives, the COO can remain present with the project to guide and support both the division leaders and the focus group members. The future goals of the focus groups (C) are important to consider when planning the next action steps, but without digging into the root causes of the project's initial challenges, progress and positive change will be limited.

69. A: The most likely resulting culture in the organization would be fear based. Employees would likely be fearful of making contributions as they may make a mistake and would be fearful of losing their jobs or speaking up in meetings.

70. B: It's best to hire a neutral third-party expert to come in and make an unbiased assessment. The CEO is more likely to be receptive to feedback from a professional who has made a thorough analysis of the organization's leadership.

71. A: Under Title II of the Genetic Information Nondiscrimination Act (GINA), it is illegal for employers to base any type of hiring decision (promotions, hiring, and/or firing) on genetic information, such as family medical history or the likelihood that they may contract a disease or illness.

72. A: When determining the cause of employee turnover, it is best to separate out involuntary terminations from voluntary terminations. Counting involuntary terminations in the calculation will skew the separation rate and will not help determine the cause for attrition.

73. A: Before traveling to Chennai or collecting sample documents, a political, economic, social, and technological (PEST) analysis should be conducted from an HR viewpoint. Political, economic, social, and technological factors will influence most decisions that need to be made, so thorough research and analysis is critical.

74. C: The most effective approach to improving daily communication is a short status call that occurs every day. The attendees can discuss pressing topics for the day or just catch up, and this allows attendees to build relationships and feel connected.

75. B: Senior leaders who are focused in finance are usually most interested in how much things will cost and what the return on investment will be. Furthermore, usually their time is short and valuable, so a more succinct delivery of this information is better.

76. C: A successful mentor does not necessarily need to be the most senior. Even a less experienced mentor can provide insight and guidance to a mentee in an area the mentee is not familiar with.

77. C: Although HR may contact the medical professional to confirm the validity of the certification and ask clarifying questions, to protect the employee's privacy, they may not ask for more information about the condition. HR may require a second or third opinion at the employer's expense.

78. B: A PEST analysis is conducted as part of a strategic market analysis of several factors: political, economic, social, and technological.

79. A: Automatic enrollment in a 401(k) for new hires, although not a requirement, is a recommended strategy to boost participation in the plan. There is not usually backlash from employees against this provision; however, communication to new hires and current employees is essential to avoid mistrust.

80. B: A nine-box grid is a matrix with three degrees of performance on one axis and three levels of potential on the other axis. Names are generally plotted in the different grid squares to identify individuals who have potential to move into leadership roles in the organization.

81. A: The Age Discrimination in Employment Act (ADEA) requires an employee over 40 to receive 21 days to review a severance agreement before signing. Once the employee signs the agreement, he or she has seven days from the date of signature to change his or her mind and revoke the agreement. Agreements should not contain any type of language that would prevent employees from filing a complaint with the Equal Employment Opportunity Commission (EEOC).

82. D: Organizations should never base any hiring decision on race, gender, age, or any other protected visual attributes, even if the intent is to "hire for more diversity." Also, whereas the other two suggestions would help create a more inclusive workplace, the most effective strategy is to expand the reach of recruitment efforts toward underrepresented groups.

83. B: The stability period is the duration of time that coverage must be offered to all full-time employees. This period of time must be at least six months and not less than the defined measurement period.

84. A: Intermittent Family and Medical Leave Act (FMLA) leave is not mandated for baby bonding time; however, an employer may allow it. In this particular instance, it would present a hardship on the department, and asking others to work extra hours to fill in for this employee would likely be perceived as unfair.

85. D: To gain buy-in for a large change management initiative, the first step is to create a sense of urgency with your audience so that they understand the importance of the project.

86. C: Given the fact that this is a high-tech digital company, a printed newsletter would likely be the least effective. Newsletters mailed to employees' homes are generally best for messages that need to be delivered to employees' spouses and/or family members, such as open enrollment for benefits or retirement plan updates.

87. A: Using lay terms about a human resource information system in a room full of software engineers may elicit a few eye rolls. Similarly, a complex presentation with acronyms and tech jargon may confuse the less tech-savvy employees. It is best to tailor the message based on the audience you're speaking to. That could mean explaining a concept in several different ways to ensure comprehension.

88. C: Defining an employee's behavior as insubordination must meet three criteria: the employer gives a clear directive to the employee, and the employee acknowledges the directive in some manner then refuses to follow directions.

89. D: Under several change management models, employees' reactions to large organizational changes evolve from indifference to rejection, then doubt, neutrality, experimentation, and finally commitment. When employees are in the commitment phase, this is the optimal stage to implement the change.

90. C: A matrix organizational structure is one in which employees may report to multiple supervisors or managers; often one is a functional relationship and the other may be project based.

91. A: When a company keeps electronic employee files, they have to be able to produce paper versions in a timely manner if a request is made. This could occur as part of a compliance audit or a lawsuit.

92. B: Choice B is the correct answer because data cleansing is used to validate that the information gathered is accurate, and this generally requires a review to ensure all of the data is complete, relevant, and contains no duplications.

93. A: According to the attribution theory of motivation, individuals judge people based upon how they view the reason for their behavior. If the manager believes that the lateness is due to an external factor beyond the late employee's control (such as a labor strike that shuts down the public transportation the employee uses), then the manager may impose a lesser form of discipline, or none at all. Here, because the manager attributes the lateness to a factor within the employee's control, he judges the conduct harshly.

94. D: The first phase of the ADDIE process, the analysis phase, involves collection of information to identify gaps. This analysis of needs is followed by the other stages of the process.

95. D: A compa-ratio is calculated by dividing the pay of the employee ($31) by the midpoint of the range ($29). If the compa-ratio is below 1.00, then the wage rate is below the midpoint. If the compa-ratio is greater than 1.00, the wage rate is greater than the midpoint.

96. A: The retention rate is calculated by dividing the number of employees who remained employed (85) by the number of employees who were employed at the beginning of the time being measured (100).

97. D: An ATS (applicant tracking system) is used to organize and track certain components of the recruitment process, such as tracking whether all of the necessary information has been submitted.

98. C: Compliance and ethics are distinct, but in some situations, they may overlap. For example, if a company discovers a legal violation that they know is unlikely to be detected, they should still correct it from both a compliance and ethical perspective.

99. C: When an employee is laid off, their employment relationship is terminated. When an employee is furloughed, they are placed on leave for what is usually a specific amount of time after which are returned to their role.

100. C: Workspace accommodations can come in a wide variety of options and costs. For example, an accommodation like closed-captioning in virtual meetings can be implemented at low-to-no cost with zero facility footprint impact; however, installing an elevator requires significant financial resources and facility space. Once the needs of employees are collected and acknowledged, leadership will be better informed to create the necessary budgets (A), determine legal requirements (B), and address any possible building change proposals (D).

101. B: A comparable worth approach to compensation pays individuals based upon how much that work is worth to the company. Under this theory if a company determines that a member of the sales team and an employee working as a social media marketer provide the same value to the employer, they would be paid the same.

102. B: Cost per candidate by source is calculated by dividing the total cost of the source (in this case, the total cost of the career fairs) by the number of candidates generated by the source. This metric can then be compared to the cost of alternate sources of generating candidates to prove its efficiency.

103. D: Because you report to the CFO, you should tread lightly when telling him he's wrong but still have a direct and private conversation about it. It's obvious that he's concerned about cost, so it's best to provide a solution to mitigate those costs while still meeting your objective of attending the career fairs.

104. A: Remuneration surveys are used to evaluate the full scope of direct and indirect compensation paid to employees, which includes base pay, PTO, and benefit entitlements.

105. B: The steps of a progressive discipline process usually include a verbal warning, written warning, suspension, and termination.

106. C: In contrast to a traditional mentor-mentee relationship where the mentor generally provides guidance to the mentee, a reverse mentorship allows both parties to benefit from the knowledge and experience of the other. Generally, a newer or less experienced employee is paired with a more experienced employee so that both can learn from each other. Reverse mentorships can be a useful tool in the global context and in workforces that have diverse employee populations.

107. B: The greatest drop-off in representation rates between men and women occurs between front-end managers and store managers. Women represent 49% of the workforce as front-end managers, but they only represent 24% as store managers and maintain somewhat comparable rates of representation through to the C-suite level of the organizational hierarchy. While all levels of the hierarchy can offer useful data for the human resources professional, the level immediately before the representation drop-off (front-end managers) is more likely to offer impactful insight into what mechanisms may be causing the drop-off, such as disparate impact, discrimination, lack of mentors, inadequate benefits, etc. Following the data collection from front-end managers, the human resources professional will have additional information that can help inform the next step. Is there a lack of leadership buy-in that may lead to interviewing VPs and C-suite level employees? Are there concerning matters raised that call for attention to the 5.8% promotion rate for male employees from entry-level workers to front-end managers versus the 4.7% promotion rate for female employees? Are there matters raised that call for the next data collection to come from the female employees promoted to store managers to ascertain how their promotion process went?

108. D: An ATS (applicant tracking system) is a system used by an employer to handle information related to applicants that move through its system. The other three responses are metrics used to evaluate the effectiveness of the talent acquisition process.

109. A: An employer will generally have control over how and where the work of an employee is completed, and employees are paid on a W-2 form. In contrast, independent contractors are generally hired for a specific project, are not subject to the control of the employer, and are paid on a 1099 form.

110. C: Job rotation refers to working in a different role. Job enlargement and enrichment refers to broadening of the scope of an individual's current role, but the employee will be working in a different role for one day per week in this case.

111. B: It is best practice for organizations to conduct exit interviews with their departing employee to obtain feedback about the individual's experience.

112. B: An employer can assert the BFOQ defense when a decision based upon a protected class (here, sex) is reasonably necessary for the individual to carry out a job function. The BFOQ defense is narrowly-applied but generally accepted as a defense within the context of privacy issues such as in this case.

113. B: Succession planning refers to the process an organization uses to identify the most crucial roles in an organization and establish a plan to replace the individuals working in those roles as they depart.

114. D: Phishing, catfishing, and spearing pose a threat to the confidentiality of workplace data, but a departing employee is an insider threat because they have access to the information that an outsider would generally not have.

115. C: An affinity bias can occur when an individual creates a stronger bond with another due to perceived similarities in upbringing, backgrounds, and personal characteristics. This particular bias may cloud the hiring manager's judgement because he or she sees himself or herself in the candidate rather than seeing all the candidates for their relevant experiences and qualifications. An extroversion bias (A) is the tendency to select or trust outgoing, charismatic individuals over those who appear more reserved. Social comparison bias (B) occurs when an individual compares oneself to others that he or she perceives to be better off than the individual is in a certain quality. In-group bias (D) is the tendency to show a preference for those who are part of the same social group as opposed to those perceived as outsiders.

PHR Practice Test #2

1. Which of the following statements about the performance appraisal process is LEAST accurate?

    a. Ranking is the most effective method for appraising large groups of employees.
    b. Annual performance appraisal cycles are becoming less prevalent in favor of review cycles that are more frequent and regular in design.
    c. Forced ranking systems assume that most employees are neither exceptionally good nor exceptionally bad.
    d. A behaviorally anchored rating system isolates each job's most important tasks.

2. The head of the administrative department for a major university has asked Raisa, a human resources professional at the school, for a team-building exercise that will benefit the administrative department. The administrative department is composed of employees who work closely together daily but often experience conflicts that indicate a clash of personalities. The department head hopes to find a team-building exercise that will improve the relationships among staff members in the department. Which of the following should Raisa recommend to the department head?

    a. A team obstacle course
    b. Role-playing situations
    c. Team scavenger hunts
    d. The Meyers-Briggs Type Indicator

3. For their first few months, new employees at Flanders Company receive frequent praise and encouragement from their supervisors. After a while, though, supervisors pay less attention to these employees. Performance evaluations indicate that employee productivity declines at this point. What are the supervisors at Flanders Company practicing?

    a. Punishment
    b. Positive reinforcement
    c. Negative reinforcement
    d. Extinction

4. When considering the purchase of an HRIS that includes ATS capabilities, which of the following metrics would be the MOST important as it relates to increasing recruiting volume?

    a. Candidate demographics ratios
    b. Employee participation rate
    c. Application conversion rate
    d. Return on investment ratio

5. Lewis is in charge of collecting feedback from employees about a new program that his company has implemented. The company has a number of locations, spread out across four different countries. Which of the following methods of data collection would be most effective for Lewis to employ?

    a. Focus group
    b. Interviews
    c. Questionnaire
    d. Observation

6. Which of the following HRIS functions is the MOST impactful when reducing the transactional responsibilities for a human resources team?

    a. Employee self-service
    b. Data reporting and analytics
    c. Performance management
    d. Training platform

7. After an initial business assessment, an organization has determined that it needs to invest in a new HRIS. Which of the following steps should the organization's HR and business team take first?

    a. Set an implementation timeline.
    b. Determine the budget.
    c. Request HRIS vendor quotes.
    d. Perform an organizational needs assessment.

Refer to the following for questions 8 - 10:

> Initech is a healthcare company with 500 employees based out of the home office in Seattle. They have 150 employees working remotely from their homes all over the country. The Initech office is always buzzing with activity and events—company meetings, Friday social hour, summer BBQ, and holiday parties for employees and their families. The remote employees have been complaining because they feel disconnected from the home office. Unfortunately, the budget doesn't allow for frequent visits for the remote employees to visit the home office.

8. What would be a creative solution to help the remote employees feel more included while keeping costs low?

    a. Post photos of the events on the company intranet so remote employees can see them.
    b. Invite the remote employees to attend the holiday party and summer BBQ; however, they would be responsible for covering the cost of their own transportation and lodging.
    c. Organize periodic social meet-ups for remote employees who live near one another.
    d. Set up a dial-in/webcam for the company meetings and social events so that remote employees can hear and see the activity.

9. What could be the biggest advantage of having a remote workforce from a human resource perspective?

    a. Lower overhead costs—less office space and equipment required
    b. No commute for remote employees, resulting in fewer emissions for the environment
    c. No need for child care for remote employees
    d. Better overall work-life balance for remote employees, resulting in higher morale and more successful recruitment efforts

10. Of the following options, what is generally the biggest disadvantage of having a remote workforce?

    a. Communication can be particularly challenging
    b. Stress often increases for employees who work remotely
    c. It is more difficult to establish a sense of camaraderie and connection between the in-office team and remote workers
    d. Having a remote workforce increases a company's carbon footprint

11. What is true regarding dependent enrollment with COBRA continuation coverage?
   a. It is required if the primary beneficiary is enrolled.
   b. It is allowed even if the primary beneficiary is not enrolled.
   c. It is only permitted if the primary beneficiary is enrolled.
   d. It is generally not permitted in any instance.

12. Best practice for initial completion of the U.S. Citizenship and Immigration Services (USCIS) Form I-9 does NOT include that _____
   a. the employee should fill out the form no later than the first day of work.
   b. the employer may specify that the employee should supply a passport to verify identify.
   c. the employee may use a translator for purposes of completing the form.
   d. the employer must review the original documentation supplied by the employee.

13. Which question should interviewers NOT ask candidates during an interview?
   a. Are you able to work for our company without immigration sponsorship?
   b. Are you able to perform the work duties without accommodation?
   c. Do you live close to our office?
   d. It sounds like you have an accent. Where are you from?

14. H-1B work visas may only be obtained for employees who _____
   a. reside in either Mexico or Canada and work in a specialty occupation.
   b. pass a rigorous test to prove their knowledge of the United States.
   c. work in a specialty occupation and have a bachelor's degree equivalency.
   d. are a recent college graduate and wish to work in the same field of study.

15. In the context of the Fair Labor Standards Act (FLSA), which statement is true regarding the concept of workers being "engaged to wait" versus "waiting to be engaged"?
   a. An employee who is "engaged to wait" is effectively on duty and must be paid for that time.
   b. An employee who is "waiting to be engaged" is usually required to remain at the workplace or nearby in case they are needed.
   c. An employee who is "engaged to wait" is generally on call and can use his or her time freely as long as they're able to make it to the workplace in the event they are called.
   d. An employee who is "engaged to wait" is relieved of duty, so he or she does not need to be paid unless he or she is called to work.

16. Under Fair Labor Standards Act (FLSA) guidelines, what are employees entitled to?
   a. One 30-minute lunch and two 15-minute breaks for every eight hours worked
   b. No required lunch or rest periods
   c. One hour lunch and two 10-minute breaks for every eight hours worked
   d. One 30-minute lunch break for every four hours worked

17. A technology company hires three new information technology professionals. To fill the positions, the company incurs both internal and external costs totaling $60,000. The total first-year compensation of the three new hires is $300,000. What is the Recruitment Cost Ratio?
   a. 2%
   b. 5%
   c. 20%
   d. 50%

18. Which of the following tools would be most useful in correcting the historically pervasive discrimination in compensation?
    a. Compensation survey
    b. Pay audit
    c. Job analysis
    d. Performance evaluations

19. What tasks needs to be performed continuously throughout the entire risk management process?
    a. Invest and set direction
    b. Reevaluate and direct
    c. Monitor and review
    d. Engage and motivate

20. What is the final step when putting a knowledge management system in place?
    a. Training employees on how to access and use the knowledge database
    b. Integrating the knowledge database into the company's information technology system
    c. Creating a dashboard for easy information access
    d. Revising and adding new information on an ongoing basis

21. An HR manager wants to determine if there is a correlation between an employee's score on a pre-hire assessment test and their sales performance as measured by the number of closed sales in the last quarter. What tool can he use?
    a. Trend diagram
    b. Pie chart
    c. Scatter diagram
    d. Pareto chart

Refer to the following for questions 22 - 25:

> Over the past six years, a local restaurant chain has been successfully building its internal DE&I practices. Across each of its seven locations, employee culture scores are at an all-time high, turnover rates have dropped, and customer satisfaction scores have increased.
>
> The restaurant's president and other executives task the marketing team with more effectively communicating the upgraded practices and policies to the workforce and to customers. Communication team leaders elect to seek the guidance of the HR department to advise in giving the most appropriate messaging and most accurate communication of programs and initiatives. Together, the marketing and HR team decide to start with internal statements and then address external communications.

22. When assessing the use of internal statements in support of DE&I policies and practices, which of the following types of statements would be the most practical to refer to when communicating the company's values with new employees?
    a. Equal Employment Opportunity Commission affirmation statement in employee handbook
    b. Companywide email from president supporting DE&I development
    c. DE&I affirmation posters in each break room
    d. Dedicated DE&I section in the weekly newsletter affirming organizational support

23. Which of the following policy upgrades would be most effective at combining internal policies with external recruiting practices?
   a. Exclusively advancing candidates in the hiring process that are recommended by applicant tracking software screenings
   b. Publishing accurate pay scales with job requisitions
   c. Designing recruiting flyers with diverse individuals
   d. Listing the diversity dimension preferences within job requisitions

24. When reviewing the internal DE&I programs available to the workforce, the HR team notes employee feedback celebrating the recent changes promoting diversity and equity; however, some employees suggest they still do not feel a sense of belonging. In response, the HR team seeks the communication team's guidance to determine the most effective first step to establishing employee resource groups. Which of the following is the most effective first step?
   a. Craft a comprehensive mission statement for each of the ERGs.
   b. Create a flyer to share with the company president to garner buy-in for the new program.
   c. Develop a marketing plan to recruit employees to the newly established ERGs.
   d. Design a survey for the workforce to determine which diversity dimensions should be represented by ERGs.

25. Which of the following marketing strategies would be most effective when communicating the restaurant's commitment to DE&I to the community and to potential customers?
   a. Including as many diversity dimensions as possible within the restaurant's television commercials
   b. Featuring diverse employees in digital ads speaking about their genuine experiences with the restaurant
   c. Publishing the restaurant's diversity statement on a local billboard
   d. Liking and sharing pro-DE&I content on social media from other local organizations.

26. While at work, two employees get into a serious argument that results in a physical altercation on company property. The employees have a clear understanding that this violates company policy. The manager pulls both employees into the office to terminate their employment. What step should the manager have taken beforehand?
   a. Establish a baseline for the termination.
   b. Review the company's performance management system.
   c. Interview the employees as part of an investigation.
   d. Consult with legal counsel.

27. A new marketing manager is assigned a mentor by the human resources (HR) department. The mentor is a senior business partner of the company with many years of experience. They are meeting once a month, and the mentor prepares for the meetings by setting learning objectives and creating training material for the mentee. Why might this mentorship NOT be successful?
   a. Meetings should take place weekly.
   b. Communication should be a two-way street and objectives set together.
   c. The mentor should be a peer and not a senior colleague.
   d. The mentor should not be assigned by HR, but selected by the mentee.

28. Sarah is a carpenter on a construction crew tasked with framing a series of residential houses. As the only female on the team, Sarah feels pressured to avoid wearing makeup at work or talking about her young children in an attempt to secure respect from her team and supervisors. This scenario is a demonstration of which of the following barriers to success for diverse workers?

   a. Imposter syndrome
   b. Microaggressions
   c. Identity covering
   d. Cultural taxation

29. New procedures are being rolled out from the company headquarters to offices located all over the country. The communications director created a detailed slide show presentation to share with all general managers virtually. What type of groupware is intended to be used for this purpose?

   a. Web conferencing
   b. Video presence
   c. Virtual meeting
   d. Network seminar

30. In what stage of a workforce analysis would a flow analysis be conducted?

   a. Supply analysis
   b. Demand analysis
   c. Gap analysis
   d. Solution analysis

31. What pay system rewards long-term employment instead of high performance?

   a. Merit pay
   b. A straight piece-rate system
   c. A differential piece-rate system
   d. Time-based step-rate pay

32. What is a characteristic of a polycentric talent acquisition orientation?

   a. Each country has its own unique talent acquisition approach.
   b. Headquarter staffing policies are mimicked in other countries.
   c. The company has a global talent acquisition plan.
   d. Each region establishes its own staffing policies.

33. A company is experiencing low productivity and therefore plans to restructure its workflows. A team of organizational and employee development (OED) specialists develops a plan for the restructure and implements it. After the change initiative has been completed, the company notices employees resisting the changes. What is likely to be the reason for their resistance?

   a. The changes were implemented too quickly.
   b. The restructure was developed with insufficient data.
   c. Employees were not included in the development.
   d. No feedback was provided after the implementation.

34. What is the MOST significant reason why a company would want to invest in leadership development and succession planning?
   a. It results in higher employee engagement and lower turnover.
   b. A competitive labor market makes it difficult to hire leaders externally.
   c. Employees are more likely to meet and exceed performance expectations.
   d. Sharing leadership responsibilities allows companies to succeed in a rapidly changing environment.

35. What should organizational and employee development (OED) specialists be aware of during the entire OED process?
   a. Organizational structure
   b. Employees' emotional reactions
   c. Leadership succession plans
   d. Institutionalized practices

36. A pharmaceutical company that employs 1,000 sales representatives determines during a supply analysis that its current attrition rates are at 16%. Conducting a demand analysis, they set a future goal of attrition rates being at 6% or less. What is the attrition gap that they need to close to accomplish their goal?
   a. 6%
   b. 10%
   c. 16%
   d. 37.5%

37. How should diversity and inclusion (D&I) strategies be put into effect?
   a. Strategies should be put into effect identically.
   b. Strategies should be put into effect justly.
   c. Strategies should be put into effect simultaneously.
   d. Strategies should be put into effect consecutively.

38. What protects a company from having to pay for legal costs and settlement fees in case an employee sues?
   a. COBRA
   b. ADR
   c. EPLI
   d. EAP

39. As a step to reduce workplace accidents, a company assesses how many workers are wearing personal protective equipment. What kind of indicator are they studying?
   a. A preceding indicator
   b. A leading indicator
   c. A dominant indicator
   d. A lagging indicator

40. A company introduces a new human resources system that allows managers to view and generate reports, write employee reviews, and process transfers, leaves, and terminations in one application. What kind of system is this?

  a. Decision-maker service
  b. Employee self-service
  c. Service point application
  d. Manager self-service

41. A company operates in an area that is subject to a reoccurring tornado and earthquake risk. As part of their disaster preparedness plan, they set up an employee text alert system that will allow the company to quickly communicate information to all employees in case of emergency. What is this risk strategy called?

  a. Transfer
  b. Alleviate
  c. Mitigate
  d. Enhance

42. A company was recently certified as a B Corp. What stage of the corporate social responsibility (CSR) maturity curve is the firm in?

  a. Adaptation
  b. Integration
  c. Assimilation
  d. Transformation

43. What is a feature of an asynchronous learning environment?

  a. Employees can access learning modules using different types of technology.
  b. Employees receive real-time feedback.
  c. Employees can study anywhere and anytime.
  d. Employees interact with each other in real time.

44. A manager tells his employee that he will be demoted if he votes for the union. What are possible consequences if the employee reports the incident?

  a. The National Labor Relations Board (NLRB) will investigate the charge.
  b. The union and employer will engage in mediation.
  c. The NLRB will file a complaint on behalf of the employee.
  d. There will be no consequences because the employer can demote, but not terminate, the employee.

45. What is a key benefit of conducting stay interviews?

  a. Improved retention
  b. Development of performance objectives
  c. Not needing exit interviews
  d. Data gathered for performance appraisals

46. A call center is looking to fill some of their open management positions. They receive a total of 250 applications, of which 100 are from female candidates. What is the yield ratio of female applicants to total applicants?
   a. 20%
   b. 25%
   c. 40%
   d. 60%

47. Why is it essential that a company works hard to build a comprehensive diversity and inclusion program?
   a. Because it has a direct impact on the company's profitability
   b. Because it is necessary for building a positive company reputation
   c. Because it helps employees and managers approach situations from different perspectives
   d. Because it is difficult to change deeply held beliefs, assumptions, and habits

Refer to the following for questions 48 - 51:

> A nationwide organization operates with leadership and management teams working remote or from one centralized location and then with small teams of a handful or fewer employees working at service locations across the country.
>
> After a visit from the off-site manager and other leadership figures to a small service location, an on-site team member is let go for misuse of company property and gross negligence. Two months later, a new staff member is selected as a replacement and starts working. The new staff member is a woman in her late twenties, and her coworkers are two men in their mid-to-late fifties.
>
> Almost immediately, the new staff member begins reporting back to the management team regarding condescension and inflexibility from her coworkers. Over the course of six months, she reports instances of disregard for organizational directives, discriminatory side comments, and, eventually, feeling uncomfortable in the workplace. After several incidents, the off-site manager seeks guidance from the team's HR representative for best practices and next steps.

48. Which of the following would be the most effective first step for the HR representative to present for the manager?
   a. The manager should relocate his or her office to be able to work on-site and better understand the working dynamic.
   b. The manager should design and implement a performance improvement plan for the male team members to improve overall morale.
   c. During the next team meeting, the manager should join virtually to remind staff members of the organizational values.
   d. The manager and the HR representative should schedule one-on-one meetings with each of the team members individually to better understand the workplace dynamics.

49. Which of the following is more likely to be positively correlated with a highly performing, diverse team?
    a. Psychological safety
    b. Disparate impact
    c. Conflict-free collaboration
    d. Team dissatisfaction

50. After meeting with each of the on-site team members, the manager and HR representative discover that some of the miscommunications likely stem from the differences in life experiences and expectations that come with team members being from different generations. How should the manager most effectively coach a multigenerational workforce?
    a. Assign tasks that align with the generational strengths of each employee, such as computer work for the younger employee and mentoring roles for the older employees.
    b. Determine each team member's individual strengths and challenges through individual coaching sessions and set goals for each individual to use his or her strengths to contribute to the team.
    c. Observe team meetings and when miscommunication arises, mediate the conversation to aid each team member in better understanding the other.
    d. Assign projects that force each team member to work one-on-one with the other in order to fast-track communication strategy development.

51. Which of the following DE&I tools would be most effective at creating a sense of belonging for employees of a diverse workforce who are spread across the country?
    a. Employee surveys
    b. Unconscious bias training
    c. Employee resource groups
    d. Performative allyship

52. An organization decides to partner with two employment service agencies for a temp-to-lease program. HR is asked to write the staffing contract. What best practice should they keep in mind?
    a. Refrain from pricing negotiations.
    b. Utilize a standard contract.
    c. Consult with legal counsel.
    d. Specify an end date of service in the contract.

Refer to the following for questions 53 - 56:

> After a string of discrimination-related incidents and consistently low workplace culture scores, a medium-sized financial advising firm launched a series of unconscious bias trainings in an attempt to create a more inclusive workplace.
>
> The trainings consisted of six 30-minute virtual sessions with interactive capabilities and a short answer debrief at the end of each session to gauge participant experience. Employees were instructed to attend a minimum of four out of the six trainings, which were scheduled across the span of nine months.
>
> After the final training, the HR team met to review participation metrics, the debrief answers, and updated workplace culture scores.

53. When developing the next phase of unconscious bias trainings and DE&I programs, which of the following actions would be the most effective?
   a. Increase the number of trainings offered and required to improve exposure.
   b. Eliminate the unconscious bias training due to poor participation rates and negative debrief results.
   c. Demand a higher rate of participation among organizational leaders during the next series of trainings.
   d. Link the virtual trainings to supplemental in-person follow-up sessions within each facility.

54. In addition to adding in-person elements to the training, the HR team is also tasked with improving the virtual portion of the unconscious bias training. After analyzing the first iterations of the training, which of the following steps should come next?
   a. Implementing a pilot training prior to a companywide launch
   b. Developing effective and appropriate content to fill training sessions
   c. Evaluating the results of the first training through surveys and focus groups
   d. Designing an efficient delivery structure that is scheduled with respect to its participants work responsibilities

55. Consider the chart below detailing the number of employees who participated in the training series stratified by organizational function.

Trainings completed	Financial Advisors	Loan Officers	Accounting Specialists	Marketing Team Members	Team & Facility Leaders	Executive Leadership
0	2	9	0	1	5	2
1-3	7	13	1	2	4	1
4	75	14	8	9	9	3
5-6	4	0	3	3	2	1
Total:	88	36	12	15	20	7

Which of the following conclusions would be most appropriate to draw from the available data?
   a. The loan officers are the likely root cause of the discriminatory behaviors and sentiment within the organization.
   b. Current and future DE&I programs and policies will likely benefit from stronger leadership buy-in.
   c. The strategy used to achieve the accounting specialists' participation rates should be duplicated for underperforming groups.
   d. The unconscious bias training was most effective among the teams with fewer employees.

56. In collaboration with facility leaders, the HR team launches the next series of unconscious bias trainings with a reduced requirement for the virtual session attendance but with added elements of in-person, unconscious bias team reflections and activities. Which of the following business outcomes would be most effective to track immediately following these changes that could suggest the actual impact of the new training design?
   a. Employee engagement rates
   b. Net facility income
   c. Employee retention rates
   d. Performance management scores

57. What approach can be used to evaluate HR's performance and alignment with organizational strategy?
   a. Internal customer satisfaction rate
   b. Employee retention rate
   c. Human capital return on investment
   d. Balanced scorecard

58. What is one advantage of a group interview?
   a. More candidate comfort during the interview
   b. Elimination of unqualified candidates
   c. Increased control for the interviewer
   d. Time-savings for both companies and job seekers

59. A company recently went through an organizational and employee development (OED) intervention. How can HR help the company promote and support adherence to the new processes?
   a. Utilize HRIS to track data.
   b. Support leaders through ongoing training and development initiatives.
   c. Ensure new processes and goals are reflected in performance reviews.
   d. Establish a mentorship program.

60. A group of seven managers is meeting to discuss restructuring the geographic areas that their sales teams support. They make a list of factors that will support the restructure as well as a list of what might hinder it. They then rate each factor depending on its importance. What kind of decision-making tool are they using?
   a. Cost-benefit analysis
   b. SWOT analysis
   c. Multi-criterion decision analysis
   d. Force-field analysis

61. A consulting firm determines that the average annual salary for project analysts in their area is $60,000. They are looking to hire a new project analyst and post the position with an annual pay rate of $70,000. What pay strategy does the company pursue?
   a. Top market competition
   b. Match market competition
   c. Lead market competition
   d. Lag market competition

62. What is an example of a business outcome that can be measured to gauge the effectiveness of an employee engagement initiative?
   a. Employee problem-solving abilities
   b. Employee motivation
   c. Managerial skills
   d. Employee absences

63. What is an important part of administering an employee survey to avoid employees becoming disappointed and disengaged?
   a. Conducting surveys at regular intervals, for example, annually
   b. Using online surveys for higher response rates
   c. Communicating the results to the employees
   d. Asking primarily open-ended questions in the survey

64. Which of these is most important for having a successful focus group?
   a. Encourage discussion.
   b. Have an agenda.
   c. Recognize conflicts early on.
   d. Summarize statements.

65. An employee has been selected for a global assignment and is getting ready to move in the coming weeks. What is an important step in preparing the assignee for departure?
   a. Determining a competitive pay rate for the employee while on assignment
   b. Analyzing the return on investment
   c. Identifying how the assignment fits with the employee's career aspirations
   d. Attending a cultural awareness training program

66. A company introduces a new product and needs its call center employees to go through extensive product training so that they can answer customer questions. The training is conducted through an online learning portal, set up as a labyrinth, that employees have to navigate through. Along the way, they learn about different aspects of the product, take quizzes, collect points, and move up levels to access more information. What type of learning is this?
   a. Scenario-based learning
   b. Maze product training
   c. Gamification
   d. Play-based learning

67. What tool can you use to make sure all of the firm's risk management strategies and processes are compliant with local laws?
   a. Attestation
   b. Audit
   c. Risk analysis
   d. Security report

68. A company aims to reduce occurrences in which employees violate company policy and have to be disciplined. What steps can they take?
   a. Implement strict disciplinary actions as a deterrent.
   b. Monitor employees closely throughout their shifts.
   c. Take away employees' company discounts if violations occur.
   d. Create a company culture of open two-way communication.

69. How would you respond to the CEO?
   a. Explain that, although unfortunate, this is a common response from employees when asked how they feel about HR. HR's role is to be an enforcer of laws and policies, and that is usually not well received.
   b. Explain that you will be looking into this further by conducting an audit of all HR processes and protocols to see what needs to be improved.
   c. Based on the results it's clear that your HR staff needs to work on their customer service skills—tell the CEO that you'll be mandating customer service training for all HR staff immediately.
   d. Tell the CEO that you will be issuing another company-wide survey; this time it will be regarding only HR internal services to identify the exact source of dissatisfaction.

70. What will be your first steps in initiating an HR audit?
   a. Identify the key HR staff for interviews and feedback.
   b. Create a comprehensive audit checklist.
   c. Collect benchmark data for comparison to findings.
   d. Determine the scope of the audit.

71. Given the original reason for the HR audit, what would be the MOST appropriate type of audit?
   a. An audit to ensure all HR functions are aligned with best practices
   b. An audit to ensure compliance with applicable regulations
   c. An audit to ensure HR function is aligned with organizational goals
   d. An audit focused on employee relations

Refer to the following for questions 72 - 73:

> You are a human resources manager for a small software start-up company. The organization is relatively flat with several software engineers reporting to one lead and all five leads reporting to the director. A common complaint among the engineers is that there is no opportunity for advancement. In fact, this is prompting some high performers to look for jobs elsewhere.

72. What approach would you take to address this source of discontent?
   a. Spearhead a significant wage increase for all engineers in the company to make up for the fact that they may never receive a promotion.
   b. Make it clear to engineers that promotions are difficult to come by in smaller organizations and instead emphasize all the perks that they enjoy by working for a small, dynamic company.
   c. Encourage engineers to identify the gaps in their skills in relation to the lead position and improve upon those skills to prepare for a potential promotion.
   d. Train the leads to encourage the engineers to assess and communicate their needs and act—pursue learning opportunities and set goals.

73. What types of human resource metrics would you calculate to quantify the severity of the issue?
   a. Time since last promotion
   b. Turnover rate
   c. Retention rate
   d. Performance and potential

74. If an employer declines to move a candidate forward in the interview process because she disclosed that she has a family history of breast cancer, this would likely be a violation of:

   a. ADA
   b. GINA
   c. Title VII
   d. FMLA

75. A job applicant who was invited to interview with your organization requests to have the questions in print format during the interview so that he can read along as the questions are asked. The applicant mentions that he is hard of hearing, and this will help him respond appropriately to the questions. But you have not done this for the other candidates in the process. What do you do?

   a. Offer to read the questions loudly and slowly during the interview.
   b. Decline the request, as it is important to treat every candidate consistently, and interview candidates do not have the same Americans with Disabilities Act (ADA) protections as employees.
   c. Accommodate the candidate, and print out the interview questions for him, as it is an accommodation request under the ADA.
   d. Provide a special hearing device for the candidate to use during the interview.

76. If three companies merge, what does it mean when a number of employees' salaries are red-circled?

   a. The employees will be prohibited from receiving any further salary increases.
   b. The employees are paid over the rate of others at the company in the same role but their rates will continue to be paid.
   c. The employees are paid over the rate of others at the company in the same roles so their rates will gradually be decreased to align with their counterparts.
   d. The employees are paid under the rates of others at the company and the rates will be gradually increased to match their counterparts.

77. If an executive starts a bargaining session by stating that the best base compensation offer they can offer is $175,000 and the candidate responds that the lowest base salary he will accept is $192,000, what type of bargaining in this?

   a. Principled bargaining
   b. Auction bargaining
   c. Position-based bargaining
   d. Interest-based bargaining.

78. If a group of hotel employees are on strike and a group of delivery workers joins the strike in support of the hotel employees this is called:

   a. A support strike
   b. A sympathy strike
   c. A secondary strike
   d. A boycott

Refer to the following for questions 79 - 80:

Two manufacturing companies merge, and two middle-level managers learn that they are being paid substantially less than their new counterparts. The employees demand a meeting with their manager and HR to discuss the issue. In that meeting both employees indicated that they believe they are entitled to a salary increase to match their new colleagues. HR is aware that the company relies on these two employees and the company needs to retain them for at least another three months to ensure they finish their post-merge projects.

79. How should HR respond?
   a. Tell the employees that their salaries will be immediately raised to the level of their counterparts, and future increases will be based on merit.
   b. Tell the employees that their salaries will be adjusted, but it may take a few months for them to reconcile the financial assets of the two new companies.
   c. Suggest that the employee take some time to research the market rate for individuals working in substantially similar roles in the industry and submit a report with data to support their requested increase.
   d. Make a commitment to review the compensation structure of the individuals working in substantially similar roles and to circle back with them with your findings.

80. As the merger progresses, the HR team learns that the post-merged HRIS system is capable of streamlining a number of payroll processes that could reduce the number of employees needed to work in that department.
What should HR do with this information?
   a. Keep the information to themselves because it would be unethical to make suggestions that would lead to layoffs.
   b. Share the information with leadership, but only after providing the payroll department with a heads-up about the system's capabilities so they have time to prepare for potential layoffs.
   c. Create a detailed report about the capabilities of the post-merged HRIS system, explaining how it can be used to further the strategic objectives of the merger.
   d. Reach out to other companies that use the same system to gather information about how they realigned their payroll staff as they rolled out the technology.

Refer to the following for questions 81 - 83:

Over the objections of HR, a company lays off more than 40% of its workforce to reduce payroll costs and redirect funding to acquiring a new company. The company merges with the acquired company, and employee morale drops to an all-time low. Leadership notices a decline in productivity and becomes concerned about employee engagement and retention, especially because they know that the current level of staffing will be insufficient to complete a number of critical projects. In addition, the company is fairly certain they will not be able to meet the commitment it made to provide a minimum number of volunteers for an annual summer run which it oversees with a number of other companies in the industry. Furthermore, they will not be able to adequately staff the annual holiday gift drive. The gift drive is incredibly important for the community members that rely on the holiday gifts. It is also incredibly important to the company because it bolsters its reputation on the national stage which leads to stock price increases and increased market share.

Leadership first approaches HR about its concerns about being able to provide enough volunteers for the upcoming summer fun run.

81. How should HR respond?
a. Tell leadership that they knew this was going to happen, which is why they objected so strongly to the layoffs.
b. Suggest that leadership require all employees to attend the run.
c. Suggest that all managers personally ask their employees to attend the run as a way to compel their attendance.
d. Offer to reach out to some of their colleagues at other companies to see if they might be able to sign up additional volunteers.

82. When leadership approaches HR about its concerns regarding how it will adequately staff the holiday gift drive, how should they respond?
a. Tell leadership "we told you so," and explain that they should have considered this before gutting their workforce.
b. Suggest that managers re-prioritize the current workload of their employees to free up some of their time to work on the gift drive.
c. Suggest the company downsize the event in the coming year and explain that it plans to revert back to the original size after it has had time to move through its current transition.
d. Offer to reach out to staffing companies that specialize in placing seasonal workers.

83. To minimize turnover, HR is asked to review the job descriptions of the current workforce to evaluate how work tasks can be distributed to make workloads more manageable. Within a few weeks, HR is able to streamline some of the work and to eliminate redundancies, but the turnover rate continues to increase. Leadership then informs HR that they should redirect their resources to recruit for the roles that were eliminated. How should HR respond?
a. Remind leadership that this situation could have been avoided had they not laid off the employees in the first place.
b. Suggest that HR continue to review the job descriptions because it might be too early to determine if their work is paying off.
c. Start to recruit for all open roles.
d. Prioritize recruitment of some of the open roles while simultaneously continuing to review the job descriptions to determine if any adjustments should be made.

Refer to the following for questions 84 - 86:

> At a midsize retail provider, a recent initiative in its DE&I strategy led to the creation of a handful of employee resource groups (ERGs) that were designed to help create more inclusive spaces. The chief HR officer requested each of the groups discuss and propose other ways that the organization could create more welcoming and inclusive practices with the workforce.
>
> One of the first recommendations to be put into action came from the African American ERG, which suggested designing and launching a global festivities calendar. The calendar would include celebrations beyond the typically celebrated ones (e.g., Christmas and Thanksgiving), such as the Chinese New Year, the Jewish holiday of Passover, and the cultural celebration of Kwanzaa.
>
> After the rollout of the calendar to the organization, initial feedback was gathered via a survey. The response was mixed. Some employees were excited by the changes

and other employees complained that the change was too "politically correct" and took away from the usual holiday season celebrations.

84. Employees who are expressing concerns about the changes are displaying what type of barrier to diversity and inclusion?
   a. In-group bias
   b. Microaggressions
   c. Social comparison bias
   d. Stereotyping

85. Before launching a global festivities calendar, which of the following practices would be most effective at appealing to the greatest number of employees?
   a. Require attendance at events to improve employee education of other cultures.
   b. Only celebrate secular holidays to separate religion from the workplace.
   c. Collect input from team members to better understand which holidays are celebrated across the workforce.
   d. Ensure traditional holidays still headline the internal communications to keep from ostracizing employees.

86. The employee survey also elicited responses that claimed the company did not go far enough with the calendar, and it was just lip service rather than a genuine recognition of other holidays. Which of the following solutions would be the best in helping the company demonstrate respect for holiday diversity among its workforce?
   a. Substitute all holiday days for paid time off that employees can take whenever they choose.
   b. Introduce floating holidays that allow employees to designate a limited number of days to be off.
   c. Develop a series of holiday schedules based on a variety of cultures and allow employees to select their preferred schedule.
   d. Issue a follow-up survey to determine what additional holidays employees would want off.

Refer to the following for questions 87 - 88:

A company hires a new HR manager with extensive payroll experience to join its team. The new manager has been asked to review current payroll practices to look for ways to increase efficiency. On her first day of work the HR manager learns that the company requires employees to complete paper timesheets each week. She also learns that the company has a policy that all employees are required to enroll in direct deposit but continues to pay a significant amount of money to continue to provide hard copy checks, which is a known contributor to payroll inefficiencies.

87. The manager is shocked that the company is still using paper time sheets to track time due to its environmental impact. What should she do next?
   a. Ask her manager whether the company is aware of the environmental impact of using paper time sheets in a company of its size.
   b. Use the staff directory to see if any employees are responsible for ensuring that the company is engaging in socially responsible business practices and start to develop relationships with those individuals or teams.
   c. Submit an anonymous complaint through the company's compliance hotline informing them of excess waste of paper.
   d. Make a note of this potential concern but do nothing further at this time.

88. When the manager asks why so many employees have not enrolled in direct deposit, she is informed that all employees were provided with the option to enroll in direct deposit, but many declined. What should the manager do next?
   a. Recommend that the company stop issuing hard copy checks.
   b. Recommend that the company make an announcement that hard copy checks will no longer be issued after a certain date.
   c. Impose discipline upon any employees who do not sign up for direct deposit by a certain date.
   d. Ask for additional information about when and how employees were informed.

89. What is the name for a neutral third party who is retained to assist an employer and an employee resolve a dispute but has no power to decide how it will be resolved?
   a. Mediator
   b. Arbitrator
   c. Panel review board
   d. Hearing officer

90. A company that is using a balanced scorecard to map out its strategic plan will review the company from which of the following perspectives?
   a. Financial, business processes, customers, and organizational capacity
   b. Political, societal, and environmental
   c. Financial, political, environmental, and organizational
   d. Customers, investors, and employees

91. Indirect compensation is:
   a. A cash benefit paid to employees outside their base salary
   b. Additional compensation earned by an hourly employee for working overtime hours
   c. Non-cash benefits such as health insurance coverage
   d. The portion of an employee's salary that is paid by a third party such as a client

92. If a company offered its new sales director $250,000 in annual compensation and reports that its internal recruiters allocated $25,000 in internal costs to the role and paid an external recruiter $25,000 for its support in the process, what is the RCR?
   a. 10%
   b. 20%
   c. 25%
   d. 50%

93. An organization that stores art reports that the single loss expectancy of its air conditioner is $3,000,000. What does this mean?
   a. This is the amount of insurance it will need to ensure that all of its assets are protected.
   b. This is the amount of money that should be budgeted to fix the air conditioner in the event it breaks down.
   c. This refers to the loss that can be expected if the air conditioner breaks.
   d. This refers to the amount of risk the organization undertakes each time it takes on a new piece of art.

94. When considering flexible scheduling practices such as hybrid work, compressed hours, job sharing, and vacation time policies, which of the following planning elements is most critical?
    a. Return on investment
    b. Company policy
    c. Industry trends
    d. Program cost

Refer to the following for questions 95 - 98:

The HR team is tasked with setting up a new compliance hotline designed to supplement the other processes in place for employees to report concerns. The hotline provides employees with the opportunity to call a phone number or to use a website to anonymously file a report. The department is leading the project and partnering with IT to ensure that the technology is set up properly to guarantee confidentiality. The HR team is also working with the general counsel's office to draft communications to educate the workforce about the hotline.

The department determines it will need a total of four communications from the general counsel's office to alert the workforce to each stage of the process.

95. How should HR communicate this information to the general counsel's office?
    a. Contact the general counsel and ask them how they envision working together.
    b. Provide the general counsel with a project plan that includes the proposed content for each communication, the deadline for submission of each first draft, the anticipated turnaround time for delivery of feedback, and the anticipated dissemination date for each communication.
    c. Provide the general counsel with a list of the proposed content for each communication and ask them to provide feedback.
    d. Provide the general counsel with three weeks' notice of when you will need each communication and ask them to adhere to the timeline to ensure that the project stays on schedule.

96. As the project moves forward the department decides to use the negotiated "out" clause to invalidate the agreement with the initial vendor and work with a second vendor. This pushes out the timeline by six months. How should the department communicate the situation to the general counsel's office?
    a. They should not communicate this information to the general counsel's office. The content for the communications will not change, so the department should just continue to move forward with that part of the project plan to ensure that the communications are ready in advance of when they are needed.
    b. They should let the general counsel's office know that they decided to move forward with a new vendor and request that the communications still be completed on the same schedule, but that the vendor change allows for some flexibility with regard to timing.
    c. They should send the general counsel's office a detailed memo explaining the issues the department faced with the vendor, the process used to select the new vendor and negotiate the new terms, and the new proposed timeline for the project.
    d. They should inform the office that some elements of the project have changed but they do not need the details because their part of the project will move forward as planned.

97. Supervisors are provided with the first communication and asked to present it to their respective teams at their next staff meeting. The document is a simple statement from the CEO of the organization explaining its commitment to learning about potentially problematic situations and resolving them. One supervisor calls HR and asks them to send a representative to their next staff meeting to educate their team about the new hotline. How should HR respond?
    a. They should decline the invitation because it would not be appropriate for someone from HR to attend a department staff meeting and their presence might make the employees uncomfortable.
    b. They should decline a meeting because the meeting specifically states that the supervisor is responsible for letting their employees know about the project.
    c. They should ask the supervisor why they would like someone from HR to attend the meeting.
    d. They should thank the supervisor to the invitation, accept it, and attend the meeting.

98. Another supervisor emails HR and asks for guidance regarding how to communicate the information to his team because there have been a number of discrimination complaints within his department in the past six months. How should HR respond?
    a. Decline to meet with the supervisor because this first communication is merely an announcement of the project and provides very few details. Suggest that a meeting to discuss delivery of information will be more appropriate at a later date when more details about the hotline are shared.
    b. Decline to meet with the supervisor because they should be able to convey basic information to their team members. HR involvement has potential to undermine the supervisor's authority.
    c. Set up a time for the meeting but provide strict parameters around what will be discussed at the meeting and what will be considered outside the scope.
    d. Set up a time for the meeting.

99. An employee presents data to her employer to support her position that she is paid $3,000 below market rate. She asks for an adjustment and the company said they value her work and understand she is underpaid but they simply do not have the budget to increase her salary. If the parties agree that the employee will continue to be paid her current salary but will be given an additional week of paid vacation, what type of conflict resolution mode will the parties have used?
    a. Accommodate
    b. Assert
    c. Collaborate
    d. Compromise

100. What does it mean when an organization conducts a staffing gap analysis and they determine they have deployment and time gaps?
   a. Employees are leaving the organization to work for their competitors, and it is taking too long to fill their roles.
   b. Too much money is being used to poach talent from other companies, and it takes too long for employees to be hired.
   c. Employees cannot be sent to the areas of the organization where they can bring the most value, and the work is taking too long to be completed.
   d. Employees need to be sent externally to get the appropriate level of training, and it takes too much time for them to get up to speed.

Refer to the following for questions 101 - 104:

An HR director is leading an investigation related to whether a supervisor discriminated against an employee when he denied the vacation requests of two women on his team because they did not submit the request using the online request form required by the company. According to the women, a number of men have had requests via email routinely approved.

101. If the complaint includes 50 email requests and approvals from the male colleagues of the accusers from the past year, what should the investigator do next?
   a. Initiate an investigation but create a truncated plan because there is sufficient evidence to support the allegation.
   b. Draft an investigatory report confirming that the women have been discriminated against.
   c. Consider the emails part of the evidence to be reviewed during the investigatory process.
   d. Disregard the emails because they were provided by the accuser, who would have had a motive to submit false documents.

102. During the investigatory interview the supervisor becomes visibly upset about the allegations. How should the investigator respond?
   a. Ask the supervisor if he would like to take a break so he can collect his thoughts
   b. Ignore the situation unless the supervisor requests a break.
   c. Suggest to the supervisor that if he did nothing wrong, then there is no reason for him to be upset.
   d. Inform the supervisor you would like to ask an HR colleague to join the interview to observe the discussion in case things escalate.

103. When the investigator provides her boss with a daily recap of the investigatory meetings and explains that the supervisor got emotional, the boss replies that "real men don't cry." How should she respond?
   a. Ignore the comment because it is her boss.
   b. Ignore the comment because she is conducting the interview and writing the investigatory report, so the comment will not have any impact on the investigation.
   c. Explain that she could understand how both men and women might find participating in this type of process to be an upsetting experience.
   d. Make light of the situation by referencing the fact that her husband cries in movies.

104. On the morning after the investigator concludes her investigation she receives an email from the supervisor explaining he has additional information to share. How should she respond?

a. Ignore the email because the investigation is closed.
b. Respond to the email and explain to the supervisor that the investigation is over and to be fair she will not accept any additional information from either party.
c. Respond to the email and ask the supervisor whether he would like to schedule a time to speak.
d. Escalate the email to the CHRO so she is aware that the supervisor is attempting to influence the investigation.

Refer to the following for questions 105 - 108:

A company is expecting to launch its new video game on November 1st, and it anticipates that fans will line up to purchase it days before launch. The company store is open from 9 am-5 pm, and the marketing team requests that HR reach out to the union representing the cashiers and security officers to arrange for a schedule change. The department is requesting the appropriate level of staffing to enable the store to keep its doors open from 12:01 am until 11:59 pm on launch day to accommodate potential crowds.

105. How should HR respond to this request?

a. Inform the marketing team that they are in full support of this adjustment and will do what it takes to make it happen.
b. Inform the marketing team that the unionized employees are working under a collective bargaining agreement and their schedules cannot be changed.
c. Inform the marketing team that they should consider working within the parameters of the current store hours to avoid a potential labor issue.
d. Inform the marketing team that the unionized employees are working under a collective bargaining agreement, then contact the union to attempt to negotiate an agreement to allow for this temporary schedule change.

106. HR arranges to meet with the union to discuss a potential schedule change for employees to work extended shifts during launch of the new product. In response, the union states that a contract is a contract, and they have no interest in making any changes. How should HR respond?

a. Thank the union for their time and inform the marketing team they will have to adjust their plans for the launch to coincide with the current store hours.
b. Tell the union that they are being unreasonable and demand that they reconsider the request.
c. Provide the union with examples of prior agreements between the company and the union that temporarily adjusted the schedules of employees, in response to a union request, to allow as many employees as possible to attend a national labor conference.
d. Explain to the union that if they are not willing to discuss any accommodation the company will plan to use other employees to cover the times that the union employees are not scheduled to work.

107. If the union responds that it is not interested in making any schedule changes even though some adjustments have been made in the past, how should HR respond?
   a. Tell the union that it is unfortunate that they are unwilling to participate in the company's success, and plan to remind them of their response next time they ask for a concession.
   b. Thank the union for their time and let them know you plan to escalate the situation to your supervisor, and they should expect a call from the head of the department.
   c. Review the union contract to see what rights the company might have to staff the marketing event without any union involvement.
   d. Immediately inform the marketing department that the union is unwilling to make a concession so they can start to develop an alternative plan.

108. When the HR team learns that the union does not want the company to assign the extra shifts to their employees, they decide that they will bring in their family and friends to volunteer to cover the extra shifts. After the event, the general counsel informs HR that their conduct violated the law because individuals who perform work for the company must be paid.

How should the HR team respond?
   a. Respond that it is already done and suggest everyone moves on.
   b. Ask the marketing department to reach out to the general counsel's office to explain they were just trying to support their initiatives.
   c. Explain that they were unaware that use of volunteers was problematic and agree to use discretionary funds to compensate anyone that should have been paid for their time.
   d. Explain to the general counsel's office that had the Union been more willing to partner with them the entire mess would have been avoided.

109. What does a performance management system allow?
   a. Managers can adjust or calibrate the questions used to review their direct reports based upon their roles.
   b. Managers use the same standards to evaluate their employees across the organization.
   c. Managers receive a dashboard of data related to each direct report that can be incorporated into the evaluation.
   d. Managers ask their direct reports to complete a self-evaluation, then incorporate any components they may have overlooked in the final evaluations.

110. If a supervisor is given a list of four statements that might describe one of their direct reports, and they are asked to indicate which single statement best describes them and which single statement is least representative, what type of appraisal method is being used?
   a. Comparative method
   b. Forced choice
   c. Ranking
   d. Graphic scale

111. An employee continues to have mail sent to an incorrect address even after changing his address in the HRIS system. What type of issue is this?
   a. Analytical issue
   b. Typographical issue
   c. Data integrity issue
   d. Data integration issue

112. What is the name of the law that provides expanded job-protected leave for family members to care for other family members who are covered members of the military?
   a. ADA
   b. NDAA
   c. FLSA
   d. OWBPA

Refer to the following for questions 113 - 115:

> Alison, who recently started within the past two months, is the newly hired manager for a team of education professionals who specialize in adult learning and career skills community development. She supervises Sandra, the newest employee to the team and a recent college graduate; Andrew, the most experienced member of the team known for his networking skills; and Mark, the most organized member of the team.
>
> After being tasked to send two of her team members to an industry conference, Alison selects Sandra and Mark, citing the desire to increase Sandra's exposure to other professionals and her confidence in Mark's organizational skills to bring home all the knowledge and resources they gain while there. While Sandra and Mark are away at the conference, Andrew meets with Alison to discuss typical daily tasks and brings up her selection criteria for the conference. He asks if he could have done anything different to be considered for the opportunity.
>
> Alison reassures Andrew that his work is high quality, but she mentions she selected his other coworkers because she assumed navigating travel and the conference convention center would be too difficult for Andrew as he uses a wheelchair. Flustered at the response, Andrew lets the conversation drop but later decides to speak with the department's HR manager to discuss his frustrations.

113. Which of the following actions would be the most effective first step for the HR manager following his or her conversation with Andrew?
   a. Put Alison on a performance improvement plan for team management.
   b. Mandate that Alison retake the annual virtual diversity and inclusion trainings.
   c. Schedule a meeting with Alison to discuss the situation and gauge her ideas for possible solutions.
   d. Review Alison's previous performance assessments of her team to identify any other mistreatment.

114. In the counseling meeting, Alison expressed genuine surprise and remorse at how her decision-making process was ableist and was eager to learn more about working with team members with physical disabilities. Alison expressed the desire to apologize to Andrew and offered some ideas for how to make things right after her mistake. In addition to an apology, which of the following ideas would be the most effective for the HR manager to encourage Alison to pursue?
   a. Send Andrew to the next local industry conference three months from now.
   b. Arrange a team meeting with Sandra, Mark, and Andrew to acknowledge the mistake and establish the expectations moving forward.
   c. Offer a one-time performance bonus in appreciation for his high-quality work.
   d. Have a one-on-one meeting with Andrew to discuss career goals and development.

115. After meeting with Andrew to discuss his career aspirations and the methods by which Alison can empower growth, Alison realizes she has much to learn about managing a diverse team. Which of the following DE&I programs would be most effective for Alison to help her better support and learn about employees with diverse backgrounds?

   a. Allyship events
   b. Executive sponsorship
   c. Mentoring programs
   d. Virtual diversity trainings

Answer Key and Explanations for Test #2

1. A: Ranking is not an effective method for appraising large groups of employees. The ranking method simply entails placing employees in order from most important to least. In a large organization, it will be difficult to make comparisons between jobs. Also, many job groups will be so different that comparisons will be worthless. The other answer choices are true statements. Annual performance reviews are waning in favor of the higher engagement levels required for regular reviews. In a forced ranking system, the appraisers place all employees on a bell curve, and therefore the vast majority end up close to the middle. Behaviorally anchored rating systems (BARS) assess employees based on the behaviors deemed critical to their particular job.

2. D: In the workplace, the Meyers-Brigg Type Indicator is primarily used as a personality test to enable individuals to understand their personalities better and to assist staff members in appreciating how to interact with their co-workers more effectively. Due to the nature of the administrative department and its situation—employees who work together quite frequently and run into personality conflicts—the Meyers-Brigg test will be Raisa's best recommendation. Answer choices A and C are incorrect because research has suggested a lack of long-term value in team-building activities such as obstacle courses and scavenger hunts. Answer choice B is also incorrect. While role-playing situations might be beneficial to those who work in highly active and often sensitive fields, they will not necessarily be as useful for employees whose jobs are more focused around completing and maintaining paperwork or projects.

3. D: The supervisors at Flanders Company are practicing extinction, though they are most likely unaware of doing so. Extinction occurs when the positive reinforcement that followed a behavior ceases, and the behavior gradually ceases as well. Punishment is a negative consequence to a behavior. The absence of positive reinforcement is not considered punishment. Positive reinforcement is a reward, while negative reinforcement is the removal of a punishment. Positive and negative reinforcement are both used to encourage certain behaviors.

4. C: An applicant tracking system (ATS) can be a standalone software or can be packaged within an overarching human resources information system (HRIS). The application conversion rate is the percentage of candidates who complete a job application after the first click on the "apply" button or link. Factors that can affect the application flow include the number of clicks from start to finish, the presentation of the ATS program compared to the company's website, and other barriers, such as forcing applicants to create system logins or re-input their resume data after uploading the original document. Improved application flow leads to an increased number of applications and an increased pool of candidates to consider when recruiting. Candidate demographics ratios can be important for a company focusing on employee diversity but may not affect the overall volume of candidates. Employee participation rate focuses on candidates after they've completed the hiring process and are using other elements of the HRIS. The return on investment focuses on the financial impact of the system and can include a number of outcomes within the measurement—not just recruiting.

5. C: The widespread nature of the company locations means that a questionnaire is going to be the most effective way to acquire feedback; the questionnaire can be sent out, and employees can then complete it and return it by a certain time. A focus group is impractical, as it might be difficult to get enough people together for the discussion. Interviews and observation can prove to be cumbersome, both to employees and management, because they might require extensive travel and/or arranging of schedules.

6. A: An Employee Self-Service (ESS) function with HRIS allows employees to perform transactional tasks for themselves instead of going through their manager or human resources representative. These tasks can include requesting time away from work, selecting benefits, updating personal data, filing expense reports, and more. The other functions listed can also help reduce the transactional responsibilities for a human resources team but still require intervention in the design, collection, and use of the other functions. Additionally, functions like training, performance management, and data analytics can play critical roles in the transformational side of human resources responsibilities.

7. D: The critical first step when purchasing a new HRIS is determining what the organization needs from a system as well as what it may want from a system. A comprehensive needs assessment sets the foundation for then determining a system budget and project timelines. Once needs, budget, and timelines are defined, then an organization can seek vendor quotes within each of these parameters.

8. C: Organizing a social meet-up for remote employees to connect with one another would encourage strong working relationships and a kind of support group where they can share remote working experiences and tips. Posting photos would probably make remote workers feel even more left out of the fun. Also, if given the choice, remote workers would probably prefer not to attend the company party if it meant paying for travel and lodging. The dial-in and webcam would not be a bad idea but, again, may make the remote workers feel more left out.

9. D: The biggest advantage is offering a better work-life balance for employees. Overhead costs may be slightly less for a remote worker; however, the employer should still pay for home office supplies and equipment. A lack of commute does have a positive impact on the environment, but that is not necessarily the focus from a human resource perspective. Finally, a remote work arrangement is not a substitute for child care, as the employee's focus should be on working, not tending to other responsibilities.

10. A: Communication is generally the biggest challenge when it comes to having a remote workforce. Employees and managers must be more proactive in communication efforts with remote workers—a simple face-to-face chat is not an option. Option C may also be true, but the effects are less far-reaching than the effects of poor communication. Options B and D are incorrect because generally the opposite is true. Usually stress decreases for remote workers and they are more productive.

11. B: Dependents may enroll with COBRA continuation coverage even if the primary beneficiary (employee or former employee) is not enrolled.

12. B: The employer should provide a comprehensive list of acceptable documentation to an employee and allow him or her to choose the documentation that meets the criteria. Requiring a new hire to supply a passport would discriminate against those who are not U.S. citizens.

13. D: Even if a candidate appears to be originally from the United States, interviewers should not ask where the candidate is from, as national origin is a protected class. If not selected, a candidate could claim discrimination based on this criterion.

14. C: H-1B visa applicants are eligible if they possess a bachelor's degree or foreign equivalent and work in a specialty occupation as defined by the U.S. Citizenship and Immigration Services (USCIS).

15. A: An employee who is "engaged to wait" is one who must stay at the workplace until his or her work assignment is given. Therefore, he or she must be paid for that time, as he or she is effectively on duty. An employee who is "waiting to be engaged" is relieved of his or her work duties, and can use his or her time freely, but must return to the workplace if a work assignment requires his or her presence.

16. B: Federal law does not require lunch or rest periods for employees; however, many states do have these provisions.

17. C: The Recruitment Cost Ratio is calculated by dividing the total amount of recruitment costs ($60,000) by the total first-year compensation of new hires in a given time period ($300,000) and then multiplying the result by 100. $60,000/$300,000x 100 = 20%.

18. B: Pay audits are designed to assess the rates of pay for all comparable positions and their compensable factors devoid of the individuals performing the job. Pay audits can help to identify pay discrepancies that may have been persisting for an individual because of past pay inequities, and they can identify pay practices to be corrected. Pay audits are most useful in correcting historical pay inequities as they are designed to identify when those inequities may have started and occurred. Compensation surveys (A) and market data about compensation trends can be useful for a company when setting pay rates for future hires or in times of pay restructuring. A job analysis (C) can be a useful tool prior to conducting pay audits to affirm that job descriptions and duties are accurate across different positions. Performance evaluations (D) are important within the context of pay equity to reward employees in clear, tangible ways that directly correlate to their work performance.

19. C: Throughout the entire risk management process, it is important that strategies are monitored and reviewed to ensure alignment with the process' goals and the organization's overall strategy.

20. D: The final step in creating a knowledge management system is to update, revise, and add information on an ongoing basis to keep the database relevant and current.

21. C: A scatter diagram is used when one wants to determine if there is a correlation between two variables. One axis would be the test scores, and the other axis the number of closed sales. The diagram will show a dot for each employee. If the dots resemble a line, it would suggest that there is a correlation between the two variables.

22. A: Designing an EEOC statement or diversity statement to include with the employee handbook can help to connect any external promises of DE&I to internal accountability standards. By including the DE&I expectations and values in the onboarding stage right next to dress code and attendance standards, the organization is demonstrating that diversity is a core function and expectation for all its employees. A companywide email (B), if worded and timed correctly, can be a powerful sentiment; however, a new employee has not yet necessarily built trust in the company leadership, so the message may not have the intended effect. DE&I affirmation posters (C) can be useful as a supplement to other communication strategies but are passive modes of communication for new and veteran employees. A weekly DE&I spotlight (D) could be an engaging idea but similarly to a companywide email might not have the intended effect for new employees that haven't built trust with the company.

23. B: Pay transparency helps to empower candidates from traditionally disenfranchised diversity dimensions to apply for and negotiate their worth based on their work rather than on their pay history. By posting the pay ranges for each job, the company begins to build trust with candidates while also demonstrating an internal culture built on work outcomes and transparency. Applicant tracking software (A) can be useful to thin out large volumes of resumes but can also maintain biases depending on its build; employers should take care to utilize ATS as a tool and not as the be-all and end-all. Recruiting flyers (C) that feature diverse individuals can be useful in the fact that representation is a powerful thing; however, this can also be seen as performative in nature when compared to actual practices that support workforce inclusion. Listing the preferred diversity dimensions within the job requisition (D) can be interpreted as disparate treatment and would not be recommended in this scenario.

24. D: Employee resource groups can be a powerful program when embraced by the workforce. By surveying the workforce for the desired ERGs, the organization will be more likely to set the program up for success. ERGs can represent a wide variety of dimensions across protected classes, such as sex, race, religion, national origin, and ability, among others, and establishing the ERGs that are most meaningful to the workforce is critical. This data will also be critical when the HR team seeks out leadership buy-in (B) as the team will be presenting not just DE&I best practices but the direct feedback from the workforce that informed the ERG designs.

25. B: In order to shift the messaging from performative to genuine, the company will benefit from featuring actual employees who are speaking about their actual experiences with the company. Representation in commercials (A), advertisements (C), and social media (D) are important but are not as powerful as a demonstration of the action the company has taken in support of DE&I progress and values.

26. C: The company should conduct a thorough investigation before making the decision to terminate an employee. As part of the investigation, the manager should interview each of the employees to hear their side of the story. The employees should then be suspended pending investigation. This will give HR time to research and review all relevant information, including any prior similar instances, before making a final decision.

27. B: A successful mentorship is a two-way street in which both parties exchange knowledge and learn from each other. The mentee must help shape the overall mentoring relationship, and goals should be set together. The frequency of meetings can vary. Generally, a mentor is a senior colleague or a peer. In a formal mentorship, the mentor and mentee are usually paired by HR. In an informal mentorship, the mentee often selects someone as a mentor for themselves.

28. C: Identity covering occurs when a worker feels the need to downplay or hide part of their personality or personal life in order to better fit in with the majority. Identity covering can prevent employees from feeling like they truly belong in the workplace and can prevent them from reaching their true potential. Imposter syndrome (A) is the phenomenon in which an employee doubts their abilities or feels as if they are not qualified for the role. Microaggressions (B) are intentional or unintentional comments or behaviors that have a discriminatory effect. Cultural taxation (D) is the burden borne by minority employees to participate in DE&I initiatives and to represent others of the same diversity dimension.

29. A: Web conferencing allows a presenter to share presentation slides on each participant's computer. The participants can see the slide show presentation slides on their device and can hear the presentation over their computer's speakers or headphones. They also have the opportunity to directly communicate with the presenter through a webchat or their computer's microphone.

30. A: A flow analysis looks at how employees move around in the company. It follows each team member throughout the employee life cycle, including any promotions, demotions, or transfers. It is a critical part of evaluating the skill and talent that exists within the organization (supply analysis). The demand analysis forecasts future talent needs of the company. The gap analysis contrasts the demand against the supply to identify possible talent shortfalls. During the solution analysis, a company identifies ways to fill any talent gaps.

31. D: Time-based step-rate pay rewards tenure over performance. Pay increases are granted on a previously established timeline. On the contrary, merit pay, also called performance-based pay, grants pay increases based on an individual's performance. With a straight or differential piece-rate system, an employee is paid a base wage plus additional pay for completed work up to an established standard. They may receive a premium for work accomplished that exceeds this standard.

32. A: In a polycentric organization, each country has its own unique talent acquisition approach. In an ethnocentric organization, headquarter staffing policies are mimicked when expanding into other countries. A geocentric organization has a global talent acquisition plan. Each region establishes its own staffing policies in an egocentric organization.

33. C: The employees affected by the change were not included in the development of the restructure, which can lead to resistance.

34. D: Succession planning and leadership development are imperative because the environment in which organizations operate changes rapidly. Shared leadership, in contrast to having single leaders, allows for quicker and more efficient responses to external change.

35. B: During the entire OED (organizational and employee development) process, the specialists should be aware of the employees' emotional reactions to proposed and implemented changes. They should also find ways to improve their ability to adapt to the changes.

36. B: The company has determined that 16% of their sales representatives are leaving the firm. Their goal is to reduce this number to 6%. Therefore, the gap between the current attrition and the future targeted attrition is 10% (16%-6%). Given that the company has 1,000 sales representatives, this change would result in only 60 employees leaving the organization (6%), rather than 160 (16%).

37. B: Diversity and inclusion (D&I) strategies need to account for differences in cultural backgrounds, organizational departments, and geographical locations. Therefore, they should not be put into effect identically across the entire organization. It is important that the implementation is adaptable, just, and fair, taking into account the uniqueness of individuals and teams.

38. C: EPLI (employment practices liability insurance) is insurance for companies that protects them in case they get sued by an employee. It covers legal costs and settlement fees related to the suit.

39. B: Wearing personal protective equipment is considered a leading indicator because it affects the rate of future workplace accidents. The opposite is a lagging indicator, which had an impact on the number of workplace accidents that occurred in the past.

40. D: This is an example of a manager self-service (MSS) application. It allows managers to handle the HR part of their role through one portal. It can be used for reporting and the performance management process. Tasks that are traditionally handled by the HR department can now be performed by the managers themselves.

41. C: This is an example of risk mitigation. The company reduces the severity of the potential consequences by creating a plan to quickly communicate with employees and share information that will help keep them safe.

42. D: There are three stages on the corporate social responsibility (CSR) curve: compliance, integration, and transformation. The company is at the transformation stage. They have successfully integrated sustainability into their core strategy by receiving the B Corp certification. A company can obtain this certification if they meet a number of environmental and social performance standards.

43. C: E-learning, which is learning conducted via electronic media, can be either synchronous or asynchronous. Asynchronous learning means that employees can access the material anytime and anywhere. With synchronous learning, employees go through the training material at the same time and communicate with each other in real time.

44. A: Telling an employee that he will be demoted if he votes for the union is an unfair labor practice (ULP). After the employee reports the ULP to the NLRB, the NLRB will investigate the allegation.

45. A: Stay interviews can improve retention by allowing managers to find out early on if an employee is happy and satisfied or unhappy and disengaged. If the employee is unhappy or disengaged, the manager has an opportunity to address their concerns. With exit interviews, it's usually too late to prevent the employee from resigning.

46. C: The yield ratio is calculated by dividing the number of female applicants by the number of total applicants: 100/250 = 40%.

47. D: It is important for a company to invest in a comprehensive diversity and inclusion program because the goal is to change deeply held beliefs, assumptions, habits, and processes, which is a difficult undertaking. If the company does not truly care about making these difficult changes and putting in the necessary effort, the initiative will not be successful. Further, the company will not be able to profit from the advantages of a diverse workforce.

48. D: In a working environment where management and team members are geographically dispersed, it is important that dialogue with each employee is conducted to better understand the team dynamics and motivations and to separate facts from emotions. Conducting conversations with both the manager and HR representative demonstrates to employees that their complaints are being addressed, and it also allows each team member to communicate his or her point of view without any interruptions. Relocating the manager on-site (A) would be an extreme reaction that could take away from other sites he or she manages and other organizational responsibilities he or she oversees. While performance improvement plans (PIP) may be required after further conversation (B), immediately placing just the employees of one gender on PIPs without additional investigation may cause backlash and additional discrimination claims. The manager joining the team meetings to discuss organizational values (C) can be a positive action, but it fails to address the specific behaviors that are causing the tension among the team.

49. A: Diverse teams, even high-performing diverse teams, typically experience higher levels of conflict due to differences in experiences, beliefs, and behaviors. Psychological safety is the critical element in which, despite the differences among team members, everyone feels comfortable offering opposing ideas, trying new things, adjusting their point of view, and taking risks. Disparate impact (B) (or unintentional discrimination) and team dissatisfaction (D) are less likely to be found positively correlated with high-performing, diverse teams. Collaboration (C) in and of itself is a style of conflict that leads to new solutions and added value.

50. B: It is important for managers to not get lost in the stereotypes of generational differences (A) and recognize each employee for his or her individual strengths and challenges. Those strengths may or may not align with generational expectations, and they will vary by individual and must be addressed as such. By focusing on the strengths of each employee, the manager can help the team to see the value in each other and lean into each member's strengths in order to improve the work outcomes of the site. As an off-site manager, mediating all conversations (C) is inefficient and unlikely to be effective. Forcing conflicting team members to work together (D) without addressing the challenges at hand can end up exacerbating the conflicts and lead to more drastic negative outcomes.

51. C: Employee resource groups can serve as an important tool to bring together groups of employees with a common trait to feel as if they are truly part of a team. These groups can go beyond just social gatherings, as they can discuss issues and challenges facing the organization and propose solutions to improve the working experiences for a diverse workforce. Employee surveys (A) are important tools for understanding how the workforce feels, and how it views the company, but they do not necessarily pull employees together. Unconscious bias training (B) can be a useful tool, but it can be difficult to effectively plan and map the belonging metrics that result. Performative allyship (D) is a negative phenomenon in which companies say the right thing in support of diverse workforces while neglecting to take actual action.

52. C: HR should consult with legal counsel when writing a staffing contract. They should avoid setting end dates in the contract so it can be terminated in case of dissatisfaction. They should also stay away from generic contract forms. Finally, they should negotiate the price of the staffing company's service.

53. D: Unconscious bias trainings are at higher risks of failure if they are used as stand-alone bandages that simply check a "DEI training" box. In general, DEI trainings benefit from a variety of modalities, interactions, and workplace-specific applications. Simply adding additional trainings (A) runs the risk of backfiring if employees refuse to attend or feel their time is being wasted. Eliminating the trainings altogether (B) could also cause backlash from employees because they may view the action as an abandonment of DEI strategy. Higher leadership participation (C) can be a helpful change to the next series of trainings, but the participation must be due to a genuine desire to contribute to DEI advancement and not due to threats or demands.

54. D: In the ADDIE method of training design and evaluation, the design stage comes after the analysis stage (analyze, design, develop, implement, evaluate). Designing prior to developing (B) is important in this scenario because without knowing how many sessions the training will include, the length of each session, and the capabilities of the virtual platform, the development stage lacks the context for the depth and breadth of topics to be covered. Evaluating the results of the first training (C) occur as part of the analysis portion that has already been conducted; formal training evaluations will be held again after the next training sessions.

55. B: Nearly half of the team leaders, facility leaders, and executive leadership members failed to meet the standards set for the organization. Whether the leaders felt they were above the training, were not the problem, or were too busy, this lack of participation can be observed by lower-level employees, and thus the lack of commitment demonstrated by organizational leadership can be detrimental to the future participation and buy-in from the rest of the workforce. While the numbers for the loan officers are discouraging (A), it is not possible to discern from the data if the reason the participation rate was low was because of discrimination or because of other issues inhibiting employees from attending the trainings. While the accounting team's participation rates (C) are encouraging, the strategy used to mobilize a team of 12 is not likely to have the same effect when duplicated for a team of 36 or 88. While the smaller teams may have recorded higher levels of participation (D), participation rates are not equivalent to training effectiveness, and additional follow-up and measurements are required to make such conclusions.

56. A: Unconscious bias trainings are not intended to change beliefs necessarily but to influence behaviors and improve the interactions between employees, customers, and stakeholders. Tracking the employee engagement rates through volume of communication, opened emails, and communication maps can be evidence of shifting behavioral patterns. Net facility income (B) may be measured as a long-term outcome, but unconscious bias trainings are unlikely to affect financial outcomes immediately. Employee retention rates (C) and performance management scores (D) may shift in response to unconscious bias training, but the short-term changes to these metrics can be misleading. For example, employee retention may decrease, which can be read as a negative outcome of the trainings, but the employees leaving may be those who do not support a diverse workforce. Thus, in the long run, the turnover results in positive outcomes.

57. D: A balanced scorecard shows if the HR strategy is in alignment with and supports the company's strategic direction. It can be used to assess the performance of the HR department and gauge the value it provides for the organization.

58. D: In a group interview, one or several managers interview a number of job candidates. They can be conducted as either team interviews or panel interviews. The main advantage is that they reduce the time spent on the interview and candidate selection process.

59. C: HR professionals can support adherence to new processes by incorporating goals that reflect those processes into performance reviews. Performance objectives should be transparent and easy for employees to understand. They should also reflect the new goals and responsibilities that resulted from the change initiative.

60. D: The managers are conducting a force-field analysis and identifying factors that help and hinder the proposed restructure. As a result, the team can determine which possibilities they should pursue further and which ones to stay away from.

61. C: To attract the best talent, the company pursues a lead market strategy and offers higher wages than the market. A match market strategy would be to offer pay rates similar to other companies. A lag market strategy would aim to save on personnel costs by offering lower-than-average wages.

62. D: The employee absence rate is a measure that can be calculated and used to assess the effectiveness of an engagement action plan. Problem-solving abilities, employee motivation, and managerial skills are not outcomes that can be measured explicitly.

63. C: Employee surveys are a tool to increase employee engagement. But it is important that managers communicate the results honestly to their employees, take the feedback seriously, and respond in a meaningful manner. The greatest mistake companies can make with employee surveys is ignoring or not responding to the survey results. This can lead to frustrated and disengaged employees.

64. A: The leader of a focus group should put his emphasis on drawing out information from the participants. He can do this by involving all of them equally and encouraging deep discussion of the topic.

65. D: Once the employee has been selected for the global assignment, it is important for him to learn about the local culture. This will prepare him for a successful start overseas. Setting pay rates, analyzing the potential return on investment, and assessing fit with the employee's career aspirations should take place well before selecting an employee for the assignment.

66. C: This is an example of gamification, a technique frequently used in mobile learning (m-learning), where educational material is delivered in the form of a game. It is intended to make learning more fun and the material more engaging.

67. B: Conducting a compliance audit at the last step of the risk management process will ensure that all implemented changes comply with applicable regulations and laws.

68. D: Companies that want to minimize having to discipline their workforce should practice open communication with their employees. It allows employees to develop a good understanding of company policies and expectations. And, managers who are in regular communication with their employees understand reasons for their behavior and can correct it before a violation occurs.

69. B: In this instance, you should gather more information before instituting a plan of action. The cause of the poor ratings could be anything from bad internal customer service to inefficient processes. Another survey would probably give employees survey fatigue, so it's best to launch an internal audit.

70. D: The first step in a human resources audit is to determine the type and scope of the audit. Will you focus on one specific function, such as recruiting or employee relations? Or will it be more exhaustive of all processes? Will it be strategic or compliance-oriented, or will it identify best practices?

71. A: This audit should address all HR functions, not just employee relations. The poor survey results could be prompted by other processes such as performance reviews, benefits enrollment, promotional opportunities, and so on. Although compliance is important, it is not the goal of this audit. Industry best practice will provide a useful benchmark to identify deficiencies in the HR function.

72. D: In this situation, you don't want to imply that the engineers only need to improve upon their skills to get a promotion, but you also don't want to stifle their ambition. The leads should work with the engineers to identify exactly what they need—is it just more money? More recognition? More responsibility? More autonomy? Perhaps some of these needs can be met with a creative solution rather than a promotion.

73. A: The best way to quantify this situation is to calculate the time since last promotion for each employee and average it out across the organization. Whereas a turnover rate may indicate a problem with higher-than-average employee exits, it will not identify the reason for exits.

74. B: The Genetic Information Nondiscrimination Act (GINA) prohibits employers from discriminating against individuals based upon their genetics, which would include discrimination related to an applicant's family medical history.

75. C: The Americans with Disabilities Act (ADA) protects job applicants as well as employees, and this candidate's request is a reasonable one; the employer should provide this reasonable accommodation so that the candidate has a fair opportunity to compete for the position.

76. B: Red circling is used to indicate that an employee is overpaid but that they will continue to be paid at this rate. There are number of reasons why a rate may be red circled.

77. C: In position-based bargaining, both sides state their position, and they view the process as a zero-sum game where one person "wins" and one person "loses." When parties engage in position bargaining, both sides usually state their opening positions, then both sides offer concessions, and the agreement generally, but not always, is reached when the parties agree upon a figure that is somewhere in the middle of the two opening positions.

78. B: A sympathy strike occurs when a group of non-striking employees joins the strike as a way to show support for their cause. Many collective bargaining agreements contain contract language that prohibits employees working under it from participating in a sympathy strike.

79. D: Choice D is the correct answer because HR professionals should ensure that their decisions are data driven and should not simply increase compensation based upon an employee request.

80. C: Choice C is the best answer because HR professionals are obligated to use all available business information and technologies to increase the efficiency of the company, even if it results in loss of jobs. It would be unethical not to share this information with leadership as a way to maintain jobs that may not be needed. It would also not be appropriate to share information about potential layoffs when there is no clear indication of when or if they might occur.

81. D: Because employee morale is at an all-time low, it is unlikely that requiring employees to volunteer at an event or asking managers to use their influence to compel them to attend is going to be an effective path forward. HR professionals should develop and maintain a strong network so they can reach out for support. In this case, another company that participates in the event may be able to secure additional volunteers to compensate for the company's shortfall.

82. D: Because the holiday drive is a priority for the company for its reputation, its stock price, and its customer acquisition, HR should look for a short-term solution to the staffing shortfall. While it might be useful to reprioritize the workload of existing employees, it is unclear whether this will be sufficient to ensure a successful event.

83. D: Choice D is the best path forward. Ideally, review of the job descriptions would be completed before HR starts to recruit for the vacant roles. However, the increased turnover rate requires a short-term strategy to stabilize the current workforce. HR should start to recruit new employees to address the short-term need, while also developing a long-term strategic plan.

84. A: An in-group bias refers to one's preference to work and associate with others that they perceive to be as part of the same social group. This can also be referenced as an out-group bias, which is when individuals expressing concerns may be feeling threatened by others that they perceive to be from outside of their social group. By identifying this particular bias, the HR team and ERG can reassess the announcement and design of the global festivities calendar to reemphasize the intent of adding to celebrations without downplaying or "canceling" the traditional celebrations that can be of high importance to workforce members. While the concerns raised may offend other employees, these particular comments are private and in response to a survey as opposed to being directed at others; therefore, they do not necessarily qualify as stereotyping (D) or microaggressions (B), but they can raise HR's awareness to be on the lookout for possible changes in team dynamics. Social comparison bias (C) refers to comparing ones' achievements and status to another's, often negatively.

85. C: When introducing new elements to the employee experience, it is important to understand who the employees are and what they value in workplace holiday observations. By collecting input first, the calendar organizers can ensure that no holidays or celebrations get missed in the calendar launch and may discover key allies to help promote the calendar. Employees who celebrate these other holidays may be willing to act as spokespeople for these celebrations to help introduce them to others. Putting a recognizable face to the holiday may help employees who feel threatened by change to empathize with these coworkers they already know and thus recognize the importance of the celebration. Requiring attendance (A) at any holiday gatherings can create uncomfortable situations for employees and increase the levels of hostility toward what should be culture-building events. Eliminating all religious holiday celebrations (B) will, at best, further entrench the divide between workers from different cultures and, at worst, put the company at risk of discrimination claims. While it is important to be conscientious of employees who may feel threatened by the new calendar, downplaying the changes in favor of only specific holiday celebrations (D) would undermine the work of the global festivities calendar and keep the workforce from growth and development within the DE&I sphere.

86. B: Floating holidays can serve to support employees who may celebrate holidays that they usually need to save vacation time for, as opposed to peers who may already have days off built in for the holidays they celebrate. Floating holidays can also make it easier for managers to balance personnel needs with operations instead of using a more drastic measure, like developing multiple holiday schedules for employees to choose from (C). Substituting all holiday days for vacation days (A) may not be feasible for a retail organization that may need to balance operational demands when serving customers. While issuing a survey (D) to better understand the needs of employees may be useful, issuing a second survey on the heels of the first without any tangible actions to address concerns that were raised may cause that second survey to be taken less seriously or disregarded.

87. D: Choice D is the best answer because this is the manager's first day of work and she likely has very little knowledge about whether the company's business operations and its strategic objectives align with her personal views. The manager should learn more about the company's business and operations before taking any action.

88. D: Choice D is the best answer because this is a critical gap in the data that is being presented. The problem seems to be that a large number of employees have not complied with the policy, and the first step should be to gather all of the data necessary to identify the scope of the problem. If an employee never received the communication, received it a long time ago, or simply needed assistance in making a change in the system, the situation might be easily resolved.

89. A: A mediator is a third-party neutral who assists the parties in reaching a resolution but has no authority to impose the resolution. An arbitrator is a neutral third party who acts in a role similar to a judge who, after a hearing, will issue a decision as to how the dispute will be resolved.

90. A: Choice A is the correct response and lays out the four perspectives that are analyzed when organizations use a balanced scorecard to measure their success.

91. C: Indirection compensation refers to non-cash payments that employees receive outside of their base pay, overtime, and other benefits. Assistance in repayment of student loans, medical insurance, and retirement contributions are all examples of indirect compensation.

92. B: The RCR (recruitment cost ratio) is calculated by adding the external costs ($25,000) to the internal costs ($25,000), dividing that figure by the annual compensation ($250,000), and multiplying it by 100.

93. C: Single loss expectancy refers to how much money an organization will lose each time an asset (such as a piece of equipment) breaks down.

94. A: While each of the options are important to consider when implementing new practices, return on investment will provide the most insight into the long-term benefits that the company can expect as well as a timeline for when the company can expect to experience those benefits. A return on investment can be as simple as calculating the cost-to-revenue ratio forecasted by the change or as complex as considering the return for the long-term development of the workforce (and their future contributions to the company); the return for communities and the environment (if the practice reduces the amount of commuting required); and the return for the employer brand in its ability to attract new talent (and the future contributions of that new talent to the organization). Company policies (B) may be outdated but can be useful in suggesting how future changes may be received depending on the company's culture and level of agility. Industry trends (C) can be useful for inspiration to solve different workforce challenges, but each company will require unique solutions. Initial program cost (D) is important to understand so the company can assess the proper scope of program implementation while retaining fiscal responsibility.

95. B: Because HR is leading the project, they should tightly manage the project by providing stakeholders with information about their deliverables, when they can expect feedback, and the proposed deadlines. Once the plan is distributed, the HR department should be open to feedback and make adjustments based on any concerns, but they should develop the path forward.

96. B: Choice B is the best answer because the department should keep its stakeholders informed about significant changes to the project, but there is no need to provide them with extensive details that do not impact their work. Choice D is not the correct answer because best practice is to provide enough information to keep the stakeholders updated rather than making assumptions related to how they might perceive the information.

97. C: Choice C is the best path forward. The communication seems fairly straightforward, so HR should ask the supervisor follow up questions to understand the reason behind the invitation. Once they understand the underlying concerns, they will be in a better position to know how to respond to the invitation.

98. D: Choice D is the best answer because HR professionals should be prepared to provide guidance to non-HR managers regarding how to communicate HR issues. There is no need to ask for further information about the meeting agenda because the supervisor included a specific request in their email.

99. C: Choice C is the correct answer because the parties reached an agreement that met both of their needs. Compromise is incorrect because the company did not move from its position (the salary was less than what the candidate proposed) because they were unable to do so. Instead, the parties identified a third option that satisfied both parties.

100. C: A deployment gap occurs when employees cannot be directed to the work locations where they can make the greatest contribution to the organization and a time gap refers to a situation where it takes too long for the organization to achieve its desired results.

101. C: Choice C is the best response because HR professionals should be able to review data and identify any potential gaps and seek missing information. In this case, the information is probative and should be considered, but it is too early to draw conclusions.

102. A: Choice A is the best response because HR professionals have an obligation to respect all employees and should do their best to demonstrate concern for their well-being.

103. C: Choice C is the best response because HR professionals have an obligation to recognize biases and act to increase awareness and accountability. Even if the comment will have no impact on the investigation, it is still a best practice to call out biases when they materialize.

104. C: Choice C is the best answer because the role of an investigator is to conduct a thorough investigation. If new information is presented it should generally be considered.

105. D: Choice D is the correct answer because HR professionals are obligated to support their stakeholders and to advise them of potential impediments to implementation of any new initiatives.

106. C: Choice C is the best answer because HR professionals should strive to provide data and other evidence to support their positions. The HR professional should work to address the interests of the marketing team in planning this event and not immediately conclude it is not an option. Telling the union they are being unreasonable is not likely to enhance the working relationship between the parties. Suggesting that other employees will be hired to do the work would harm the relationship between the two parties and could potentially violate the collective bargaining agreement.

107. C: Choice C is the best answer because HR professionals should look for ways to overcome obstacles. It is possible that the union contract may grant the employer the right to staff the event in a way that would not violate the contract.

108. C: Choice C is the correct answer because HR professionals must be accountable for their decisions, including admitting when mistakes are made and remedying the situation.

109. B: In an organization that uses a calibration performance management system, HR and managers generally meet to discuss the rating system they will use to evaluate their team members to ensure that there is consistency across the organization.

110. B: When using the comparative method, employees are compared against one another, the ranking method lists the employees from the top performer to the poorest performer, and the graphic scale requires the evaluator to assign a number (usually from 1-5) to represent how well each individual performs each task.

111. C: Data integrity refers to whether information gathered is accurate, complete, and valid. If a system does not produce correction information even after it has been entered correctly in the system this suggests a lack of data integrity at the organization.

112. B: The National Defense Authorization Act (NDAA) provides family members of certain members of the military expanded unpaid job-protected leave. The ADA prohibits discrimination based upon disabilities, the FLSA regulates payment of minimum wage, overtime, and child labor, and the OWBPA established provisions that must be included in a separation agreement on individuals 40 years of age and above to create a valid waiver.

113. C: Before taking action that assumes Alison's intent, it is important for the HR manager to understand Alison's point of view and her interpretation of what had occurred. The data from this initial meeting can then inform if corrective action is required (A), if additional investigating is required (D), or if additional training would be useful (B). This puts the power in Alison's hands to understand where she may have misjudged a situation and gives her the opportunity to grow and make things right.

114. D: While it was a conference that Andrew missed out on initially, just sending him to the next conference on the docket (A) may appear as a quick fix to the problem (especially if the conference is less renowned and as it eliminates the experience of traveling for career development). By meeting with Andrew to discuss career goals, Alison is no longer making assumptions about what is best for him but is engaging him in that conversation and empowering his ability to steer his developmental opportunities. Offering a bonus (C) can also come off as a quick fix and does not get to the root of what went wrong in the first place. Arranging a team meeting (B) to discuss the situation may put Andrew in an uncomfortable situation if he is more of a private individual (especially with possible medical information).

115. A: Allyship events are opportunities for employees to learn from those who are from different diversity dimensions and show their support and desire to learn. Executive sponsorship (B) is more relevant for empowering DE&I initiatives in a general context. Mentoring programs (C) are more intended for one-on-one relationships as opposed to trying to get Alison to be better across-the-board with regard to managing diverse teams. Virtual trainings (D) certainly have their place in DE&I programs but are not as impactful as actual connections between people from different diversity dimensions.

PHR Practice Test #3

1. Which of the following types of employee rating systems usually results in rating employees along a bell curve?

   a. Paired comparison
   b. Forced distribution
   c. Ranking
   d. Nominal scale

2. The Williamson Company is using the paired comparison method to appraise performance. There are seven people in the sales job group. With how many people will each member of this group be compared?

   a. One
   b. Two
   c. Six
   d. Seven

3. Helena is the human resources professional for a large legal firm. The upper management is interested in polling employees about ideas for improvements, but the firm has a solid hierarchy in place. As a result, many of the lower-level employees have confided in Helena that they do not feel comfortable speaking up. Which of the following ideas might Helena recommend to allow employees to voice their opinions without fear of upsetting higher-ranking employees?

   a. Brown bag lunch
   b. Focus group
   c. Email
   d. Suggestion box

4. Which of the following retention strategies would be most effective for a human resources professional to leverage in an effort to reduce the turnover rates of valuable seasoned employees?

   a. Internal mobility
   b. Job description review
   c. Streamlined onboarding
   d. Remote work

5. Which of the following is a rating method of performance appraisal?

   a. Checklist
   b. Field appraisal
   c. Essay
   d. Critical incident review

6. To save costs, a call center located in Ohio has decided to outsource one of its largest departments to a country overseas. The manager of this department, Gina, has the task of informing her employees about this event. She consults the human resources professional, Silvia, about the best approach to take. What advice should Silvia give to Gina?
    a. Recommend that Gina provide all employees with a hand-written note explaining the situation.
    b. Recommend that Gina assist employees in finding new positions once their jobs end.
    c. Recommend that Gina be honest and share with her employees as many facts as possible.
    d. Recommend that Gina petition the call center to retain the department by proving the employees' value.

7. Not all employees will agree on all topics of conversation when communicating with one another in the workplace; topics such as politics, current events, technology, and the economy can all elicit emotional responses that affect workforce collaboration and output. Which of the following would be the MOST effective approach to addressing divisive topics of employee conversation in the workplace?
    a. Update company policy to restrict topics of conversation to be only work-related.
    b. Emphasize an open door policy for employees to know where they can go if faced with challenging conversations.
    c. Closely monitor employees' social media accounts to identify confrontational personalities.
    d. Take a hands-off approach to respect employees' right to free speech.

8. Which of the following is a true statement about a company's compensation philosophy?
    a. Although an employer should strive to ensure that its compensation strategy is easy to understand and communicate, the best philosophies are challenging to communicate due to the complexities of total rewards.
    b. If a company is new, one should expect a philosophy that is not competitive because a company in its growth phase will likely be allocating revenue to long-term investments such as technology and infrastructure.
    c. A compensation policy should include the company's guiding principles for employee compensation and the relevant portions of the company's handbook.
    d. A compensation philosophy should be a short but broad statement outlining the company's values that guide its compensation decisions.

9. How is position control defined?
    a. A process by which positions are created, maintained, and tracked according to budgetary constraints
    b. A process by which only the highest human resource leader has authority to add new positions
    c. A process by which all recruitment activity is paused, and no new employees will be hired
    d. A process by which a position is defined by the person in it

10. Which of the following is a true statement about workplace investigations?
   a. It is best practice to have HR conduct all investigations since they would likely be in the best position to understand the company's policies and procedures.
   b. It is best practice to review each investigation on a case-by-case basis to determine whether HR or an outside investigator should investigate the claim.
   c. It is best practice to hire an external investigator to investigate a situation that implicates more than 10% of the workforce.
   d. It is best practice to decline to retain an outside investigator to look into a claim of misconduct that implicates a single employee.

11. If a hiring manager explains that he plans to interview candidates in the spring and summer for an anticipated fall vacancy, why would you want to be sure to note the anticipated start date in the job posting to support a positive candidate experience?
   a. A number of state legislatures have passed transparency laws that require employers to provide this information.
   b. Candidates should be advised of the start date to be considerate of their time in the event they have a need to find a new role in a different time-frame.
   c. It is best practice to provide candidates with an opportunity to provide at least 3 months' notice of their intent to resign from a position.
   d. Candidates have the right to know details regarding why an incumbent is leaving and when.

Refer to the following for questions 12 - 14:

A long-term remote employee is feeling unsatisfied in her role but is eager to make changes and remain with the company. The employee approaches her supervisor and explains that she feels excluded from her team, as the rest of the team are typically present at team meetings prior to her logging in and are already engaged in discussion.

12. How should the supervisor respond to this employee?
   a. Explain to the employee that employees are consistently engaged in different conversations throughout the day, and she likely also has conversations with her coworkers that do not include the entire group.
   b. Explain to the employee that this is a challenge of being a remote employee with a company that has hybrid, face-to-face, and remote employees, and she should consider whether returning to the office one or more days per week would be beneficial.
   c. Create a waiting room for the team Zoom meetings so everyone enters the meeting at the same time and promptly end the meeting at its scheduled end time.
   d. Speak with the team members who join the meeting early, inform them that their behavior is making the employee feel excluded, and ask that they make a concerted effort to include the remote employee in their conversations.

13. After the manager explains his plan of action to address the employee's concerns, he explains that she is a valued employee, and he wants to do what he can to make her happy. The employee says that working with a larger group of employees across different departments might help her to feel more connected to the organization. Assuming the manager intends to provide the employee with exactly what she is asking for, what should be his next step?
   a. Reach out to his colleagues to find the employee a mentor.
   b. Reach out to his colleagues to find the employee a sponsor.
   c. Reach out to his colleagues to see if they are aware of any opportunities for cross training.
   d. Speak with HR about the possibility of offering the employee a promotion.

14. As a follow-up to this conversation, the employee explains that she has prior work experience in the food services industry and would be most interested in working on projects with the company's dining services team because she has ideas that could significantly reduce waste in the company cafeteria. The manager knows the department is not interested in environmentally friendly initiatives because of additional cost.

Based on this, the manager should:
   a. Explain to the employee he will take the lead in finding an opportunity that best meets the needs of the organization, but does not believe there are any opportunities in the area she identified.
   b. Explain to the employee that she should provide additional suggestions because he does not think leadership will support any changes that might increase costs.
   c. Explain to the employee that the new assignment will be more beneficial to her if she selects an area that is geared toward remote employees.
   d. Explain to the employee that he does not believe the department has a current need for additional support, but if she has any specific ideas he will share them with the department.

15. A recruiter is on a tight deadline to fill two new roles focused on managing the logistics of its warehouses using a new program used by a limited number of companies around the world. In this situation, which is the best approach?
   a. Use social media to identify passive talent.
   b. Reach out to all of the managers at the company asking for internal candidate referrals.
   c. Reach out to all employees at the company asking for external candidate referrals.
   d. Research upcoming career fairs to ensure they have access to the largest possible applicant pool.

16. If an employee reports an allegation of sexual harassment to human resources and explains that he just wants to notify them of the situation but does not want HR to act, how should HR respond?
   a. Explain that HR will protect the confidentiality of the information the employee shared until the employee is ready to file a complaint.
   b. Explain that HR will maintain the confidentiality of the information for a reasonable time to provide the employee an opportunity to resolve the situation on their own.
   c. Explain that HR cannot maintain the confidentiality of this information and that it must be logged into their internal tracking system to protect the company and the employee.
   d. Explain that information about potentially harassing behavior cannot remain confidential but it will only be shared on a "need-to-know" basis.

17. What is one major differentiating factor that distinguishes an independent contractor from an employee?
   a. Independent contractors work for a short, defined duration of time, typically less than six months.
   b. Independent contractors work less than 20 hours per week.
   c. Independent contractors are usually not located at the employer's site.
   d. Independent contractors' work is typically for a defined assignment or project, not ongoing.

Refer to the following for questions 18 - 20:

Human resources has had a number of difficult conversations with the C-suite, explaining that it has received a growing number of complaints from employees suggesting unfair treatment and a toxic work culture. The leadership team insists that because employees generally go to HR with their complaints, HR has a skewed view of the workplace. To address the situation, the leadership team brings in an outside consultant to develop and conduct an employee engagement survey. The results of the survey show high employee engagement with more than 85% of the workforce participating. Leadership concludes that this information is clear evidence that the workforce is engaged.

18. What should you do next?
   a. Thank the leadership team for listening to your concerns and taking the necessary steps to ensure that there are no systemic problems.
   b. Tell the leadership team that the results are inconsistent with what has been reported to you and you are not confident that the survey results are accurate.
   c. Suggest that the leadership team disseminate the survey results to the workforce so that perhaps those who are unhappy will realize they are the minority.
   d. Suggest to the leadership team that they request further details about the survey responses.

19. The detailed survey results become available to you online and leadership points to the anecdotal data that consistently shows employees are pleased with their compensation, benefits, and opportunities for advancement. They conclude that this was a valuable exercise but now feel like it is time to redirect resources to the many other company initiatives that are in progress.
What do you do next?
   a. Move on to the next project, but only after confirming that the anecdotal data is consistent with what you have been told.
   b. Explain to leadership that you are still not convinced that the results of the survey paint an accurate picture of the workforce.
   c. Explain to leadership that you would like to dedicate some additional time to review the data.
   d. Escalate the situation to your manager because you disagree with the proposed path forward.

20. You feel very strongly that a deeper dive into the results would be beneficial to the workforce, and you know the reason everyone wants you to move on is because you have two upcoming deadlines related to other projects that are a priority for the company. How should you resolve this situation?

   a. Move on to your other projects. You have gone as far as you can go.
   b. Escalate this to your manager because you need additional support.
   c. Suggest that leadership allow you to continue to review the data as soon as you submit all of your deliverables for the upcoming project.
   d. Provide your two-week notice because it is clear that leadership is not interested in the value you can bring to your role.

Refer to the following for questions 21 - 24:

> A large legacy law firm is seeking to revamp and improve its approach to DE&I strategy and outcomes. Traditionally, the company has participated in more performative diversity actions, but after recent events, the company's leadership feels it is important to start being more proactive.
>
> Rachel, an up-and-comer within the HR management team, was handpicked for a promotion to the newly created position of vice president of talent development and tasked with improving the company's DE&I practices and policies. She has been tasked with addressing both the company's recruiting practices and the development and support available to current employees.

21. When approaching the company's recruiting practices, what step should Rachel take first?

   a. Interview hiring managers to learn the common interview styles and questions.
   b. Plan a recruiting calendar to attend job fairs in a variety of communities and target specific audiences.
   c. Set hiring quotas for hiring managers to abide by when filling out their teams.
   d. Collect and analyze recruiting data stratified by diversity dimensions.

22. Rachel's initial recruitment data collection suggests there may be a disparate impact effect that is discouraging older candidates from applying for certain positions. Which of the following phrases from the job descriptions could be contributing to this effect?

   a. Candidates should possess a relevant graduate degree or relevant work experience with an undergraduate degree from an Ivy League institution.
   b. Preferred applicants will thrive in a competitive environment and fit in to the work-hard, play-hard culture of our sales teams.
   c. Seeking an energetic team member with three to five (but no more than seven) years of relevant work experience.
   d. Looking for a team member to join our family of supportive and nurturing professionals.

23. While researching benefit programs aimed at more effectively supporting a diverse workforce, Rachel narrows down her recommendations to the following options. Which of these options would be most likely to support the greatest number of employees?

   a. Hybrid work options
   b. Tuition assistance
   c. Caregiver reimbursement
   d. Parental leave

24. In reviewing the representation rates among the varying organizational hierarchical levels, Rachel observes a drop-off from the number of women working in the operations-heavy store manager positions to the executive-heavy VP positions. While interviewing current female store managers, Rachel finds that one of the prominent barriers to ascension at that level is the intimidation factor to joining the primarily male teams at the executive levels. Which of the following DE&I programs might be most effective at tackling this particular barrier?
    a. Diversity council
    b. Employee resource groups
    c. Allyship events
    d. Mentorship program

25. **What is considered a breach of confidentiality?**
    a. Granting an employee's request to view his or her personnel file
    b. Disclosing an employee's drug test results
    c. Sharing the hire and termination dates of a former employee
    d. Providing employee data to the company's benefits vendor

26. **When an individual's wage amount is "red circled," what does it mean?**
    a. The wage is above the set range for the position.
    b. The wage is below the set range for the position.
    c. A cost-of-living adjustment has not been made yet.
    d. The wage includes some kind of additional incentive, like a sign-on bonus or educational premium.

27. **When an organization assumes direct payment for its employee's medical claims rather than partnering with an insurance provider for coverage, what is it called?**
    a. Self-funded insurance plan
    b. Fully insured insurance plan
    c. Disability insurance plan
    d. Health maintenance organization (HMO)

28. **What is a stretch assignment?**
    a. Upskilling
    b. A job redesign
    c. Forecasting
    d. Transfer to a new department

29. **There are several different types of employees who work on an international work assignment. What is an expatriate, or expat?**
    a. An employee who permanently relocates back to his or her home country after working abroad
    b. An employee who takes on an assignment in a country outside of his or her home country
    c. An employee who is brought into an organization from another country
    d. An employee who works in the country he or she is originally from

Refer to the following for questions 30 - 31:

At a recent management meeting, during one manager's presentation, he made a joke that others reported later as being insensitive. Apparently, he had laughed

241

when he saw a person he referred to as a "he-she" at the grocery store the evening prior and "ran the other way." Two employees have now come to you with a similar account of what happened and asked what will be done to handle this situation.

30. What would you say in response to the complainants?
 a. "This is completely unacceptable. We do not tolerate insensitive remarks at our organization. We will address this right away, and the manager will be dealt with appropriately."
 b. Ask clarifying questions such as these: "What was the context of discussion when the remark was made? Was it said in a joking manner?"
 c. "Thank you for bringing this to my attention. You are not the only person who has reported this incident. We will be launching an investigation shortly regarding this matter."
 d. "Thank you for bringing this to my attention. We will look into this immediately. Is it OK if I contact you again for questions or clarification regarding the facts of the situation if needed?"

31. Assuming you launch an investigation and confirm the comments were made in the meeting, what would be your course of action with the manager who made the offensive comments?
 a. Create a performance improvement plan (PIP) with a six-month plan for addressing his biases.
 b. Enroll the manager in a diversity and inclusion-focused coaching program.
 c. Rather than focus on the individual manager, explore cultural sensitivity training for the entire organization.
 d. This individual should not be in a leadership role in the organization—demote him to be an individual contributor.

Refer to the following for questions 32 - 33:

> As a human resource manager for a manufacturing organization, you've been noticing a general feeling of low morale among workers on the production floor. There's not a lot of talking among coworkers and no joking or even smiles. Attendance hasn't been stellar, and you've noticed more employees than usual resigning lately. Supervisors have reported that employees are feeling burned out because of the strict deadlines they must meet.

32. Given the fact that these deadlines are nonnegotiable due to client commitments, what could be a creative, low-cost solution to boost morale on the production floor?
 a. Conduct "stay" interviews, and give employees an outlet to voice their concerns.
 b. Implement an employee recognition program.
 c. Hire additional workers to ease the workload of current employees.
 d. Encourage coworker relationships by holding on-site social events during work time.

33. What is the most important component of a successful employee recognition program?
 a. Plentiful budget
 b. Program structure: simple to administer, meaningful rewards
 c. Management buy-in
 d. Communication and training

Refer to the following for questions 34 - 35:

Each year you send your lead recruiter to the same conference to recruit financial analysts. Each year he extends four offers for the fall cohort and four offers for the spring cohort. The recruiter calls you from the event and explains he only extended three offers because only three individuals were qualified for the role. The recruiter then says he does not plan to return to the conference next year, and within the next two weeks will provide you with a recommendation for a replacement.

34. Which of the following is your best next step?
   a. Explain that he should first focus on filling the vacant roles, and once that is completed you would like to have a conversation with him about why he did not meet your expectations this year.
   b. Thank him for being so diligent in his role and let him know you look forward to reviewing his recommendations.
   c. Recommend that the recruiter immediately contact the conference organizer to explain his dissatisfaction with the talent pool in attendance and request a partial refund of his registration fee.
   d. Recommend that the recruiter start by speaking with other recruiter attendees to determine if they also noticed a change in the quality of the job applicant attendees.

35. The recruiter attends happy hour and overhears a group of people complaining that there were fewer attendees at the conference this year because organizers decided they could save money by reducing marketing costs. What should the recruiter do next?
   a. Call you to report that he discovered the reason for the decreased quality of the applicant pool.
   b. Find the conference organizer, explain what he heard, and demand an explanation.
   c. Reach out to the conference organizer and request a post-meeting conference to discuss his experience with the conference.
   d. Ignore the information because he has already decided he will attend a different conference next year.

Refer to the following for questions 36 - 38:

> A midsize contracting facility with a multi-floor office space has set aside one of its smaller conference meeting spaces to use as a multipurpose workspace for employees with varying daily needs. Some employees use the room regularly for prayer or meditation while others use it for private meetings or as a quiet work area.
>
> One employee, who has been gone for several months on maternity leave, returns to work and begins using the space as a lactation room where she can pump unencumbered. Soon, conflicts begin to arise as employees seek to use the room at the same time.

36. When the HR manager is called in to aid with the multipurpose room scheduling conflicts, which of the following would be the most effective first step to addressing the challenges?
  a. Ask if the lactating employee can utilize the bathroom to pump so she will have access to a sink and other counter space.
  b. Dedicate a second conference room to add to the multipurpose spaces for employees.
  c. Collect data from room users to learn more about the timing and space needs for the area.
  d. Award permanent priority for the pumping mother and instruct other room users to utilize their personal desk spaces.

37. After collecting the data from users regarding requested multipurpose room usage, the HR manager discovers that the employees who were most likely to request conflicting room times were individuals from different floors and departments who previously had not had any interaction with one another. Which of the following plans of action would be most effective?
  a. Mediate a brainstorming session to discuss the needs of each employee and create mutually acceptable solutions.
  b. Assign a virtual calendar that allows employees to book needed time in advance.
  c. Send an introductory email between the employees so they can work out their schedules together.
  d. Assign each department an allotment of time for its employees to use the space to decrease competition.

38. The contracting facility is in a state with protections for pumping mothers that differ from federal protections. Under state law, the employee is required to be compensated for pumping time and a non-stall private bathroom could be considered an appropriate location. However, federal law does not require employers to compensate employees for time spent pumping but does expressly prohibit any kind of bathroom space as an appropriate place to pump. How must the HR manager proceed in accommodating the employee with pumping needs?
  a. The employer must follow the local state laws by compensating the employee during pumping breaks but does have the flexibility to offer the employee a non-stall bathroom space.
  b. The employer must follow federal laws by providing a non-bathroom space but is not required to compensate the employee for pumping breaks.
  c. The employer must provide the greater protections from each set of laws by providing a non-bathroom space and by compensating the employee for pumping breaks.
  d. The employer may elect which provisions of the laws to follow so he or she may provide a non-stall bathroom space for pumping and is not required to compensate for pumping breaks.

39. In the 2012 Q12 Engagement Survey, Gallup researchers found that certain company performance measures correlate with employee engagement. What did they find in organizations with high employee engagement compared to those with low employee engagement?
  a. Increased number of applicants per job posting
  b. Fewer employee safety incidents
  c. Increased brand value recognition
  d. Fewer involuntary employee terminations

40. A male manager demoted one of his female employees because she turned him down when he asked her out on a date and tried to kiss her. What type of harassment is this?
   a. Offensive conduct
   b. Quid pro quo
   c. Forced arrangement
   d. Hostile environment

41. A company deciding to relocate its headquarters to an area of the country that has lower labor costs is an example of:
   a. Offshoring
   b. Onshoring
   c. Nearshoring
   d. Undershoring

42. What is one major difference between a cost-benefit analysis (CBA) and a return on investment (ROI) calculation?
   a. ROI is displayed as a dollar value, whereas CBA is displayed as a percentage or ratio.
   b. CBA is generally conducted before the expense is made, whereas ROI is generally calculated after the investment is made.
   c. CBA is displayed as a dollar value, whereas ROI is displayed as a percentage or ratio.
   d. CBA tends to focus on tangible financial gains, whereas ROI is more in depth and takes into account tangible and intangible gains.

43. In the context of a retirement plan, how is graded vesting defined?
   a. The employee receives complete ownership of employer contributions after a certain number of years (no more than six).
   b. The employee has elected to fully manage his or her own fund allocations and investments.
   c. If a fund's performance drops below a certain threshold, the employer will cease to offer it as an option for employees.
   d. The employee's ownership of employer contributions grows partially each year of participation.

44. Which of the following scenarios would NOT result in a COBRA-qualifying event for an employee?
   a. A reduction in hours below plan eligibility requirements
   b. Voluntary termination of employment
   c. Family and Medical Leave Act (FMLA) protected leave
   d. Involuntary termination of employment for reasons other than gross misconduct

45. Which of the following scenarios is covered by FMLA?
   a. Care for the employee's grandmother who needs ongoing medical care
   b. Care for the employee's aunt with a serious health condition
   c. Care for the employee's brother who is recovering from a surgery
   d. Care for the employee's child after adoption

46. The corporate social responsibility (CSR) strategic process starts with a committed leadership team. What is the second step?
    a. Assessment
    b. Plan development
    c. Brainstorming
    d. Communication

47. Which recruitment method takes into account an employee's desire to move into a certain position even though there are no current openings?
    a. Intraregional recruiting
    b. Job bidding
    c. Open house
    d. Inside moonlighting

48. When considering the benefits and challenges associated with a multigender workforce, which of the following diversity dimensions is most likely to be predictive of how these benefits and challenges will affect workplace outcomes?
    a. Racial diversity
    b. Diversity of religion
    c. Diversity of ability and disability
    d. Cultural diversity

49. A 9-box grid is used to do which of the following?
    a. Compare the work performance and productivity of team members
    b. Compare the work performance of team members across different departments
    c. Develop a succession plan within a team
    d. Compare an individual's work performance with their potential for development

50. An organization is assessing the compliance program it put in place. As part of the program, all employees watch a short video and then take a quiz to ensure understanding of the information. What type of evaluation takes place when the HR team looks at the number of completed quizzes?
    a. System evaluation
    b. Process evaluation
    c. Method evaluation
    d. Outcome evaluation

51. If a female restaurant host is paid less than a male sous chef, which of the following is a true statement?
    a. The female host will have a valid claim for sex discrimination under Title VII.
    b. The female host may have a valid claim for sex discrimination under Title VII.
    c. The female host will have a valid claim for discrimination under the EPA.
    d. The female host may have a valid claim for discrimination under the EPA.

52. What are the five components of the ADDIE instructional design process?
    a. Analysis, development, design, implementation, execution
    b. Announcement, development, debrief, implementation, external review
    c. Analysis, design, development, implementation, evaluation
    d. Announcement, development, dress rehearsal, implementation, evaluation

53. What can be a possible downside of extending the use of technology in a human resource department?
   a. Discourages teamwork
   b. Potential employee lack of computer literacy
   c. Difficult to use for employees with disabilities
   d. Cost intensive for the company

54. What is an example of HR's strategic role?
   a. Anticipating the knowledge, skills, and abilities needed in the future
   b. Conducting background and reference checks for new hires
   c. Utilizing HR's information system to maintain employee data
   d. Conducting team-building initiatives to reduce turnover

55. Which of the following is a component of a personalized onboarding process?
   a. Providing a new hire with the company vision, values, and mission statement prior to their first day of work
   b. Providing a new hire with access to the internal job postings, explaining when they will be eligible to apply for promotion opportunities
   c. Providing a new hire with a mentor to work with them as they become acclimated to the new workplace
   d. Making sure a new hire knows the location of the restroom and where they can find the best lunch deals within the first few days of their employment

56. Which is an expense that a flexible spending account (FSA) may NOT be used for, as governed by the Internal Revenue Service (IRS)?
   a. Acupuncture
   b. Hearing aids
   c. Contact lenses
   d. Electric toothbrush

57. What best practice increases employee engagement during onboarding?
   a. Implementing a "buddy program"
   b. Conducting an employee engagement survey
   c. Providing positive feedback to new employees
   d. Reviewing company policy documents with new employees

58. The executive team of an organization is selecting employees for succession planning. What should they look for in potential candidates?
   a. Readiness to take on responsibilities of aspired position right away
   b. Display of growth potential
   c. A current management employee
   d. Participation in the company's mentorship program

Refer to the following for questions 59 - 60:

The CEO of a company plans to hire a new social media manager. The executive explains he wants HR to review the applications received through the online application portal and present him with the resumes of the three top candidates so his assistant can schedule the initial screening interviews. The HR manager reminds the CEO that he will need to select five candidates for the initial screenings, and the CEO responds that he is aware of the policy, but he has already received two referrals that he believes would be strong candidates.

59. What should the HR manager do next?
   a. Follow company policy and provide the department chair with the five top candidates for the role based upon her review of the online applications.
   b. Provide the CEO with three candidates but document the fact that this was based upon his request.
   c. Speak with her manager to determine how to best approach the situation since it involves the CEO.
   d. Suggest that the department chair direct his referrals to submit their applications through the online portal so they can be reviewed alongside the other applicants.

60. The HR manager provides the selected applicants to the CEO's assistant and explains that she is confident the CEO will be pleased with her selections because they are all recent graduates with active social media accounts. The assistant rolls her eyes and says she is sixty-two years old and has thousands of followers across three different platforms. What should be the HR manager's next step?
   a. Ignore the comment, thank the assistant for her assistance, and go back to her office.
   b. Thank the assistant for her assistance, ask her to return the applicant list, and go back to her office.
   c. Politely suggest that the assistant focus on her own job responsibilities.
   d. Speak to the CEO about the assistant's inappropriate behavior.

61. A women's shoe designer advertises a job seeking two female models for catalog photos. Is this considered discrimination?
   a. Yes, because basing a hiring decision on an applicant's gender is considered discriminatory.
   b. No, because the gender is a bona fide vocational criterion.
   c. No, because the gender is a reasonable accommodation.
   d. No, because the gender is a bona fide occupational qualification.

62. What types of factors are reviewed as part of a PESTLE analysis?
   a. Political, economic, social, technological, legal, and environmental factors
   b. Political, economic, societal, training, legal, and educational factors
   c. Purchasing power, economic, social, technological, leveraging of debt, and educational factors
   d. Political, export-import, social, transition assistance, legal, and environmental factors

63. If an employer uses software as part of its recruiting process to assist in organizing and tracking the number of applicants that are applying to different versions of its job posting, what tool is the employer using?
   a. Chat bots
   b. Artificial intelligence
   c. An ATS
   d. An LMS

64. An organization restructures itself and removes some management layers. Having fewer levels of middle management between staff and executives give individuals more autonomy in their decision-making. What kind of pay structure is a probable result of this restructure?
   a. Broadband structure
   b. Graded structure
   c. Market-based structure
   d. Hybrid structure

65. A food and beverage manufacturer has four open account manager positions that they asked the recruiting manager to fill. After posting the position, the company receives a total of 240 applications, of which 80 applicants meet all minimum qualifications. After the final interviews, the company extends offers to four candidates. What is the yield ratio of offers extended to qualified applicants?
   a. 2%
   b. 5%
   c. 12%
   d. 20%

Refer to the following for questions 66 - 68:

An underperforming employee is placed on a 90-day performance improvement plan due to repeated careless errors on invoices he is expected to process, which has caused the employer to lose thousands of dollars. On day 72 of the plan, the employee files a complaint against his supervisor alleging his vacation day request was denied in a discriminatory manner because the requests for all his younger colleagues were approved. The supervisor speaks with HR and communicates that this is another example of the employee being difficult to manage and requests immediate termination because the employee will be terminated at the end of the 90-day period anyway.

66. What is the next step HR should take?
   a. Do nothing until the end of the 90-day performance improvement plan period. If the employee has not adjusted his behavior as required by the performance improvement plan, then terminate him.
   b. Initiate an investigation into the alleged claim of age discrimination.
   c. Train the manager on the concept of retaliation.
   d. Assign the employee to a new supervisor and direct both the supervisor and employee to avoid each other.

67. The HR director assigned to investigate the claim is aware that the employee had previously filed a frivolous discrimination claim against her cousin. What should the director do with this information?
   a. Ask the employee if he has previously filed a claim for age discrimination within the context of the investigatory interview.
   b. Decline to share the information with anyone because it is irrelevant to the current situation.
   c. Disclose the information to her supervisor and request that the investigation be assigned to another investigator.
   d. Contact the prior employer to determine if they are willing to share information that may be relevant to this investigation.

68. The HR director is removed from the case. Months later the HR director receives a message from the external HR director who investigated her cousin's case. She indicates that she heard about the pending complaint and felt that sharing information could be mutually beneficial to their respective companies. How should the HR director respond?
   a. Decline to return the call because it would be inappropriate to share information.
   b. Return the phone call, gather all relevant information, and share it with the current investigator.
   c. Return the phone call, explain that she is not involved in the investigation, and provide the contact information of her colleague that is handling the investigation.
   d. Return the phone call. Explain that she cannot comment on whether there is a pending investigation and that she would be unable to share any information due to confidentiality concerns.

69. A company is planning to redesign its organizational structure. What is one of HR's responsibilities during this process?
   a. Develop the company's pay structure, and set pay rates for all positions.
   b. Analyze organizational problems through structural diagnosis.
   c. Lead a workforce committee on organizational change.
   d. Develop succession plans for all key positions.

70. What do you call the sum of all interrelated actions, inputs, and processes that create a company's product until it ends up in the hands of a customer?
   a. Supply channels
   b. Logistic cooperation
   c. Value chain
   d. Production system

71. An organization provides company cars with full insurance coverage to their management employees. An employee drives faster than usual with the company car because he would not be responsible for any costs should something happen to the car. What is this an example of?
   a. Moral hazard
   b. Loss expectancy
   c. Ethical dilemma
   d. Principal-agent problem

Refer to the following for questions 72 - 74:

In a facility of more than 100 employees, there is a team of 12 dedicated customer service representatives (CSRs) led by the customer relations manager. Traditionally, the customer service team has led the facility with the highest performance ratings and employee attendance ratings.

Two months ago, one of the CSR team members came out to the organization as a transgender man and requested that the team use he/him pronouns and his new name Benjamin as opposed to his deadname Bernadine. The majority of the team and organizational leaders were supportive of Benjamin and adjusted to the name and pronoun change with little trouble. One member of the team, Clarice, has continued to use the incorrect pronouns of "she" and "her" and slip between "Ben" and "Bern" while referencing or speaking to Benjamin.

After correcting Clarice several times for using the incorrect identifiers, Benjamin speaks to their manager. The manager agrees that Clarice's actions are disrespectful and that she needs to be spoken with but also downplays the impact by claiming that Clarice is from a "different generation" and that she probably doesn't know any better.

72. Which of the following statements regarding the use of preferred pronouns in the workplace is NOT true?

a. Using an employee's preferred pronouns is considered a civil right under the umbrella of protections within the prohibition of discrimination based on sex.
b. Employee records can remain the same for a transgender employee so long as that employee is referred to and spoken to using the preferred names and pronouns.
c. In addition to he/him and she/her, some employees may also use gender expansive terms such as they/them or ze/hir.
d. Offhand comments and nonserious isolated incidents of misgendering an employee do not necessarily qualify as discrimination.

73. After meeting with Benjamin, the manager meets with Clarice in a counseling session to discuss the appropriate ways to address coworkers. Following the meeting, Clarice no longer acknowledges Benjamin at all and goes out of her way to work with other CSR associates. This shift in collaborative energy negatively impacts CSR team outcomes, and Benjamin again seeks the manager's support. Which of the following DE&I concepts can be most clearly identified in this stage of the conflict?

a. Cultural taxation
b. Intersectionality
c. Imposter syndrome
d. Retaliation

74. Following Benjamin's second complaint, the manager seeks HR for advisement regarding the appropriate next steps. In a meeting with the manager, Clarice, and the HR representative, Clarice claims she is feeling discriminated against because her religion does not support the concept of transgender individuals. Which of the following would be the most appropriate initial response for the HR representative and manager to take?

a. Set a hard expectation with Clarice that her retaliatory actions are considered harassment and will be responded to as such.
b. Propose moving Benjamin to a different team to protect both employees' civil rights.
c. Continue genuine discussions regarding behaviors versus beliefs and prioritizing organizational outcomes in decision-making.
d. Request that Benjamin make an exception for Clarice in order to recognize her religious beliefs.

75. If your CEO insists that each prospective candidate meet with every member of the 20-person team they will be working with, which of the following would be the most appropriate response?
    a. Explain that you fully support this idea because studies show candidates appreciate a comprehensive hiring process.
    b. Explain that you do not support this idea because studies show that candidates appreciate a quick hiring process.
    c. Explain that you support this process but strongly recommend they have no more than 2 interviewees meet with the candidate at any given time.
    d. Explain that you support this process, but you strongly recommend that they limit the rounds of interviews.

76. A company is planning to expand its headcount by two employees and is seeking guidance as to the most appropriate compensation strategy for each role. Their priority is to fill the senior development officer vacancy, which is a critical revenue-producing role. If funding is available, they would also like to hire an administrative assistant. If the company decides it wants to recruit for both roles simultaneously, which would be the best strategy to adopt?
    a. Use the lead-lag strategy for both roles.
    b. Use the lead strategy for both roles.
    c. Use the lead strategy for the senior development officer role and the lag strategy for the administrative assistant role.
    d. Use the match strategy for the senior development role and the lead-lag strategy for the administrative role.

Refer to the following for questions 77 - 80:

> A midsize wellness company has recently enjoyed glowing reviews from employees following an overhaul of the performance and benefits policies, which created a more inclusive working environment.
>
> Performance review standards were upgraded after job analyses and evaluations revealed measurable work metrics for employee ratings that replaced the previously used subjective rankings. Additionally, parental and caregiver leave and policies were expanded along with developmental benefits such as tuition reimbursement and company perks for employee families.
>
> While employee feedback was overall positive, the organization's leadership team is seeking the guidance of the HR director to better understand the potential business impact of the performance and benefits upgrades.

77. Given the wide variety of workforce and business data, which of the following would be the most effective first step for HR to take?
    a. Issue an official employee feedback survey to collect additional data and perspectives.
    b. Select the highest-grossing department to identify its best practices.
    c. Design a measurement map to lay out data points and identify possible relationships.
    d. Stratify the employee feedback according to performance to determine the relationship between performance and benefits.

78. Review the initial draft of the HR director's measurement map below and select which of the following conclusions would be the most appropriate to draw from the map structure.

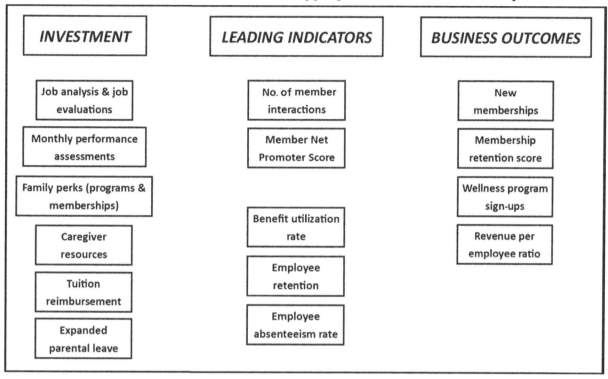

a. Tuition reimbursement is causing an improved revenue-per-employee ratio by increasing employee retention.
b. An increased benefit utilization rate may be linked to the added family perks.
c. A decreased employee absenteeism rate is a result of the improved monthly performance assessments.
d. The increase in member interactions is a direct cause of the increased wellness program sign-ups and the membership retention score.

79. In order to better understand the relationship between the DE&I policy changes and employee effectiveness, how might the HR director further assess the data associated with the measurement map?

a. Create a scatter plot comparing monthly performance assessment scores to number of member interactions.
b. Filter employee feedback data by seniority.
c. Stratify leading employee indicator data by diversity dimension.
d. Interview employees using the tuition reimbursement program regarding member relations best practices.

80. The HR director is assembling a proposal for the company's leadership team to better understand the possible causal relationships at play between the different DE&I investments and business outcomes. Which of the following suggestions would be most effective in this pursuit?
    a. Future benefits upgrades should target employees with higher performance scores to tie the investments together.
    b. Weekly employee surveys can track the employee experience in real time for additional data.
    c. The revenue-per-employee metric should be the primary focus, as it deals with both employee data and financial data.
    d. Future program or policy upgrades could be introduced as a pilot program to compare results between facilities.

81. Which of the following would NOT be maintained in an HRIS system?
    a. Employee benefit selections
    b. Time and attendance records
    c. FMLA policies
    d. Employee names and addresses

82. Suggestion mechanisms, predictive attrition analysis, and personalized onboarding are all examples of concepts and best practices related to:
    a. Employee engagement
    b. Employee development
    c. Employee advancement
    d. Employee retention

83. HR policies that establish parameters for employees to securely use their personal devices for work purposes are called:
    a. BYOD policies
    b. BYOE policies
    c. BYO policies
    d. Securing your personal device policies

84. How is an organization's vision statement different from the mission statement?
    a. It is a set of core principles that guides the organization's decision-making.
    b. It is forward looking and higher level, describing the organization's strategic direction.
    c. It remains constant throughout the organization's life cycle.
    d. It is more specific, describing how business is conducted.

85. When presented with a harassment complaint from an employee, which statement should human resources NOT say to the victim?
    a. "Thank you for bringing this to our attention; however, this does not sound like harassing behavior."
    b. "Please keep any investigation details confidential."
    c. "We do not tolerate retaliation."
    d. "The information you're giving me today is completely confidential."

86. What does the SMART goal acronym stand for?
    a. Smart, metric-driven, actionable, relevant, and time bound
    b. Specific, measurable, accurate, relative, and time bound
    c. Specific, measurable, achievable, relevant, and time bound
    d. Specific, masterful, achievable, relevant, and time bound

87. Which is an example of a Bona Fide Occupational Qualification (BFOQ)?
    a. A job applicant supplying documentation of his or her college degree
    b. A fast-food restaurant with Christian values only hiring Christian employees
    c. An airline only hiring attractive female flight attendants to draw in more male passengers
    d. A sheriff's office refusing to hire police deputies over the age of 50

88. What is the biggest risk in conducting an employee satisfaction survey?
    a. Skewed results because only the most satisfied employees respond
    b. The potential for employees to not be truthful in their responses
    c. The potential for the responses to not be anonymous
    d. No employer follow-through on the results gathered from employees

89. In the instance of Family and Medical Leave Act (FMLA)-protected leave, new mothers' and fathers' rights differ in what way?
    a. New mothers can take the entire 12 weeks; new fathers may only take leave for bonding purposes.
    b. New mothers can take the entire 12 weeks; new fathers may only take leave to care for their spouse during the period of disability, which ranges from six to eight weeks.
    c. They have the same rights; however, they may not take the leave at the same time.
    d. They have the same rights—both can take time for bonding with the newborn, and the mother can take time for the period of disability. A new father can take the time to care for his spouse during the recovery period.

90. If an employee requests a day off, citing a religious holiday that he or she wishes to observe, is the employer obligated to grant the request?
    a. The employer should if the employee has enough vacation time or paid time off.
    b. If it is not a company-observed holiday, the employer is not required to allow the day off.
    c. The employer should grant the request if it does not present undue hardship.
    d. To avoid claims of discrimination, an employer should allow the request no matter the circumstances.

91. Which of the following is NOT an effective approach for a supervisor delivering feedback to a struggling employee?
    a. The supervisor should list each area of deficiency and how it impacts the team and/or organization.
    b. The supervisor should provide specific examples of instances in which the employee had a misstep.
    c. The supervisor should make performance expectations clear.
    d. The supervisor should provide some praise around the things the employee is performing well.

92. If a company offers its employees an additional paid day off each year to volunteer at an organization that is in close proximity to the company's headquarters, this is part of their:
   a. Compensation philosophy
   b. CSR plan
   c. BYOD plan
   d. Strategic staffing plan

93. If an employer reassigns an employee to an undesirable shift after he files a complaint with OSHA alleging that there was mold in the restrooms, this is called:
   a. Retribution
   b. Reallocation
   c. Retaliation
   d. Reverse discrimination

94. A junior sales manager is told that that maximum salary increase he can receive is $6,000 because a raise in excess of that amount would result in a salary higher than that of his boss. This is an example of:
   a. Pay depression
   b. Pay compression
   c. Comparable worth
   d. Equitable distribution

Refer to the following for questions 95 - 96:

Due to the excessive absenteeism rate every Friday before a holiday weekend, the company has a three-day weekend policy. According to the policy, individuals who call out sick on a Friday before a long holiday weekend will not be paid for the holiday unless they provide a doctor's note confirming they were ill. HR was charged with developing the policy and has been administering it for the past twelve years. An employee calls out sick on a Friday and informs his manager he is too sick to get out of bed. In response, the manager advises him to contact HR to obtain information about how to ensure he will get paid for the Monday holiday. The HR manager receives a voicemail message from the employee relaying the conversation with his manager and requesting HR guidance.

95. How should the HR manager respond?
   a. Return the employee's call, ask about his symptoms to evaluate whether he is actually sick, and discuss the situation with the manager.
   b. E-mail the link to the policy to the employee to avoid having to pay the employee for any time spent on the phone.
   c. Return the employee's call and explain the policy and the reason for it.
   d. Contact the manager, explain the policy and the reason behind it, and suggest he return the employee's call.

96. If the employee reports back to work the following week and requests a meeting with HR to discuss potential ways to change the policy, how should HR respond?
   a. Agree to the meeting.
   b. Agree to the meeting, but only if the manager agrees to attend.
   c. Decline to have the meeting and reiterate to the employee that he should direct any questions to the manager.
   d. Decline to have the meeting and explain to the employee that the policy has been in effect for more than 12 years and the company has no intention of changing it.

97. An organization traditionally had its employees work in departments based upon the role they played at an organization. However, as part of a merger the organization acquires the rights to develop two new movie productions. As a result they want to change the structure so that all of their employees work for one production or the other. What type of structure will the company move from and to?
   a. They will move from a product structure to a functional structure.
   b. They will move from a functional structure to a product structure.
   c. They will move from a functional structure to a matrix structure.
   d. They will move from a matrix structure to a functional structure.

98. If an organization wants to outsource the majority of its HR functions it will most likely work with:
   a. A temporary staffing company
   b. A leasing company
   c. A PEO
   d. An external payroll company

Refer to the following for questions 99 - 101:

A company is facing a significant short-term budget deficit and needs to find ways to quickly free up some of its cash reserves. An announcement is made outlining a 2-part plan to quickly cut costs and manage the budget. The company imposes an immediate wage freeze and also asks every department to review all of their spending and eliminate any expenses that are not critical to their essential job tasks.

99. Each week HR provides employees with coffee and donuts in the main lobby as a way for the workforce to build relationships and exchange information about workplace issues. How should HR proceed?
   a. Continue with their weekly event because it is critical to their role, which is to ensure that the workforce feels welcome and heard. The events are also a valuable source of information that enables HR to effectively do their jobs and the cost savings resulting from canceling it would be minimal.
   b. Agree to reduce the cost by hosting the event twice per month.
   c. Agree to stop offering donuts at the event to reduce costs and find money for the coffee from another budget line.
   d. Refrain from offering coffee and donuts at the event.

100. After the wage freeze is announced, an HR coordinator notices a 500% increase in the number of bonuses submitted for processing. He also notices that, unlike in the past, the majority of the bonuses are dated retroactively, prior to the date the directive was issued. As a practical matter, the coordinator's role is only to process the bonuses. He does not review them because each department has full control over its own budget. How should the Coordinator proceed?
   a. Process the bonuses pursuant to the documentation received as he has always done in the past. He should not do anything outside the scope of his job responsibilities.
   b. Reject the bonus payments and send them back to the department for further review in light of the recent announcement.
   c. Escalate the situation to his supervisor for guidance on how to proceed.
   d. Contact the department heads to share his concern and ask for additional support for the bonus payment.

101. Two days after the wage freeze and elimination of discretionary funding were announced, HR was scheduled to meet with its vendor to sign a national contract for new copy machines. The new contract includes significant up-front costs but will save the company money over the next 10-15 years. How should HR proceed?
   a. Move forward with the national contract since it is not discretionary spending and outside the scope of the directive.
   b. Move forward with the contract because not signing it could detrimentally impact its future relationship with the vendor.
   c. Speak with the vendor to see if there is a way to delay the up-front costs to address the company's immediate short-term budget concerns.
   d. Cancel the contract because the current machines likely work fine and will be able to sustain the company for a bit longer.

102. If you subtract the total costs of goods sold from the total sales, and divide that figure by total sales, what is the result figure?
   a. Gross margin
   b. Profit margin
   c. P/E ratio
   d. Return on investment

103. If a US-based company decides it will not market a specific product in one of its global offices because it would like not be considered legal there and would also likely subject the global office to political pressure to resign, they likely used what type of analysis to reach its decision?
   a. A SWOT analysis
   b. An ethnocentric analysis
   c. A PESTLE analysis
   d. A functional analysis.

104. A company is looking to reduce its head count and asks each manager to create a list of the roles in their department from most important to least important. This is called:
   a. Job analysis review (JAR)
   b. Job ranking
   c. Job-content based job evaluation
   d. A review of key performance indicators (KPIS)

105. If a company engages in benchmarking they are:
   a. Comparing jobs with the same titles across different departments in their organization.
   b. Comparing jobs with the same titles across their national and international offices.
   c. Creating a hierarchy of all jobs and evaluating how each contributes to the organization's long-term strategic goals.
   d. Comparing jobs against those of similarly situated organizations.

Refer to the following for questions 106 - 107:

A company has rolled out annual sexual harassment training in response to a new state law that requires all employees to be trained on an annual basis by their current employer. HR is responsible for administering the program. An employee requests to be excused from the program because she is a certified sexual harassment trainer.

106. How should HR respond to this request?
   a. Grant the exception.
   b. Grant the exception if the employee can provide documentation to support her claim that she is an expert in the field.
   c. Grant the exception if the employee agrees to facilitate at least one training session so HR will have the ability to certify that the employee is an expert.
   d. Deny the exception.

107. If a male employee explains to HR that he is uncomfortable sitting with a room of men and women discussing issues related to sexual harassment because in his culture these types of issues are not discussed openly with members of the opposite sex, how should HR respond?
   a. Explain to the employee that the law requires him to attend the session.
   b. Recommend that the employee sit in the back of the room and not participate.
   c. Inform the employee that you will inform the facilitator not to ask him any questions and allow him to leave the room if he feels uncomfortable at any point.
   d. Modify the invite list for one session, so all invited employees are men and invite this employee to that session.

Refer to the following for questions 108 - 109:

A company's IT department is responsible for tracking whether employees across the company have completed all of their mandatory annual training programs. Every year the IT department provides the HR department with a list of non-compliant employees for follow-up. The general counsel's office is consistently frustrated by the HR department's inability to maintain a 95% compliance rate, but the HR department is unable to meet this goal because they receive the data from IT with only a few days to work with those employees who did not complete the program by the deadline.

108. How should HR handle the situation?
   a. Ask the IT department to provide a specific date they can expect to receive the non-compliance list so they can develop an "all hands-on deck" strategy to reach out to all non-compliant employees quickly.
   b. Request a meeting with the general counsel's office to explain that they should direct their concerns to the IT department because they are responsible for the delay.
   c. Request a meeting with the IT department to explain that they should work to revise their processes because the general counsel's office is displeased with the non-compliance rate and they need the data earlier to satisfy them.
   d. Request a meeting with the general counsel's office and the IT department to develop the best path forward.

109. The head of HR decides to have a meeting with the head of IT to discuss the situation and asks one of the managers to prepare notes for her for the meeting. How should the HR manager proceed?
   a. Gather data on the impact of training on workplace productivity and company profits.
   b. Gather historical data to show the average number of times HR has had to reach out to non-compliant employees on the list before they completed the training.
   c. Gather data on any recent fines levied against its industries for non-compliance.
   d. Gather data on the number of new projects HR has taken on in the previous two years.

110. Which of the following diversity measurements would be most useful when identifying possible disparate impact of an organizational practice or policy?
   a. Four-fifths rule
   b. Demographic yield ratios
   c. Turnover rates
   d. Performance review scores

111. If a cashier is hired to work in a department store and is advised that she may sometimes be required to work on inventory projects in the event that the warehouse is short-staffed, what is the inventory work?
   a. An essential function
   b. A nonessential function
   c. Must be paid at a higher rate
   d. Cannot be required for more than one day a week

Refer to the following for questions 112 - 115:

A company realizes that a recent technological advancement could eliminate 10% of its workforce. The impacted employees work in 5 different departments across the company. Leadership intends to speak with the board at their next board meeting to confirm the effective date of the layoffs. They speak with HR about the need to handle the situation delicately because they are extremely concerned about any potential backlash from their employees and from the general public once the layoffs are announced. The board's primary goal is to eliminate, or at least reduce, any negative impact to their reputation as a result of this organizational change.

112. What is the first step HR should take once leadership informs them that they want to eliminate these jobs?
   a. Immediately start to prepare the paperwork necessary to execute the layoffs so they will be ready as soon as the board decides on the effective date.
   b. Immediately review their schedule of upcoming projects to determine which can be pushed out into the future because the layoffs will be a top priority and will require a substantial amount of work.
   c. Research whether there are any company policies, employment agreements, or union contracts in place that would prevent the layoff or require certain administrative steps prior to execution of the layoffs.
   d. Review the vacant roles at the organization to see whether any of the impacted employees are qualified to fill them.

113. One member of the HR team is familiar with several names on the layoff list because their supervisors have had numerous discussions with HR about the need to provide them additional training. According to their supervisors they were hard-working and loyal employees but were not being provided with the resources necessary to keep up with the changing natures of their roles. What should the team member do with this information?
   a. They should do nothing because leadership generated the list and best practice is to eliminate everyone with the same job title.
   b. Bring the issue to the attention of her supervisor and suggest they start to look for opportunities for training or upskilling.
   c. Request a proactive meeting with these employees and suggest that they start to look for new opportunities because the programs in use are going to continue to be used.
   d. Remove these employees from the layoff list because they may have a viable legal claim against the company.

114. The HR team meets to discuss the process for deciding how the layoffs will be rolled out across the organization. One member of the HR teams suggests that the employees be laid off based upon their anniversary dates to ensure that as few bonuses are paid as possible. The individual explains this will save the company a lot of money, which will be incredibly appealing to the leadership team. How should you respond?
   a. Agree to move forward with this plan because using anniversary dates to determine the order of the layoffs is an objective factor that can result in significant cost-savings for the company and poses little risk.
   b. Create a plan that is based on another objective factor that is not tied to the payment of bonuses.
   c. Refuse to follow this directive and escalate the matter to leadership to ensure they are aware of what was proposed.
   d. Explain the ethical concerns related to the proposed method for determining the order of layoffs and suggest an alternative selection method such as use of seniority.

115. How should HR communicate the layoffs to the impacted employees?
   a. Send out letters to the impacted employees so they will have hard copies of all the documents they need to review. Use a mailing service that requires a signature upon receipt to be sure everyone receives the notification.
   b. Send out a mass email to employees so that everyone gains access to the information at the same time to prevent equity issues.
   c. Because the managers have the most direct relationships with the employees, they should be provided with the information the impacted employees will need and should be directed to share this information with each employee by a certain deadline.
   d. Plan for individual meetings with the manager of the employee and an HR representative.

Answer Key and Explanations for Test #3

1. B: A forced distribution usually results in rating employees along a bell curve. In a paired comparison, each employee's performance is viewed in the context of another employee's performance. A ranking system is usually better for a smaller group of employees but can be difficult to organize with a larger group. A nominal scale is not recognized as a type of employee rating system.

2. C: Since the Williamson Company is using the paired comparison method, each member of the sales job group will be compared with six other people. The paired comparison method requires every member of the job group to be compared to every other member. This means that each member of the Williamson Company's sales group will be compared to the other six members. The paired comparison method is a good way to rank employees systematically.

3. D: A suggestion box offers employees a measure of anonymity in proffering ideas to the company's upper management. Brown bag lunches and focus groups require employees to participate actively, and as the scenario indicates, many employees would be uncomfortable with this. Email might be private, but it certainly is not anonymous, so it would not represent the best recommendation for Helena to make.

4. A: Streamlined onboarding is a valuable retention tool for newly hired employees who are just being introduced to the organization. Remote work may be a valuable perk or working condition for some employees, but it is not a one-size-fits-all strategy nor is it feasible for all positions or organizations. Job description reviews can be useful during job analysis processes, but if an employee has taken on responsibilities and grown in their role to the point of a job description review, leveraging internal mobility is a more impactful way to recognize the value the employee brings to the organization. Recognition for value added and a job well done in the form of a promotion or other career enhancement encourages employees to stay and continue to grow within the organization.

5. A: A checklist is a rating method of performance appraisal. In a checklist system, the various elements of the job description are listed, and the employee receives a check mark for each element he performs with competence. This is considered a rating system because the number of checks can be converted into a score, which makes it possible to compare employees. In a field appraisal, someone besides the employee's supervisor observes and reports on the employee's performance. In an essay appraisal, the evaluator writes a short prose passage about the employee's performance. In a critical incident review, the supervisor discusses the especially positive and negative aspects of the employee's performance.

6. C: When addressing complex and emotional situations, the most effective approach is one that is honest, transparent, and active. Advising Gina to write hand written notes each employee is inefficient and takes can take away from transparency if not all employees receive the same message. Assisting employees in their job search may be appropriate as a secondary course of action but is not Gina's primary concern or responsibility. Advocating to retain the department likely falls outside of Gina's scope of the business and may take away from the communication needed first and foremost with the employees.

7. B: In order to build trust and respect within the workplace, it is important for human resources professionals and organizational leaders to set the example for open communication. Establishing and maintaining open door policies can give employees somewhere to go if they need to talk through interpersonal challenges, seek advice pertinent to their working team, or file a complaint or report inappropriate behavior. Restricting topics of conversation is unrealistic and unlikely to be an effective approach. Monitoring social media is a passive approach that may also breach employee privacy. While some parts of employee speech are protected, the First Amendment does not apply to employees in the private sector; additionally, speech that causes harm can fall into the buckets of harassment or discrimination and is not protected.

8. D: The most effective compensation philosophies are clear and concise, but present overriding themes that explain the company's views on how it makes compensation decisions.

9. A: Position control is often a feature of a human resource information system (HRIS)/financial tool within which employees are tracked separately from positions. Positions are often approved according to available budget and then maintained and tracked in the position control system.

10. B: Choice B is the correct answer because the employer has an obligation to conduct an impartial and thorough investigation. Whether HR or an outside investigator would be in the best position to secure this result would depend upon the specific facts of the situation.

11. B: Choice B is the best answer because one aspect of supporting a positive candidate experience is to be considerate of the applicant's time as you move through your hiring process. Most state transparency laws focus on salary information, not whether a job is vacant. Furthermore, a notice period of 3 months for a resignation is rare and not expected. A candidate may ask questions related to the incumbent, but they do not have the right to know details of the separation, and the employer may be obligated to maintain the confidentiality of a separation.

12. C: Choice C is correct because managers of employees with different working conditions should use the technological tools that are available to build an inclusive workforce. While employees do speak with different coworkers throughout the day, managers should work to build an inclusive environment where possible.

13. C: Choice C is the best answer because cross training occurs when an employee works on a project in an area other than the one to which he or she is assigned. The employee may benefit from a sponsor or mentor, or may appreciate a promotion, but the specific request is for cross training.

14. D: Choice D is the correct answer because an organization should be open to new opportunities and initiatives to reduce waste and promote environmentally friendly initiatives. Even if the dining service department is resistant to new ideas, the manager should still be open to learning about them. In addition, the manager should use this opportunity to enhance inclusion of the remote employee rather than reinforcing the idea that remote employees have interests that are not aligned with the non-remote workforce.

15. A: Choice A is the best answer because the recruiter can narrowly target potential applicants who work at the companies that currently use the program the company is going to be using. The other strategies may be helpful, but use of social media will be the most likely to produce qualified candidates in the shortest period of time.

16. D: Choice D is the correct answer because once HR is notified of potentially problematic workplace conduct, it is obligated to investigate the situation and respond as appropriate. HR should work to maintain confidentiality to the extent it is possible.

17. D: Independent contractors' work is independent—specifications are provided by the employer with a required deliverable, and they determine how, what, and where the contractor performs the work to complete the task.

18. D: Choice D is the best answer because additional information is needed to understand the information that was collected by the survey. The results may be inconsistent with what has been reported to you, but you do not have any information to suggest the results are not accurate.

19. C: Choice C is the best answer because those anecdotes alone do not prove that the results are not flawed. If you have concerns about the survey or the results, you should continue to raise those concerns, even if you are pressured to move forward. In addition, you should continue to work to obtain the data you need to draw evidence-based conclusions.

Influence > "Shares opinions about important issues, regardless of risk or discouragement from others."

20. C: Choice C is the best answer because you need to review the data further to gain a better understanding of the results. You are more likely to obtain buy-in for this work if you craft a path forward that addresses the concerns raised.

21. D: Rachel's first step should be to understand the recruiting environment to the best of her ability and within the scope of diversity dimensions. This data can then inform her line of questioning when she speaks with hiring managers (A) and suggest what the target audience should be for future hires and job fairs (B). Setting hiring quotas (C) is an extreme action that should be taken with caution, and Rachel should include leadership and legal input before instituting it.

22. C: Words or phrases such as "energetic," "digital native," "recent college graduate," or any other specification that sets a cap for the amount of experience a candidate can possess can be discouraging to older, more experienced candidates. Requiring degrees from certain institutions (A) may be viewed as classist or elitist. Wording regarding "competitive environment," and "work hard, play hard," can be discouraging for female candidates (B); conversely, wording like "family" and "nurturing" can be discouraging for male candidates (D). It is important to review the job descriptions used for postings for possibly biased language and to ensure that the job descriptions are as succinct as possible without making assumptions about possible candidates.

23. A: Hybrid work options are more likely to apply to a larger number of employees as a support tool. Employees who could utilize tuition assistance (B) could also find value in a hybrid schedule that better empowers them to balance work and school. Employees who would benefit from a caregiver reimbursement (C) or parental leave (D) could also benefit from a hybrid working environment to balance family responsibilities with work responsibilities.

24. D: Mentorship programs would be the strongest option to connect store managers with executive leaders to learn more about the transition, build their skills and confidence, and create networking connections to bridge the gap between hierarchical levels. Options like diversity councils (A), employee resource groups (B), and allyship events (C) can be useful in building a sense of belonging within the organization, but they do not provide the opportunity for targeted one-on-one relationships designed specifically to empower female store managers to pursue executive-level positions.

25. B: HR must protect confidential employee information. Data that cannot be shared includes medical information, such as drug test results.

26. A: When a wage is "red-circled," it means that the individual is paid above the set salary range for the position. Red-circled wages are often either frozen or reduced to be in the correct range for the position.

27. A: When an organization is self-funded, or self-insured, it typically purchases stop-loss coverage for larger claims over a predefined amount but pays for all other claims directly.

28. A: Upskilling refers to the process of developing new skills for the purpose of career advancement.

29. B: An expatriate, or expat, is an employee who takes on an international assignment, usually for three to five years.

30. D: In the instance of an employee complaint, it's important to remain calm and professional toward the complainant and all other parties involved. Asking follow-up questions is a good idea; however, neither the context nor the manner of delivery would change the severity of the offensive remarks. Also, the fact that others have complained is best kept confidential.

31. B: Performance improvement plans (PIPs) are best used when the behavior that needs correction is quantifiable, but this is a qualitative behavior issue. It seems to be an isolated incident with multiple employees reporting that the comments were inappropriate, so organization-wide training is likely not the best avenue, and neither would demotion be the best choice if this is not a recurring problem.

32. B: An employee recognition program can vary from formal and structured to inexpensive and casual and generally promotes positive results from employees with minimal expense. It would be an effective approach to ensure that employees feel appreciated for working hard without significantly altering the working conditions.

33. C: Leadership buy-in is critical to create a culture of appreciation, not only as it relates to the tangible rewards in a formal recognition program but setting the tone of direct verbal kudos and thank-yous for a job well done.

34. D: If the recruiter has had success at the conference in the past, he will want to pinpoint the source of the problem before implementing a change. There might be a number of explanations for the drop in qualified candidates and he should start to gather information before changing course.

35. C: Choice C is the best response because the recruiter should seek information to understand the decline in quality of the applicant pool, then use that information to support his decision. He should not share the information with his manager because he has no data to support it, and he will likely receive the best quality information if he has a meeting with the organizer explaining his concerns, rather than demanding answers at a social event. He should not ignore the information because he might decide the best strategy is to continue to attend the conference.

36. C: In a space that serves as an integral accommodation space for several employee needs (religion, breast pumping, mental health, etc.), it is critical that the HR manager collects all pertinent data related to the users' needs, schedules, and expectations. Federal pumping protection laws prohibit the designation of bathroom space (A) for breast-pumping employees; however, automatically awarding the breast-pumping employee the primary use of the multipurpose space (D) without any attempt at problem-solving or collaboration can result in employee frustration at best and claims of religious or ableist discrimination at worst. Dedicating additional space as a

second multipurpose room (B) could solve the problem at hand but will take away from the workplace footprint and other organizational workspaces.

37. A: By mediating a solutions meeting, the HR manager communicates not just that all employees' needs are valued but that the organization has trust in them to communicate and problem solve. By meeting with the involved employees together, solutions can be as simple as discovering a mutually agreed upon schedule or as creative as making an outdoor meditation space with a rooftop garden. Because of the serious nature of some of the accommodations, it is important that the HR manager remain involved to ensure the protection of each employee's civil rights; therefore, an email (C) simply introducing the employees would be inappropriate. A virtual calendar (B) may be part of the ultimate solution but does not necessarily encourage collaboration among the employees and may backfire if individuals book times that are also required by other team members. Assigning time to each department (D) for its employees to use would be inappropriate as the needs for the room likely span throughout the day and could infringe on workers' rights if the department is not assigned time conducive to its team's needs.

38. C: When determining practices and policies within the scope of employment law, the employer must provide the highest level of protection between the competing issuing bodies. Therefore, the company is required to abide by the state law requiring paid breaks for pumping employees but must also abide by the federal law requiring that the pumping space be a non-bathroom space.

39. B: The study showed that there were significantly fewer employee safety incidents in companies with high employee engagement. The other performance outcomes were: customer ratings, profitability, productivity, turnover, thefts, absenteeism, and quality defects.

40. B: This is an example of quid pro quo (this for that). The manager asks for a sexual favor in return for the employee's continued employment. Quid pro quo and hostile work environment are two types of harassment that can occur at a workplace.

41. B: Onshoring is the opposite of offshoring, which refers to a relocation to outside of the country.

42. C: Cost-benefit analysis (CBA) is calculated by subtracting costs from benefits, and the result is potential profit as a dollar value. Return on investment (ROI) is costs subtracted from benefits divided by costs, resulting in a ratio or percentage.

43. D: Vesting is the process by which employees receive ownership of the employer contributions made into their retirement savings plans. Graded vesting is a common plan design strategy and allows employees to earn an increased portion of the employer contributions each year of their participation.

44. C: All the other scenarios listed are qualifying events that allow an employee to elect into COBRA to continue health insurance coverage for employees who are on a protected leave.

45. D: The Family and Medical Leave Act (FMLA) grants unpaid time off to an employee who is caring for a newborn or a child placed for adoption or foster care. The employee may also use this time to provide care for immediate family members that are experiencing a serious health condition. Immediate family members are limited to the employee's spouse and parents. Finally, if the employee is unable to work due to their own serious health condition, they may apply for FMLA to take care of themselves. FMLA does not apply to extended family members such as grandparents, aunts, uncles, or siblings.

46. A: The second step of the corporate social responsibility (CSR) process is to conduct an assessment of the organization's current state. The assessment will review company structure, strategy, and processes.

47. B: Job bidding allows current employees to express interest in positions even though there might not be any openings at the moment. Inside moonlighting means that an employee works a second job at the same company before or after his or her regular working hours. Intraregional recruiting and open houses are external recruiting sources.

48. D: The productivity and impact of a multigender workforce can be heavily influenced by a team's culture. A workplace culture that values gender diversity is more likely to experience the benefits often attributed to a multigender workforce. Culture in the workforce can be influenced by both internal elements like organizational trust, values, and structure, as well as external elements such as language, national origin, and political climate. Religion (B), race (A), and ability (C) can heavily influence a team's or individual's perspectives, but they are each just a single piece of the bigger picture of cultural diversity.

49. D: A 9-box grid can be an important part of an employee's career development plan.

50. B: This is an example of a process evaluation, which looks at the details of the conducted program and assesses which activities have been completed. The opposite would be an outcome evaluation, which looks at the effects of the program. These effects could be changes in behavior as a result of the newly acquired information.

51. B: The given information is not enough to show whether the pay differential is based on sex, which is why choice A is incorrect. Answer choices C and D are incorrect because the jobs being compared must be substantially similar (with respect to skill, effort, and responsibility) to have a viable EPA claim. Host and sous chef are not substantially similar positions.

52. C: The five-step ADDIE framework includes analysis, design, development, implementation, and evaluation.

53. B: One concern companies have to take into consideration when moving parts of the HR function to an online portal is that not all employees are computer literate. Therefore, they might need training on how to use a computer and access different functions.

54. A: Anticipating and developing the knowledge, skills, and abilities needed for the organization's strategic direction is an example of HR's strategic role. Maintaining employee data in the HRIS and conducting background and reference checks are examples of HR's administrative role. Team-building initiatives are an example of HR's operational role.

55. C: Choice C is the best answer because a personalized onboarding experience provides a new hire with specific information they will need to successfully acclimate to a new role. A mentor selected based on knowledge that would be most relevant to the new hire can be a valuable source of this information.

56. D: Flexible spending account (FSA) funds may not be used to purchase an electric toothbrush. The other items are eligible expenses according to the Internal Revenue Service (IRS), and an FSA may be used for those purchases.

57. A: Implementing a "buddy program" increases employee engagement. The company assigns the new employee a "buddy" who has been with the company for a significant amount of time. The "buddy" can provide guidance and help the new employee settle into his or her new role.

58. B: Succession planning builds a talent pool of potential future leaders within the company. Therefore, it is important to select candidates with growth potential. Candidates can come from all levels of the organization. After candidates have been selected, they receive training and development, which can include, for example, a mentorship program.

59. D: Choice D is the best response because HR professionals should adhere to company policies in a uniform and non-discriminatory manner across all job functions and job levels. While the HR manager might want to speak with her manager about the situation, the best approach is to handle it directly.

60. B: Choice B is the best answer here because, the HR manager's comments suggest she may have been biased when reviewing the applicant pool, and the assistant's comment may have alerted her to an unconscious bias if she did not intend to select the finalists in a discriminatory manner.

61. D: Hiring females to model women's shoes is a bona fide occupational qualification (BFOQ). This hiring practice is not discriminatory because only females would be able to model women's shoes.

62. A: A PESTLE analysis considers political, economic, social, technological, legal, and environmental factors.

63. C: An applicant tracking system (ATS) is software used by employers to monitor different elements of the recruitment and selection process. This is different than a chat bot, artificial intelligence, or learning management system (LMS).

64. A: A flatter organizational structure often results in fewer, but broader pay ranges, which is called broad banding.

65. B: The yield ratio is calculated by dividing the number of offers extended by the number of qualified applicants: $\frac{4}{80} = 5\%$.

66. C: Choice C is the best answer because an employer should ensure its managers understand that retaliation is prohibited, which prevents employers from imposing an adverse action on an employee in response to their assertion of their legal right to report a case of potential age discrimination. The situation requires HR to initiate an investigation, and the employer must immediately ensure that any prohibited retaliatory action stops. The employer should not change the working conditions of the employee because this could be viewed as retaliation.

67. C: The HR director should disclose this knowledge and request that the investigation be assigned to another investigator to eliminate any potential conflicts of interest. The employer should not ask the current employee about a past claim or investigate any past claim because it is not relevant to the current situation.

68. D: Choice D is the best answer because an employer has an obligation to maintain the confidentiality of its employees and to ensure that the process is fair. Informing another HR professional that you are unable to share information may be uncomfortable, but the call should be returned to maintain a professional relationship.

69. B: During an organizational intervention, it is the role of HR to conduct a structural diagnosis, analyze problems the organization faces, and identify the root cause of those problems.

70. C: A company's value chain is the sum of all interrelated actions, inputs, and processes that contribute to the design, creation, and production of a product or service until it is received by a customer.

71. A: This is an example of a moral hazard, which describes a situation where one person does something (employee driving fast) but another suffers the consequences for it (company and/or insurance company).

72. B: The Equal Employment Opportunity Commission guidance directs employers to recognize the preferred gender and name of their employees both in communications and interactions with the employees and also within their employee records and written terms. Using an employee's preferred pronoun (A) falls within the federal civil rights protections of sex, gender identity, and sexual orientation. The gender expansive terms (C) such as ze/hir can be used by individuals who wish to be identified by terms that do not specify gender or for other reasons personal to them. Offhand comments, nonserious isolated incidents (D), and genuine mistakes do not necessarily qualify as discrimination immediately; however, if these behaviors become pervasive or intentionally damaging in nature, then they can be considered harassment.

73. D: Retaliation is any adverse action or change in behavior toward an employee who raises concerns about harassment or discrimination. Clarice's refusal to interact with or acknowledge Benjamin negatively affects Benjamin's ability to complete his job and the team's ability to communicate effectively. Additionally, this behavior singles Benjamin out for his differences and create feelings of isolation and hostility. Cultural taxation (A) refers to the burden on underrepresented individuals to represent their diversity dimension in formal and informal settings. Intersectionality (B) may be at play between different diversity dimensions but the most obvious and pervasive barrier at play is retaliation. Imposter syndrome (C) refers to an individual's fabricated self-doubt regarding his or her achievements and responsibilities.

74. C: Managing conflicting civil rights in the workplace can be complicated, and it is essential for organizational leaders to engage in genuine conversations that respect the beliefs of employees while also prioritizing behaviors that contribute to organizational outcomes. In the long run, any knee-jerk reactions without an authentic and well-meaning dialogue (A) may harm the organization in terms of team morale and discrimination suits. Proposing to move Benjamin (or Clarice) to a different team (B) immediately does not address the root of the problem and may also be interpreted as retaliation. Asking Benjamin to make an exception for Clarice (D) would be an inappropriate request to protect her religious beliefs over his gender identity instead of working toward a mutually beneficial solution.

75. D: While candidates appreciate a comprehensive interview process where they can learn about the role and the people with whom they will interact, one of the most effective strategies to support a positive candidate experience is to limit the number of interview rounds.

76. C: Because the senior development role is a critical position, the company should use a lead pay strategy, which offers a compensation package that is higher than the market rate. This is the most effective compensation strategy to attract and retain top talent. Because the administrative role is not a priority, the company could use the lag strategy, which offers compensation that is lower than the market rate. There is no indication that the lead-lag strategy, which offers higher wages in the first part of the year and offers below-market rates in the second half of the year, would be useful here.

77. C: A measurement map is a tool to help make sense of possible relationships between different data sets that can have complex relationships. By building out the map first, the HR director can then start to make hypotheses regarding the possible relationships between these data sets. This data can then inform future feedback surveys (A), show which are the appropriate departments to discern best practices from (B), and demonstrate the relationship between employee performance and benefits utilization (D).

78. B: Mapping out data can suggest correlations between investments, leading indicators, and business outcomes, but does not automatically illustrate causal relationships. An assumption such as "Tuition reimbursement causes increased revenue per employee" (A) can be dangerous, as it does not consider external influencing factors that may be causing the positive relationship instead. By assuming causation from correlation, employers may increase or decrease their investments in ways that hurt business outcomes because they failed to consider confounding factors.

79. C: In order to better understand how employee-related leading indicators affect the diverse workforce, the HR director should stratify the data by diversity dimensions in order to more effectively observe any successes or inequities otherwise hidden by averaging the data. A scatter plot (A) comparing monthly performance scores to member interactions does not demonstrate the impact of this investment on different diversity dimensions. Filtering feedback by seniority (B) is unlikely to be useful as it could skew the results to represent older employees or could disregard new employees who joined the company during the policy changes. Interviewing just employees utilizing the tuition reimbursement program (D) would only identify the population who are still in school or have the time to pursue education outside of work.

80. D: One of the key methods to making the case for causation over correlation is designing a controlled study. By utilizing a pilot program for the next set of policy changes, the company can track the differences in leading indicators and business outcomes and compare those results to locations that were not running the pilot programs. Targeting the higher-performing employees for benefits upgrades (A) may end up influencing business outcomes, but without any controlled data to compare, there are too many possible confounding factors to claim causation. Weekly surveys (B) may help to bolster causation claims but are less likely to succeed due to the logistical burden on the survey takers and interpreters. The revenue-per-employee metric (C) would be a useful business outcome to better understand but is influenced by a wide variety of leading indicators and other influencing factors that makes claims of causation very challenging.

81. C: An HRIS system is used to store and maintain employee data, but company policies, such as those related to FMLA, would not be stored in the system.

82. D: Each of these terms is related to employee retention.

83. A: Bring your own device (BYOD) policies establish rules employees must follow when using personal devices for work to ensure the information is secure.

84. B: A vision statement should be aspirational and strategic, describing where the organization wants to be in the future and how they plan to achieve that goal.

85. D: Human resources should never guarantee confidentiality to complainants. In the case of an investigation, details of the complaint will likely need to be shared with the accused and/or witnesses.

86. C: A SMART goal is specific, measurable, achievable, relevant, and time bound.

87. D: A Bona Fide Occupational Qualification (BFOQ) is only legitimate if it is a criterion (e.g., gender, religion, or national origin) that is required for business operations. There is a business need and safety consideration for hiring police officers and deputies who are younger than 50.

88. D: The biggest organizational risk when conducting an employee satisfaction survey is the potential for not taking any action based on the findings of the survey. This may backfire and create ill will among employees.

89. D: Both new mothers and new fathers have the same rights under the Family and Medical Leave Act (FMLA)—that is, 12 weeks of job and benefit protection following the birth or adoption of a child. This includes bonding time, physical incapacity from the delivery, and/or care for the spouse who is recovering.

90. C: It is a good idea to grant the employee's request but only if it does not present undue hardship to the employer. Some examples of undue hardship could be cost, staffing shortages, or a decrease in workplace efficiency.

91. A: When providing feedback, a supervisor should limit the focus to one or two areas of deficiency. Otherwise, it tends to make the employee feel defensive.

92. B: A Corporate Social Responsibility (CSR) plan represents an organization's commitment to enhancing their local and global community.

93. C: Employers are prohibited from imposing adverse employment actions in response to their assertion of a legal right, such as a filing a complaint with an agency.

94. B: Pay compression occurs when there is minimal or no difference between an individual's salary and those who are more experienced than them. In some situations, pay compression will result in an individual earning the same or more than their supervisor.

95. D: Choice D is the best answer because HR professionals are obligated to assist non-HR managers in effective communication of policies to their direct reports. Although HR is responsible for administering the policy, the best initial path forward is to ensure the manager is equipped to explain the policy and the reason behind it without HR involvement.

96. A: Because HR developed and administered the policy, they should be open to hearing employee feedback. Questions related to the reason for the policy or proposed changes would be appropriate to discuss with HR.

97. B: The company initially organized its employees based on their functions (i.e., HR, sales), but then moved to organize its employees based on the product (i.e., which move they were assigned to work on).

98. C: A PEO (short for professional employer organization) generally acts as a leasing company that handles payroll and benefits administration for a group of individuals who are then leased back to the company to complete the job responsibilities.

99. D: Choice D is the best answer because HR should ensure that its actions are aligned with the organization. If everyone is being asked to eliminate discretionary spending, they should follow this directive. If HR has extra money in another budget line that can be used for coffee, then that money could also be considered discretionary and should also be examined. There are other no-cost alternatives HR could use to foster employee engagement.

100. C: All HR professional should act with personal integrity, and the increased rate of bonuses with retroactive dates suggests that some departments may be trying to act in a way that is not aligned with the company's directives. Reaching out to speak with the departments about the submitted paperwork may be outside the Coordinator's responsibilities, particularly because his role is limited to processing the paperwork. However, the facts suggest that the situation should be escalated for review.

101. C: Because HR is aware of this immediate but short-term deficit, they should proactively look for ways to alleviate the financial burden on the organization. In this case, it is unlikely simply requesting an adjustment would impact the vendor relationship. Based on the announcement there is no indication of a long-term financial issue, so canceling a contract that would provide long-term savings is likely not the best path forward.

102. A: Choice A is the correct answer because it describes the formula used to determine the gross margin. The P/E ratio is calculated by dividing the stock price per share by the earnings per share. Return on investment is calculated by subtracting the cost of investment from the gain from the investment, then dividing that figure by the cost of the investment.

103. C: A PESTLE analysis considers political, economic, social, technological, legal, and environmental factors to make operational decisions.

104. B: When using a job ranking, all roles are reviewed based upon the value that they add to the overall organization.

105. D: When engaging in benchmarking, organizations may compare processes, employee performance, or other data to evaluate where there may be gaps or areas of improvement.

106. D: Choice D is the best answer because HR has an obligation to comply with the law when administering its policies and procedures. In this case, HR might consider reaching out to their legal counsel to inquire about potential exceptions to the law, but absent confirmation that exempting the employee would be consistent with the law, HR has an obligation to comply with the law.

107. D: Choice D is the best answer because HR professionals should work to apply policies in a uniform manner but with respect for differences in business operations and cultures.

108. D: Choice D is the best answer because the situation likely will need a multi-pronged approach to reach a resolution. There may be valid reasons IT cannot provide the data earlier and the general counsel should be aware of the reasons why HR is unable to meet its directives. While it might be useful to meet with the teams individually, a single meeting with both stakeholders would be the best path forward to indicate a commitment to partnering with them, rather than looking to cast blame on a particular department.

109. B: Choice B is the best answer because the purpose of the meeting is to provide information to the IT department to explain why HR is requesting the reports be delivered earlier. Training is important and non-compliance is a serious issue. However, these are not explanations for why HR is consistently asking for the data earlier. While choice D might be relevant because it could be used to show that HR is faced with an increased workload, choice B is a better answer because it is more closely tied to the central issue.

110. A: Disparate impact occurs when practices or policies intending to be nondiscriminatory in nature result in discriminatory outcomes. The four-fifths rule measures the rate at which a protected group experiences an employment action when compared to the majority group. The experience occurrences of each group should occur at similar rates; the protected group should experience the action at 80 percent or higher when compared to the majority group. Yield ratios (B), turnover rates (C), and performance review scores (D) can be helpful when identifying potential disparate impact but lack a standard of comparing majority and minority groups to determine the measurable difference in treatment.

111. A: An essential function of a job is a main job responsibility which the individual must be able to do with or without reasonable accommodations. In contrast, a nonessential function is a task that is not required but is desired. There is no requirement to pay an individual a higher rate for a nonessential task, and a nonessential function might be performed on more than one day per week.

112. D: The best way to reduce any negative impacts of layoffs is to work to prevent them. Offering employees other roles in the organization will be a win-win situation for the company and the employee. The company will be able to reduce the number of layoffs and reduce the negative reaction, and the employee will have the opportunity to continue employment. HR should research whether there are limitations on the right to layoff the employees on the list, but they should do this after they determine whether any of the layoffs can be avoided.

113. B: Choice B is the best answer because training or upskilling employees to ensure they have skills aligned with the organization may qualify the individuals for new roles in the organization, which is aligned with HR's obligation to support employees. It may also qualify the individual for a new role which is aligned with the organizational goal to minimize the impact of the layoffs by potentially reducing the number of impacted employees.

114. D: Selecting employees for layoff on the basis of avoiding upcoming bonus payments is unethical. While it would be acceptable to simply create a plan based on another selection criteria, it would be best to also communicate to the team member that suggested the problematic plan the reasons why it isn't right.

115. D: Choice D is the best answer because best practice for a layoff is to have a face-to-face meeting with the manager and a member of HR or another representative who has knowledge about the process and will be able to answer any questions.

How to Overcome Test Anxiety

Just the thought of taking a test is enough to make most people a little nervous. A test is an important event that can have a long-term impact on your future, so it's important to take it seriously and it's natural to feel anxious about performing well. But just because anxiety is normal, that doesn't mean that it's helpful in test taking, or that you should simply accept it as part of your life. Anxiety can have a variety of effects. These effects can be mild, like making you feel slightly nervous, or severe, like blocking your ability to focus or remember even a simple detail.

If you experience test anxiety—whether severe or mild—it's important to know how to beat it. To discover this, first you need to understand what causes test anxiety.

Causes of Test Anxiety

While we often think of anxiety as an uncontrollable emotional state, it can actually be caused by simple, practical things. One of the most common causes of test anxiety is that a person does not feel adequately prepared for their test. This feeling can be the result of many different issues such as poor study habits or lack of organization, but the most common culprit is time management. Starting to study too late, failing to organize your study time to cover all of the material, or being distracted while you study will mean that you're not well prepared for the test. This may lead to cramming the night before, which will cause you to be physically and mentally exhausted for the test. Poor time management also contributes to feelings of stress, fear, and hopelessness as you realize you are not well prepared but don't know what to do about it.

Other times, test anxiety is not related to your preparation for the test but comes from unresolved fear. This may be a past failure on a test, or poor performance on tests in general. It may come from comparing yourself to others who seem to be performing better or from the stress of living up to expectations. Anxiety may be driven by fears of the future—how failure on this test would affect your educational and career goals. These fears are often completely irrational, but they can still negatively impact your test performance.

Elements of Test Anxiety

As mentioned earlier, test anxiety is considered to be an emotional state, but it has physical and mental components as well. Sometimes you may not even realize that you are suffering from test anxiety until you notice the physical symptoms. These can include trembling hands, rapid heartbeat, sweating, nausea, and tense muscles. Extreme anxiety may lead to fainting or vomiting. Obviously, any of these symptoms can have a negative impact on testing. It is important to recognize them as soon as they begin to occur so that you can address the problem before it damages your performance.

The mental components of test anxiety include trouble focusing and inability to remember learned information. During a test, your mind is on high alert, which can help you recall information and stay focused for an extended period of time. However, anxiety interferes with your mind's natural processes, causing you to blank out, even on the questions you know well. The strain of testing during anxiety makes it difficult to stay focused, especially on a test that may take several hours. Extreme anxiety can take a huge mental toll, making it difficult not only to recall test information but even to understand the test questions or pull your thoughts together.

Effects of Test Anxiety

Test anxiety is like a disease—if left untreated, it will get progressively worse. Anxiety leads to poor performance, and this reinforces the feelings of fear and failure, which in turn lead to poor performances on subsequent tests. It can grow from a mild nervousness to a crippling condition. If allowed to progress, test anxiety can have a big impact on your schooling, and consequently on your future.

Test anxiety can spread to other parts of your life. Anxiety on tests can become anxiety in any stressful situation, and blanking on a test can turn into panicking in a job situation. But fortunately, you don't have to let anxiety rule your testing and determine your grades. There are a number of relatively simple steps you can take to move past anxiety and function normally on a test and in the rest of life.

Physical Steps for Beating Test Anxiety

While test anxiety is a serious problem, the good news is that it can be overcome. It doesn't have to control your ability to think and remember information. While it may take time, you can begin taking steps today to beat anxiety.

Just as your first hint that you may be struggling with anxiety comes from the physical symptoms, the first step to treating it is also physical. Rest is crucial for having a clear, strong mind. If you are tired, it is much easier to give in to anxiety. But if you establish good sleep habits, your body and mind will be ready to perform optimally, without the strain of exhaustion. Additionally, sleeping well helps you to retain information better, so you're more likely to recall the answers when you see the test questions.

Getting good sleep means more than going to bed on time. It's important to allow your brain time to relax. Take study breaks from time to time so it doesn't get overworked, and don't study right before bed. Take time to rest your mind before trying to rest your body, or you may find it difficult to fall asleep.

Along with sleep, other aspects of physical health are important in preparing for a test. Good nutrition is vital for good brain function. Sugary foods and drinks may give a burst of energy but this burst is followed by a crash, both physically and emotionally. Instead, fuel your body with protein and vitamin-rich foods.

Also, drink plenty of water. Dehydration can lead to headaches and exhaustion, especially if your brain is already under stress from the rigors of the test. Particularly if your test is a long one, drink water during the breaks. And if possible, take an energy-boosting snack to eat between sections.

Along with sleep and diet, a third important part of physical health is exercise. Maintaining a steady workout schedule is helpful, but even taking 5-minute study breaks to walk can help get your blood pumping faster and clear your head. Exercise also releases endorphins, which contribute to a positive feeling and can help combat test anxiety.

When you nurture your physical health, you are also contributing to your mental health. If your body is healthy, your mind is much more likely to be healthy as well. So take time to rest, nourish your body with healthy food and water, and get moving as much as possible. Taking these physical steps will make you stronger and more able to take the mental steps necessary to overcome test anxiety.

Mental Steps for Beating Test Anxiety

Working on the mental side of test anxiety can be more challenging, but as with the physical side, there are clear steps you can take to overcome it. As mentioned earlier, test anxiety often stems from lack of preparation, so the obvious solution is to prepare for the test. Effective studying may be the most important weapon you have for beating test anxiety, but you can and should employ several other mental tools to combat fear.

First, boost your confidence by reminding yourself of past success—tests or projects that you aced. If you're putting as much effort into preparing for this test as you did for those, there's no reason you should expect to fail here. Work hard to prepare; then trust your preparation.

Second, surround yourself with encouraging people. It can be helpful to find a study group, but be sure that the people you're around will encourage a positive attitude. If you spend time with others who are anxious or cynical, this will only contribute to your own anxiety. Look for others who are motivated to study hard from a desire to succeed, not from a fear of failure.

Third, reward yourself. A test is physically and mentally tiring, even without anxiety, and it can be helpful to have something to look forward to. Plan an activity following the test, regardless of the outcome, such as going to a movie or getting ice cream.

When you are taking the test, if you find yourself beginning to feel anxious, remind yourself that you know the material. Visualize successfully completing the test. Then take a few deep, relaxing breaths and return to it. Work through the questions carefully but with confidence, knowing that you are capable of succeeding.

Developing a healthy mental approach to test taking will also aid in other areas of life. Test anxiety affects more than just the actual test—it can be damaging to your mental health and even contribute to depression. It's important to beat test anxiety before it becomes a problem for more than testing.

Study Strategy

Being prepared for the test is necessary to combat anxiety, but what does being prepared look like? You may study for hours on end and still not feel prepared. What you need is a strategy for test prep. The next few pages outline our recommended steps to help you plan out and conquer the challenge of preparation.

STEP 1: SCOPE OUT THE TEST

Learn everything you can about the format (multiple choice, essay, etc.) and what will be on the test. Gather any study materials, course outlines, or sample exams that may be available. Not only will this help you to prepare, but knowing what to expect can help to alleviate test anxiety.

STEP 2: MAP OUT THE MATERIAL

Look through the textbook or study guide and make note of how many chapters or sections it has. Then divide these over the time you have. For example, if a book has 15 chapters and you have five days to study, you need to cover three chapters each day. Even better, if you have the time, leave an extra day at the end for overall review after you have gone through the material in depth.

If time is limited, you may need to prioritize the material. Look through it and make note of which sections you think you already have a good grasp on, and which need review. While you are studying, skim quickly through the familiar sections and take more time on the challenging parts.

Write out your plan so you don't get lost as you go. Having a written plan also helps you feel more in control of the study, so anxiety is less likely to arise from feeling overwhelmed at the amount to cover.

STEP 3: GATHER YOUR TOOLS

Decide what study method works best for you. Do you prefer to highlight in the book as you study and then go back over the highlighted portions? Or do you type out notes of the important information? Or is it helpful to make flashcards that you can carry with you? Assemble the pens, index cards, highlighters, post-it notes, and any other materials you may need so you won't be distracted by getting up to find things while you study.

If you're having a hard time retaining the information or organizing your notes, experiment with different methods. For example, try color-coding by subject with colored pens, highlighters, or post-it notes. If you learn better by hearing, try recording yourself reading your notes so you can listen while in the car, working out, or simply sitting at your desk. Ask a friend to quiz you from your flashcards, or try teaching someone the material to solidify it in your mind.

STEP 4: CREATE YOUR ENVIRONMENT

It's important to avoid distractions while you study. This includes both the obvious distractions like visitors and the subtle distractions like an uncomfortable chair (or a too-comfortable couch that makes you want to fall asleep). Set up the best study environment possible: good lighting and a comfortable work area. If background music helps you focus, you may want to turn it on, but otherwise keep the room quiet. If you are using a computer to take notes, be sure you don't have any other windows open, especially applications like social media, games, or anything else that could distract you. Silence your phone and turn off notifications. Be sure to keep water close by so you stay hydrated while you study (but avoid unhealthy drinks and snacks).

Also, take into account the best time of day to study. Are you freshest first thing in the morning? Try to set aside some time then to work through the material. Is your mind clearer in the afternoon or evening? Schedule your study session then. Another method is to study at the same time of day that you will take the test, so that your brain gets used to working on the material at that time and will be ready to focus at test time.

STEP 5: STUDY!

Once you have done all the study preparation, it's time to settle into the actual studying. Sit down, take a few moments to settle your mind so you can focus, and begin to follow your study plan. Don't give in to distractions or let yourself procrastinate. This is your time to prepare so you'll be ready to fearlessly approach the test. Make the most of the time and stay focused.

Of course, you don't want to burn out. If you study too long you may find that you're not retaining the information very well. Take regular study breaks. For example, taking five minutes out of every hour to walk briskly, breathing deeply and swinging your arms, can help your mind stay fresh.

As you get to the end of each chapter or section, it's a good idea to do a quick review. Remind yourself of what you learned and work on any difficult parts. When you feel that you've mastered the material, move on to the next part. At the end of your study session, briefly skim through your notes again.

But while review is helpful, cramming last minute is NOT. If at all possible, work ahead so that you won't need to fit all your study into the last day. Cramming overloads your brain with more information than it can process and retain, and your tired mind may struggle to recall even previously learned information when it is overwhelmed with last-minute study. Also, the urgent nature of cramming and the stress placed on your brain contribute to anxiety. You'll be more likely to go to the test feeling unprepared and having trouble thinking clearly.

So don't cram, and don't stay up late before the test, even just to review your notes at a leisurely pace. Your brain needs rest more than it needs to go over the information again. In fact, plan to finish your studies by noon or early afternoon the day before the test. Give your brain the rest of the day to relax or focus on other things, and get a good night's sleep. Then you will be fresh for the test and better able to recall what you've studied.

STEP 6: TAKE A PRACTICE TEST

Many courses offer sample tests, either online or in the study materials. This is an excellent resource to check whether you have mastered the material, as well as to prepare for the test format and environment.

Check the test format ahead of time: the number of questions, the type (multiple choice, free response, etc.), and the time limit. Then create a plan for working through them. For example, if you have 30 minutes to take a 60-question test, your limit is 30 seconds per question. Spend less time on the questions you know well so that you can take more time on the difficult ones.

If you have time to take several practice tests, take the first one open book, with no time limit. Work through the questions at your own pace and make sure you fully understand them. Gradually work up to taking a test under test conditions: sit at a desk with all study materials put away and set a timer. Pace yourself to make sure you finish the test with time to spare and go back to check your answers if you have time.

After each test, check your answers. On the questions you missed, be sure you understand why you missed them. Did you misread the question (tests can use tricky wording)? Did you forget the information? Or was it something you hadn't learned? Go back and study any shaky areas that the practice tests reveal.

Taking these tests not only helps with your grade, but also aids in combating test anxiety. If you're already used to the test conditions, you're less likely to worry about it, and working through tests until you're scoring well gives you a confidence boost. Go through the practice tests until you feel comfortable, and then you can go into the test knowing that you're ready for it.

Test Tips

On test day, you should be confident, knowing that you've prepared well and are ready to answer the questions. But aside from preparation, there are several test day strategies you can employ to maximize your performance.

First, as stated before, get a good night's sleep the night before the test (and for several nights before that, if possible). Go into the test with a fresh, alert mind rather than staying up late to study.

Try not to change too much about your normal routine on the day of the test. It's important to eat a nutritious breakfast, but if you normally don't eat breakfast at all, consider eating just a protein bar. If you're a coffee drinker, go ahead and have your normal coffee. Just make sure you time it so that the caffeine doesn't wear off right in the middle of your test. Avoid sugary beverages, and drink enough water to stay hydrated but not so much that you need a restroom break 10 minutes into the test. If your test isn't first thing in the morning, consider going for a walk or doing a light workout before the test to get your blood flowing.

Allow yourself enough time to get ready, and leave for the test with plenty of time to spare so you won't have the anxiety of scrambling to arrive in time. Another reason to be early is to select a good seat. It's helpful to sit away from doors and windows, which can be distracting. Find a good seat, get out your supplies, and settle your mind before the test begins.

When the test begins, start by going over the instructions carefully, even if you already know what to expect. Make sure you avoid any careless mistakes by following the directions.

Then begin working through the questions, pacing yourself as you've practiced. If you're not sure on an answer, don't spend too much time on it, and don't let it shake your confidence. Either skip it and come back later, or eliminate as many wrong answers as possible and guess among the remaining ones. Don't dwell on these questions as you continue—put them out of your mind and focus on what lies ahead.

Be sure to read all of the answer choices, even if you're sure the first one is the right answer. Sometimes you'll find a better one if you keep reading. But don't second-guess yourself if you do immediately know the answer. Your gut instinct is usually right. Don't let test anxiety rob you of the information you know.

If you have time at the end of the test (and if the test format allows), go back and review your answers. Be cautious about changing any, since your first instinct tends to be correct, but make sure you didn't misread any of the questions or accidentally mark the wrong answer choice. Look over any you skipped and make an educated guess.

At the end, leave the test feeling confident. You've done your best, so don't waste time worrying about your performance or wishing you could change anything. Instead, celebrate the successful completion of this test. And finally, use this test to learn how to deal with anxiety even better next time.

> **Review Video: Test Anxiety**
> Visit mometrix.com/academy and enter code: 100340

Important Qualification

Not all anxiety is created equal. If your test anxiety is causing major issues in your life beyond the classroom or testing center, or if you are experiencing troubling physical symptoms related to your anxiety, it may be a sign of a serious physiological or psychological condition. If this sounds like your situation, we strongly encourage you to seek professional help.

Additional Bonus Material

Due to our efforts to try to keep this book to a manageable length, we've created a link that will give you access to all of your additional bonus material:

mometrix.com/bonus948/phr